T0358182

This book reveals a new generation of researchers redirecting the agenda of agrifood studies. The authors create an original synthesis of convention theory, neoinstitutional theory and practice theory, captured in the concept of social orders. In an ambitious and convincing work, the great transformations of the Brazilian agrifood system since the early twentieth century are reinterpreted in the light of this new analytical framework.

—**John Wilkinson**, Professor of Economic Sociology, Federal Rural University of Rio de Janeiro

Understanding reality as a "social order," the authors propose an innovative review of the evolution of agrifood system in Brazil. Their conclusions about the instability and contradictions of social orders are not only a contribution to the Sociology of Agriculture and Food, but also an important contribution to Sociological Theory.

—**Alessandro Bonanno**, Regents' Professor of Sociology, Sam Houston State University

A remarkable and challenging book. Few authors can combine so well such a pluralist theoretical inspiration and detailed historical analysis. The dynamics of Brazilian agriculture and agrifood system are analyzed in its multiple facets, revealing countless contradictions and complementarities.

—**Sergio Schneider**, Professor of Sociology of Food, Federal University of Rio Grande do Sul, Porto Alegre

For everybody interested in the dynamics of food and eating, this book offers an exciting and original panorama of the theme, clearly connecting the theoretical framework that guides the authors and the reality of the Brazilian context. No doubt this is a must-have and must-read.

—**Livia Barbosa**, Professor of Political Anthropology and Consumption, Pontifical Catholic University of Rio de Janeiro

A reference book to understand the transformations in the food system. By means of the innovative approach of the "food orders," the authors trace a broad panel of the dynamics of food production and markets. This is a must-read for academic, entrepreneurs and policymakers.

—**Walter Belik**, Professor of Agricultural Economics, State University of Campinas

Agrifood System Transitions in Brazil

This book explores the agrifood system transitions in Brazil to provide a new understanding of the trajectory of agriculture and rural development in this country. It accentuates the increasing diversification and hybridization of food production and consumption practices throughout history.

With a framework that combines convention theory, neoinstitutional approaches and practice theory, this book suggests the concept of "food orders" which represents different arrangements of practices, institutions and sociotechnical artifacts. By exploring the interrelations between these elements, the book looks at six different food orders: industrial, commercial, domestic, aesthetic, civic and financial, in tandem with examples of practices, sectors and territories to understand the dynamics of each one. This aids in understanding the main tendencies of the agrifood sector in such a vast country that, being a major player in global food markets, also affect production and consumption dynamics in several other countries. Besides, this book also seeks to comprehend the current institutional changes in Brazil that may be critical to interpret the global dissemination of populist and autocratic governments.

Offering key insights into the contemporary sociology of agriculture and food, this book demonstrates how strengthening democracy and supporting the organization of civil society are major challenges when we think about transition for sustainable food systems.

Paulo André Niederle is Professor of Rural and Economic Sociology at the Federal University of Rio Grande do Sul, Porto Alegre, Brazil.

Valdemar João Wesz, Junior is Professor of Rural Development at the Federal University of Latin American Integration, Foz do Iguaçú, Brazil.

Critical Food Studies

Series editors: Michael K. Goodman, *University of Reading, UK* and Colin Sage, *Independent Scholar*

The study of food has seldom been more pressing or prescient. From the intensifying globalisation of food, a worldwide food crisis and the continuing inequalities of its production and consumption, to food's exploding media presence and its growing reconnections to places and people through "alternative food movements," this series promotes critical explorations of contemporary food cultures and politics. Building on previous but disparate scholarship, its overall aims are to develop innovative and theoretical lenses and empirical material in order to contribute to – but also begin to more fully delineate – the confines and confluences of an agenda of critical food research and writing.

Of particular concern are original theoretical and empirical treatments of the materialisations of food politics, meanings and representations, the shifting political economies and ecologies of food production and consumption and the growing transgressions between alternative and corporatist food networks.

Digital Food Cultures
Edited by Deborah Lupton and Zeena Feldman

Food Insecurity
A Matter of Justice, Sovereignty, and Survival
Edited by Tamar Mayer and Molly D. Anderson

Shifting Food Facts
Dietary Discourse in a Post-Truth Culture
Alissa Overend

Agrifood System Transitions in Brazil
New Food Orders
Paulo André Niederle and Valdemar João Wesz, Junior

For more information about this series, please visit: www.routledge.com/ Critical-Food-Studies/book-series/CFS

Agrifood System Transitions in Brazil

New Food Orders

**Paulo André Niederle and
Valdemar João Wesz, Junior**

Translated by Regina Vargas

Routledge
Taylor & Francis Group

LONDON AND NEW YORK

First published 2021
by Routledge
2 Park Square, Milton Park, Abingdon, Oxon OX14 4RN

and by Routledge
52 Vanderbilt Avenue, New York, NY 10017

Routledge is an imprint of the Taylor & Francis Group, an informa business

First published in Portuguese by UFRGS Publishing Press, 2018

British Library Cataloguing-in-Publication Data
A catalogue record for this book is available from the British Library

Library of Congress Cataloging-in-Publication Data
A catalog record has been requested for this book

ISBN: 978-0-367-46318-2 (hbk)
ISBN: 978-1-003-02812-3 (ebk)

Typeset in Times New Roman
by Newgen Publishing UK

Contents

Figures

Tables

Preface

How to understand the coexistence between the rising concentration of the agrifood markets in the hands of a small group of transnational companies allied with financial capital and the proliferation of increasingly diversified food practices? This book seeks an answer to this question by offering an original interpretation of the agrifood system transitions in Brazil. Over the past two decades, this country has become the object of growing academic and political interest, either because of the aggressive practices of its agribusiness corporations in some global food chains, or by virtue of its domestic food security policies legitimated by the recognition family faming has achieved in the course of strong social struggles.

Brazil is a country full of contrasts and inequalities. In 2019, according to the Global Human Development Report published by the United Nations Development Program, the group of the 10% richest people in this country concentrated 42% of the total income. The richest 1% holds 28%. This inequity is still worse in rural areas. Last Brazilian Agricultural Census reveals that, in 2017, only 51,000 farms with more than 1,000 ha– out of 5 million farms – accounted for 48% of the total agricultural area. It means that 1% of the largest farms occupy 167 million hectares, while, in the other extreme, 2.5 million farms with less than 10 ha, each one represent together an area of only 8 million ha.

This inequity has hitherto underpinned dualistic interpretations about Brazilian agriculture. One of the most remarkable is precisely that between agribusiness and family farming, two identities that have been consolidated not only in the political discourse, but also in the institutional structure of the State, with one ministry for each group. However, following the aggravation of the crisis resulting from institutional ruptures that took place with the impeachment of the president Dilma Roussef in 2016, while some actors and authors still emphasize the differences between these two agricultures, usually to call for social support to marginalized sectors, others more aligned with the dominant elites, do everything to hide all differences and inequities. They prefer to talk about a single agriculture, so that family farmers would be integrated into the modern agribusiness. Accordingly, they extinguished the

Ministry of Agrarian Development and transferred public policies for family farming to a department within the Ministry of Agriculture.

This book demonstrates that Brazil is not a country of a single agriculture. Not even two. From data collected in researches we have conducted over the last decade in different regions, we demonstrate a process of historical diversification of models of food production, supply and consumption. We define these models as "food orders," with the purpose of identifying the new analytical approach we want to introduce to the debates of the sociology of agriculture and food. This approach emerged from a multidisciplinary dialogue between the Practice Theory, the French Convention School and the Neoinstitutional Sociology. Merging these unconventional theories, we were able to identify six arrangements of practices, institutions and artifacts that we named industrial, commercial, domestic, civic, aesthetic and financial food orders. For us, these orders explain much better the diversity of the Brazilian agrifood system than any dualist conception opposing agribusiness and family farming.

A first edition of this book, entitled simply "The new food orders" (*As novas ordens alimentares*), was published in 2018 by the Federal University of Rio Grande do Sul, Porto Alegre. In comparison to that edition, this one presents some noteworthy changes. Besides adapting the text to foreign readers, several data were updated and reinterpreted. To the extent that these data made it possible to grasp dynamics that were not evident before, some arguments also changed. In this same direction, we tried to explain the most relevant effects of the deep economic and political ruptures Brazil has faced over the last years, emphasizing, however, that this is an ongoing process and that uncertainties prevail at this critical time.

Acknowledgements

Arguments presented in this book have been compiled in the course of a decade of researches in different Brazilian regions. Most of these researches were associated to projects of the Research Group on Agriculture, Food and Development at the Federal University of Rio Grande do Sul (GEPAD-UFRGS); the Observatory on Public Policy for Agriculture (OPPA) and the Research Group on Social Change, Agribusiness and Public Policy, both at the Federal Rural University of Rio de Janeiro (UFRRJ); the Observatory on Latin American Family Farming, located at the Federal University for Latin American Integration (AFLA-UNILA); and the Network on Public Policy and Rural Development in Latin America and the Caribbean (PPAL).

This book would not have been feasible without the support of some institutions. We are especially grateful to the Graduate Programmes in Sociology (PPGS) and Rural Development (PGDR) of the Federal University of Rio Grande do Sul, as well as the Graduate Programme in Public Policy and Development (PPGPPD) and the undergraduate Course in Rural Development and Food Security (DRUSA) of the Federal University for Latin American Integration. Especially at the present difficult time for Brazilian science, assaulted by increasingly drastic budget cuts, we also have to highlight the support of the National Council for Scientific and Technological Development (CNPq) and the Coordination for the Improvement of Higher Education Personnel (Capes).

Finally, our thanks to some colleagues who have most directly contributed to the publication of this book. Mike Goodman and Colin Sage for the invitation to publish it in the Routledge's Critical Food Studies Series. Sergio Schneider and Marcelo Conterato, editors of the UFRGS's Rural Studies Series, made it possible to publish the Brazilian version of the book. The UFRGS Press has freely granted the rights to publish this new English version. John Wilkinson has been a particularly important inspiration for this book, especially for the knowledge shared during the research we conducted together. Fabiano Escher and Maycon Schubert made valuable comments and suggestions on previous versions of the book. Regina Vargas for her careful review and translation of the manuscript. Finally, Catia and Simone deserve special thanks for their patience and support to our endeavor, which extends far beyond this book and research.

Abbreviations

AATR	Association of Lawyers of Rural Workers
ABCAR	Brazilian Association of Credit and Rural Assistance
ABCCD	ADM, Bunge, Cargill, Cofco and Dreyfus
ABCD	ADM, Bunge, Cargill and Dreyfus
ABIMAPI	Brazilian Association of Cookie Industries
ABIR	Brazilian Association of Soft Drinks
ABNT	Brazilian National Standards Association
ABRA	Brazilian Association of Agrarian Reform
ABRACERVA	Brazilian Association of Craft Beer
ABRAS	Brazilian Association of Supermarkets
ABRASCO	Brazilian Association of Collective Health
ADM	Archer Daniels Midland Company
AENDA	Brazilian Association of Generic Pesticides
AGF	Direct Government Purchases
AGU	Office of the Attorney-General
ANA	National Articulation of Agroecology
ANFAVEA	Brazilian Association of Automotive Vehicle Manufacturers
ANM	Mining National Agency
ANVISA	Brazilian Health Regulatory Agency
ASSOCON	Brazilian Association of Intensive Livestock Farming
BM&F	São Paulo Commodity and Futures Exchange
BMSP	São Paulo Commodity Exchange
BNDES	National Bank for Economic and Social Development
BRF	Brazil Foods
BSE	Bovine Spongiform Encephalopathy
CADE	Administrative Council for Economic Defence
CAPES	Coordination for the Improvement of Higher Education Personnel
CAR	Rural Environmental Registry

CBD	Brazilian Company of Distribution
CBT	Brazilian Company of Tractors
CDA	Agricultural Deposit Certificate
CDCA	Agribusiness Credit Rights Certificate
CFN	Federal Council of Nutritionists
CFS	Committee on World Food Security
CNA	National Confederation of Agriculture and Livestock
CNPCT	National Council of Traditional Peoples and Communities
CNPO	National Committee of Organic Products
CNPQ	National Council for Scientific and Technological Development
COFCO	China Oil and Food Corporation
CONATRAE	National Commission for the Eradication of Slave Labour
CONSEA	National Council for Food and Nutrition Security
CONTAG	National Confederation of Agricultural Workers
COREXPORT	Articulated Export Corridors
CPR	Rural Product Security
CPRM	Mineral Resources Research Company
CPT	Pastoral Land Commission
CRA	Agribusiness Receivables Certificate
CTC	Centre for Sugarcane Technologies
DFID	Department for International Development
EAP	Economically Active Population
ECLAC	Economic Commission for Latin America
EGF	Federal Government Loan
EMBRAPA	Brazilian Agriculture Research Corporation
EMBRATER	Brazilian Company of Technical Assistance and Rural Extension
FAO	Food and Agriculture Organization of the United Nations
FBSSAN	Brazilian Forum on Food and Nutrition Sovereignty and Security
FDA	American agency, Food and Drug Administration
FDI	Foreign Direct Investment
FETRAF	National Federation of Family Farm Workers
FNDE	National Fund for Development of Education
FSS	Food Sovereignty and Security
GI	Geographical Indication
GPA	Pão de Açúcar Group
GPD	Gross Domestic Product
GVP	Gross Value of Production
Ha	Hectares

HACCP	Hazard Analysis and Critical Control Point
HRAF	Human Right to Adequate Food
IBA	Brazilian Tree Industry
IBGE	Brazilian Institute of Geography and Statistics
IC	Intermediate Consumption
IDEC	Brazilian Institute of Consumer Protection
IGPM	Brazilian General Market Price Index
ILC	The International Land Coalition
ILO	International Labour Organization
INCRA	Brazilian Institute for Colonization and Agrarian Reform
INESC	Institute of Socioeconomic Studies
INPE	National Institute for Space Research
INPI	National Institute of Industrial Property
IPCA	Brazilian Consumer Price Index
IPHAN	Institute of National Historical Heritage
IPO	Initial Public Offering
ISO	Organization for Standardization
ITR	Rural Territorial Tax
LCA	Agribusiness Letter of Credit
M&A	Mergers and Acquisitions
MAPA	Ministry of Agriculture, Livestock and Supply
MATOPIBA	Maranhão, Tocantins, Piauí and Bahia
MDA	Ministry of Agrarian Development
MDIC	Ministry of Development, Industry and Foreign Trade
MLP	Multilevel Perspective
MMA	Ministry of Environment
MME	Ministry of Mines and Energy
MPA	Small Farmers Movement
MPF	Federal Public Prosecution Service
MPT	Labour Prosecutor's Office
MST	Landless Movement
MTE	Ministry of Labour and Employment
NGO	Non-governmental organization
OECD	Organisation for Economic Cooperation and Development
OPEC	Organization of Petroleum Exporting Countries
PAA	Food Acquisition Programme
PGPM	Minimum Guaranteed Price Policy
PGS	Participatory Guarantee Systems
PIN	National Integration Plan
PLANAPO	National Plan on Agroecology and Organic Production
PNAD	National Household Sample

PNAE	National School Feeding Programme
PNATER	National Policy of Technical Assistance and Rural Extension
PNDA	National Plan for Agricultural Pesticides
POLOAMAZÔNIA	Programme of Amazon Agricultural and Agromineral Hub
POLOCENTRO	Cerrado Development Programme
POLONOROESTE	Integrated Programme of Brazilian Northwest Development
PROAGRO	Production Guarantee Programme
PRODECER	Japanese-Brazilian Cooperation Programme of Cerrado Development
PRODES	Program to Calculate Deforestation in the Amazon
PRONAF	National Program for Strengthening Family Agriculture
PRONAT	National Program for Sustainable Development for Rural Territories
PROTERRA	Programme of Land Redistribution and Incentive to the Northern and North-Eastern Agro-Industry
PROVE	Programme for Verticalization of Small-scale Agricultural Processing
PVEA	Amazon Economic Enhancement Plan
REDD+	Reducing Emissions from Deforestation and forest Degradation
RENCA	Copper and Related ores National Reserve
SBC	Brazilian Society of Cardiology
SISAN	National Food and Nutrition Security System
SISBI/POA	Brazilian Inspection System for Animal Products
SISOrg	Brazilian Organic Conformity Assessment System
SNCR	National Rural Credit System
SUASA	Food Safety Unified Systems
TIAA	Teachers Insurance and Annuity Association
UFRGS	Federal University of Rio Grande do Sul
UFRRJ	Federal Rural University of Rio de Janeiro
UK	United Kingdom
UNICA	Brazilian Sugarcane Industry Association
UNILA	Federal University of Latin American Integration
US	United States
USDA	United States Department of Agriculture
WA	Agricultural Warrant
WFP	World Food Program

Introduction

Markets constitute an enigma for the social sciences. Even being at the core of classical interpretations on the organization of modern societies, they still spark vivid theoretical controversies, not only among economists, but also, and increasingly, among sociologists, anthropologists and political scientists. Today, against the idea of an impersonal mechanism aimed at seeking an illusory equilibrium, these social scientists support the idea of markets as institutional structures built by the visible hands of individuals, organizations, companies and social movements. The challenge lies in understanding the foundations of such structures, their different forms of organization, how they shape behaviors of economic actors simultaneously changing by the action of such actors.

Food markets are even more challenging. Steiner (2008) categorizes them as "special markets," as they involve values and beliefs that would never allow food to be reduced to a pure commodity. However, this characteristic is not exclusive to food. Any good, including even money, is the object of far more complex cultural meanings than the idea of commodity generally suggests (Zelizer, 1994). Thus, if in "market societies" food is a commodity, the fact is that commodities are something much more complex than it is generally assumed by economic theory (Polanyi, 1957; Appadurai, 1988). That is why, rather than referring to a generic "market logic," we prefer to consider a plurality of mercantile logics.

Nevertheless, there is something special about food markets. It is the fact that they embrace a kind of good associated with one of the most vital needs of human beings. Precisely for being so essential, it has been quite difficult to establish food as a sociological object. Poulain (2013) highlighted this "futility" of food for Western scientific thinking. According to him, it was not until the second half of the twentieth century that social theory began to pay attention to this theme. The rapid transformations in the forms of production and consumption since the advent of the urbanized society, as well as the subsequent crises unleashed by these changes, made the project of a serious sociology of food possible (Grignon, 1995).

Initially, French sociology transformed food into a social fact. It was then disseminated among various social disciplines and contexts as a biocultural phenomenon or a "biopsychosocial fact" (Contreras and Gracia, 2011). After all, no other product is capable of so broadly mobilizing the physiological and sociocultural functions of every society. As Fischler (1990) argues, foods differ from other goods because they are both physiologically (altering bodies) and psychologically (changing minds) "incorporated." People do not become what they eat only because of the ingested vitamins and nutrients, but also for the symbolic qualities of the food. Accordingly, we could say that food markets are special because food has a strong biopolitical connection to everything that surrounds life (Steiner, 2008).

Another particular aspect of food markets lies in the way they become subjects of strong scientific and political controversies. Although this is not a phenomenon restricted to food nor eminently contemporary, food is once again one of the main concerns in different public arenas. The specificity of the current context is, on the one hand, the global scale of the phenomenon and, on the other hand, the confluence of multiple crisis factors. Besides the neo-Malthusian nightmare of scarcity and hunger, we have also to consider the new food risks, health epidemics and pandemics, and the environmental and climatic effects of the our models of production, distribution and consumption (Guivant, Spaargaren and Rial, 2010).

Considering the advances of agricultural modernizing policies since the end of World War II, few could imagine that food would once again become one of the main political dilemmas of contemporary societies. Some still believe that the problem only emerged due to inability of governments to advance and disseminate the technological changes that were underway. In this case, the crisis solution would involve a further modernizing effort, now led by private capital rather than the State (Buainain, Lanna and Navarro, 2019). At the opposite pole, some view the problem as a kind of time bomb set by the Green Revolution policies themselves. In this perspective, it is argued that modernization more than failing to end hunger, has aggravated inequalities in food access and brought with it a new pattern of consumption – a diet based on carbohydrates, animal proteins and sugars – whose effects kill more than scarcity itself (Altieri and Toledo, 2011; Ploeg, 2009).

What makes the debate different now is the fact that the "food question" is no longer strictly alimentary, but is also energetic, environmental and financial (Bernstein et al., 1990). For the first time in history, food products are also raw materials, fuel and financial assets. Due to the emergence of what the literature calls 4F Crops (Food, Feed, Fiber and Fuel), agriculture has ceased to be the sole responsibility of farmers. Transnational corporations, investment funds and banks are also interested in profiting from the appreciation of agricultural assets on stock markets. Since the greater it is, the more dangerous it becomes, increasing the risk of a global food insecurity crisis. The problem is that even the possibility of profiting from anticipating a civilizing crisis feeds the appetite of financial capital.

The more intricate the food question becomes, the more complex must be both the analytical tools to interpret it and the political solutions to address its multiple and articulated crises. However, while in the political arena positions crystallize in unproductive dualism opposing supporters and critics of a new modernizing wave, the academic world faces difficulty in renewing its frameworks to interpret the new dynamics of food markets. This was the main reason that prompted us to propose a new analytical approach, built on a heterodox synthesis of contributions from the Convention Theory, which draws attention to the plurality of normative configurations of capitalism; Historical and Sociological Neoinstitutionalisms, which discusses the institutional mechanisms for building and stabilizing markets; and Practice Theory, which focuses on the analysis of the contingent evolution of different arrangements of social practices. At the heart of this approach lies the notion of "social order," which is defined as an arrangement of social practices integrated with institutions and material artifacts.

According to Schatzki (2002, 22), one of the leading authors of Practice Theory, "social orders are thus the arrangements of people, artefacts, organisms and things through and amid which social life transpires, in which these entities relate, occupy positions, and possess meanings." Our concept is not very different, since it also highlights the participation of material artifacts in shaping social orders. Nevertheless, we place a stronger emphasis on the normative, regulatory and cognitive pillars of the ordering processes. In other words, we are interested in how institutions constrain or reinforce the conformation of social practices, while being recursively altered by these latter. This question leads us to a concept of social order that dialogues with institutionalist authors who analyze the mechanisms of market coordination and stabilization (Beckert, 2009; Thévenot, 2001).

The stability of an order, and therefore of a market, depends on the formation of coherent links between three elements: practices, institutions and artifacts. Institutions guide the organization of practices, either by favoring certain discourses and actions, or by restraining them. Practices, in turn, are recursively responsible for defining patterns of interaction that, over time, shape institutions. In addition, practices arrange the positioning of the various artifacts that intermediate social relations. Yet, by their very nature, these artifacts also delimit a range of possibilities and limits for social practices. They are responsible for naturalizing the institutions, making them more resilient to changes induced by actors' practices. Finally, institutions engender technical paths that affect the selection of artifacts by humans.

The analysis proposed in this book focuses on the constitution, stabilization, crisis and change in markets (orders) as a result of changes in the links between practices, artifacts and institutions. Such approach could be "tested" in different social contexts. Two factors explain the choice of Brazil. The first is practical: it is the only country about which we have accumulated a vast set of information gathered from researches over the last decade, which could support our analyses. To exemplify the practices, artifacts and institutional mechanisms that constitute the food orders, each chapter will bring cases drawn from these researches that concern different food markets and

Brazilian regions. It is worth noting beforehand that such examples are not intended to be the most characteristic expression of each order. They are only the expression of our research themes and contexts. Even so, we believe they will suffice to support the idea of a plurality of food orders.

The second factor regards the exemplarity of the Brazilian case for the analysis. The predominant representation of Brazilian agriculture underscores a homogeneous image of its powerful agribusiness. Although this representation has been reconsidered since the 1990s, based on the dualistic (and also insufficient) contraposition between agribusiness and family farming, both advocates and critics of the modernization of Brazilian agriculture converge on the view that if diversity has not been completely eliminated, it was only because this process was interrupted. Thus, currently, while some actors and authors try to resume modernizing policies, others keep striving to stop them. Engaged in this conflict, both sides find it hard to think of diversity not as a remnant of an incomplete process, but as a structuring feature of contemporary forms of food production and consumption.

With the analytical purpose of interpreting this diversity, we distinguish six food orders: the *industrial, commercial, domestic, aesthetical, civic* and *financial orders*. Following a discussion of the main theoretical and methodological aspects of this classification (Chapter 1), we begin the analysis by defining the *industrial order* (Chapter 2). Supported by a wide range of technical (e.g., tractors, pesticides, hybrid seeds) and institutional (e.g., rural credit, banks, cooperatives, rural extension, agricultural research) artifacts established by means of strong leadership of the State, this order became dominant as of the second half of the twentieth century, bringing about radical changes in food production and consumption practices. On the one hand, it promoted mechanization of crops, specialization of labor, intensification of grain production and the chemical revolution of industrial processing. On the other hand, it intensified the standardization of food consumption, which responded to the rapid growth of urbanization and industrialization rates.

The consolidation of this mode of industrial ordering was enhanced by (and contributed to) the crisis of the commercial and domestic orders. Until 1930, the *commercial order*, heir to the traditional plantation and imperial–colonial power, was predominant in Brazil. The organization of this order dates back to preindustrial labor practices, which was relatively specialized due to the extensive monoculture. Moreover, anchored in the control exerted by the *latifúndio* over the state, this order also combines longstanding authoritarian and violent practices to access land and other natural resources. In recent decades, despite widespread criticism for such practices, this order has come back along with new forms of colonialism, which have spread among different Latin American countries, defined by increased rates of spoliation of natural resources to meet the demand from new world metropolises, mainly China.

The industrialization of agriculture also accelerated the crisis of the *domestic order* (Chapter 4). This order embraces production and consumption practices that have historically characterized peasant societies, where forms of coproduction between nature and society are anchored in the connection between traditional knowledge and artisanal objects. Considered by adepts of the agricultural modernization policies as a step prior to the entry of capitalism into the countryside, that would inevitably be overcome with the advent of industrialization – just as peasants would be replaced by agricultural entrepreneurs – the domestic order resisted and reinvented itself. This becomes clear, today, from the importance of production for own consumption and artisanal food processing, and from the growing demand for local, traditional and farm-house products.

From the 1980s onwards, the crisis of the *industrial order* not only favored the perpetuation of the domestic and commercial orders, but also made room for the emergence of new food orders. The rising criticism over the effects of the Green Revolution led to the articulation between agrarian movements and ecologists, reinforcing an "ethical critique" of the industrialization of agriculture. To a large extent, the establishment of a *civic order* (Chapter 5) was an outcome of the way these movements, guided by an ideal of food democracy, built practices of economic redistribution, recognition of family farming, protection of the commons and promotion of food and nutritional sovereignty and security. As we will show, agroecology has become the main expression of this set of civic practices.

Ethical criticism was followed by an "aesthetic critique" (Boltanski and Chiapello, 2005). In this case, the opposition movements challenged the rigidity of the industrial machine of capitalist accumulation in agriculture. Rather than uniformity and efficiency, the aesthetic critique lauded singularities, differences and hedonic aspects. In this sense, the *aesthetic order* emphasizes the "culturalization" of food economy, a process that reveals new normative bases for the valuation of food and eating practices. Such bases are associated with aesthetic representations of the human body, the nature, the countryside and the food itself. The practices most characteristic of this order are related to the expansion of the gastronome, gourmand and foodie universes.

Among the institutional transformations that succeeded the crisis of the modernization project, those deemed most significant to Sociology of Agriculture are associated with the consolidation of a *financial order*. This form of social ordering, increasingly predominant and widespread, is characterized by the specific way new artifacts and institutional devices promote, for example, financial speculation, deregulation of capital markets, flexibility of production structures, mechanisms of liberal corporate governance, capital concentration and global outsourcing. At the core of this order are institutional mechanisms that favor a short-term economic rationality responding to the aim of maximizing shareholder value. Consequently, financialization encourages, for example, speculative and despoiling investment practices, such as land, water and green grabbing.

These six orders coexist in tension, one trying to prevail over the others to enforce its own institutional logic. This was what happened in the post-World

War II, when the industrial order became hegemonic; and this is what the imperialist expansion of the financial order is announcing. However, nowhere in recent history have these orders been established as the only form of ordering the food production and consumption practices, not even during the dominance of the commercial order over the domestic one in the nineteenth century. The reactions, criticisms and changes that have characterized the development and diversification of these orders in the last century also recommend being reticent about the idea that financialization may be the last frontier. Reactions to this process can lead not only to the strengthening of other existing orders, but also to the emergence of new practices and values that do not fit into any of these orders. When and how new forms of ordering will arise is a question we are unable to answer. Since it has profoundly questioned the role of the State, the global crisis opened by the Covid-19 diffusion may be the occasion for this. However, and even if it seems that all liberal economists have once again become Keynesians, it is still too soon to proclaim a new order.

Throughout the chapters, we will also highlight various areas in which orders overlap, allowing observing that certain practices, artifacts and institutions are coherent with different logics of production and consumption. These overlapping areas also reveal movements of "appropriation," whereby a particular order tries to expand its domain by incorporating artifacts, rules, values, discourses and so on, which then will be adjusted to another arrangement of social practices. Finally, it will also become increasingly evident that the demarcation of these orders is a heuristic and normative exercise. Social reality is far more complex and contradictory. Nevertheless, just as social actors are compelled to classify the world to get some ontological security and make sense of their lives, social scientists are compelled to create models that allow them to analyze it.

References

Altieri, M. and Toledo, V. 2011. "The agroecological revolution in Latin America: rescuing nature, ensuring food sovereignty and empowering peasants." *Journal of Peasant Studies*, 38(3): 587–612.

Appadurai, A. (ed.). 1988. *The Social Life of Things: Commodities in Cultural Perspective*. Cambridge: Cambridge University Press.

Beckert, J. 2009. "The social order of markets. *"Theory and Society*, 38(3): 245–269.

Bernstein, H., Crow, B., Mackintosh, M. and Martin, C. (eds). 1990. *The Food Question: Profits versus People?* London: Earthscan.

Boltanski, L. and Chiapello, È. 2005. *The New Spirit of Capitalism*. London: Verso.

Buainain, A., Lanna, M. and Navarro, Z. (eds). 2019. *Agricultural Development in Brazil: The Rise of a Global Agro-Food power*. London: Routledge.

Contreras, J. and Gracia, M. 2011. *Alimentação, sociedade e cultura*. Rio de Janeiro: Fiocruz.

Fischler, C. 1990. *L'Homnivore*. Paris: O. Javob.

Grignon, C. 1995. "L'alimentation populaire et la question du naturel." In *Voyage en Alimentation*. Eizner, N. (ed.), 60–72. Paris: ARF.

Guivant, J., Spaargaren, G. and Rial, C. (eds). 2010. *Novas práticas alimentares no mercado global*. Florianópolis: UFSC.

Ploeg, J. D. van der. 2009. *The New Peasantries: Struggles for Autonomy and Sustainability in an Era of Empire and Globalization*. New York: Routledge.

Polanyi, K. 1957. *The Great Transformation: The Political and Economic Origins of Our Time*. Boston: Beacon Press.

Poulain, J.-P. 2013. *Sociologias da alimentação: os comedores e o espaço social alimentar*. 2nd ed. Florianópolis: UFSC.

Schatzki, T. 2002. *The Site of the Social*. University Park: Pennsylvania State University.

Steiner, P. 2008. "Les marchés agroalimentaires sont-ils des marchés spéciaux?" In *Les nouvelles figures des marchés agroalimentaires*, edited by Y. Chiffoleau, F. and J.-M. Touzard, 16–28. Montpellier: INRA.

Thévenot, L. 2001. "Organized complexity: Conventions of coordination and the composition of economic arrangements." *European Journal of Social Theory*, 4(4): 405–425.

Zelizer, V. 1994. *The Social Meaning of Money*. New York: Basic Books.

1   Food orders

Debates on the reconfigurations of the agrifood system have been characterized by several academic and political controversies. In Brazil, a major discussion is still related to the historical dependence of the country on an economic model based on production and export of agricultural commodities. Disagreements regarding this strategy encompass positions ranging from those who advocate a renewed version of the theory of comparative advantage, and who recurrently exalt the Brazilian agro-export vocation, to those who reproduce the old criticism related to deterioration in the terms of trade and criticize what they define as a process of respecialization of the Brazilian economy (Cano, 2012).

In the second half of the 1990s, the global devaluation of primary commodities led many scholars to suggest that this model could not support either farmers or national economies. At the same time, the volatility of these markets, which were increasingly at the mercy of the short-term logic of financial capital, prompted analysts to suggest that, instead of a model anchored in economies of scale from export monocultures, the new agrifood economy would require diversification and specialty products, so that to respond to growing consumer demand for organic, artisanal, local, ethical and ethnic foods (Wilkinson, 2008; Goodman and Sage, 2014). A decade later, however, the global commodity market resumed momentum. Its boom in the 2000s encouraged many researchers to analyze the reconfiguration of the "global food regime" and its impacts on the reorganization of rural spaces (McMichael, 2016a). In Brazil, special attention was paid to the formation of the "soy-meat complex" caused by Chinese demand (Sauer, Balestro and Schneider, 2018; Wesz, Jr., 2016).

Critics of the "commodity return" immediately engaged in demonstrating that this phenomenon is unstable, given, for example, the fluctuation in international prices and the rising of production costs. Moreover, critics highlighted how this regressive specialization would deplete natural resources and disrupt the socioeconomy of territories (Sassen, 2013). At the same time, they strived to identify rural development alternatives locally devised by farmers in opposition to the commodity expansion, discovering a myriad of short food supply chains that are rendered invisible to official statistics

(Cruz, Matte and Schneider, 2016). They also pointed to the role of public policies in supporting these alternatives, especially those based on the food security approach (Maluf et al., 2015). Even so, some analysts continued to challenge the significance and resilience of these small "niches," suggesting that these alternatives would be nothing than academic "neo-populism" (Bernstein, 2011).

The confrontation between these different interpretations of the agrifood system dynamics has favored the reproduction of dualistic conceptions that oppose global and local dynamics. In this case, global is usually the space of inequalities, asymmetrical powers, relations of domination and degradation of resources, whereas local is seen as positive through a set of ethical, ecological and aesthetic attributes. There is no room, here, for considering the problems of a "defensive localism," whose chauvinistic configuration may imply inequalities even greater than those found in the so-called global markets. These forms of "nonreflexive localism" may be associated with authoritarian and exclusionary mechanisms whereby local elites create a narrative of justice that mistakes social relations for spatial relations (Hinrichs, 2003; Goodman, Dupuis and Goodman, 2012).

In critical agrarian studies such dualism is reflected, for example, in differences between the approaches built on the concepts of "food regimes" and "farming styles." The first is heir to Marxist political economy, also retrieving elements from the World-System Theory and from French Regulation School (Friedmann, 2005; McMichael, 2013). The second represents the constructionist synthesis built by post-1980 sociology around the "problem of agency" and is based primarily on Giddens's structuration theory (Long, 2001). In our view, despite their different origins, both approaches share the same kind of difficulty in escaping the global–local dualism. While the food regimes approach is underpinned by metanarratives about the transformation of agriculture in the context of global capitalist economy, finding difficulties in explaining spatial variations, studies in terms of farming styles favor the heterogeneity of localized forms of agriculture, but are unable to generalize their conclusions on the organization of the agrifood systems.

It is true that in recent years there have been efforts to broaden the analytical framework of both approaches, bearing in mind the dialogue with the sociologies of markets and the sociotechnical transition studies (Friedman, 2016; Ploeg, 2017). Nevertheless, the difficulty in reconciling approaches still subject to the straitjacket of actor–structure dual language with the new theories that handle other ontologies confirms the contradiction of this new theoretical movement. On this account, although formulations based on the concepts of food regimes and farming styles are not representative of the various frameworks used for the analysis of food practices, their relevance in the contemporary debate within sociology of agriculture and food, coupled with the efforts of both perspectives to move towards "new sociologies," leads us to take them as privileged interlocutors for the debate proposed in this book.[1]

The sociology of agriculture and food

Until the late 1980s, sociology of agriculture was largely dominated by controversy between the rational-utilitarian modernization theory and its Marxist rival theory of commoditization (Long et al., 1986). While the former praised the market, the latter demonized it. Both, however, coincided in formulating it as an impersonal and fictitious structure. Since then, the many "turns" (cultural, pragmatic, ontological, decolonial) that have revitalized the social sciences contributed to produce new approaches to market analysis, which distance themselves from structural narratives in order to get closer to the social actors, albeit without falling into the methodological individualism of the utilitarian tradition (Carolan, 2012).

As to food markets, one of the approaches most widely applied in this period was known as "actor-oriented perspective" (Long, 2001). Building on criticism of neo-Marxist theories of simple commodity production, this approach guided the elaboration of new explanations about the maintenance of noncapitalist social forms (the peasantry) in advanced capitalist societies. Instead of focusing on the structural contradictions of the system, attention has been redirected to the organization of agricultural production units (Ploeg, 2009). In general, it was sought to reconcile a Chayanovian view of agrarian changes, which prioritizes the socioproductive logic of farmers, with theoretical innovations produced by the cultural turn in the social theory (Buttel, 2001).

Among the main merits of this proposition was the emphasis on social heterogeneity in the countryside, which would derive from farmers' ability to withstand structural pressures exerted by both the market and the State (Long, 2001). In this perspective, it was Ploeg (2009) who has advanced most empirical evidence, demonstrating how, in different regions of the world, from Dutch Friesland to Peruvian mountains, farmers create alternatives to the commoditization of agriculture (market action) and institutional incorporation (State action). For that, this author associated the concept of "farming style" with "a cultural repertoire, a composite of normative and strategic ideas about how farming should be done" (Ploeg, 1993, 241).

The concept of farming styles was one of the main developments of the actor-oriented perspective. Employed by Hofstee (1946) in *The Causes of Diversity in Dutch Agriculture*, the concept was originally connected with the dimensions of culture and locality, representing "the complex but integrated set of notions, norms, knowledge elements, experiences etc., held by a group of farmers in a specific region, that describes the way farming praxis should be carried out" (Ploeg, 1994, 17). Accordingly, the definition initially referred to interregional differences of European agriculture. Nevertheless, say Ploeg (1993, 243), as heterogeneity within the same community became evident, "farming styles have become mainly an intra-regional phenomenon." In this case, in accordance with the Chayanovian framework, the concept refers more directly to farmers' productive and social logics. Therefore, a style involves a specific mode of organization through which farming is defined by a cultural repertoire that, in turn, is tested, corroborated and, if necessary, adjusted by practice.

Operationally, the use of the concept varied along two axes. On the one hand, an eminently hermeneutic perspective that focuses on farmers' representational discourses about their social identities. On the other hand, a realistic perspective that emphasizes the organization of production practices, as well as their connection with the material environment, creating sociotechnical arrangements that define different ways of doing farming. As compared with the first one, this second use distances the concept from the cultural theory getting closer to the new relational sociologies, especially those based on the actor–network theory and, then, to a broader set of approaches on sociotechnical transitions. Two consequences are particularly relevant regarding this theoretical movement. First, the incorporation of sociotechnical networks theory requires abandoning the actor–structure dualism (Callon and Latour, 1981). It no longer makes sense to talk about structure if this is the very network formed by the "*actants*" (actors and objects). Second, and as a result, structuring notions such as that of "market" are replaced by heterogeneous arrangements of actors and artifacts (Callon, 1998).

While redirecting the theoretical path of the actor-oriented perspective, a major challenge was posed to it. Interesting as studies on agricultural styles may have been, revealing the plurality of production practices connected to different cultural repertoires and sociotechnical arrangements, they prove unable to build analytical generalizations. It means they fail to extrapolate a broader explanation of the organization of agrifood systems from the accumulated knowledge on locally situated styles. It was in this sense that Goodman (2004) criticized the excessive "localism" of the approach, a problem that became even more instigating in view of the new dynamics of globalization of food markets, which, especially for neo-Marxist authors, required a new look into the more structuring processes of agrarian capitalism (Edelman and Borras, Jr., 2016; Bernstein, 2016).

It was precisely because of this understanding that, in recent years, sociohistorical narratives have recovered space in agrarian studies. Among those, the food regime approach became one of the most widespread. It was initially formulated to understand "the role of agriculture in the development of the capitalist world economy, and in the trajectory of the state system" (Friedmann and McMichael, 1989, 93). However, over time, the approach has become a broad and heterogeneous global platform for renewing agrarian studies through combined research efforts on the structuring forces of the globalized agrifood system. Despite internal differences among its proponents, a commonality can be found in the recognition of, at least, two major historical periods of stability of the processes of capitalist accumulation and regulation in agriculture.

The first regime (1870–1920) is defined as Imperial–Colonial and is characterized by the transformation of peripheral countries into exporters of raw materials (rubber, cotton, flax fiber) and food (sugar, coffee) to sustain the emerging European industrial class. Organized under the hegemony of the British Empire, this regime established its institutional foundations on the gold standard, and its moral foundations on the free market rhetoric. The second regime was consolidated in the 1940s, following the postwar restabilization of global markets, and is defined by the formation of a new mercantile–industrial pattern of accumulation–regulation under the control of national states. Based on the establishment of the modern agro-industrial grain complex, it was formed under the insignia of the Green Revolution. Institutionally, the British Empire gave way to US hegemony, the gold to the dollar standard and the liberalism to the Developmental State (McMichael, 2013, 2009).

Nevertheless, as to the third regime, interpretations regarding its existence, nomenclature and configuration diverge. On the one hand, Friedman (2005) suggests that it simply defines an emerging configuration that still lacks clear contours, what would be a result from the resilience of the second regime by circumventing crises and readjusting (Niederle, 2018). The very emergence of a "corporate–environmental food regime" would demonstrate the ability of "green capitalism" to appropriate socioenvironmental criticism. McMichael (2005), in turn, argues that the transnationalization of the financial sector would have already become the marks of a new spirit of capitalism, leading to the emergence of a "corporate–neoliberal food system." More recently, the author has even suggested that, while it is premature to define a future food regime, China's current global strategy associated to the Belt and Road Initiative offer a lens on a new transitional process (McMichael, 2019).

Food regimes are represented by a series of regulatory frameworks that organize the relations of production and circulation of food and raw materials. Despite its legacies from earlier regimes, the corporate food regime would represent "a new moment in the political history of capital, which can be conceptualized as the 'project of neoliberal globalization'" (McMichael, 2016a, 71). Thus, for the author, instead of the postwar developmental project, in which states ruled the markets, now "states serve the markets" (*ibid.*, 72). The reason is the increasing centralization of power by transnational corporations and financial capitals, as well as the normative logic of liberalization driven by the reform agenda imposed by the World Trade Organization (Bonanno, 2012; Weiss, 2007). Reactions to such dynamics, in turn, would be basically led by the organization of agrarian social movements that also act at a transnational scale, such as Via Campesina, considered by McMichael (2016a) as the main front of resistance to the advancement of food corporations.

The food regime approach has allowed characterizing a set of signs that, especially since the 2000s, came to define some of the greatest social phenomena in the sphere of agriculture and food, such as: liberalization, supermarketization and financialization. The relevance of these phenomena furthered the criticism from political economy, which had showed so far a defensive theoretical position, against the "postmodern and neoempiricist" thinkers who, disregarding food regimes analysis, reverted to the analysis of "anomalous" and "local" case studies, which would be a kind of "agrarian particularism that, in getting rid of the superfluous, dispensed with the essential." Therefore, according to McMichael (2016b, 27), "while postmodernism promotes abstract localism, the concept of food regime concretizes historical relations."

However, at the same time as this approach became widespread, it also began to be recurrently challenged. The main criticisms targeted the overestimation of institutional ruptures to the detriment of transitions; lack of empirical evidence; too much emphasis on Western capitalisms; dualism of power relations; tendency to a normative reasoning; and excessive confidence in the ability of agrarian social movements to react (Niederle, 2018; Wilkinson and Goodman, 2017). In short, by reapproaching structuralism, the food regime theory would have solved the "generalization problem"– to which farming styles studies do not offer adequate answer – but at the cost of losing sight of heterogeneity. This would be expressed in the construction of an excessively unitary image of the agrifood system. According to Wilkinson and Goodman (2017, 278), "the homogenizing depiction of 'regimes' and 'hegemonic strategies' fails to recognize the diversity of agrarian trajectories and the variety of institutional landscape that exist since the second half of the nineteenth century."

Unexpectedly, the same kind of problem was then also becoming apparent in the work of some authors who had been more concerned with understanding the fragmentation of the rural world. An example is the way Ploeg (2009) borrowed from Hardt and Negri (2001) the notion of Empire to explain the broader tendencies of agrarian capitalism. Such shift in his focus was consistent with the reinterpretations of the effects of globalization and was also a response to the criticisms towards the localism of his analyses. This also denoted an effort to avoid the metanarrative of regimes, as the notion of Empire defines a more fluid and contingent configuration of relations of control on a global scale. Unlike imperialism – and therefore contrary to contemporary views on neoimperialism that prevail in debates surrounding food regimes – the Empire does not establish a territorial center of power, nor is it based on boundaries or fixed barriers. It is rather "a decentralizing and de-territorializing apparatus" that "controls hybrid entities, flexible hierarchies and multiple exchanges by means of regulatory structures. The various national colours of world imperialism have convened and merged into a single global imperial rainbow" (Hardt and Negri, 2001, 12). As we can see, this perspective attaches a lower weight to the State and to organized social movements as actors in either support or opposition to contemporary capitalism. They rather highlight the power of transnational corporations and the response of the "multitude" as the focal point of resistance to the privatization of commons triggered by the imperial dynamics.

The dialogue with these postmodern Marxist philosophers about the contemporary dynamics of global capitalism, allowed Ploeg (2009) to present the Empire as "an increasingly monopolistic complex, multifaceted, and expanding set of connections (i.e., a coercive network) linking processes, places, people, and products in a specific way" (Ploeg, 2009, 279). Despite the incredible malleability of the concept, the image of a "monopolistic" control structure still prevails, the new superstructure of globalizing markets against which peasant resistance movements are supposed to rise, whose practices are similar to those conceived by the authors of *Multitude* (Hardt and Negri, 2004). According to this perspective, beyond large mass mobilizations, the strategies of resistance to the Empire develop in connection with the constitution of technical and organizational "novelties" that allow farmers to achieve the level of autonomy required for their social reproduction (Ploeg, 2017; Schneider and Niederle, 2010).

In recent years, both understandings of agrifood systems have sought to move away from the dualism that opposes, on the one hand, a cohesive and unitary regime acting globally as a true "world-system" or "empire"; and, on the other, several localized alternatives, different styles of agriculture that would configure multiple and erratic niches that resist system pressure. One of the most fruitful paths taken by this debate is the rapprochement of both extremes to the Multilevel Perspective (MLP) on sociotechnical transitions, which comprises three heuristic levels: *regime*, *landscape* and *niche* (Geels, 2002). The "regime" is the level of the dominant and stable patterns of production relations, in which only incremental innovations take place without altering substantially the established configurations of power and domination. Substantial changes depend, on the one hand, on the ability of radical innovations produced in the "niches" to destabilize the regime. To this end, firstly, they must be able to shield themselves from pressures of the regime, so that to survive, and then leverage scaling up processes that enable them to decisively affect the regime's configuration (Wiskerke and Ploeg, 2004). On the other hand, both regime and niche can be profoundly impacted by landscape transformations, a level that represents the broadest articulation between the accumulation–regulation structures at a given historical moment.

This dialogue with the MLP leads us to three main questions. The first one concerns the diachronic aspect of the interpretation given to the concept of food regime. The food regime approach emphasize moments of historical disruption (crises), which are usually marked by events from outside the agrifood system (i.e., those associated with the level of the "landscape"). This is evident from factors that characterize the change from one regime to another (coinciding with the crises of capitalism). Nevertheless, this interpretation based on external shocks has been challenged by authors who discuss more gradual processes of transition from a social order to another, and who emphasize the analysis of the internal factors of change related to the ability of actors to drive changes inside the regime, which do not stem from exogenous institutional disruptions (Scott, 2008; Thelen, 2005). As Marsden (2016) points out, we have "to recognize that the dominant neo-liberalised 'socio-technical regime' is in itself vulnerable and potentially becoming far more 'decentred'."

The second question relates to the synchronic aspect of social changes. For paying little attention to localized agrifood systems, the food regime approach shows difficulty in explaining how these experiences operate and expand in the face of global pressures. The problem is that, by building an excessively homogeneous representation of both the regime and the countermovements that contest it, the approach reinforces the dualist view we criticized above. Everything that mismatches the representation of the regime is imprecisely treated as a kind of niche. Therefore, in this case, only three options are left for alternative forms of production and consumption: (1) to challenge the regime and change it (conversion); (2) to be appropriated by the regime (conventionalization); or (3) to keep forever as a niche (marginalization) (Niederle, 2018).

As several authors have pointed out, MLP has several limits when it comes to analyzing the complex interactions between levels. For instance, according to Marques, Ploeg and Dal Soglio (2012, 42), "the difficulties in establishing connections between an innovation niche and the socio-technical regime represent not only a barrier to transition, but also an obscure and uncharted theoretical area. "Trying to solve this problem, Elzen, Leeuwis and van Mierlo (2008) break with the idea of hierarchical levels, offering a reading of a chaotic arrangement of overlapping niches, regimes and landscapes. However, this makes it difficult to understand what defines each of them: what is a niche within a regime, if not the regime itself? Indeed, the changes proposed by these authors are so radical that it is hard to see what is left of the original approach, except for a confusing overlap of institutional spaces where the actors perform.

Finally, studies based on the MLP generally pay little or no attention to the landscape. The definition provided by Rip and Kemp (1998, 334), for instance, states that the landscape "is something around us that we can travel through; and in a metaphorical sense, something that we are part of, that sustains us." A little more precisely, though still quite broadly, Geels (2002, 1260) defines landscape as "a set of heterogeneous factors, such as oil prices, economic growth, wars, emigration, broad political coalitions, cultural and normative values, environmental problems." In this case, it would be necessary to define more precisely the boundaries between landscape and regime, so that not to confuse them nor to make undue generalizations that hinder the clear definition of how these levels are dynamically interconnected.

The trajectory of Brazilian agriculture

During the first food regime, Brazilian agriculture seemed to meet most of the conditions to legitimize the conceptualization proposed by McMichael (2016a). It comprised an export-led plantation model closely linked to British interests, whose companies had control over railways, ports, banks, sugar and coffee manufacturers, meat processing plants and large tracts of land (Linhares and Silva, 1979). In the early twentieth century, however, British dominance was already shared with French and American companies besides the national oligarchy. Furthermore, the "imperial-colonialist" thesis is surrounded by several controversies in Brazilian historiography. The prevailing image of the colonial system and the purpose of colonization as part of the expansion of commercial capitalism, supported by Marxist economists such as Caio Prado, Jr. (1942), was challenged by Fragoso and Florentino (2001), who, underling the endogenous processes of capitalist accumulation, point to a mosaic of noncapitalist forms of production as the foundation of Brazilian social formation.

In any case, it was the image of colonial plantation that became established in historiography, decisively contributing to the organization of time and space according to successive cycles of export commodities (gold, sugarcane, cotton, rubber, coffee). Plenty of evidence supports this narrative. At the end of the first regime, between 1921 and 1930, coffee accounted for 70% of the total value of Brazilian exports (49% to Europe, 26% to the United States). Therefore, the dependence of trade balance on a single crop is undeniable and occurred not only in this first regime, but all over the Brazilian history in the world economy. Even so, the trade balance structure does not allow for generalizations about the internal dynamics of agriculture and rural areas. The 1920 Agricultural Census, the first carried out in the country, corroborated the importance of coffee, since it represented one-third of the cultivated area and one-quarter of the value of production. Nevertheless, its presence was limited to 20% of the rural establishments, as its cultivation was concentrated in the southeast region, which accounted for over 90% of Brazilian coffee plantations. In turn, production of staple food for domestic consumption had a higher incidence among rural establishments, especially maize (present in 76%), followed by beans (63%), rice (37%) and cassava (26%). Maize production even exceeded that of coffee in terms of area and matched the same production value (IBGE, 1924).

In the 1980s, several Brazilian scholars strived to demonstrate that plantation has always been closely connected with a variety of domestic farming styles, which developed both within and adjacent to large farms. As described by Maria Yeda Linhares, a renowned historian of rural Brazil, to circumvent the misconception of an excessively homogeneous representation, a research effort was set in motion aiming for "going beyond the plantation in search of heterogeneity" (Linhares, 1995, 83). As a result, these studies recognized the diversity of local agrarian systems – comprising indigenous groups, freed black communities (*quilombolas*) and several settlements of European immigrants of different nationalities – allowing to "reconsider the relationship between food crops and commercial export farming, what meant reconsidering the view of the colony's agriculture as marked by monoculture exclusively destined for or imposed by the metropolitan dominant class" (Linhares, 1995, 84).

The end of the first regime coincides with a radical change of capitalism. The 1929 crisis is a key factor for understanding this historic moment, corroborating the connection between Brazilian coffee production and the world economy. There are though other equally relevant political–institutional elements less discussed in the literature on food regimes. In Brazil, the 1930 Revolution allowed the rise to power of Getúlio Vargas (who would remain until 1945), partially countering the interests of the coffee oligarchy. Since then, the State channeled efforts into urbanizing, industrializing and modernizing the country. The production of primary commodities for export continued to be privileged, though being now, on the one hand, connected to a nationalist strategy and, on the other, confronted with domestic food supply crises and famine (Castro, 1984).

The debates about domestic food supply revealed an aspect scarcely considered in the discussion on the configuration of the first regime, namely, the importance of the colony as importer of food from the metropolis (cod, wheat, beans and potatoes). In some years, total Brazilian imports have even exceeded exports. Furthermore, the control of foreign companies over food distribution went far beyond the dynamics of global trade. In fact, the major political disputes focused on the effects of stocks withholding by foreign companies that profited from inflation and food shortages in the domestic market (Linhares and Silva, 1979). There is no way to measure it, but this type of practice may have had effects as significant or more so on the disruption of localized agrifood systems than the US food aid would have from the 1950s onward (a prevailing factor in the debate on food regimes).

In Brazil, the second regime was marked by efforts of developmental plans to promote industrialization via "import substitution." At first, the priority given by the US to the Marshal Plan in Europe allowed Latin America to experiment with industrializing theories and policies led by the Economic Commission for Latin America (ECLAC). This, however, did not mean a break with the new center of global power and, in the mid-1950s, cooperation with the US had already intensified. The food aid to tackle the still unsolvable supply problem was just one aspect of a broader platform to "avert the risk of contagion from ideologies alien to Latin America" (Lessa, 2008). Another important face of this strategy was the entrance of foreign capital. Between 1955 and 1963, the value of foreign direct investment (FDI) in Brazil totaled US$497.7 million, 73% of which was concentrated between 1957 and 1960. Most of the funds came from the US (43.5%), followed by Germany (18.7%), Switzerland (7.3%), England (4.8%), Japan (3.3%) and France (3.1%). Almost all of the FDI went to the manufacturing industry (97.7%), especially to the automobile sector, the main focus of the developmental state (Caputo and Melo, 2009).

In agriculture, the incorporation of the American model began with a cooperation agreement for development of agricultural technologies between the Brazilian government and the Rockefeller Foundation. Signed in 1948, this agreement is deemed to be the origin of the rural extension model later institutionalized in the Brazilian Association of Credit and Rural Assistance (ABCAR), created in 1956. However, it was only during the military dictatorship (1964–1985) that the process for modernization of Brazilian agriculture accelerated. This process was driven by the National Rural Credit System (SNCR), created in 1965, backed by large loans from US banks. Concurrent to this, the Brazilian agriculture research corporation (EMBRAPA) was created in 1973, which included a great number of Brazilian PhDs graduated from American universities. A year later was created the Brazilian Company of Technical Assistance and Rural Extension (EMBRATER), consolidating the North American model for diffusion of innovations in agriculture.

The crisis of the second regime, which again coincides with a moment of restructuring of the global capitalist economy, was revealed in the late 1970s. The "oil shocks" (1973 and 1979) and the debt crisis made the State intervention unsustainable. In Brazil, the "lost decade" (1980s) was accompanied by the dismantling of agricultural policies, failed attempts to stabilize the economy so as to tackle inflation (the plans Cruzado I and II, Bresser, Summer), and reemergence of social movements, among which the agrarian ones stood out. These movements not only stirred up the fall of the military regime, in 1985, and the enactment of the new Federal Constitution, in 1988, but afterwards also became fundamental to disclose how unequal was the modernization process – which favored commodity production and large producers, particularly in the Center–South region of the country (Leite, 1998) – legitimizing the creation of specific public policies for family farmers.

As regards the emergence of the third regime, the Brazilian context could once again be taken as an example. A process particularly relevant in this moment was the expansion of the financial capital and the transnational corporations (Sauer, Balestro and Schneider, 2018; Wilkinson, Wesz, Jr. and Lopanne, 2016). While, in 1990, six of the ten largest food retail companies operating in Brazil were controlled by Brazilian capital, in 2016, six of the top ten were foreign. These companies reached out a rapid and intense process of concentration: while in 1994 the three largest firms controlled 18.3% of gross revenues, 20 years later, this percentage jumped to 47.4%. However, Flexor (2014) observed the persistence and, in some cases, the growth of small retail establishments (groceries, bakeries, butchers, greengrocers etc.). Once considered unable to compete with these large supermarkets, these enterprises have gained locational advantages (residential neighborhoods, suburbs, small municipalities), and offer differentiated products that attract specific segments of consumers.

Segmentation and differentiation of agrifood markets have also expanded in recent decades in light of concerns over health, sustainability, food quality, tradition and origin. This has created, revived and strengthened production and consumption practices associated with agroecology, short circuits, artisanal production, geographical indications and fair trade.

Instead of food from nowhere, grown by unknown producers, packaged and transported over long distances by large corporations, other practices – either old, new or renewed – become visible, which point to a different way of producing, distributing, choosing, valuing and consuming.

(Schmitt, 2011, 4)

It was in this context that Brazilian scholars also changed their focus towards quality, revealing the emerging logic of "flexible accumulation" in the agrifood sector – a fact that helped consolidate the criticism over the food regime theory (Wilkinson, 2008).

However, as soon as a decade later, this phenomenon seemed to show its limits. The return of commodities compromised the ability of particularist (and localist) strategies to counteract new processes of transnationalization and financialization, and the literature on global food regimes regained impetus. Even so, the Brazilian path during this period reveals that it is a mistake to diametrically oppose these two narratives. Neither the quality turn was the predominant logic in this country since the 1990s nor the commodity return represented an actual "return" to the agroindustrial logic that prevailed in the second regime, as demonstrated by recent appropriation by commodity markets of differentiation processes. Beyond criticizing such dualism, this book challenges the dominant narrative that suggests a process of homogenization of the Brazilian agrifood system, which is recurrently associated to the idea of an "agribusiness society."

Over the last decade, an interpretative (and political) dispute about these phenomena has been in place in Brazil. On the one hand, based on data on land, production and income concentration, the old thesis of disintegration of peasant economy gained space in view of the advance of agribusiness. For instance, based on information from the 2006 Agricultural Census, Alves and Rocha (2010) argued that 85% of gross production value is concentrated in 8.2% of rural establishments, and that only 22,000 establishments generate 51% of national agricultural production. At the other extreme, 3.8 million establishments have an average production value of R$128.00 per month and, according to Alves and Rocha (2010, 288) "in agriculture, there is simply no solution to their poverty problem." On the other hand, contesting this thesis, some researchers have explored the social skills of these farmers in structuring practices that enable them not only to resist institutional pressures but also to create new mechanisms of interaction with markets and the state, and to refute the notion of a single viable model of agriculture in capitalist societies (Schneider and Niederle, 2010).

While the heterogeneity of family farming styles has become the subject of increasing recognition, the agribusiness representation has remained an almost indecipherable black box. Although researches on the distinct socioproductive logics of agribusiness are more recent (Bühler, Guibert and Oliveira, 2016; Desconsi, 2017; Herédia, Palmeira and Leite, 2010), they have already shown that heterogeneity is not a feature exclusive to subordinate groups, what would give it a sense of remnant. Not only the actors, but also the accumulation logics of Brazilian agribusiness have become more diverse. An example is the production of soybean. Certainly, this is not the best example to reveal the heterogeneity of the agrifood system. Nevertheless, if this can be accomplished in this segment, frequently considered the ultimate expression of commoditization, the generalization of our argument will be more plausible.

Among the main annual agricultural crops in Brazil, soybean was the only one that had significant increase in cultivated area in recent decades. Between 1965 and 2005, the area expanded by 5,000% (from 431,000 to 23 million ha). By comparison, in this same period, the area of beans crops grew by only 16.5% (from 3.3 to 3.8 million ha) and that of rice decreased by 15% (from 4.6 to 3.9 million ha). More recently, between 2005 and 2016, the soybean area jumped from 23 to 33.9 million ha, driven by the boom in international prices. In 2015, soybeans accounted for 34% (R$98.7 billion) of the gross value of national agricultural production (R$288 billion) and for 38%, or R$28 billion, of Brazilian agricultural exports. In 1997, this percentage was 33%, which represented a value of only R$5.5 billion.

Currently, the bulk of Brazilian soy production is exported to China, whose purchases amounted to 57% of the total Brazilian soy exports (R$16 billion) in 2015, while in 1997 this percentage was only 11% (R$0.61 billion). The formation of a "soy–meat complex" between the two countries may be the main sign of a new global food regime (Escher and Wilkinson, 2019; Oliveira and Hecht, 2017), though at the same time it calls concepts such as "corporate–neoliberal regime" (McMichael, 2016b) and "corporate–environmental regime" (Friedmann, 2016) into question. On the one hand, nothing suggests that this complex is moving towards a kind of "green capitalism," given the slow incorporation of social and environmental certifications. On the other hand, it challenges the thesis of decreasing importance of states and governments before powerful deterritorialized transnational corporations, given, for example, the rise of the Chinese state-owned COFCO (China National Cereals, Oils e Foodstuffs Corporation) in the Southern Cone (Wilkinson, Wesz, Jr. and Lopane, 2016).

Changes occurred in the soybean market in the last two decades point to a globalized, financialized and technified agriculture. Nevertheless, these changes show quite specific forms of production according to the extension of the farming area and the logic of organization and accumulation, sociospatial origin and economic power of the farmer. As Wesz, Jr. (2014), Desconsi (2017) and Mier and Cacho (2016) demonstrate, there is still a wide variety among soy producers, differences being not restricted to land and financial resources, but also involving management strategies, types of business negotiation, sales arrangements and production destinations. Therefore, although the expansion of soybean led to some homogenization of rural landscapes, creating uniform and continuous farming spaces, the same is not true for the farmers and their practices, which remain deeply conditioned by the social contexts in which they are rooted.

> In spite of the movements of globalization, financialization and foreignization of the agrofood commodities markets, local space remains a strategic locus for the functioning of these economic activities. Besides, this study shows that all transnational power of the ABCD companies, which seems to be so abstract and intimidating when seen in global scale, depends, in its basis, on the formation, maintenance and exploration of a relation of proximity, trust and reciprocity with local actors (especially rural producers), going through family and friendship links.
>
> (Wesz, Jr., 2016, 307)

The findings of a research conducted by Vennet, Schneider and Dessein (2015, 18) also show that "despite the implication that all soy production systems are homogenous, the farms where soy are produced have important differences." The different styles of soybean farming presented by these authors stem from different sociotechnical arrangements. Each style implies a connection of soybean production with broader universes of social practices, in which distinct links are established between people, artifacts, techniques and institutions. Therefore, equating a land reform settler's soy production destined for biofuels to the soy cultivated by an Argentinean Corporation destined for feeding pigs in China is inappropriate. In other words, production, consumption and all practices connecting these are interdependent and related to the place where they occur, thus defining different arrangements, but also different meanings and identities.

The thesis presented by Desconsi (2017) on soy production by land reform settlers in the state of Mato Grosso also elucidates the existing plurality of social nexus, refuting the more recurrent view of "soy expansion as an 'external force' affecting settlers" (Desconsi, 2017, 307). The findings of his careful ethnographic work demonstrate that "the 'soybean region' is traversed by personal, kinship, neighbourhood relationships and, in a sense, patronage relations, while being shaped by various kinds of authority, networks and by multiple identities" (ibid., 301). According to the author, although these relationships do not conceal the fact that certain dominant actors associated with transnational capital, such as plantation owners and input resellers, were instrumental in shaping soybean farming styles, they also demonstrate that the mechanisms used by these actors to exercising and legitimizing their positions are far more complex than suggested by analyses that point generically to the strict rationality of capitalist accumulation.

Recognizing the heterogeneity of agricultural models does not contradict the existence of global dynamics in the agrifood system. However, it calls for adequate analytical lenses that enable perceiving the diversity of accumulation–regulation processes and locating them in time and space as well. Just as the concepts of commoditization and externalization were at the core of interpretations of changes in agriculture in the 1980s (Long et al., 1986), the watchwords today are financialization and transnationalization. And, as before, we suggest that these processes are more heterogeneous and contingent than they may seem at first glance. In order to more accurately understand them, it is imperative to look into the universe of social practices and institutions that organize these processes.

The analytical paradox

The narrative based on the notion of food regime falls into the same kind of problem that attracted extensive criticism over World-System Theory, especially for hardly explaining variations in institutional structures that operate globally (Block, 2012). However, and somewhat unexpectedly, the same can be said also of the farming styles approach, for which diversity only emerges from the resilience of actors to the structural pressures that, by their very nature, would lead to uniformity. To a certain extent, in both cases, heterogeneity would be a feature peculiar to niches (largely residual) and not of macroinstitutional regimes or landscapes.

It is rather paradoxical that these interpretations have gained ground in sociology of agriculture just as several authors of different theoretical strands of neoinstitutional school began to argue that multiple "varieties of capitalism" coexisted (Block, 2012; Thelen, 2004). This concept defining the existence of a plurality of normative arrangements (regimes, orders, worlds or systems) has been appropriated by different theoretical traditions. On the one hand, among authors who embrace the "rational choice" models, Hall and Soskice (2001) suggest that "liberal market economies" are not the only system in force and that, in many contexts, they are less efficient than the "coordinated market economies." On the other hand, from a more structural perspective that seeks to renew the French Theory of Regulation, Boyer (2005) not only extends the typology to four varieties (market-led, mesocorporatist, social democrat and state-led), but also adopts a broader set of parameters for the state–market–society relationship (wage relation; competition patterns; currencies and finance; state configurations; international integration and modes of regulation). Based on this, he analyzes different national paths, concluding that "this institutional diversity shows up in a variety of regulation modes and accumulation regimes that differ across time and space" (Boyer, 2005, 548).

Although focusing their attention on different levels of analysis, both approaches distinguish varieties of capitalism at the nation-state level. Even Hall and Soskice (2001), who make a case for the "firm" as the basic unit of analysis, eventually distinguish varieties of capitalism at the level of national states, contrasting the liberal American model and the coordinated German economy. In another way, we argue that these different configurations can coexist within a same State (Vidal and Peck, 2012), as suggested by the debate on the simultaneous, interrelated and conflicting occurrence of neoliberal and developmental strategies in Brazil between 2002 and 2016, period during which a center–left political coalition sought to reconcile a liberal strategy based on primary commodity exports with social welfare and inequality reduction policies (Niederle et al., 2019).

The very notion of "regime" could be employed to encompass this institutional plurality, although this would require recognizing the coexistence of multiple regimes and distinguishing what exactly concerns the regime as regards the institutional landscape. One problem is that the concept is often employed as equivalent to capitalism. This reproduces the analyses of the first generation of regulation school about the transition from a Fordist regime to the flexible accumulation (Harvey, 1992). Indeed, if Boyer himself, one of the major exponents of this school, works today with the idea of spatial and temporal coexistence of multiple regimes, it is because the old conception is limited. Indeed, the regulation theory has evolved over the past two decades from a structural Marxism to a more institutional view, concerned with the normative and cognitive elements of economic coordination processes (Boyer, 2003).

An alternative for apprehending the plurality of institutional grammars is Contention Theory. Built in close dialogue with the regulation theory, this French school proposes a possible mediation between institutional economics and pragmatic sociology (Wilkinson, 1997). Its proponents criticize the Keynesian-Marxist structuralism that marks the Theory of Regulation, which, according to them, explains its analytical focus on the historical institutional development at the level of the superstructure, emphasizing the link between Market and State. As a result, its framework has difficulties in addressing the relations between large-scale institutional changes and the individual and collective behaviors of social actors. Therefore, Convention Theory was initially established as a kind of complement to the Regulation Theory at the microlevel. While the latter was concerned with institutional evolutions in broader aggregate systems, the former followed an actor-centered approach (Eymard-Duvernay, 2009).

With the advancement of discussions and the emergence of a fruitful interaction between references and publications, a process of cross-fertilization between these two perspectives led to some important convergences. On one side, conventionalists have moved from a complex methodological individualism to an institutionally situated characterization of the individual action; on the other, regulationists sought to overcome the remnants of a functionalist interpretation to address how institutions become connected to collective routines and behaviors (Boyer, 2006; Wilkinson, 2011). This, however, did not result in an "institutionalist merger." The division of intellectual work eventually resulted in competition between two heterodox schools that began to construct integral interpretations connecting different heuristic levels (Boyer, 2003). The main example in this sense is the conventionalist interpretation of the macroinstitutional dynamics of capitalism presented by Boltanski and Chiapello (2009).

The concept of convention was originally described as a "shared knowledge system" (Salais, 1989), a "system of representations" (Eymard-Duvernay,

1989) or a "collective cognitive tool" (Orléan, 1989). However, over time, the encounter with pragmatism gave the concept an "interpretive character" (Dosse, 2003). Since then, a convention comprises a normative framework whose mobilization presupposes moral engagement. It is a shared world view that guides actors in carrying out their practices. It is not merely about a routine or a habit, since it only makes sense within a social collective. It is a scheme of interpretation constructed by means of social interaction and communicative action, which prescribes a form of action to be adopted, without necessarily constituting a formal regulation. According to Batifoulier and Larquier (2001), the major difference between the "small" cognitive convention, part of actors' rationality, and the "great" normative convention, based on moral value judgments, is that the latter carries an imperative of justification. That is, it must be publicly legitimized on the basis of a "higher principle," which ultimately makes it "a justified common world." Here the concept of convention meets the model of multiple "worlds" (*cités*) proposed by Boltanski and Thévenot (1991) to analyze the actions of qualification carried out every day by individuals, when classifying and judging objects and people.

According to Boltanski and Thévenot (1991), social interactions generally are based on equivalences established in the course of a historical process of building classification systems. These systems reduce uncertainties and provide individuals with an intelligible social world, constituting an indispensable condition for the coordination of their actions. Hence, for the most part, life goes on without the need for people to make a new agreement every time they need to exchange property, gestures, words, goods and so on. This is basically the role of conventions as objective and normative resources that enable people and organizations to coordinate their activities for the production of monetary and cultural values. However, there are "critical moments" when the established classifications are subject to contestation. These are particularly interesting moments for social analysis, since the critical capacity of the actors (reflexivity) sharpens.

Nevertheless, how can actors coordinate their actions among various possible ways of establishing equivalences? How to define these forms of equivalence (worlds, orders, systems) without falling into the pitfalls of both the unitarian perspective of traditional economics, which recognizes only price as a measure of equivalence, and the postmodern relativism, which, as Boltanski and Thévenot (1991) express, make the world an anarchic confrontation of heteroclite conceptions that are deaf to each other? To solve this impasse, these authors seek in classical political philosophy different notions of justice, based on which they propose a model founded on six worlds, each organized under different moral principles: Inspirational (creativity); Domestic (loyalty); Opinion (reputation); Civic (representation); Market (competitiveness); and Industrial (productivity). Each of these worlds makes up an institutional grammar that shapes the actors' logics and is endowed with its own coherence and legitimacy.

In agrifood studies, this analytical framework made room for a fruitful research agenda on diverse institutional formats for market coordination. One of the most recent contributions was presented by Touzard and Labarthe (2017) at the seminar (see Allaire and Daviron, 2017) that discussed the advances in Convention and Regulation Theories 20 years after the publication of the book that marked the incorporation of this approach into Rural Studies: *The Great Transformation of Agriculture: Conventionalist and Regulationist Readings* (Allaire and Boyer, 1995). Based on the convergence of institutional devices and specific dynamics of capitalist accumulation, which also involve innovation processes, technological paradigms and territorial embeddedness, the authors trace the historical evolution of different "food models": (a) agroindustrial, (b) domestic (c) proximity, (d) artisanal commodity and (e) differentiated quality. According to the authors, "the *coexistence of these models in most countries* calls into question sectoral approaches to regulation" (Touzard and Labarthe, 2017, 301, our italics).

Another widely known approach derived from Convention Theory is that presented by Salais and Storper (1992) about "worlds of production." Although originally developed for industrial systems, the idea was adapted for the analysis of agrifood markets, originating the concept of "worlds of food," seeking to discern "an increasingly fragmented and differentiated food market" (Morgan, Marsden, and Murdoch, 2006, 11). Unlike the original concept, which focuses only on economic differentiation, this concept adds three complementary aspects. First, it considers the key role played by *nature* in food production and consumption. Second, it considers that *culture* defines the meanings (qualities) attributed to food, which distinguish generic and dedicated products in different social contexts. Third, it closely focuses on political *institutions* operating at different spatial levels, suggesting a dialogue with the Regulation Theory. Thus, according to Morgan, Marsden and Murdoch (2006, 23), the "worlds of food that now comprise the contemporary food sector work not just according to an *economic* logic (as implied in Salais and Storper's approach), but also according to *cultural*, *ecological* and *political/institutional* logics" (italics in the original).

Integrating consumption into agrifood system

Regulation Theory has always favored the social relations of production and labor. The same applies to part of the Convention Theory. However, the assimilation of this school in the food sector revealed greater concern over consumer practices (Wilkinson, 2011; Rangnekar and Wilkinson, 2011). This led to a fruitful dialogue with the sociology of food (Fischler, 1990; Poulain, 2013) and, thereon, to two major advances. On the one hand, the recognition that "consumer patterns also correspond to very different agrifood systems" (Morgan, Marsden, and Murdoch, 2006, 1). It means that the criticism of the complete commoditization have also to encompass the heterogeneities of food consumption. On the other hand, it led to the perception that resistance to dominant logics in the agrifood system are also heterogeneous, relatively dispersed, and go far beyond agrarian movements. In this sense, the interfaces with literature on the practices and meanings of "politicized consumption" stand out (Portilho and Micheletti, 2018).

A brief genealogy of the sociology of consumption shows that studies on this subject were initially characterized by a strong productive bias, since consumption was seen as "subordinated to, and explained in terms of, production" (Warde, 2014, 281). This stereotyped form of understanding consumption has been associated with Marxist discussions on structure and superstructure, in which cultural elements such as taste are conceived as industry-led, while consumption patterns are treated almost exclusively as markers of unequal distribution of means of production and therefore of wealth. This model was countered by an equally limited one: the neoclassical utilitarianism that considers the consumer as the sovereign actor, who makes rational decisions in view of his/her preferences. In this perspective, no social structures or shared cultural meanings help define individual consumption decisions.

Since the 1980s, new approaches influenced by the "cultural turn" in the humanities have criticized both perspectives, while redirecting attention from instrumental aspects to the symbolic dimensions of consumption. In this case, instead of mere manipulation by industry or maximization of utilities, consumption has come to be identified as a form of meaningful social interaction. According to Warde (2015), consumption has become a means by which individuals and social groups express their identities, which in turn materialize into tastes and lifestyles. Marked by discussions on the processes of globalization, aestheticization and commoditization, cultural theory has given rise to interpretations of people's aspirations, activities and possessions in terms of a "consumer culture." However, the more this perspective attracted followers, the more it was criticized. A major criticism centered on its neglect of practical activities, routines, habits, procedures and material aspects related to consumption. Because of that, "[t]he emphases of the cultural turn diverted attention away from some empirical phenomena relevant to the analysis of consumption" (Warde, 2015, 282).

The debate on the materiality of consumption were strengthened by the emergence of another theoretical movement in the humanities, which became known as the "practice turn" (Schatzki, Knorr-Cetina and Savigny, 2001). Associated with a former philosophy of social action, this movement emphasizes "practices" as the primary entities of the social world. Its ontological implication entails, firstly, the assumptions that actions precede justifications, flows and interactions prevail over units, and materiality precedes the symbolic (Schatzki, 2002). This new focus engendered a profound reconfiguration of hitherto dominant understandings of consumption, mainly by making room for questioning Marxist theses about standardization and commodity fetishism. Afterwards, rather than the existence of a generalized process of commoditization of tastes, habits, beliefs and senses, due to the control exerted by food empires (Ritzer, 1995), several authors suggest that the history of food consumption should be told in terms of production of diversity, the result of the encounter between different cultures, each one with its own practices, ways of doing, objects and meanings (Lang, 1999; Sassatelli, 2007; Warde, 2005).

While the formation of global value chains evens out certain differences imposing similar standards, especially regarding health control, it also entails the emergence of new differentiations. One of the most noticeable effects of this process is the increased access to "exotic" foods associated to the proliferation of ethnic cuisines around the world, and whose main expression is the Asian food diaspora. Apart from the access itself to differentiated food, what is most interesting in this process is the resignification of food practices. Eating "Chinese food" in China, France or Brazil are completely different experiences. The encounter of Chinese culture with the Brazilian "all-you-can-eat buffet" model, for example, makes a Chinese feel more "culturally displaced" than a Brazilian, when eating Chinese food in São Paulo. To begin with, a Chinese would not understand why rice went from main course to side dish.

In Brazil, there was also an expansion of regional cuisines. In recent years, there was a rapid spread of restaurants specialized in typical food of Minas Gerais and of north-eastern Brazil, as well as of steakhouses. Even the *churrasco* (grilled meat) presents regional differences in forms of preparation, types of cuts of meat, side dishes and the way it is served. Another example of the resignification of Brazilian regional food is açaí. Typical product of the Amazon, where it is usually consumed pure or with cassava flour and fish, in the rest of the country it is recurrently associated with guarana syrup and accompanied by strawberries, banana and/or granola. Something similar happens with tereré (indigenous drink prepared with the infusion of *yerba mate* in cold water). Much consumed in Mato Grosso do Sul due to its proximity to Paraguay, but already widespread in other regions of the country, the drink began to be prepared with artificial juice or soda.

This phenomenon is not just about incorporating new products and ingredients. Poulain (2013) also highlights the incorporation of new instruments and utensils in food preparation practices. The most common would be the microwave revolution, one of the highest symbols of food industrialization associated with urbanization and profound changes in labor society. However, the return of clay and iron pots, wooden spoons and even the incorporation of objects strange to the West such as the hashi are also part of the repertoire of objects that have altered our daily eating practices. In addition, new social actors were also incorporated. For instance, although "everyday cooking and, more broadly, food remain a primarily female territory" (Poulain, 2013, 59), men have increased their participation in domestic shopping and food preparation.

In short, as the next chapters will show, the diversification of the agrifood system is evident not only in the scope of production, which remains a privileged focus of the analyses even though many experts point to the emergence of a food system increasingly driven by consumption. We argue that, by observing the broader arrangement of eating practices – preservation (drying, smoking, preserves, packaging), preparation (threshing, filtering, cutting, grinding, cooking) and consumption (individual, collective, at the table, on the sofa, at home, away from home, at work) – it is possible to visualize a plurality of social orders.

Food orders: linking practices, institutions and artifacts

The notion of "order" is basic to understand the constitution of society, particularly the phenomena of institutional stabilization and legitimation. Based on this notion, the social sciences produced various formulations about the intertwining between the social, political, economic and legal spheres. These are present mainly in institutional theories, in which, depending on the perspective, "orders" are not distinct from "regimes" or "worlds." In our view, however, while the concept of regime of the Regulation Theory approaches the macroinstitutional landscape, and the worlds of the Convention Theory define moral principles of too wide generality, it is possible to think of a definition of orders linked to the universe of social practices and their meanings.

Most institutional theories treat institutions (habits, customs, conventions, laws, standards) as mechanisms for producing behavioral stability and regularity, which consequently result in "order" (Beckert, 2009). Accordingly, March and Olsen (2006, 3) define an institution as

> a relatively enduring collection of rules and organized practices, embedded in structures of meaning and resources that are relatively invariant in the face of turnover of individuals and relatively resilient to the idiosyncratic preferences and expectations of individuals and changing external circumstances.

Indeed, even Giddens (1984) suggested that institutions are, by definition, the most enduring elements of social life, which bestow "soundness" upon social systems.

However, a new generation of social scientists criticizes this tendency towards equating institutions to everything that remains stable in the continuous flow of social change (Fligstein, 2001; Scott, 2008; Thelen, 2005). According to this criticism, the institutions themselves are always subject to reinstitutionalization processes. As Scott (2008, 59) points out, "although institutions function to provide stability and order, they themselves undergo change, both incremental and revolutionary." Because of this, the analysis "must include not only institutions as a property or state of an existing social order, but also institutions as processes, including the processes of institutionalization and deinstitutionalization" (Scott, 2008, 59). By observing these processes, we can understand why, as said by Schatzki (2002, 16), "social orders are inherently unstable, and frequently de and restabilized."

To circumvent the uncertainties, tensions and criticisms that may endanger their perpetuity, institutions often rely on material artifacts that naturalize them, making norms, rules and standards seem an objective element of reality (Busch, 2011). Like actor–network theory, convention school also add to the analysis of institutionalization the entities that express the materiality of social life. Rarely considered by most institutional approaches, the role of artifacts has been incorporated into Thévenot's (2002) idea of "equipped humanity," for whom each order should be considered as a specific arrangement between norms and objects. As Boltanski and Thévenot (1991) point out, the notion of "worlds" aims to show "how people face uncertainty by relying on objects to produce orders and, conversely, consolidating objects by coupling them to constructed orders."

To the extent that both institutions and artifacts "always produce partial and temporary orderings" (Busch, 2011, 6), the concept of order acquires a procedural and dynamic character (Schatzki, 2002). It also confers on orders permeable boundaries through which actors and objects circulate, activating processes of criticism, contestation and social change – until a new moment of stability is created. In addition, they show overlapping points, so that some actors and objects appear in more than one order, although carrying different identities and meanings. Thus, just as "a garden rock, say, can suddenly become a paperweight and at a later moment a weapon" (Schatzki, 2002, 16), soy can be the industrial commodity of transnational corporations, and in another context, the sustainable and healthy alternative of vegetarian consumers.

In this sense, the analysis does not lie in the actors or structures, but in everything that creates a nexus between them – the practices, institutions and artifacts. These three elements configure a social order, based on their interactions, their relative positions and their identities (human) or meanings (objects). Accordingly, while Schatzki (2002) defines an order as a specific arrangement of practices, our definition emphasizes the relationship of these practices with the institutional devices and the material universe. The inclusion of institutions not only widens the ability to "capture more aggregate levels of social organization" (Warde, 2015), but also adds a historical dimension to the analysis, thus addressing two limits recurrently pointed by critics of the practice theory.

As practices, artifacts and institutions constitute three central categories in our framework, it is important to clearly define each of them. *Artifacts* are perhaps the easiest to define, even though the understanding of how they participate in social dynamics is the subject of deep controversy. This category includes all material entities that help shape and stabilize production and consumption practices (and all other intermediary practices that such as processing, packaging, distribution, storage, marketing, preparation etc.). The analysis of how artifacts contribute to the conformation of social orders involves examining their position in relation to other entities, whether they are other artifacts or human beings. At the same time, it is important to figure out how artifacts are associated with certain institutional choices, seeking to understand their role in defining sociotechnical trajectories. Operationally, this analytical stance is not very different from that suggested by Marcel Mauss in his *Manual of Ethnography*:

> Any object must be studied (a) in itself; (b) in relation to its users; and (c) in relation to the whole of the system under scrutiny ... The most insignificant tool should be named and located; by whom is it used, where was it found, how is it used and for what purpose, does it have a general purpose or a special one? ... It should be photographed as it is used, together with the object on which it is used, or with its end product; the photographs will show the various stages of production. The industrial system to which the object belongs should be identified; the study of a single tool normally implies the study of the craft as a whole.
>
> (Mauss and Hubert, 2007[1947], 27)

For Schatzki (2002, 41), "social relations, consequently, cannot be restricted to relations among humans alone." Yet, while recognizing the central role of materiality, this author does not establish a complete symmetry between humans and nonhumans, as proposed by the more radical posthumanist ontology of Latour and Callon. Otherwise, he emphasizes human ingenuity for manufacturing and handling artifacts (nature), albeit recognizing that, for their material configuration, artifacts impose conditions on human action. Although they may be qualified and manipulated in different ways, their uses partly depend on themselves. In other words, artifacts resist certain uses and, therefore, they undeniably circumscribe limits to and possibilities for action.

Practices organize the relationships, positions and meanings involving not only humans, but also all social and natural entities (people, objects, animals, artifacts ... stone and soy). Indeed, they cannot be reduced to the individual level. As Schubert (2017) suggests, they are emergent properties that take shape only in social interaction (and while immersed in a particular material context). The most basic unit of social practices comprises the sets of *doings* and *sayings*. The former includes actions that people perform with their bodies: eating, weeding, running, writing etc. The speeches involve oral language, though not exclusively, since they can also be considered a subset of bodily acts when actors manifest themselves through gestures and physical expressions. The central parameter for defining discursive practices is the production of a socially shared message (Schatzki, 2001).

On the one hand, practices create patterns of interaction that shape meanings, senses, identities and, more broadly, institutions. On the other hand, institutions establish systems of classification and appraisal of all entities that configure social orders. Institutions create a frame so that social actors can understand each other and carry out their interactions. As noted earlier, to understand how this happens, it is necessary to surpass the notion of institution that predominates in Convention and Regulation Theories, because, while the latter focuses primarily on regulatory aspects, the former divides its attention between general principles and localized cognitive references. A more comprehensive reading of institutions requires connecting the set of *normative, cognitive* and *regulatory* components that guide social action. These three institutional pillars suggested by Scott (2008) encompass broad values imposed on individuals as moral sanctions; legally sanctioned rules, norms and standards; and shared beliefs and logics that constitute the cultural and cognitive components of action.

How to delimit social practices and orders? A practice can be identified by its "regularity" in time and space (Warde, 2014). In turn, the central element to define an order is "similarity," which implies identifying the position that each element (person, artifact, object, rule, pattern etc.) occupies in relation to the others. From an eminently relational perspective, "to be 'positioned' is to take up a place among other things, a place that reflects relations between the things involved" (Schatzki, 2002, 19). But this position should not be understood as a merely spatial phenomenon. It is rather an abstraction denoting how entities create links between each other, which in turn depends on the establishment of meanings (objects) and identities (people). Hence, language stands out as a cornerstone for the architecture of social orders. This "tool of the tools" (Dewey, 1988, 134) organizes relationships, positions, meanings and identities – and not just for humans, but for all social entities, including norms, rules, laws, representations and so on (Figure 1.1).

Therefore, the institutions themselves are also reinterpreted in action, what leads to their varied incorporation into socially situated practices. Institutions

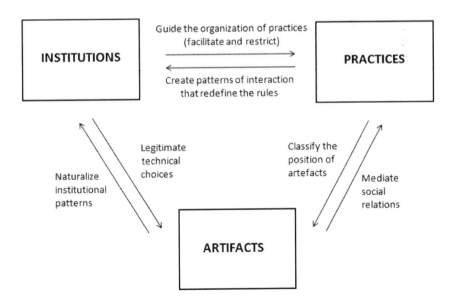

Figure 1.1 Ordering practices, institutions and artifacts.

are discursively handled to establish coherent links with other entities of the social order. This implies recognizing that the analysis of institutions requires understanding the different ways in which they are incorporated into the world of life, what breaks with the functional–structural approach that often guides the discussion about how norms "define" social behavior. As Ostrom (2007) stresses, it implies the study of "rules-in-use," that is, the analysis of institutional devices as they are actually incorporated into social practices. According to this author, insofar as institutions are not self-formulating, self-determining or self-enforcing, rather than building models that presuppose the effects of rules on individuals' behavior and on organizational strategies, the analysis should focus on "working rules," which entails considering the particularities of different social contexts.

Social change depends on the destabilization of relatively stable orders, which entails movements of contestation (Boltanski, 2009), but also, and associated with it, the circulation of social entities through the permeable boundaries of orders. Just like occurs between conventional "worlds" (Boltanski and Thévenot, 1991), actors and artifacts also move between social orders, creating complex, hybrid interconnections and, in some cases, prompting critical moments. The crisis can result in either readjustments or radical transformations, including the emergence of new orders. Throughout this process, entities change not only their relational positions, but also their meanings and identities. However, there are limits to this circulation. Just as artifacts, identities and meanings are not completely fluid or manageable, it is often this kind of movements that triggers dynamics of contestation that destabilize orders and produce social change.

By way of example, in Brazil, "family farming" and "agribusiness" delimit two distinct sociopolitical identities, to which different rural development practices are associated. Over time, the consolidation of these identities has produced a kind of institutional framing that, on the one hand, fosters social action and, on the other, limits the circulation of social actors. Thus, while these identities are managed by social actors to create collective engagement, integrating, under the same definition, different social groups that have specific identities, they also impose practices and discourses that restrict circulation of actors. As we will show later, the movements that overflow this institutional framework produce a set of social criticisms that, depending on several factors, can induce changes in practices and also in the currently established identities.

Once defined the components of an order, it is necessary to address its demarcation. As with the "varieties of capitalism" and the "worlds of production," "the demarcation of specific arrangements is ... relative to the interests and purposes of the demarcator" (Schatzki, 2002, 46). That is, orders are not an element of objective reality, but rather an analytical tool. Thus, not only the number of orders can be variable, but also the level of generalization changes according to the researcher's objectives. For this reason, in the next chapters, we analyze the conformation of six food orders that, in view of the level of aggregation we adopted, bring together the variety of production and consumption practices found in our research on food systems in Brazil: industrial, commercial, domestic, aesthetic, civic and financial.

Note

1 Some parts of this chapter have been originally published in the article "A pluralist and pragmatist critique of food regime's genealogy: varieties of social orders in Brazilian agriculture". *Journal of Peasant Studies*, 45(7): 1460–1483, 2018.

References

Allaire, G. and Boyer, R. (eds). 1995. *La grande transformation de l'agriculture.* Paris: INRA, Economica.

Allaire, G. and Daviron, B. (eds). 2017. *Transformations agricoles et agroalimentaires: entre écologie et capitalisme.* Paris: Quae.

Alves, E. and Rocha, D. 2010. "Ganhar tempo é possível?" In *A agricultura brasileira*: desempenho recente, desafios e perspectivas, edited by J. Gasques, J. Vieira Filho and Z. Navarro, 275–89. Brasília: Ipea.

Batifoulier, P. and Larquier, G. 2001. "De la convention et de ses usages." In *Théorie des conventions*. Batifoulier, P. (ed.), 9–31. Paris: Economica.

Beckert, J. 2009. "The social order of markets." *Theory and Society*, 38(3): 245–69.

Bernstein, H. 2011. *Dinâmicas de classe da mudança agrária.* São Paulo: UNESP.

Bernstein, H. 2016. "Agrarian political economy and modern world capitalism: The contributions of food regime analysis." *Journal of Peasant Studies*, 43(3): 611–47.

Block, F. 2012. "Varieties of what? Should we still be using the concept of capitalism?" *Political Power and Social Theory*, 23: 269–91.

Boltanski, L. 2009. *De la critique.* Paris: Gallimard.

Boltanski, L. and Chiapello, È. 2005. *The New Spirit of Capitalism.* London: Verso.

Boltanski, L. and Thevenot, L. 1991. *De la Justification.* Paris: Gallimard.

Bonanno, A. 2012. *The Legitimation Crisis of Neoliberalism.* New York: Palgrave-Macmillan.

Boyer, R. 2003. "Les institutions dans la théorie de la régulation." *Cahiers d'Économie Politique*, 44(1): 79–101.

Boyer, R. 2005. "How and why capitalisms differ." *MPIfG Discussion Paper*, 5(4).

Boyer, R. 2006. "L'économie des conventions 15 ans après: un point de vue à partir de la théorie de la régulation." In *L'économie des conventions: méthodes et résultats*, edited by F. Eymard-Duvernay, 45–66. Paris: La Découverte.

Bühler, E., Guibert, M. and Oliveira, V. (eds). 2016. *Agriculturas empresariais e espaços rurais na globalização.* Porto Alegre: UFRGS.

Busch, L. 2011. *Standards*: receipts for reality. Boston: MIT Press.

Buttel, F. 2001. "Some reflections on late twentieth century agrarian political economy." *Sociologia Ruralis*, 41(2): 165–81.

Callon, M. 1998. "An essay on framing and overflowing: economic externalities revisited by sociology." In *The Laws of the Markets*, edited by M. Callon, 244–69. Oxford: Blackwell.

Callon, M. and Latour, B. 1981. "Unscrewing the big leviathan: how actors macrostructure reality and how sociologists help them do so." In *Advances in Social*

Theory and Methodology, edited by K. Knorr-Cetina and A. Cicourel, 277–303. London: Routledge.

Cano, W. A. 2012. "Desindustrialização no Brasil." *Economia e Sociedade*, 21: 831–51.

Caputo, A. and Melo, H. 2009. "A industrialização brasileira nos anos de 1950." *Estudos Econômicos*, 39(3): 13–38.

Carolan, M. 2012. *The Sociology of Food and Agriculture*. New York: Routledge

Castro, J. 1984. *Geografia da Fome*. 10th ed. Rio de Janeiro, Antares.

Cruz, F. T., Matte, A. and Schneider, S. (eds). 2016. *Produção, consumo e abastecimento de alimentos*. Porto Alegre: UFRGS.

Desconsi, C. 2017. *O controle da lavoura: a construção de relações sociais e a produção de soja entre assentados do meio norte do Mato Grosso – Brasil*. PhD Thesis. Rio de Janeiro: UFRJ.

Dewey, J. 1988. *Experience and Nature, Later Works*. Carbondale and Edwardsville: Southern Illinois University.

Dosse, F. 2003. *O império dos sentidos: a humanização das ciências humanas*. Bauru: Edusc.

Edelman, M. and Borras, Jr., S. 2016. *Political Dynamics of Transnational Agrarian Movements*. Rugby, UK: Practical Action Publishing.

Elzen, B., Leeuwis, C. and van Mierlo, B. 2008. *Anchorage of Innovations: Assessing Dutch Efforts to Use the Greenhouse Effect as an Energy Source*. Working Paper. Wageningen: Wageningen Agricultural University.

Escher, F. and Wilkinson, J. 2019. "A economia política do complexo Soja-Carne Brasil-China." *Revista de Economia e Sociologia Rural*, 57(4): 656–78.

Eymard-Duvernay, F. 1989. "Conventions de qualité et formes de coordination." *Revue Économique*, 40(2): 329–59.

Eymard-Duvernay, F. 2009. "L'économie des conventions entre économie et sociologie." In *Traité de sociologie économique*, edited by P. Steiner and F. Vatin, 131–64. Paris: PUF.

Fischler, C. 1990. *L'Homnivore*. Paris: O. Javob.

Flexor, G. 2014. "Las tiendas frente a la 'revolución de los supermercados': el caso de la región metropolitana de Río de Janeiro." *Economía, Sociedad y Territorio*, 14: 130.

Fligstein, N. 2001. *The Architecture of Markets*. Princeton: Princeton University Press.

Fragoso, J. and Florentino, M. 2001. *O Arcaísmo como projeto*. Rio de Janeiro: Civilização Brasileira.

Friedmann, H. 2005. "From colonialism to green capitalism: social movements and emergence of food regimes'." In *New Directions in the Sociology of Global Development*, edited by F. Buttel and P. McMichael, 227–64. Amsterdam: Elsevier.

Friedmann, H. 2016. "Commentary: Food regime analysis and agrarian questions: widening the conversation." *Journal of Peasant Studies*, 43(3): 671–92.

Friedmann, H. and McMichael, P. 1989. "Agriculture and the State system: the rise and decline of national agricultures, 1870 to the Present." *Sociologia Ruralis*, 29(2): 93–117.

Geels, F. 2002. "Technological transitions as evolutionary reconfiguration processes: a multi-level perspective and a case study." *Research Policy*, 31: 1257–74.

Giddens, A. 1984. *The Constitution of Society*. London: Polity Press.

Goodman, D. 2004. "Rural Europe Redux? Reflections on alternative agro-food networks and paradigm change." *Sociologia Ruralis*, 44(1): 3–16.

Goodman, D., Dupuis, E. and Goodman, M. 2012. *Alternative Food Networks: Knowledge, Practice and Politics*. London: Routledge.

Goodman, M. and Sage, C. (eds). 2014. *Food Transgressions: Making Sense of Contemporary Food Politics*. London: Routledge.

Hall, P, and Soskice, D. 2001. "An introduction to varieties of capitalism." In *Varieties of Capitalism*, edited by P. Hall and D. Soskice, 1–68. Oxford: Oxford University Press.

Hardt, M. and Negri, A. 2001. *Empire*. Cambridge: Harvard.

Hardt, M. and Negri, A. 2004. *Multitude*. New York: Penguin.

Harvey, D. 1992. *A condição pós-moderna*. São Paulo: Loyola.

Herédia, B., Palmeira, M. and Leite, S. 2010. "Sociedade e Economia do Agronegócio." *Revista Brasileira de Ciências Sociais*, 25: 159–76.

Hinrichs, C. 2003. "The practice and politics of food system localization." *Journal of Rural Studies*, 19(1): 33–45.

Hofstee, E. 1946. *The Causes of Diversity in Dutch Agriculture*. Wageningen: Wageningen Agricultural University.

IBGE. 1924. *Censo Agropecuário*. Rio de Janeiro: IBGE.

Lang, T. 1999. "The complexities of globalization: the UK as a case study of tensions within the food system and the challenge to food policy." *Agriculture and Human Values*, 16(2): 169–185.

Leite, S. P.1998. *Inserção internacional e financiamento da agricultura brasileira (1980–1996)*. PhD Thesis. Campinas: Unicamp.

Lessa, A. 2008. "Há cinquenta anos a Operação Pan-Americana." *Revista Brasileira de Política Internacional*, 51(2): 5–7.

Linhares, M. Y. 1995. "A pesquisa histórica no Rio de Janeiro: a história agrária como programa de trabalho: 1977–1994." *Revista Brasileira de História*, 15(30): 77–89.

Linhares, M. Y. and Silva, F. C. 1979. *História Política do Abastecimento*. Brasília: Binagri.

Long, N. 2001. *Development Sociology*. London and New York: Routledge.

Long, N., Ploeg, J. D., Curtin, C. and Box, L. (eds). 1986. *The Commoditization Debate*. Wageningen: Wageningen Agricultural University.

Maluf, R. S., Burlandi, L., Santarelli, M, Schottz, V. and Speranza, J. 2015. Nutrition-sensitive agriculture and the promotion of food and nutrition sovereignty and security in Brazil. *Ciência & Saúde Coletiva*, 20(8): 2303–12.

March, J. And Olsen, J. 2006. "Elaborating the "new institutionalism"." In *Oxford Handbooks of Political Institutions*, edited by R. Rhodes, S. Binder and B. Rockman, 3–21. Oxford: Oxford University Press.

Marques, F., Ploeg, J. D. van der and Dal Soglio, F. 2012. "New identities, new commitments: something is lacking between niche and regime." In *System Innovations, Knowledge Regimes, and Design Practices Towards Transitions for Sustainable Agriculture*, edited by M. Barbier and B. Elzen, 23–46. Paris: INRA.

Marsden, T. 2016. "Exploring the rural eco-economy: Beyond neoliberalism." *Sociologia Ruralis*, 56(4): 597–615.

Mauss, M. 2007. *Manual of Ethnography*. New York: Durkheim Press, Berghahn Books.

McMichael, P. 2005. "Global development and the corporate food regime." In *New Directions in the Sociology of Global Development*, edited by F. Buttel and P. McMichael, 229–67. Oxford: Elsevier.

McMichael, P. 2009. "A food regime genealogy." *Journal of Peasant Studies*, 36(1): 139–69.

McMichael, P. 2013. *Food Regimes and Agrarian Questions*. Nova Scotia: Fernwood.

McMichael, P. 2016a. "Commentary: Food regime for thought." *Journal of Peasant Studies*, 43(3): 648–70.

McMichael, P. 2016b. *Regimes alimentares e questões agrárias*. São Paulo and Porto Alegre: UNESP and UFRGS.

McMichael, P. 2019. "Does China's 'going out' strategy precure a new food regime?". *Journal of Peasant Studies*, DOI: 10.1080/03066150.2019.1693368

Mier, M. and Cacho, T. 2016. "Soybean agri-food systems dynamics and the diversity of farming styles on the agricultural frontier in Mato Grosso, Brazil." *Journal of Peasant Studies*, 43(2): 419–41.

Morgan, K., Marsden, T. and Murdoch, J. 2006. "Networks, conventions and regions: Theorizing "worlds of food"." In *Place, Power and Provenance in the Food Chain*, edited by K. Morgan, T. Marsden and J. Murdoch, 7–25. Oxford University Press: Oxford.

Niederle, P. 2018. "A pluralist and pragmatist critique of food regime's genealogy: varieties of social orders in Brazilian agriculture." *Journal of Peasant Studies*, 45(7): 1460–83.

Niederle, P., Grisa, C., Picolotto, E. and Soldera, D. 2019. "Narrative disputes over family-farming public policies in Brazil: conservative attacks and restricted countermovements." *Latin American Research Review*, 54: 707–20.

Oliveira, G. and Hecht, S. B. (eds). 2017. *Soy, Globalization, and Environmental Politics in South America*. New York: Routledge.

Orléan, A. 1989. "Pour une approche cognitive des conventions économiques." *Revue Économique*, 40(2): 241–72.

Ostrom, E. 2007. "Institutional Rational Choice: an assessment of the institutional analysis and development framework." In *Theories of the Policy Process*, edited by P. Sabatier, 21–64. Cambridge: Westview Press.

Ploeg, J. D. van der. 1994. "Styles of farming: An introductory note on concepts and methodology." In *Born from Within: Practices and Perspectives of Endogenous Rural Development*, edited by J. D. Ploeg and A. Long, 7–30. Assen: Van Gorcum.

Ploeg, J. D. van der. 1993. "Rural sociology and the new agrarian question: A perspective from the Netherlands. *Sociologia Ruralis*, 32(2): 240–46.

Ploeg, J. D. van der. 2009. *The New Peasantries: Struggles for Autonomy and Sustainability in an Era of Empire and Globalization*. New York: Routledge.

Ploeg, J. D. van der. 2017. *Camponeses e a arte da agricultura*. São Paulo: UNESP.

Portilho, F. and Micheletti, M. 2018. "Politicizing consumption in Latin America. In *The Oxford Handbook of Political Consumerism*, edited by M. Boström, M. Micheletti and P. Oosterveer, 539–57. Oxford: Oxford University Press.

Poulain, J.-P. 2013. *Sociologias da alimentação: os comedores e o espaço social alimentar*. 2nd ed. Florianópolis: UFSC.

Prado, Jr., C. 1942. *The Colonial Background of Modern Brazil*. Berkeley: University of California.

Rangnekar, D. and Wilkinson, J. 2011. "(New) borders of consumption." *Environment and Planning A*, 43(9): 2007–11.

Rip, A. and Kemp, R. 1998. Technological change. In *Human Choice and Climate Changes*, edited by S. Rayner and E. Malone, 327–99. Columbus: Battelle.

Ritzer, G. 1995. *The McDonaldization of Society*. San Francisco: Pin Forge Press.

Salais, R. 1989. "L'analyse économique des conventions du travail." *Revue Économique*, 40(2), 199–240.

Salais, R. and Storper, M. 1992. "The four worlds of contemporary industry." *Cambridge Journal of Economics*, 16: 169–93.

Sassatelli, R.2007. *Consumer Culture: History, Theory and Politics*. London: Sage.

Sassen, S. 2013. "Land grabs today: Feeding the disassembling of national territory." Globalizations, 10(1), 25–46.

Sauer, S., Balestro, M. and Schneider, S. 2018. "The ambiguous stance of Brazil as a regional power: Piloting a course between commodity-based surpluses and national development." *Globalizations*, 15(1): 37–58.

Schatzki, T. 2002. *The Site of the Social*. University Park: Pennsylvania State University.

Schatzki, T., Knorr-Cetina, K. and Savigny, E. (eds). 2001. *The Practice Turn in Contemporary Theory*. London, New York: Routledge.

Schmitt, C. 2011. Encurtando o caminho entre a produção e o consumo de alimentos. *Revista Agriculturas*, 8(3): 4–8.

Schneider, S. and Niederle, P. 2010. "Resistance strategies and diversification of rural livelihoods: the construction of autonomy among Brazilian family farmers." *Journal of Peasant Studies*, 37(2): 379–405.

Schubert, M. 2017. *Comer fora de casa, as práticas e as rotinas do comer nos contextos da modernidade: uma leitura comparada entre Brasil, Reino Unido e Espanha*. PhD Thesis. Porto Alegre: UFRGS.

Scott, W. R. 2008. *Institutions and Organizations: Ideas, Interests and Identities*. 3rd ed. Thousand Oaks: Sage.

Thelen, K. 2004. *How Institutions Evolve*. Cambridge: Cambridge University Press.

Thelen, K. 2005. "Institutional change in advanced political economies." In *Beyond Continuity*, 1–39. Oxford: Oxford University Press.

Thévenot, L. 2002. "Which Road to Follow? The moral complexity of an 'equipped' humanity." In *Complexities: Social Studies of Knowledge Practices*, edited by J. Law and A. Mol, 53–87. Durham: Duke University.

Touzard, J.-M. and Labarthe, P. 2017. "Théorie de la régulation et transformations de l'agriculture." In *Transformations agricoles et agroalimentaires: entre écologie et capitalisme*, edited by G. Allaire and B. Daviron, 291–304. Paris: Quae.

Vennet, B., Schneider, S. and Dessein, J. 2015. "Different farming styles behind the homogenous soy production in southern Brazil."*Journal of Peasant Studies*, 42(2): 396–418.

Vidal, M. and Peck, J. 2012. "Sociological institucionalism and the socially constructed economy." In *The Wiley-Blackwell Companion to Economic Geography*, edited by T. Barnes, J. Peck and E. Sheppard, 595–611. Chichester and Malden: Wiley-Blackwell.

Warde, A. 2005. "Consumption and theories of practice." *Journal of Consumer Culture*, 5(2): 131–53.

Warde, A. 2014. "After taste: Culture, consumption and theories of practice." *Journal of Consumer Culture*, 14(3): 279–303.

Warde, A. 2015. *The Practice of Eating*. Cambridge: Polity.

Weiss, T. 2007. *The Global Food Economy* . London: Zed Books.

Wesz, Jr., V. 2014. *O mercado da soja e as relações de troca entre produtores rurais e empresas no Sudeste de Mato Grosso (Brasil)*. PhD Thesis. Rio de Janeiro: UFRRJ.

Wesz, Jr., V. 2016. "Strategies and hybrid dynamics of soy transnational companies in the Southern Cone." *Journal of Peasant Studies*, 43(2): 286–312.

Wilkinson, J. 1997. "A new paradigm for economic analysis?" *Economy and Society*, 26(3): 305–339.

Wilkinson, J. 2008. *Mercados, redes e valores*. Porto Alegre: UFRGS.

Wilkinson, J. 2011. "Convention Theory and Consumption." In *Encyclopedia of Consumer Culture*, edited by D. Southerton, 358–61. London: Sage.

Wilkinson, J. and Goodmann, D. 2017. "Les analyses en terme de 'food regime': une relecture." In *Transformations agricoles et agrolaimentaires: entre écologie et capitalisme*, edited by G. Allaire and B. Daviron. Versailles: Quae.

Wilkinson, J., Wesz, Jr., V. and Lopane, A. 2016. "Brazil and China: the agribusiness connection in the Southern Cone context." *Third World Thematics*, 1(5): 726–45.

Wiskerke, J. S. and Ploeg, J. D. van der (eds). 2004. *Seeds of Transition*. Uitgeverij: Van Gorcum.

2 Modernization and consolidation of the industrial order

In the mid-twentieth century, the asymmetries in international trade resulting from industrial and technological domination by advanced capitalist countries, particularly the United States, gained prominence in the international debate, while discussions on State planned economy also stood out. In Latin America, the Economic Commission for Latin America and the Caribbean (ECLAC) proposed that industries should lead the process of economic development and that, to this end, a State-led process of industrialization via import substitution would be a *sine qua non* condition for fostering domestic industry, to allow for internal accumulation of capital and reduction of external dependence. This was the accent of the Brazilian developmental project (Fonseca, 2003; Bresser-Pereira, 2010; Delgado, 2005).

As the industry became the "engine" of economic development, agriculture took on the subsidiary role of "financing" the import substitution effort, by means of exports of primary products; freeing up labor for the industrial sector, so as to avoid rising wages and decreasing industry's profit rates, which could make new investments unviable; providing food and raw materials, considering the growing urbanization and increasing demand from the industrial sector; and consuming industrial products (such as agricultural implements and fertilizers) to expand the domestic market in other sectors (Johnston and Mellor, 1961; Rodrigues, 1978). However, in Brazil, the 1950s marked a period of "stagnation of agricultural production, especially for the domestic market, [what] was seen as a serious obstacle to a continued economic growth" (Graziano da Silva, 2003, 87). Therefore, industrialization also depended on the revitalization of agricultural production.

At the same time, the discourse about technological modernization of agriculture as a solution to the problem of hunger in the world was also gaining momentum. Adherents of the theory of modernization argued that the replacement of traditional methods of farming with modern agriculture in Third World countries was fundamental, and this should be based on the technological model already established in the USA (Schultz, 1965). To this end, besides the formation of human capital at US universities, since the 1960s, several research centers were established in various countries (including

Embrapa, in Brazil), with funding from the World Bank, Rockefeller and Ford foundations, as well as other funding institutions (Albergoni and Pelaez, 2007).

From then on, Brazilian agriculture began to compulsorily implement a process of agricultural modernization understood as "capitalist technological transformations, shifting from a 'natural' agriculture to one that uses industrially manufactured inputs ... in an effort to increase productivity" (Kageyama et al., 1990, 119). A leading analyst of this process, Graziano da Silva (1980), highlighted how the introduction of new artifacts that accompanied technological advances in agriculture has decisively affected farmers' practices: mechanical innovations altered the intensity and pace of work; physicochemical innovations changed the natural conditions of the soil, thus increasing labor productivity; biological innovations affected the speed of the production process by reducing the production period and enhancing the effects of mechanical and chemical innovations.

Kageyama et al. (1990, 120) note that agricultural modernization has increased farmers' dependence on extrasectoral products and services (machines and inputs), so that agricultural production has become "increasingly dependent on other sectors of the economy, which are more intensive in the use of both fixed and circulating capital." A concise indicator of this process is the Intermediate Consumption (IC), which represents the value of all production inputs except labor force. The higher the ratio of IC to Gross Value of Production (GVP), the greater the degree of dependence of farmers on external agents. In Brazil, as Conterato et al. (2014) observe, the evolution of IC in relation to the gross value of production rose from 10% in 1939 to 38.7% in 1980 and then to 54.8% in 2006.

As a result, agricultural practices that hitherto employed artifacts that farmers reproduced in their own farms (seeds, natural fertilizers, equipment, working animals etc.) were altered by the diffusion of modern technological packages that led to a growing process of "externalization" (Ploeg, 1990). Agricultural production has integrated with the industrial sector in a relatively sudden way. As agriculture began to supply food processing industries, its "industrialization" changed productive practices to such an extent that the sector would be (almost) transformed into an industry-like production segment that buys inputs and produces raw materials aimed to other economic sectors. In this sense, the emergence of an industrial order in the agrifood system is conceived.

State-led industrialization

Within sociology of agriculture, one of the main interpretations of the emergence of an industrial order in agriculture was presented by Goodman, Sorj and Wilkinson (1987). For these authors, this phenomenon involved a series of partial and discontinuous appropriation of the rural labor and the biological processes of production by the industrial logics (machines, fertilizers, hybrid seeds, chemicals, biotechnologies), as well as the parallel development of industrial substitutes for food products. In this sense, they highlighted the transformation of different agricultural practices aimed for reducing the limitations posed by the biological cycles that underlie food production and human nutrition to the capitalist accumulation in agriculture. To this end, the authors introduce the concepts of appropriationism and substitutionism.

Appropriationism is the action taken to reduce the role of nature in agricultural production, changing it into a process subject to management and control according to industrial parameters. Indeed, it was sought to eliminate specific elements of agricultural production, transforming them into industrial artifacts incorporated into agriculture as inputs. This occurred, for example, with rural work, which was appropriated by industry by means of the manufacturing of new machines and equipment (from hand-sowing to seed drills; from oxen and horses to tractors). The natural production process was also appropriated (and speeded) by the chemical industry and by biological and genetic innovations, via industrial production of fertilizers, improved hybrid seeds and pesticides.

In turn, substitutionism led to the creation of new means of accumulation in the downstream stages of food and fiber manufacturing. Through this process, industrial activity has not only seized an increasing proportion of value added, but also agricultural products, after being reduced to an industrial input, was replaced by others of synthetic origin. Examples include both food (use of artificial sweeteners and juices, synthetic food flavorings and colorings, flavor enhancers) and nonfood products (substitution of natural fibers – cotton, wool and silk – by artificial ones – polyester, acrylic, elastane, nylon – in fabric making; use of synthetic rubber instead of natural rubber extracted from latex; use of dyes, detergents and artificial perfumes).

The emergence of this industrial order was associated with both the introduction of new technical artifacts and a substantial change in the institutional apparatus. Firstly, it should be noted that the "great depression," generated by the 1929 crisis, produced a new model of relationship between State, market and society. In the US, the New Deal was the main demonstration of a new public action based on a broader commitment of American society to industrial progress (which entailed a profound change in social values). Later, driven by the economic and technological race during the Cold War, belief in industrialization as a path to modernity spread widely around the world, and remained strongly held until the late 1970s, at least, when the Fordist model (and its underlying idea of modernity) began to show signs of crisis (Bonanno and Wolf, 2018).

In Brazil, the role of State in boosting industrialization has also gained prominence (Delgado, 1985; Leite, 1998; Resende, 2003). Although technical progress was initially dependent on the foreign market, since it relied on the importation of machinery and inputs, from the 1930s onwards, the State sought to construct policy instruments to alter this scenario, planning a new accumulation regime. The nationalist developmental project sought to internalize industrial sectors deemed important for the supply of agricultural means of production and inputs. In turn, from an institutional point of view, in line with the new Fordist mode of regulation that emerged after the war, the government of Getúlio Vargas (1930–1945) introduced significant reforms for the modernization of the State structure. Such reforms were made possible by broad agreements among different sectors of society, which included, on the one hand, diverse economic incentives for entrepreneurs and, on the other hand, the consolidation of the labor legislation and a set of basic social rights.

Vargas government showed a special concern regarding the agrifood processing, which is reflected in the regulation of the emerging industrialization in the food sector. Even so, while the Decree 19,604 of January 19, 1931 demonstrated the State's concern with the use of colorants, flavorings and other "foreign substances" in food processing, most of the new food safety legislation favored this type of practice. As Cruz and Menasche (2014) point out, the formulation of food safety standards in Brazil broadly reflected the ongoing discussions of the US Food and Drug Administration (FDA), created in 1906 to regulate and monitor medicines and food. This is clear from the first regulation on food of animal origin established by the Ministry of Agriculture in 1952 (Decree No. 30691), which was intended "to preserve the safety, identity, quality and integrity of products, as well as the health and interests of the consumer."

Regarding the 1950s, the Brazilian State's institutional action on other fronts is also worth noting, as in the case of fertilizers and pesticides markets. The Action Plan launched by president Juscelino Kubitschek (1956/61) created incentives to encourage the emergence of a national market for industrial fertilizers – a policy later expanded through the National Programme for Agricultural Fertilizers and Limestone (1974–1980), which was part of the II National Development Plan; and the II National Fertilizer Plan (1987–1995) (Dias and Fernandes, 2006). In turn, the pesticides market, which was quite incipient and dependent on imports (4/5 of domestic consumption), was boosted by the National Plan for Agricultural Pesticides (PNDA) that, from 1975 on, led a gradual increase in domestic production so that in 1980 it accounted for 50% of total supply (Martinelli, Jr. and Waquil, 2002).

As to the market of machinery and equipment, a similar process fostered internalization. In 1960, the first tractor manufacturers were installed in the country and, in 1965, the manufacture of self-propelled harvesters for grain crops started. In the 1970s, national demand for agricultural tractors was fully supplied by domestic production and the manufacture of self-propelled harvesters also expanded considerably. In the case of tractors, it is worth noting the emergence, in 1960, of the Brazilian Company of Tractors (CBT) which, in 1968, became the second largest tractor manufacturer in the country, remaining in the third position in the market until the mid-1970s (Ferreira, 1995).

These different actions aimed fundamentally at increasing domestic production capacity by fostering both domestic and foreign industries, by means of tax exemptions and by providing significant funding raised from the international financial system and channeled to the firms at very low interest rates (Kageyama et al., 1990). This process accelerated during the military regime (1964–1985), through the National Rural Credit System (*Sistema Nacional de Credito Rural* – SNCR). Created in 1965, this system aimed at encouraging rural investments in storage, processing and industrialization of agricultural products; favoring the timely and adequate funding of the production and the commercialization of agricultural products; economically strengthening the rural sector and encouraging the introduction of rational production methods, aiming at increasing productivity (Law No. 4829/1965).

The SNCR constituted the main support for modernization of Brazilian agriculture, playing a decisive role in the technical transformation of farms, in enhancing the sector's productivity, consolidating agroindustrial facilities and agrifood chains, and integrating agrarian capital into the sphere of financial capital (Delgado, 1985; Leite, 2001). In the first years (from 1967 to 1979), real interest rates on rural credit were often negative, thus providing farmers with generous subsidies. As a result, they began to allocate much of their resources to purchase tractors, machines, agricultural inputs and equipment (Búrigo, 2010). Consequently, the rural credit policy was crucial both for farmers and for the various companies involved in agricultural modernization by supplying products and services. Nevertheless, between 1967 and 1979, the funds invested via the SNCR were largely concentrated in medium and large farmers (1% of the borrowers – about 10,000 large farmers – received 40% of funds), in the South and Southeast (and subsequently the Midwest) and in products of greater commercial value, especially soybean, sugarcane, cotton, wheat, corn and coffee (Nunes and Nassar, 2000; Pinto, 1981).

Another important instrument was the Minimum Guaranteed Price Policy (*Política de Garantia de Preços Mínimos* – PGPM) that sets a base price prior to sowing to avoid large fluctuation in prices of the main agricultural products, thus guaranteeing a minimum revenue to farmers and ensuring domestic food supply. Although the fixing of minimum prices for some products (rice, beans, maize, peanuts, soybeans and sunflower) had been a practice since 1945 (Decree Law No. 77774), it was the reformulation of PGPM in 1965–1966 that created effective instruments for compulsory modernization by means of the control of prices and supply (Decree 57391/1965 and Decree-Law 79/1966). The two main operational instruments of this policy were the Federal Government Loan (*Empréstimo do Governo Federal* – EGF) – through which the State provides farmers with funds (commercialization credit), so that to enable them to stock their products during harvest time (when prices tend to be lower); and the direct government purchases (*Aquisição do Governo Federal* – AGF) – through which the State commits to purchasing the product.

In addition to credit and PGPM, three other instruments have guided state actions aimed at modernizing agriculture. In 1973, the Production Guarantee Programme (PROAGRO) was created for the purpose of insuring farmers against crop losses due to natural disasters, pests and diseases, even exempting them from paying in case the debt settlement was hampered by these circumstances (Almeida, 2007). In the same year, Embrapa was created, a public research corporation focused on fostering technological innovation, especially by adapting exotic cultivars to Brazilian ecological characteristics (Mengel, 2015). Finally, a year later, Embrater (Brazilian Company for Technical Assistance and Rural Extension) was created for the purpose of disseminating the technological package of modernization, thus being indirectly articulated with Embrapa and other research centers (Peixoto, 2008).

The military government has also promoted the expansion of the agricultural frontier into the *Cerrado* (the Brazilian "savanna") and Amazon rainforest areas by means of several policies: Amazon Economic Enhancement Plan (PVEA), National Integration Plan (PIN), Programme of Land Redistribution and Incentive to the Northern and North-Eastern Agro-Industry (Proterra), Articulated Export Corridors (Corexport), Programme of Amazon Agricultural and Agromineral Hub (Poloamazônia), Cerrado Development Programme (Polocentro), Integrated Programme of Brazilian Northwest Development (Polonoroeste), Japanese-Brazilian Cooperation Programme of Cerrado Development (Prodecer), among others. This set of policies encompassed a wide range of actions aimed at land use, infrastructure building, land distribution, generation and diffusion of technologies adapted to the Cerrado and the Amazon. The main objective was to expand agricultural production to generate foreign exchange and improve the balance of trade through exports (Fernández, 2007; Moreno, 2007).

In short, the State has set in motion a series of actions to enhance the process of modernization and industrialization of agriculture in Brazil. As Kageyama et al. (1990, 157) note, "the state was present at all stages of the process, sometimes creating conditions for change (through financing and technological policies), sometimes 'tying' various elements around a defined project for modernization of Brazilian agriculture." The configuration of an institutional framework that has in the State – and, more precisely, in a specific type of developmental State – a fundamental entity for the organization of social practices is a key component of what we define as an industrial order. Therefore, it is not just about the implications of any agricultural industrialization process; it is about the institutional logic underlying this process. This is what distinguishes, for example, the aforementioned processes of industrialization from those guided by an eminently financial logic (cf. Chapter 7), in which the presence of this State model is a less relevant component.

Finally, it should be noted that, although the consolidation of an industrial order in agriculture took place from the mid-twentieth century on, in line with what several authors define as the Fordist model in the agrifood sector (Bonanno, 1999), as we shall see later, this order remains one of the main expressions of contemporary agriculture, even as regards the presence of the State. In Brazil, although the liberal narrative holds that agribusiness develops in spite of state action, the truth is that this latter continues, to a greater or lesser extent, supporting various sectors (Ioris, 2017; Bonanno and

Wolf, 2018), such as agroindustrial inputs, which benefits, directly, from tax exemptions and, indirectly, from the credit support granted to farmers; processing infrastructure building, which consume large funds from the National Bank for Development (BNDES); and primary commodities exports subsidized through tax exemption (Kandir Law – Complementary Law No. 87/1996).

Technological innovations and productivity growth

For the past 30 years, technological innovations kept advancing in Brazil. Attending agriculture trade shows or keeping frequent contact with a company that commercializes agricultural inputs or machines can easily reveal the speed of change and the constant emergence of new artifacts: varieties of seeds with greater productive potential, resistant to certain insects, tolerant to drought; pesticides with new, more specific and potent formulations and ingredients; fertilizers produced with new raw materials and formulations; seed drills, sprayers and harvesters that cover larger areas; multifunctional machines that can be used for different purposes depending on the attached implement; irrigation stations that interact with weather sensors; defoliants, desiccants, plant growth regulators, promoters and inhibitors … well, a huge array of artifacts that have been integrated by a continuous technological revolution (Silveira, 2014).

In the livestock sector, among the practices that illustrate the extent of technological transformations, we can mention the reduction of the production cycle, increase of feed conversion, acceleration of sexual precocity and selection of animal strains that provide higher yields of noble parts (such as thighs, drumstick and breast in the case of poultry) or whose demand is increasing (less fat, softer, increased marbling etc.). Even so, it is worth noting that although genetics are of unparalleled relevance, it must be accompanied by changes in management, health and feeding techniques, and in breeding facilities, which must be adapted to specific requirements of the new races. In cattle breeding, for example, one of the innovations that is rapidly spreading among breeders is bovine semen sexing, a technique employed in artificial insemination so that the breeder can choose the sex of the calf before insemination (Zanon, 2016).

In agriculture, among the most widespread practices in Brazil are no-till farming, cultivation of transgenic seeds and, more recently, the adoption of precision agriculture, which refers to the use of high-tech tools such as Global Positioning Systems and Geographic Information Systems, which allow the management of agricultural production by controlling both spatial variability and that of production factors. One of the areas where these practices stand out is the Cerrado, formerly deemed a region of "low agricultural potential," due to its sandy soils, high acidity and low natural fertility, as well as long dry seasons. The neutralization of soil acidity (especially using limestone), improvement of natural fertility (via synthetic fertilizers) and development of early cycle plant varieties adapted to climatic conditions have made the *Cerrado* the main region of grain production in the country (Fernández, 2007).

In order to explain the expansion of Brazilian agricultural productivity, Gasques et al. (2016) analyzed the total productivity growth between 1975 and 2014. According to the authors, from 1997 onward, the average annual growth accelerated, rising from 3.02% between 1975 and 1997 to 4.28% between 1998 and 2014. The factors that account for this performance, according to them, would be the investments in research (Embrapa's role standing out), technological changes, economic stabilization (allowed by the Real Plan), currency devaluation (as of 1999), strengthening and creation of new agricultural policies (especially credit), growth of domestic consumption and expansion of exports.

Indeed, considering the yield per area of the main Brazilian crops (cotton, rice, coffee, sugarcane, beans, cassava, maize, soybeans and wheat) between 1990 and 2015, a significant increase in agricultural productivity is observed. During this period, some crops have doubled production over the same area, as occurred with rice, cotton and maize. However, productivity growth was not overarching in the last two decades. Between 2000 and 2015, rice, maize and beans crops continued to expand their yields, keeping pace with the 1990s. But the same has not happened with coffee and sugar cane, crops that in recent years have recorded yields lower than the previous levels. Soybean, cotton and cassava, in turn, are relatively stable, especially between 2007 and 2015, when the national average remained relatively constant.

Furthermore, productivity is greatly heterogeneous in terms of regions. Considering the four agricultural products that occupy the largest areas in Brazil (soybean, maize, sugarcane and beans), significant variations between microregions become evident, as shown in Figure 2.1. In general, the highest average yields occur in the most specialized areas, although other factors contribute to the substantial differences, such as climate and soil conditions, technology employed, volume of resources invested, management and technical assistance for farmers.

Farmers' capacity of technological absorption is also very uneven, varying mainly according to activity, availability of resources and size of the agricultural area. Using data from the 2017 Agricultural Census and considering those farms whose main economic activity consist of temporary crops (which are more demanding in terms of machinery as compared to permanent farming, livestock, forestry, fishing etc.), we found that 39.3% of the farms still use only animal traction, 39.7% use only mechanical traction and 21% conciliate both. Farms that have tractors represent only 14.5% of the total farms dedicated to temporary crops, indicating a modest proportion. In dairy farming, mechanized milking is also low (13.0%), the same applying to artificial insemination (7.6%) and embryo transfer (7.6%) (IBGE, 2019).

Advances in productivity, especially when coupled with labor-saving technologies, have been associated with reduced numbers of producers. In soybean cultivation, for example, despite a 439% increase in cultivated area and

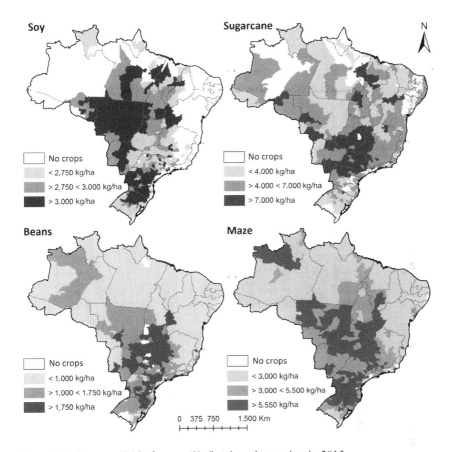

Figure 2.1 Average yield of crops (Kg/ha) by microregion in 2015.

more than 1,000% rise in production, the number of producers was halved between 1975 and 2017 (from 487,000 to 236,000). However, this has not been an overall reduction. It occurred mainly in those farms with areas of less than 100 ha (Wesz, Jr., 2016). This results, on the one hand, from the activity's own dynamics – crops with little room for differentiation, which require economies of scale, technology optimization and negotiating large volumes to reduce costs and increase profitability; on the other hand, it derives from the difficulty encountered by these farms to achieve yields that compensate the expansion of production costs.

Table 2.1 reveals that the same occurred with other crops. For sugarcane, out of four farms involved in the activity in 1975, there were only three left in 2017, even though the cultivated area underwent a fivefold increase and production has grown eightfold during this period. As to maize production, one of each two producers remained, even though productions increased

Table 2.1 Number of crop-producing farms (A), production in metric tons (B) and harvested area in hectares (C) in 1975, 1985, 1995, 2006 and 2017 – selected crops

		1975	1985	1995	2006	2017	1975/2017
Cotton	A	248.822	436.480	88.749	13.290	3.081	−98.8%
	B	935.979	2.178.455	814.188	2.350.132	3.664.808	291.5%
	C	1.014.005	2.048.772	619.627	786.974	909.829	−10.3%
Rice	A	1.780.825	1.679.963	927.619	396.628	179.588	−89.9%
	B	7.548.930	8.986.289	8.047.895	9.447.257	11.615.634	53.9%
	C	5.662.875	5.173.330	2.977.019	2.409.587	1.772.147	−68.7%
Sugarcane	A	260.281	402.542	377.207	192.845	170.466	−34.5%
	B	79.959.024	229.882.037	259.806.703	384.165.158	638.064.292	698.0%
	C	1.860.401	3.798.117	4.216.427	5.577.651	9.122.607	390.4%
Maize	A	3.267.880	3.461.551	2.539.892	2.030.122	1.628.805	−50.2%
	B	14.343.556	17.774.404	25.510.505	42.281.800	90.822.485	533.2%
	C	10.741.210	12.040.441	10.602.850	11.724.362	16.381.799	52.5%
Soybeans	A	486.872	420.204	242.999	217.015	235.766	−51.6%
	B	8.721.274	16.730.087	21.563.768	46.195.842	103.739.460	1089.5%
	C	5.656.928	9.434.686	9.479.893	17.883.297	30.469.918	438.6%

Source: Brazilian Agricultural Censuses (several years).

by 533%. The cotton and rice cases are even more emblematic. The cereal counted 1.7 million growers in 1975, and fell constantly at each decade, dropping to less than 200,000 by 2017 (a 90% decrease). The area harvested also decreased in the period (-68.7%) but production grew by 54%. In the case of cotton, there has been an impressive 99% drop in the number of producers, although production has grown by almost 300% and the area has been reduced by 10.3%.

In short, the conformation of an industrial order involved significant changes in production practices, which were fundamental for increasing agricultural production, even though their incorporation was uneven. Considering products such as rice, beans and cassava, key components of Brazilians' diet, all three underwent a decrease in the cultivated area between 2000 and 2015 (by respectively -41.6%, -29.5% and -11.5%), although the yield per area has increased, thus ensuring production growth or at least its maintenance over the same period (10.5%, 1.1% and 0.1%, respectively). On the other hand, there are products whose increase in production is mainly due to the expansion of cultivated area, even though the increase in productivity has its contribution. In the case of soybeans, for example, if the same cultivated area had been maintained between 2000 and 2015, considering only the increase in productivity, production in 2015 would have been 41.4 million tons and not the 97.4 million that were harvested in that year.

Expansion of the agricultural frontier

The advancement of the agricultural frontier has been widely discussed in Brazil, both by representatives of the agricultural sector and by academics, NGOs and the government. Although in many discussions the frontier appears as unoccupied areas that will be incorporated into the development dynamics, Bernardes (2005) shows that this is a misrepresentation. According to the author, in most cases, this is not an advance towards "empty" lands, where the "pioneers" bridge the gap between the wild and civilization, leading progress. On the contrary, in these areas there are usually indigenous people, squatters, artisanal miners, rubber tappers, riverine people, *quilombolas* (habitants of rural communities made by the descendants of African-American slaves) and other traditional communities.

In Brazil, there were numerous initiatives for frontier expansion, particularly after the 1930s (Vargas government), which encompassed a multiple set of objectives and intentions, such as filling the "demographic voids," guaranteeing national integrity, unifying economic and political boundaries, promoting the development of agricultural projects and reducing agrarian conflicts in southern and north-eastern Brazil (Ianni, 1979; Martins, 1996). As argued by Schallenberger and Schneider (2010), the construction of new agricultural frontiers has been directly influenced by the dynamics of both public policies and private capital. Regarding State action, we have already enumerated various programs that promoted tax incentives, land concession, infrastructure building, modernization of agriculture and occupation of the territory.

Although the exploitation of wood and minerals may be among the first resources that lead to the exploration of new regions, in the last decades, the agricultural frontiers expansion has been mainly related to cattle breeding and soy cultivation. However, there are distinct views as to who leverages these practices. The question that often permeates debates is whether cattle ranching expands "on its own" as a strategy of ranchers to extend the breeding area into new zones, or it is "pushed by soy" that occupies the current live-stock areas, making this activity move on. We will not discuss it here, since several studies have already done it (Brandão, Rezende and Marques, 2006; Domingues, Bermann, and Manfredini, 2014; Oliveira, 2006; Rivero et al., 2009), but rather we will spatially contextualize the paths followed by cattle breeding and soybeans in recent years.

In the case of cattle, its production in Brazil started with the Portuguese colonization, initially in the Northeast, and over time expanding to the South, Southeast and Pantanal region. The analysis of livestock figures over the last 40 years shows that it more than doubled in the period (from 102.5 million to 215.2 million head). In addition, new regions have become breeding grounds (Figure 2.2). Although the map does not show major changes in the South, Southeast and Northeast (except for Maranhão), in the Midwest and North there was a substantial transformation. Between 1975 and 2015, the cattle herd grew over 2,000% in the North, making the national participation of

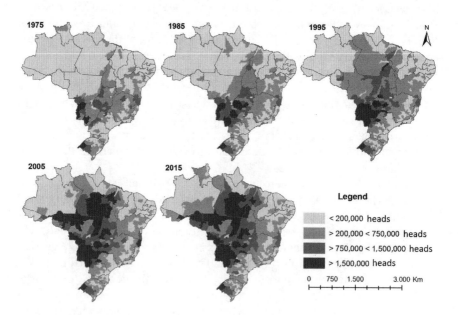

Figure 2.2 Cattle herd (heads) by microregion.

this region to jump from 2.1% to 21.9%. In the case of the Center-West, the growth was 192.4% in the same period, consolidating the region as the most important in number of heads (33.8% of the national total). These two regions are now consolidated as the country's main cattle ranching areas, holding more than half of the herd (compared with a quarter in 1975).

Soy has a more recent presence in Brazil. Although the first varieties were made available to farmers at the beginning of the twentieth century, in the state of Rio Grande do Sul, for 50 years this grain was destined to produce fodder for dairy cattle and pigs raising on small farms. It was with the national program of incentive to wheat cultivation, in the mid-1950s, that the soybean began to be encouraged as a crop option for rotation with the wheat, which is planted in winter. In the 1960s and early 1970s, soybean acted as a secondary crop, and from then on it began to establish itself as an economically important crop, taking advantage of the set of public policies for agriculture as well as the favorable international context (increased demand and price) (Wesz, Jr., 2016). From 1975 to 2015, soybean advanced dramatically, with its area increasing from 5.8 to 32.2 million hectares (IBGE, 2016).

Figure 2.3 illustrates the huge spread of soybean production over the last 40 years, highlighting two related processes: expansion into new regions and intensification in some more traditional areas. Regarding the expansion, the advance of cultivation over the Cerrado is clearly seen in the Center-West and Northeast regions. In parallel, there was also an expansion of the cultivated area in the south of the country, especially during the last 15 years, which

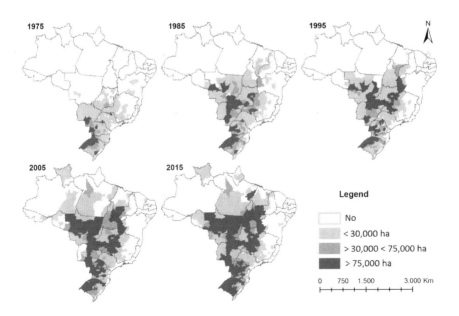

Figure 2.3 Area cultivated (hectares) with soybean per microregion.

reveals that, even in the most traditional regions, there was a new phase of soy expansion. The microregions with the highest concentration in terms of cultivated area (darker color on the map) were also enlarged. While in the early 1970s they were located mainly in the southern west, nowadays, they are spread over many Brazilian regions, especially in the states of Mato Grosso and Paraná, south of Goiás, border region between Maranhão, Tocantins, Piauí and Bahia (commonly called Matopiba), north-western of Rio Grande do Sul, border between Goiás and Minas Gerais and the central stripe of Mato Grosso do Sul.

These data demonstrate that, beside the rise of productivity, derived from the incorporation of technologies, territorial expansion still holds a significant role in the leverage of agrolivestock production. As Delgado (2012) notes, the competitiveness of this sector is based on the productivity of natural resources and any increase in demand imposes a greater pressure on nature, either because of the exploitation of nonrenewable resources (a frequent practice in the Commercial Order), or for the intensified use of the technological package (characteristic of the Industrial Order). Be that as it may, the central issue is that the narrative of increased productivity as an almost exclusive determinant of agribusiness economic dynamism does not match the reality of countless Brazilian regions. Especially in the regions of expansion of the agricultural frontier, the development of the industrial order is based on practices that, to a certain extent, lie in the intersection of this type of order and the commercial order (Chapter 3). An example refers to working conditions. While, on the one hand, the current technological standard has reduced the number of jobs and the need for some physically degrading labor (such as manual sugarcane cutting), and has expanded the demand for skilled workers who can operate increasingly modern machines (such as tractors, harvesters and self-propelled sprayers) and who earn relatively higher wages, on the other hand, farming practices associated with precarious and slave-like labor have also expanded.

Mergers, acquisitions and transnationalization of agrifood companies

As of the 1990s, important changes have affected the organization of the agrifood sector. Processes of liberalization, globalization and deregulation (or reregulation based on new institutions and forms of governance) championed and driven by international bodies (especially the International Monetary Fund, World Bank and World Trade Organization) paved the way for growing incorporation of agrifood products into global value chains and for establishing transnational companies (Gilpin, 2011). Nevertheless, it is important to recognize, as reminded by Flexor (2006), that such phenomena are not new, but rather reflect the escalation of practices already present during the constitution of Brazilian agro-industrial complexes, which are no longer the exception, having become the rule. These processes were driven by the Real Plan (1994) which, beyond the launch of a new currency, has reduced tariff protection and State regulation, implementing an economic model based on privatization, restrictive monetary policy and trade liberalization. Taken together, these measures have changed the equity structure of companies, something evident from both the expansion of Foreign Direct Investment (FDI) and the increasing number of mergers and acquisitions (M&A).

In this section, we discuss how these practices were adopted by different actors to eliminate competitors; skip steps in the process of horizontal growth of companies; reach scale of production; be on a level with or overcome competitor firms; and quickly access new markets (Benetti, 2004; Castro, 2002). Although these practices contribute to structuring the industrial order, they also configure a financial order, establishing other links with accumulation practices and logics that are characteristic of financial capital (Chapter 7). Such intersection stems from what Delgado (2012) calls the "articulation between agro-industrial and financial capitals." However, rather than considering them as practices driven by speculative gains, what matters now is understanding them as practices that companies use to achieve economies of scale and consolidate their sectoral power. To this end, let's look at some specific markets: agricultural machinery, fertilizers, seeds, agrochemicals and processing (grain, ethanol and meat).

We start by examining the industry of agricultural tractors and harvesters that both in Brazil and in the rest of the world experienced a strong concentration after the 1990s. In Brazil, John Deere acquired full control of the Schneider Longman & Co. (SLC); CNH emerged from the worldwide merger of Case IH and New Holland; AGCO acquired Ideal, SFIL, Caterpillar, Valtra and Massey Ferguson; and the Brazilian Company of Tractors (CBT) closed its activities (Silva, 2015). The only national company that resisted in the market was Agrale, which specialized in small tractors (up to 50 hp). According to Anfavea (2017), in 2016, 34,356 tractors were sold in Brazil, which were manufactured by basically three transnational companies: AGCO (44.2%), John Deere (26.8%) and CNH (25, 8%). In turn, the harvester segment is even more concentrated, with CNH controlling 47.5% of national sales in 2016, and John Deere, 42.4%, leaving 10.1% for AGCO.

In the segment of fertilizers, there was also a reduction in the number of companies and strong concentration. According to Heringer (2016), 48% of the Brazilian NPK market was in the hands of six main manufacturers in 1995, while in 2008 the concentration level increased to 86%. These include Bunge (owner of brands such as Fertisul, IAP, Ouro Verde and Manah), Mosaic (originated from the merger of IMC Global and Cargill Crop Nutrition) and Yara (which owns the brands Adubos Trevo and Fertibrás), beside the Brazilian companies Fertipar and Heringer. In recent years, mergers and acquisitions in this market have continued, with Norwegian Yara acquiring Bunge Fertilizantes (2013), Galvani (2014), Adubos Sudoeste (2016) and Vale Cubatão Fertilizantes (2018). Mosaic purchased ADM's fertilizer units in Brazil and Paraguay (2014) and acquired part of Vale's fertilizers assets (2016). Heringer, in turn, had 9.5% of its equity share acquired by the Canadian Potash Corp (world leader in potash production) and another 10% by OCP (the world's largest exporter of phosphates). Despite these initiatives, Heringer remains largely nationally owned, as is Fertipar. In 2014, these four companies accounted for 74% of fertilizers market in Brazil, with Yara holding the largest share (25%), while Mosaic, Heringer and Fertipar held 16–17% each (Heringer, 2016).

In the pesticides and seeds market, the share of the two main firms in sales increased from 27.5% in 1980 to 31.5% in 2000 and to 37.6% in 2015 (Aenda, 2016; Pelaez, Terra and Silva, 2010). However, in this sector, the leading firms remained the same (Syngenta and Bayer). Ranking first was Ciba-Geigy (which merged with Sandoz, becoming Novartis that, in turn, merged with Astra/Zeneca and became Syngenta). In second place was Bayer that, despite many mergers and acquisitions in recent years, retained its name. The market share of the main four companies also grew significantly from 1980 to 2015, stabilizing in the last decade at about 55% (Aenda, 2016). The seven leading transnational companies in the Brazilian pesticide and seed market in 2015 (Syngenta, Bayer, Basf, Monsanto, DuPont, Dow and FMC) were the same that controlled the global market (Silva and Costa, 2012).

Notwithstanding the high concentration in this sector, mergers and acquisitions have continued to intensify in recent years. The first news came from FMC, in 2015, when it announced the acquisition of the Danish Cheminova, which was among the fifteen largest pesticide companies in the world. In turn, at the end of 2015 and throughout 2016, three more megamergers were announced: between the Swiss Syngenta and the Chinese ChemChina (which in 2011 had acquired Makhteshim Agan Industries, forming Adama); between the American Dow and DuPont; between German Bayer and American Monsanto. Considering the impact of these three mergers on the Brazilian market, the three new companies now control about 60% of the domestic market of pesticides and seeds.

In the downstream segment, a simultaneous movement of concentration and transnationalization has been observed. In the grain sector, Brazil's six main soybean processors in 1995 were Ceval, Santista, Cargill, Sadia, Incobrasa and Gessy Lever, which accounted for 34% of soybean crushing capacity. In the following years, Bunge acquired Ceval, Santista and Incobrasa; Dreyfus bought Gessy Lever; ADM took over Sadia's industrial soybean plants; and Cargill incorporated Matosul's soybean operations. American ADM, Bunge and Cargill and the French Dreyfus, commonly referred to as ABCD, after coincidence of their initials, now control more than half of the processing, refining and filling capacity of vegetable oils and have become the national leaders in exports of the grain (Wesz, Jr., 2011,2016). In the fifth position was the Brazilian Amaggi, which in recent years lost the position to Cofco, a Chinese state-owned company that, in 2014, acquired two important companies (Noble and Nidera) that already operated in the country (Wilkinson, Wesz, Jr. and Lopane, 2016). According to Reuters data (2018), in 2017

ABCCD companies – where the second C refers to Cofco – accounted for 48.5% of the Brazilian soybean and maize exports.

It is important to note that these processes are not limited to commodity markets. In the segment of chocolate and derived products, for example, over 90% of national production is under the control of 35 industries (Silva et al., 2015). However, the leader in Brazil is the Swiss Nestlé, which holds a 43% market share, being known by the brands Alpino, Baton, Charge, Chokito, Garoto, Kit Kat, Prestígio, Sensação, Suflair, Serenata de Amor, Talento, among others. Ranking second, with a 31% market share, is the global vice-leader Mondelez (Kraft Foods segment for the candy industry), which controls the brands Bis, Confeti, Diamante Negro, Lacta, Laka, Sonho de Valsa, Ouro Branco, Milka and Toblerone. It means that three quarters of chocolates consumed in Brazil belong to only two transnational companies.

Mergers, acquisitions and joint ventures make it increasingly difficult to identify the origin or nationality of companies. An example is the case of Anheuser-Busch InBev (AB InBev), a beer and beverage company established in 2004 through the merger of the Belgian Interbrew and the Brazilian Ambev, which bought, in 2008, the American Anheuser-Busch. The AB InBev, which names itself a Belgian-Brazilian company, is established as a world leader in the beer sector (Ferreira, 2016). In Brazil, it controls well-known brands (Antarctica, Skol, Brahma, Original, Polar, Serramalte, Stella Artois, Budweiser, Caracu, Corona, Bohemia, Franziskaner, Leffe, Beck's, Quilmes, Norteña, Patagonia, among others) and two out of three beers consumed in the country are from AB InBev. The second largest beer company in Brazil was Petrópolis Group, which controlled 11.3% of the market via the Itaipava, Crystal, Lokal, Black Princess and Petra brands. In 2017, however, the Dutch Heineken (Heineken, Desperados, Sol, Kaiser, Bavaria, Xingu, Amstel, among others) bought the Japanese Brazil Kirin (Schin, Baden Baden, Devassa, Eisenbahn, Glacial and Cintra brands), becoming second in the ranking, with a nearly 20% market share.

Although the cases observed so far indicate high concentration in foreign companies (or mixed ones, as AB InBev), there are also leading national firms in some segments. In the pulp and paper industry, for example, there is a prevalence of groups whose capital is mostly Brazilian, such as Suzano Papel e Celulose, which, in May 2018, bought Fibria (established in 2009, following the acquisition of Aracuz Celulose by Votorantim Celulose e Papel), becoming the largest global company in the segment of hardwood pulp, and controlling 30% of the global supply (Vizzaccaro, 2018). Other companies operating in the pulp and paper business in Brazil are: Klabin, a Brazilian company that became the largest paper producer and exporter in Brazil, the Japanese Cenibra, the Chilean CMPC, the Swedo-Finnish Stora Enso (through Veracel, joint venture with Fibria), the American International Paper and the Dutch Paper Excellence. The latter acquired, in 2017, Eldorado Brasil Celulose, previously owned by JBS (Marques, 2016; Silva, Bueno and Neves, 2017; Sperotto, 2014).

In the meat sector, a movement like that of pulp and paper market is observed, involving concentration led by large firms whose capital is mostly Brazilian. In the beef industry, three companies controlled 53% of slaughtered animals in 2014: JBS (35%), Marfrig (10%) and Minerva (8%) (Carvalho, 2016). The poultry and pork segment is controlled by BRF, a Brazilian company established in 2009 through the merger of Sadia and Perdigão. According to the company, at the end of 2015, it "had a 63.9% market share of the ready meals segment, 63.3% of the cold cuts segment, 67.3% of the margarine segment and 41.3% of sausages segment" (BRF, 2016).

A practice scarcely explored in academic analyses refers to the expansion of Brazilian agrifood firms to other countries. This practice has been significant in the meat sector, in which JBS, Marfrig, Minerva and BRF have stood among the world's largest animal protein-based food companies (Coletti, Franculino and Mota, 2016). Among the four, there is no doubt about the role of JBS, whose internationalization started in 2005, when it began to acquire several companies in different countries. Today, JBS is a global leader in animal protein, as a result of a wide range of products sold in over 150 countries. As the company itself points out, JBS

> has a diverse brand and product portfolio with options ranging from fresh and frozen meat to added value, ready-to-eat, prepared and processed products … operating a global and diverse food production and distribution platform, with production units and commercial offices in over 20 countries and approximately 235,000 team members.
>
> (JBS, 2017, 28)

In turn, BRF maintains 54 units in seven countries (Argentina, Brazil, United Arab Emirates, Netherlands, Malaysia, United Kingdom and Thailand) and, at the end of 2016, acquired 2% of the equity share of Chinese state-owned Cofco Meat aiming to strengthen its presence in the Asian market. As to Marfrig Global Foods it has units in nine countries (Brazil, Uruguay, Argentina, Chile, United States, China, Malaysia, Thailand, South Korea and Australia), besides two joint ventures with Chinese companies (Cofco and Chinwhiz Poultry Vertical Integration). Minerva Foods serves several countries with meat, cold cuts and other meat products, from its processing plants located in Brazil, Uruguay, Paraguay and Colombia.

Other agrifood sectors have also seen the internationalization of Brazilian companies, albeit much more modest in terms of volume of investment and area of coverage, this latter often limited to South America. Among the firms, we can mention Camil (rice, beans and other grains) that, in 2007, started its internationalization process, which now includes 27 plants –12 in Brazil, 9 in Uruguay, 3 in Chile, 2 in Peru and 1 in Argentina. Another case is that of Amaggi, which, since 2009, has been operating in Norway (with a crushing unit), the Netherlands and Switzerland (with export and import of agricultural products units), and also in Argentina and Paraguay (purchase of grain for export). Finally, among companies with a more limited performance, we can mention Lar and Cooperativa Vale, both of which operate in Paraguay, selling products, financing inputs to rural producers, providing technical assistance and buying grain production. The first has 13 units in the neighboring country and the second has 3 units.

An aspect that is almost undetectable in this process of concentration is the central role of the State in consolidating the sectoral power of some agrifood companies, either through the approval of mergers and acquisitions by the Administrative Council for Economic Defence (Cade), or through granting public financing for that. Regarding credit, loans from the Brazilian National Bank of Development – BNDES have been of paramount importance, benefiting most of the abovementioned national companies, as well as some foreign ones. Data available from BNDES (2018) on all financing contracted either directly from the bank (direct contracts) or through accredited financial institutions (indirect contracts) allow reckoning the total amount of funds accessed by each company (which includes several contracts) between 2002 and 2017. The loans, which were assigned to various purposes (capacity expansion, working capital, logistics etc.) were massive. Among those, the following stand out: Klabin (R$8.1 billion), Suzano (R$6.2 billion), Fibria (R$5.7 billion), Ambev (R$4.2 billion), BRF – including Perdigão (R$3.9 billion), Raízen (R$3.8 billion), El Dourado (R$3 billion), CMPC (R$2.5 billion), Veracel (R$1.8 billion), Heineken (R$1 billion), Cofco (R$922 million), CNH (R$895 million) and Cargill (R$547 million).

Although these data indicate that BNDES loans went to numerous firms, one case gained high visibility: the one regarding the state's role in leveraging JBS. In the last 20 years (from 1996 to 2016), the company had a net income evolution from R$300 million to R$170 billion. Between 2007 and 2010, the company got loans of about R$8.1 billion from BNDES, R$5.6 billion of which went to JBS and R$2.5 billion to Bertin, a firm that was later acquired by JBS). More impressive than these figures – which, strictly speaking, represent no more than 2% of the bank's total disbursements in this period (R$460.5 billion) – was the public repercussion of the case, due to the disclosure of spurious relationships between the owners of the company and State authorities involving reciprocal favors. This case has not only revealed a complex web of corruption, accentuating the credibility crisis of high-level politicians, including the then President Michel Temer, but also undermined the image of that agribusiness, whose success would supposedly lie on its own efforts.

Changes in consumption practices

Associated with changes in production and processing, important modifications have also been triggered in food consumption practices. Indeed, it is simply impossible to understand the consolidation of an industrial food order without paying attention to these changes, which, in turn, are linked to at least two other social processes that have played a key role in shaping industrial societies, namely the rapid urbanization and the profound reconfigurations of the work. These processes were closely connected to each other and were central to the Fordist strategy. For instance, the release of people from the countryside to the city (rural exodus) was not an unintended and awful consequence of agricultural modernization. It was rather a state-orchestrated action aimed at making workers available to the industry. But the strategy still depended on another factor: the capacity of agriculture to produce cheap food to reduce workers' reproduction costs, thus ensuring low wages and high profits.

To enable this process, the industrialization of agriculture was announced by governments as an indispensable measure for large-scale production of cheap energy sources. In the United States, where this phenomenon has most rapidly advanced, corn has become the main component of diets, though not in the form of fresh maize or its directly derived products like flour. The US food industry has transformed maize into numerous derivatives that have been incorporated into food in the form of starch, sweetener, glucose, maltose, gluten, acids (citrus, ascorbic, sorbic), as well as others less known as polydextrose, maltodextrin, diglycerides and xanthan gum. As Pollan (2007, 55) has shown, "maize has adapted brilliantly to the new industrial regime, consuming prodigious amounts of fossil fuel-based energy to produce ever-increasing amounts of energy in the form of food."

Nowadays, added to maize derivatives, there are those products derived from soybean, wheat and, more recently, palm oil. The uses of this latter product have also become illustrative of the transformations brought about by the food industry. Valued for its high productivity (1 ha of palm produces about 5 tons of oil, while the same area of soybeans produces only 0.5 ton) and its great versatility (provides about 150 derivatives), palm oil has been considered as an economic alternative for Brazilian agribusiness. Mainly produced in Indonesia and Malaysia, which together account for 85% of world production, palm plantations have occupied a growing area in the Brazilian Amazon. Studies indicate a potential area of 30 million ha for cultivation in this region, especially in the states of Amazonas and Pará (Embrapa, 2016). Ongoing investments aim not only to increase Brazilian participation in the international market (currently of only 0.5%), but also to supply the product to the domestic market. However, the expansion of production has been opposed by researchers and environmental organizations, which deem this process as one of the main causes of worldwide destruction of tropical forests, and of displacement of many traditional communities (Nahum and Santos, 2016).

Like maize and soybeans, palm oil is also widely used in food production (margarines and creams, ice cream, cookies, chocolates, fillings, cocoa butter substitutes and cooking oil) and increasingly in nonfood products (candles, cosmetics, crayons, detergents, diesel substitute, fatty alcohols, glycerin, hair conditioner, tinplate, dyes, lubricants, plasticizers, polishers, resins, shampoos, steel sheets, soaps). Among vegetable oils, this is the most traded in the world, capturing over 30% of the oils market and 45% of the food-specific oils market. Although most consumers are unaware of this fact, palm oil has become one of the most recurring components in contemporary diets, especially in the composition of the "ultraprocessed foods," which, for many authors, are the most emblematic examples of the massive, standardized and artificial food consumption. Its most widely known expressions are the various types of cookies, ice cream, candies and sugars in general; ready mixes and instant seasonings for cakes, soups, sauces and noodles; frozen and precooked products such as hamburgers, breaded cutlets, sausages and other cold cuts.

As relevant as the expansion of agricultural production, the emergence of the industrial order as a hegemonic model in the agrifood system throughout the twentieth century results from the way it was able to create, through industrialization, biochemical and technological innovations, a bridge between large-scale grain production and mass consumption of this ultraprocessed cheap foods with high energy value (carbohydrates and sugars). The cookie market is one of the most emblematic. In 2016, the segment reached a total revenue of R$21.8 billion in Brazil – much higher than the R$8.7 billion of, for example, the pasta segment. Dominated by "sandwich cookies," which account for a quarter of total sales, followed by Cream Crackers (21%), the segment has shown a continuous growth in the last years, except for 2016 when, as other sectors, it endured impacts of the economic crisis. In terms of volume, 1,676 million tons was sold in the country in 2012. This amount increased to 1,731 million tons in 2015 and then fell to 1,684 million in 2016. In terms of values, sales continued to increase in these years, despite the crisis: R$15 billion, R$21 billion and R$21.8 billion, respectively (Abimapi, 2018).

Regarding sugars consumption, the soft drink market is particularly interesting for analysis, either because of its economic significance (in 2015, 14 billion liters were sold in Brazil), or because of the huge amount of criticism it attracts. Associated with numerous dietary problems, notably the dramatic expansion of obesity rates (19.8% of the Brazilian population in 2018 against 11.8% in 2006), the product has faced strong opposition not only from experts but also from society at large. Data from the Brazilian Association of Soft Drinks (Abir, 2017) show that while per capita consumption of soft drinks was 88.9 liters in 2010, it decreased to 70 liters in 2016. In the same period, the consumption of mineral water had a significant increase from 34.3 to 62.8 liters per person. This explains why industry giants such as Coca-Cola – which accounted for 60.70% of the Brazilian soft drink market in 2016 (Nielsen, 2017) – have invested heavily in this segment, as well as in the production of readymade whole juices, another market that, although not significant in volume (361 million liters in 2015), has shown a strong expansion trend (Valor Econômico, 2017).

In addition to carbohydrates and sugars, over time, the industry has also sought to expand access to cheap proteins. Thus, while human consumption of cereals has declined over time, consumption of meat, milk and dairy products has expanded significantly, creating an alternative for the global grain overproduction. In Brazil, the most striking aspect of this phenomenon was the accelerated expansion of poultry meat consumption in the 1990s. The new contracting systems between industry and farmers in southern Brazil led poultry produce (in tons) to exceed that of beef, while becoming one of the cheapest sources of animal protein consumed in the country. Since then, poultry has become a basic component of the Brazilian diet, especially of the poorer social classes. In 2016, the per capita consumption was 41 kg of chicken meat, surpassing the consumption of pork and beef (respectively 14.4 and 36.1 kg). Brazil also became the second largest world producer of poultry, reaching 13600tons in 2016, behind only the USA (18,000 tons). In terms of consumption, it ranks fourth globally, with consumption of 9,500 tons in 2016. In terms of exports, Brazil is the global leader, with 4,000 tons exported in 2016 (Embrapa Suínos e Aves, 2016).

Changes in consumption patterns and practices have been both effect and cause of transformations not only of agricultural production and agro-industrial processing, but also of strategies implemented by the distribution, retail and catering sectors. In this regard, a phenomenon most often mentioned in literature is the so-called "supermarket revolution" (Reardon, Timmer and Berdegué, 2005). A fact both spatially and temporally heterogeneous among countries, in Brazil it gained relevance since the 1990s, as a result of trade liberalization and the entry of foreign capital, accompanied by significant reduction of state participation in food supply and distribution. In just a decade, between 1990 and 2000, supermarkets' share of total food and beverage sales jumped from 30% to 75%. By comparison, in this same period, in urban China, this expansion ranged "only" from 30% to 48% (Streeter, 2015).

An equally relevant phenomenon involves transformations in the restaurants. The world's most important example is related to the expansion of fast food sector, in which McDonalds is the leading company, controlling about 50% of the Brazilian market with a turnover of R$6.3 billion in the in 2016. Nevertheless, the expansion of other chains such as Burger King, controlled by the 3G Capital investment fund (see Chapter 7) with a turnover of R$1.77 billion (second place), and Subway, which has the largest number of stores in the country (1,800 in 500 cities, compared to 840 McDonalds units) is also illustrative of the importance of this sector. While contributing to expansion of "eating out," which, in 2018, for the first time in Brazil, represented more than 50% of household expenditure on food – compared to 24% in 2003 (Schubert, 2017) – this "revolution of restaurants" has exacerbated the problems of public health, given the excessive intake of foods with low nutritional value.

More recently, two new forms of restaurants have also drawn attention in the literature: on the one hand, takeaway systems, that is, places where ready meals are prepared and sold to be consumed elsewhere; on the other hand, the expansion of deliveries, driven by online ordering devices such as iFood, Just-Eat, PedidosJá and UberEats. According to data compiled by Schubert (2017), in 2015, iFood registered over half a million orders on its website every month. According to the author, although no consolidated data on this business are available in Brazil, its growth is evident, following a trend already identified in other industrialized countries. In the United Kingdom, for example, in 2014, 12.7% of households spending on food away from home were spent on food delivery.

Not every service of this kind, nor even traditional buffet restaurants, can be per se considered an expression of an industrial food order. As we will see further on, an increasing number of such catering also offer natural, healthy and minimally processed foods. Even so, it is undeniable that the spread of those restaurants favored the dissemination of what Pollan (2007, 134) described as the "industrial meal," whose purpose, in the author's words, is not to make us feel "satisfied, exactly, but simply, regrettably, full." These were accompanied of other proliferating changes in eating practices, involving not just what you eat, but how (standing, driving, with hands, answering messages on the cell phone), with whom (alone, with coworkers, with partners) and when you eat (at any time, all the time). The artifacts have also changed. Forks, plates, and tables are no longer indispensable artifacts of modern Western eating practices (they were never for the rest of the world).

Although evidence for the consolidation of an industrial order of consumption is much broader and more diverse than the presented so far, we believe that our argument is sufficiently substantiated. Nevertheless, it is relevant referring two controversies that gained much attention recently in Brazil. The first involves the plan of the mayor of São Paulo, João Doria, to add to school meals a flour made with foods close to expiration date, which would be discarded by the industry. Launched in the second half of 2017 as a product that could end hunger in the state, it became known as "human feed" and was targeted with criticism from different sectors of society (Folha de São Paulo, 2017). The second controversy concerns BRF's announcement, in early 2018, about the launch of a new brand, Kidelli, priced 15% below the average price of its more traditional brands, such as Sadia and Perdigão. The company intended to have a third brand of processed foods based on poultry and pork. The controversial point was the statement by the company's vice president of operations in Brazil that the new brand would be produced with leftovers from the other brands of the company (Exame, 2018).

To close this section, we would like to add a brief comment about the norms that regulate consumer practices. The advancement of the industrial order has established a conception of food quality centered on the physicochemical characteristics inherent to the products, as well as on the technical control of the production processes (Stanziani, 2005). Accordingly, "best" production practices were disseminated, whose judges are the technical experts who handle the codified and functional language of this order (Boltanski and Thévenot, 1991). At the international level, the main reference is the *Codex Alimentarius*, a collection of standards, codes of conduct, guidelines and recommendations on food production instituted by FAO in 1981. It served as a benchmark for national organizations – such as the National Health Surveillance Agency (ANVISA) in Brazil – to establish their own requirements. In general, these institutional devices respond to the exacerbation of risks produced by industrial practices themselves, as evidenced in the 1990s by the crisis with global repercussions of the "mad cow disease" (*Bovine Spongiform Encephalopathy*). Since then, such food crises have repeatedly appeared on the front page of newspapers around the world.

This sort of normative tool – and its underlying value conceptions – while restricting other forms of production and processing to the benefit of industrial practices, did not touch the true "Achilles heel" of the industry, namely the deliberate and unrestricted use of numerous potentially harmful components, whether pesticides or the paraphernalia of synthetic ingredients and additives. Thus, while public opinion remained focused on the most punctual food crises (horse meat, swine flu, avian influenza, caustic soda in milk and other such events), chronic problems such as excess salt, sugar or agrochemicals gained less media repercussion and public interest. In Brazil, this type of concern has only recently begun to impact production and consumption practices, but advances in regulation and control are still rare. And even worse has been the recent action of the State. For instance, only in 2019 the government of Jair Bolsonaro approved 446 new agrochemicals, which represent almost three times more than the average of approvals per years between 2010 and 2015, that is, before the political crises related to the impeachment of the president Dilma Roussef.

As noted by Pelaez and collaborators (2015), Brazilian consumption of agrochemicals, which reached 500,000 tons in 2015, accounts for 20% of all agrochemicals consumed worldwide. Between 2012 and 2014, an average of 8.33 kg per hectare was used. Soybean, maize and sugarcane crops alone account for 72% of this volume. At the top of the list of most commonly used active ingredients is Glyphosate (Bombardi, 2017). Also noteworthy is the fact that Brazil has more than 100 active ingredients approved out of which are prohibited in the European Union (Bombardi, 2017). Among them is acephate, the third best-selling pesticide in Brazil, which, according to ANVISA carries "marked neurotoxicity" and is associated with "suspected carcinogenicity" (Bombardi, 2017). The pesticide market in Brazil has a fragile regulatory system that do not provide for periodic review of permitted products, and which actually only comes into play when severe and widespread poisoning crises are identified – even if thousands of people have already lost their lives before that.

Another example concerning the regulatory framework, in this case more focused on consumption than on agricultural production, is the control over salt, sugar and fat in processed foods. Apart from companies' own initiatives (such as Hellmann's differentiating strategy of substituting sugar for honey in its ketchup), which respond to consumer pressures and competition strategies, the Brazilian state has shown relative inertia in regulation of the agrifood sector. This view is corroborated by the fact that even Chile – the neoliberal laboratory in Latin American – established a labeling system more advanced than the Brazilian one regarding identification of hazardous ingredients. In Brazil, while profits from the expansion of the industrial order are appropriated by few, the costs are paid by all, insofar as the state bears the problems arising from a serious public health crisis. These and other contradictions of the industrial order make room for criticism and, consequently, for the emergence of other models of production and consumption.

Metamorphoses and dilemmas of the industrial order

As we have seen in this chapter, the industrial order represents a model of food production, processing, distribution and consumption established during the post-war, which is grounded on continuous increase of volume and productivity by means of incorporating technical innovations aimed at overcoming the conditions imposed by nature on agricultural practices. This order has not emerged spontaneously as a result of a supposed technical superiority over other forms of production and consumption. It was rather built by the strong hand of the state, whose institutional mechanisms (including public policies) were active in shaping a new universe of food practices that, once established, contributed to strengthening and, over time, restructuring those mechanisms. As of the 1990s, new organizational arrangements were created, and the State assumed a less interventionist and more regulatory role. Despite the crises that followed this process, the industrial order did not collapse, rather it adjusted to the new reality.

From an institutional point of view, the consolidation of this order involved various regulatory mechanisms (rules, norms, standards, policies) that, although initially being controlled almost exclusively by the state, soon were also under control of nonstate actors, as illustrated by the increasing relevance of private standards from the 1990s on (Loconto and Fouilleux, 2014), particularly those defined by supermarkets, which, according to some authors, became leading actors in this order (Reardon, 2015). Whether public or private, these mechanisms were connected to certain references, either normative (the belief in progress and technique) or cognitive (the representation of a modern and innovative agribusiness). These references legitimized the technical choices implemented, such as intensive mechanization, the spread of synthetic inputs and the advance of ultraprocessed foods; all this coordinated with the emergence of new eating practices and, more broadly, with the social practices that emerged from urban transition and changes in the world of work (Figure 2.4).

From the late 1970s onwards, this model began to be challenged, because of the strong criticism over its social and environmental effects. The answer, however, has been more technology. The belief in technical progress as a solution to problems created by the very technical progress has never ceased to govern this order. Artifacts, rules and practices change, though without

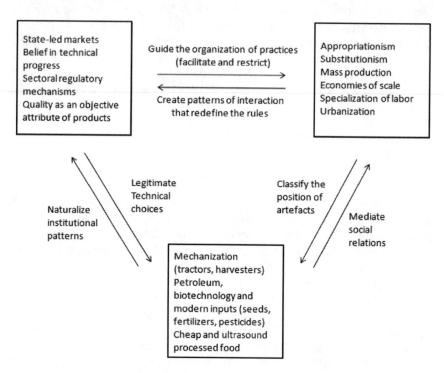

Figure 2.4 Components of the industrial order.

compromising the stability of the previously configured arrangement. Incremental innovations prevail. No-till farming solves the problem of soil loss generated by intensive mechanization. Precision agriculture solves problems stemming from uncontrolled and abusive use of inputs. The addition of lab synthesized vitamins corrects the problem of low nutritional value of ultraprocessed foods – and *voilà* the fortified, nutraceutical, functional foods ... and even "medical foods."

More drastic changes in the industrial order, also starting from the 1970s, resulted from the increasing scarcity of two elements that are essential to its constitution: money and oil. First, the two oil shocks led the price of a barrel to skyrocket, making the whole agricultural technological base, distribution and food processing much more expensive. In 1973, the member states of the Organization of Petroleum Exporting Countries (OPEC) raised the price of one barrel by more than 400%. A year later, nominal prices increased from 3 to 12 dollars per barrel. Between 1979 and 1981, the nominal price jumped from 13 to 34 dollars. Since then, this has become one of the most critical factors in the stability of the industrial order. Even with the emergence of biofuels in recent years – again a technological solution to circumvent the model's limits without changing its foundations – the problem tends to get worse because the production of ethanol and biodiesel is unlikely to meet the demand, not to mention the risks it poses to food security.

The restriction on international credit resulting from the external debt crisis has also limited the State's capacity to continue financing agriculture modernization. The problem was directly related to the increasing oil prices and, consequently, to the inflationary pressure that led the US government, whose banks were the main international creditors, to substantially raise interest rates to curb prices rise. Besides generating the first economic recession since the postwar period, this measure destabilized the global economy. In Latin America, it has decisively impacted the economic foundations that sustained the military dictatorships. In Brazil, the "economic miracle" (1969–1973) quickly fell apart. Even so, to stay in power, the government tried at all costs to maintain policies, what aggravated public debt. The outcome of this process was the crisis of the 1980s, the rise of social movements and the end of the military dictatorship (Medeiros, 2000; Schneider, 2010).

With regard specifically to agriculture, the impacts of the crisis were not devastating only because the private sector has gradually taken up practices that had been almost exclusively carried out by the State: technical assistance, rural credit, supply and distribution, agricultural insurance, regulation and standardization (Leite, 2001; Maluf and Flexor, 2017). This entailed the creation of new institutional and technical mechanisms, some of which were later incorporated into the logic of the State, such as private agricultural financing securities, new mechanisms of price guarantee and trading via auctions brokered by the Commodities and Futures Stock Market, hiring of nonstate actors for rural extension services, among others (Grisa and Schneider, 2015).

The rearrangement of practices, technical artifacts and institutional mechanisms enabled the industrial model to survive, though also creating the conditions for the emergence of new orders. The main novelty from the 1990s onwards was the process of "financialization" (Delgado, 2005). Differently from what happens in the industrial order, in which farmers, agro-industrial companies, distributors and even supermarkets resort to credit (public or private) to make their "productive" investments viable, in the new financial order, which according to various authors became predominant, it is the banks and investment funds that include the agro-industrial sector in their "investment portfolios." In this case, the practices and their meanings change – land, natural resources, commodities and food, more than goods, become highly valued financial assets. Yet, the financial order was not the only one to broaden its space thanks to the crisis of the industrial model, which, despite being dominant, was never the only existing. Other orders have also emerged, bringing to light a very diverse set of food practices.

References

Abimapi. 2018. *Abimapi registra estabilidade do setor em 2017*. Accessed March 1, 2018. www.abimapi.com.br/release-detalhe.php?i=Mjk3Mg.

Abir. 2017. *Estatísticas Refrigerantes 2017*. Accessed December 13, 2017. www.abir. org.br/o-setor/dados/refrigerantes.

Aenda. 2018. *Imprensa*. 2016. Accessed March 22, 2018. www.aenda.org.br/midia.

Albergoni, L. and Pelaez, V. 2007. "Da Revolução Verde à agrobiotecnologia: ruptura ou continuidade de paradigmas." *Revista de Economia*, 33(1): 31–53.

Almeida, W. 2007. "Massificação das operações do seguro rural: o grande desafio brasileiro." *Revista de Política Agrícola*, 16(4): 21–26.

Anfavea. 2017. *Anuário*. Accessed March 28, 2018. www.anfavea.com.br/anuarios. html.

Benetti, M. 2004. *Globalização e desnacionalização do agronegócio brasileiro no pós 1990*. Porto Alegre: FEE.

Bernardes, J. A. 2005. "Circuitos espaciais da produção na fronteira agrícola moderna: BR-163 mato-grossense." In *Geografia da soja BR-163: fronteiras em mutação*, edited by J. A. Bernardes and O. Freire Filho. Rio de Janeiro: Arquimedes.

Bndes.2018. *Consulta de Operações*. Accessed July 22, 2018. www.bndes.gobr/wps/portal/ site/home/transparencia/consulta-operacoes-bndes/consulta-op-dir-ind-nao-aut.

Boltanski, L. and Thévenot, L. 1991. *De la Justification*. Paris: Gallimard.

Bombardi, L. 2017. *Geografia do uso de agrotóxicos no Brasil e conexões com a União Europeia*. São Paulo: USP.

Bonanno, A. 1999. "A globalização da economia e da sociedade: fordismo e pósfordismo no setor agroalimentar." In: Globalização, Trabalho, Meio Ambiente. Edited by J. Cavalcanti. Recife: UFPE.

Bonanno, A. and Wolf, S. (eds). 2018. *Resistance to Neoliberal Food Regime: A Critical Analysis*. New York: Routledge.

Brandão, A., Rezende, G. and Marques, R. 2006. "Crescimento agrícola no período 1999/2004: a explosão da soja e da pecuária bovina e seu impacto sobre o meio ambiente." *Economia Aplicada*, 10(2): 249–66.

Bresser-Pereira, L. C. 2010. *Do antigo ao novo desenvolvimentismo na América Latina*. São Paulo: FGV.

BRF. 2016. *Institutional Website*. Accessed April 15, 2017. www.brf-br.com/imprensa/ release-detalhe.cfm?codigo=600&idioma=PT.

Búrigo, F. 2010. "Sistema Nacional de Crédito Rural: uma trajetória de privilégios, crises e oportunidades." In *Ensaios sobre o cooperativismo solidário*, edited by A. Volles, 426–58.Francisco Beltrão: Infocos.

Carvalho, T. 2016. *Estratégias de crescimento e reestruturação da indústria de carnes no Brasil: o papel de políticas públicas discricionárias*. PhD Thesis. São Paulo: USP.

Castro, A. C. 2002. *Localização e identificação das empresas processadoras de soja, suas áreas de influência, preços e custos de transporte relacionados*. Rio de Janeiro: UFRRJ.

Coletti, G., Franculino, K. and Mota, M. 2016. "A internacionalização das empresas frigoríficas brasileiras." *Blucher Engineering Proceedings*, 3(4): 59–73.

Conterato, M., Schneider, S, Fernandes, L. and Libardoni, P. 2014. "O consumo intermediário na agricultura: uma comparação entre agricultura familiar e não familiar no Brasil e nas regiões Sul e Nordeste." *Revista Econômica do Nordeste*, 45: 54–70.

Cruz, F. and Menasche, R. 2014. "O debate em torno de queijos feitos de leite cru: entre aspectos normativos e a valorização da produção tradicional." *Vigilância Sanitária em Debate*, 2(4): 34–42.

Delgado, G. C. 1985. *Capital financeiro e agricultura no Brasil*: 1965–1985. São Paulo: Ícone.

Delgado, G. C. 2005. "A questão agrária no Brasil, 1950–2003." In *Questão social e políticas sociais no Brasil contemporâneo*, edited by L. Jaccoud, 51–90. Brasília: IPEA.

Delgado, G. C. 2012. *Do capital financeiro na agricultura à economia do agronegócio– mudanças cíclicas em meio século*. Porto Alegre: UFRGS.

Dias, P. and Fernandes, E. 2006. "Fertilizantes: uma visão global sintética." *BNDES Setorial*, 24: 97–138.

Domingues, M., Bermann, C. and Manfredini, S. 2014. "A produção de soja no Brasil e sua relação com o desmatamento na Amazônia." *Revista Presença Geográfica*, 1(1): 32–47.

Embrapa. 2016. *Alimentos biofortificados buscam reduzir a desnutrição da população*. Accessed May 24, 2016. www.embrapa.br/busca-de-noticias/-/noticia/3254365/ alimentos-biofortificados-buscam-reduzir-a-desnutricao-da-populacao.

Exame. 2018. *BRF anuncia marca mais barata de alimentos com sobras de produção*. Accessed April 22, 2018. www.exame.abril.com.br/negocios/ brf-anuncia-nova-marca-para-mercado-de-alimentos-processados.

Fernández, A. 2007. *Do Cerrado à Amazônia: as estruturas sociais da economia da soja em Mato Grosso*. PhD Thesis. Porto Alegre: UFRGS.

Ferreira, G. S. 2016. *Análise da estrutura de mercado da cerveja: a competitividade e estratégias de mercado da indústria cervejeira e micro cervejarias*. Florianópolis: UFSC.

Ferreira, M. J. 1995. A *indústria brasileira de tratores agrícolas e colheitadeiras: as estratégias de suas empresas e o desenvolvimento de vantagens competitivas*. Master Dissertation. Campinas: Unicamp.

Flexor, G. 2006. "A globalização do sistema agroalimentar e seus desafios para o Brasil." *Economia Ensaios*, 21: 63–96.

Folha de São Paulo. 2017. *Doria agora quer incluir farinata na merenda de alunos da rede municipal*. Accessed September 22, 2017. www1.folha.uol.com.br/cotidiano/ 2017/10/1928046-doria-agora-quer-incluir-farinata-na-merenda-de-alunos-da- rede-municipal.shtml.

Fonseca, P. 2003. "O processo de substituição de importações." *Formação Econômica do Brasil*, edited by J. Rego and R. Marques. São Paulo: Saraiva.

Gasques, J. G., Bacchi, M., Rodrigues, L., Bastos, E. and Valdes, C. 2016. "Produtividade da agricultura brasileira: a hipótese da desaceleração." In Vieira *Agricultura, transformação produtiva e sustentabilidade*, edited by J. E. Vieira Filho et al., 143–64. Brasília: IPEA.

Gilpin, R. 2011. *Global political economy: understanding the international economic order*. Princeton: Princeton University Press.

Goodman, D., Sorj, B. and Wilkinson, J. 1987. *From Farming to Biotechnology*: A Theory of Agro-industrial Development. Basil: Blackwell.

Graziano da Silva, J. (ed.). 1980. *Estrutura agrária e produção de subsistência na agricultura brasileira*. 2nd ed. São Paulo: Hucitec.

Graziano da Silva, J. 2003. *Agricultura familiar e tecnologia*. Porto Alegre: UFRGS.

Grisa, C. and Schneider. S. (eds). 2015. *Políticas de Desenvolvimento Rural no Brasil*. Porto Alegre: UFRGS.

Heringer. 2016. *Mercado Mundial e Brasileiro de Fertilizantes*. Accessed August 13, 2016. www.heringer.com.br.

Ianni, O. 1979. *Colonização e Contra-Reforma Agrária na Amazônia*. Petrópolis: Vozes.

IBGE. 2016. *Produção Agrícola Municipal*. Rio de Janeiro: IBGE.

IBGE. 2019. *Censo Agropecuário*. Rio de Janeiro: IBGE.

Ioris, A. 2017. *Agribusiness and the Neoliberal Food System in Brazil: Frontiers and Fissures of Agro-Neoliberalism*. London: Routledge.

JBS. 2017. *Relatório anual e de sustentabilidade*. Accessed April 22, 2017. www.brf-global.com/brasil/responsabilidade-corporativa/relatorio-anual.

Johnston, B. and Mellor, J. 1961. "The role of agriculture in economic development." *American Economic Review*, 51(4): 566–93.

Kageyama, A. et al. 1990. "O novo padrão agrícola brasileiro: do complexo rural aos complexos agroindustriais." In *Agricultura e políticas públicas*, edited by G.Delgado, J. Gasques and C. Villaverde, 113–223. Brasília: IPEA.

Leite, S. P. 1998. *Inserção internacional e financiamento da agricultura brasileira (1980–1996)*. PhD Thesis. Campinas: Unicamp.

Leite, S. P. 2001. "Padrão de financiamento, setor público e agricultura no Brasil." In *Políticas Públicas e Agricultura no Brasil*, edited by S. P. Leite. Porto Alegre: UFRGS.

Loconto, A. and Fouilleux, E. 2014. "Politics of private regulation: ISEAL and the shaping of transnational sustainability governance." *Regulation and Governance*, 8(2): 166–85.

Maluf, R. and Flexor, G. (eds). 2017. *Questões agrárias, agrícolas e rurais: conjunturas e políticas públicas*. Rio de Janeiro: E-papers.

Marques, M. 2016. "Considerações sobre a expansão da indústria de papel e celulose no Brasil a partir do caso da Suzano Papel e Celulose." GEOgraphia, 17(35): 120–47.

Martinelli, Jr., O. and Waquil, P. D. 2002. "Tendências recentes na indústria de defensivos agrícolas no Brasil." *Análise Econômica*, 20(38): 123–42.

Martins, J. de S. 1996. "O tempo da fronteira. Retorno à controvérsia sobre o tempo histórico da frente de expansão e da frente pioneira." *Tempo Social*, 8(1): 25–70.

Medeiros, L. S. 2000. "Conflitos sociais no meio rural no Brasil contemporâneo." *Revista del Observatorio Social de la America Latina*, 1(2): 37–44.

Mengel, A. 2015. *Modernização da agricultura e pesquisa no Brasil: a Empresa Brasileira de Pesquisa Agropecuária – Embrapa*. PhD Thesis. Rio de Janeiro: UFRRJ.

Moreno, G. 2007. *Terra e poder em Mato Grosso: política e mecanismo de burla (1892 a 1992)*. Cuiabá: UFMT.

Nahum, J. S. and Santos, C. 2016. "A dendeicultura na Amazônia paraense". *Geousp*, 20(2): 281–94.

Nielsen. 2017. *Relatório do Mercado de Sucos e Refrigerantes*. São Paulo: Nielsen.

Nunes, R. and Nassar, A. 2000. Agricultura, crédito e securitização. In: *Descentralização, autonomia e geração de renda rural: proposta para o Sistema Brasileiro de Crédito Rural*, edited by G. Dias and R. Abramovay. São Paulo: Fipe.

Oliveira, A. U. 2006. "A Amazônia e a nova geografia da produção da soja." *Terra Livre*, 1(26): 13–43.

Peixoto, M. 2008. *Extensão rural no Brasil: uma abordagem histórica da legislação*. Brasília: Senado Federal.

Pelaez, V., Silva, L., Guimarães, T., Dal Ri, F. and Teodorovicz, T. 2015. "A (des) coordenação de políticas para a indústria de agrotóxicos no Brasil." *Revista Brasileira de Inovação*, 14: 153–78.

Pelaez, V., Terra, F. and Silva, L. 2010. "A regulamentação dos agrotóxicos no Brasil: entre o poder de mercado e a defesa da saúde e do meio ambiente." *Revista de Economia*, 36(1): 27–48.

Pinto, L. 1981. Notas sobre a política de crédito rural. Campinas: Unicamp.

Pollan, M. 2007. *O dilema do onívoro*. Rio de Janeiro: Intrínseca.

Ploeg, J. D. van der. 1990. *Labor, Markets, and Agricultural Production*. Boulder: Westview.

Reardon, T. 2015. "The hidden middle: The quiet revolution in the midstream of agrifood value chains in developing countries." *Oxford Review of Economic Policy*, 31(1): 45–63.

Reardon, T., Timmer, P. and Berdegué, J. 2005. "Supermarket expansion in Latin America and Asia: implications for food marketing systems." In: New Directions in Global Food Markets. Edited by A. Regmi and M. Gehlhar. Washington: USDA.

Reuters. 2018. *Cofco e ADM têm maior salto em exportação de milho e soja do Brasil em 2017*. Accessed May 23, 2018. https://br.reuters.com/article/topNews/idBRKCN1GJ2JB-OBRTP.

Rezende, G. C. 2003. *Estado, macroeconomia e agricultura no Brasil*. Porto Alegre: UFRGS.

Rivero, S., Almeida, O., Ávila, S. and Oliveira, W. 2009. "Pecuária e desmatamento: uma análise das principais causas diretas do desmatamento na Amazônia." *Nova Economia*, 19(1): 41–66.

Rodrigues, J. A. 1978. "O papel da agricultura no processo de desenvolvimento econômico e as políticas governamentais para o setor agrícola." *Revista de Administração Pública*, 12(3): 9–37.

Schallenberger, E. and Schneider, I. 2010. "Fronteiras agrícolas e desenvolvimento territorial – ações de governo e dinâmica do capital." *Sociologias*, 12(25): 202–22.

Schneider, S. 2010. "Situando o desenvolvimento rural no Brasil: o contexto e as questões em debate." Revista de Economia Política, 30(3): 511–531.

Schubert, M. 2017. *Comer fora de casa, as práticas e as rotinas do comer nos contextos da modernidade: uma leitura comparada entre Brasil, Reino Unido e Espanha*. PhD Thesis. Porto Alegre: UFRGS.

Schultz, T. 1965. *A transformação da agricultura tradicional*. Rio de Janeiro: Zahar.

Silva, A., Fachinello, A., Boteon, M., Julião, L. and Pozelli, R. 2015. "Cadeia produtiva do cacau e chocolate: perfil e desafios." In *Proceedings of the Brazilian Congress of Rural Economy and Sociology*. João Pessoa: Sober.

Silva, C., Bueno, J. and Neves, M. 2017. "A indústria de celulose e papel no Brasil." In *Fornecedores e Fabricantes*, edited by Associação Brasileira Técnica de Celulose e Papel, 6–15.São Paulo: ABTCP.

Silva, M. and Costa, L. 2012. "A indústria de defensivos agrícolas." *BNDES Setorial*, 35: 233–76.

Silveira, J. M. 2014. "Agricultura brasileira: o papel da inovação tecnológica." In *O mundo rural no Brasil do Século 21*, edited by A. Buainain et al., 373–94. Brasília: Embrapa.

Sperotto, F. 2014. "A expansão do setor de celulose de mercado no Brasil: condicionantes e perspectivas." *Indicadores Econômicos FEE*, 41(4): 85–100.

Stanziani, A. 2005. *Histoire de la qualité alimentaire: XIXe–XXe siècles*. Paris: Seuil.

Streeter, J. 2015. "Supermarket revolution and food demand in China." *Economics Bulletin*, 35(1): 452–59.

Valor Econômico. 2017. *Fertiláqua quer dobrar vendas até 2018*. Accessed August 14, 2018. www.valor.com.br/agro/5055724/fertilaqua-quer-dobrar-vendas-ate-2018.

Vizzaccaro, C. 2018. *Nasce uma gigante*. Accessed May 7, 2018. www.dinheirorural.com.br/nasce-uma-gigante-2.

Wesz, Jr., V. J. 2011. *Dinâmicas e estratégias das agroindústrias de soja no Brasil*. Rio de Janeiro: E-papers.

Wesz, Jr., V. J. 2016. "Strategies and hybrid dynamics of soy transnational companies in the Southern Cone." *Journal of Peasant Studies*, 43(2): 286–312.

Wilkinson, J., Wesz, Jr., V. J. and Lopane, A. 2016. "Brazil and China: The agribusiness connection in the Southern Cone context." *Third World Thematics*, 1(5): 726–45.

Zanon, J. E. 2016. *Uso de aptâmeros na sexagem de sêmen bovino*. PhD Thesis. Araçatuba: Unesp.

3 The reinvention of the commercial order

The economic, political and social transformations that followed the crisis of the 1930s and, especially, the end of World War II were fundamental for consolidating the industrial food order. As we saw in the previous chapter, this process involved the consolidation of modern agro-industrial facilities, increasing dependence of agriculture on the input and processing industries, accelerated expansion of grain production, international diffusion of a technological package through the Green Revolution, and a strong developmental State. All of these changes could be associated with both the emergence of a Fordist regime of capitalist accumulation (Bonanno, 2017; Bonanno and Wolf, 2017) and the formation of the "second global food regime" (Friedman and McMichael, 1989; Lang and Heasman, 2015).

However, the practices and institutions that preceded the formation of this order were not completely replaced. Rather, as we will demonstrate in this chapter, not only those practices subsisted, but also the crises of the industrial model made room both for the emergence of civic, aesthetic and financial orders, and even for the reinvention of "preindustrial" practices and institutions. This means that the "new spirit of capitalism" (Boltanski and Chiapello, 2005) still holds much of the old one; it coexists with practices, artifacts, rules, values and cognitive references whose origin precedes the conformation of the industrial order, whether in agrifood markets or in other social orders. These practices gather but are not limited to those that part of social theory – mainly in the Latin American postcolonial sociology – has termed "neoextractivism" (Acosta, 2016a; Gudynas, 2012).

To a great extent, this order brings together characteristics that define the first (imperial–colonial) food regime, such as the organization of the plantation, the centralization of geopolitical power by certain imperialist nations and an extractive economy based on the spoliation of natural resources (McMichael, 2016). In some way, it can be associated with what historiography defines as the "commercial or mercantile capitalism." Considered "precapitalism" by many historians, today this mode of ordering can be conceived as a kind of capitalism that besides a specific regime of accumulation also involves a culture of authoritarian, centralizing and populist control. Indeed, it is not surprising that the rise of this order is associated with the crisis of the model of democracy sustained by the Fordist regime (Levitsky and Ziblatt, 2018; Peters, 2017).

Some authors refer to a "postdemocracy" era to mean that capitalism would be waiving the normative foundations that underpinned postwar industrial development (Dardot and Laval, 2009). All over the world, industrial democracy has become a hindrance to certain forms of capitalist accumulation, leading to the resurgence of authoritarian and even fascist stances. This is the case with the commercial order, whose expansion is connected to this dangerous institutional metamorphosis of the highest social values. In Brazil, the expansion of practices such as Amazon deforestation and violent attacks against indigenous people has not only been allowed but also encouraged by the autocratic government of President Jair Bolsonaro.

What evidence allows us to so categorically postulate the "reinvention" of this order? Nontransparent rules of public control of property are associated with aggressive land grabbing practices; policies aimed to encourage exportation of ores and agricultural commodities are linked to the resumption of deforestation; patterns of conspicuous consumption are connected to contemporary forms of slave labor, and so on. The purpose of this chapter is to analyze how these practices and institutions define an order that has profound implications for the functioning of contemporary agrifood systems. Although this analysis is specific to the Brazilian context, recent literature evidences the generality of this process in other countries (Borras, Jr. et al., 2016; Scoones et al., 2018).

The fifth century of latifundium

The variety of capitalism that prevailed between the fifteenth and nineteenth centuries was marked by some basic characteristics: expansion of imperial domains, colonialism, mercantilism, despotic governments, different forms of servitude and primitive capital accumulation. In Brazil, the economic, social and political reforms implemented by the Marquis of Pombal in the eighteenth century encouraged manufacturing in Portugal and intensified the mercantilist exploitation of the colony. Despite the enactment of the Land Law in 1850, which regulated private property, and the formal abolition of slavery in 1888, this regime remained dominant until, at least, the 1930s. Throughout this period, the exporting latifundium has been the backbone of this regime, the one which dictated the pattern of economic accumulation and the forms of political domination based on physical and symbolic violence (Faoro, 1989).

It means that the characteristics of the latifundium during the first global food regime (1870–1920) are consistent with the type of colonial-mercantilist capitalism that marked the Brazilian agrarian economy. Throughout the Old Republic (1889–1930), this model was largely favored by the liberal politics that facilitated the subordinate integration of the country to central capitalist markets. This agrarian model has created within the Brazilian society a self-image that persists to this day: an "agricultural essence associated with an 'oceanic vocation' as exporter of primary goods supplied at risible prices thanks to the richness of the land and cheap labour" (Linhares and Silva, 1979, 68). This image became so deeply embedded that, at the beginning of the twentieth century, the emerging industry "was 'intimately' linked to farming and was therefore unable to either rise to the position of hegemonic sector or challenge the composition of the bloc in power" (ibid., 21).

Plentiful evidence supports this conception of "agroexport vocation." At the end of the first regime, between 1921 and 1930, coffee accounted for 70% of the total value of Brazilian exports, which confirms the wide dependence of the Brazilian trade balance on export crops. However, as already pointed out in Chapter 1, the trade balance does not allow generalizations about the whole of agriculture and economy, given, for example, the concentration of this commodity in the south-eastern region of the country. Moreover, although coffee occupied one-third of the cultivated area and represented 25% of the gross value of production in 1920, its cultivation was limited to a quarter of rural establishments. Other products such as beans, rice, cassava and maize were more widespread among Brazilian farmers, the latter exceeding coffee in terms of cultivated area and matching it in terms of value of production (IBGE, 1924).

The conception of export monoculture as the mainstay of Brazilian economic formation has been widely criticized by historiography. Highlighting the endogenous processes of capitalist accumulation, several authors have challenged the view of exporting latifundia as an almost exclusive underpinning of the colonial economy. As Fragoso (1992) demonstrates, the various forms of production, labor and territorial occupation invigorated the domestic market, establishing complementary exchanges between regions, which were more relevant than exports. Furthermore, besides those products typical of domestic supply, such as meat, beans, maize, rice and flour, some "products traditionally referred to as 'export commodities' circulated internally by sea and most of them supplied the domestic market, such as sugar, tobacco and leather" (Marcondes, 2012). Even the main export product of the period, coffee, circulated among the provinces, so that its domestic consumption represented almost a third of total production. This importance of the domestic market persisted during the Old Republic (1889–1930) and, between 1925 and 1944, has further expanded due to growing international geopolitical tensions and to the policies set in motion by the Vargas government (Linhares and Silva, 1979).

Even so, the continued strength over time of the colonial-mercantilist model of accumulation is undeniable. Indeed, in the 1960s, the Brazilian agrarian debate was still focused on the analysis of the persistence of practices and institutions characteristic of the "colonial capitalism." A reference in this debate was the "feudal remnants thesis" developed by Alberto Passos Guimarães (1963) in *Quatro Séculos de Latifúndio* (Four centuries of latifundium), which argued that the Brazilian economic system had experienced a transition from feudalism to capitalism, retaining many characteristics of the former regime. These characteristics, according to the author, hampered both the expansion of the domestic market and the industrialization and, hence, the constitution of industrial capitalism. In this sense, agrarian reform was presented as necessary to break with the obstacles posed by the latifundium – or, more precisely, by the practices and institutions that it combined – in order to develop capitalism.

According to Guimarães, the latifundium restricted productivity growth and technological progress for reproducing archaic labor practices and power relations, based on extraeconomic parameters. "These old relations of production that hinder the development of our agriculture are not capitalist, but legacies of colonial feudalism" (Guimarães, 1963, 34); and, "the fact that land is the fundamental means of production in agriculture indicates a lower stage of agricultural production, peculiar to pre-capitalist historical conditions" (ibid., 35). Therefore, land reform would mean a radical break with the latifundium model and thus with the "extraeconomic" power of the local political elites.

The thesis of feudal remnants had been refuted by Roberto Simonsen in 1937 and was again rejected by Caio Prado, Jr. (1979a), for whom Brazil has been, since its creation, a country integrated into the international capitalist economy. For this author, the main dilemma of Brazil was not the reproduction of precapitalist relations, but rather the kind of social organization that was engendered by capitalism. In his view, this would require a more focused examination of working conditions and of class conflict between capitalists and agricultural waged workers. Differently from what Alberto Passos Guimarães proposed, for Caio Prado, Jr. the agrarian question laid on changing the precarious working conditions and living standards of the rural population, which were outcomes of low wages and lack of a modern labor law.

The 1930s are generally defined as the historical milestone of the "end of agrarian-exporting hegemony and the beginning of the urban-industrial-based production supremacy" (Oliveira, 1977, 10). The end of this hegemony does not mean, however, the overcoming of practices and institutions that sustained the old regime. The latifundium is a "continued past–present" says Antonio Houaiss in the introduction to Alberto Passos Guimarães's book, and he also argues that "the contemporary historical (and sociological) practice ... has highlighted ... that the access to a subsequent mode in a sector of humanity does not automatically or ultimately rules out the enduring of previous mode or modes." This "results, first, in the recognition that, in the present state of human evolution, all these modes exist and coexist; second, in that none of them is exempt from contamination by the others" (Houaiss, 1963, xiii).

To some extent, the coexistence of modes of production has been recognized by the concept of "structural dualism," which defines underdevelopment as a specific variant of the capitalist development (rather than an earlier stage of a linear path, as presupposed by Walt Rostow). As Celso Furtado (1963) points out, part of the explanation for the reproduction of underdevelopment can be found in the unequal relations between center and periphery (new terms for metropolis and colony), which internally underpin the reproduction of hybrid social structures. The notion of structural dualism points to the coexistence and articulation of modern and backward sectors, because of the kind of asymmetry generated by such economic and geopolitical relations.[1]

In *The Economic Growth of Brazil*, Furtado (1963) shows that, throughout various economic cycles, Brazil has been characterized by a mode of production able to compete in international markets (commercial agriculture), despite being grounded in an archaic internal social structure, whose main characteristics were precarious labor relations, excessive concentration of land ownership and wealth, backward technology and "unproductive consumption." This latter variable was further analyzed in *O Mito do Desenvolvimento Econômico* (The myth of economic development) (Furtado, 1974), where the author suggests that, underlying the social structures that maintained underdevelopment, there was a "cultural dependence" that steered the use of surplus towards conspicuous consumption by the Brazilian elite. In short, the thesis of "structural dualism" maintained that an underdeveloped economy had "segments that operated at different technological levels, as if different epochs coexisted in it" (Furtado, 1992, 19).

Conversely, Francisco de Oliveira, in his *Crítica à Razão Dualista* (Critique of dualist reason) (1977), opposed this thesis and what he called the "false dilemma" of the traditional–modern binomial: the backward agriculture comprising an obstacle to urban-industrial development. For Oliveira, the traditional Brazilian agricultural sector has always constituted a form of primitive accumulation, grounded on the power bestowed by land ownership, which was present not only at the origin of capitalism, but is rather structural, i.e., reproduced over time. Indeed, according to the author, this supposed "duality can be found not only in almost every system, but also in almost every period" (Oliveira, 1977, 12). It follows that "the expansion of capitalism in Brazil occurs by introducing new relations in archaic practices and reproducing archaic relations in new practices" (*ibid.*, 36).

Neoextractivism

The practices and institutions that define a commercial (or mercantile) order in today's societies are not exactly the same as those that defined it two centuries ago. Contemporary slave labor, for example, does not occur in the same way as it did in the past. Therefore, to understand the reinvention of this mode of ordering, it must be contextualized into the present time. As we have already mentioned, interesting examples can be found in the modern sociological literature on "neoextractivism," which deals with a regime of accumulation based on spoliation of natural resources, and which also combines the subordinate integration into scarcely diversified international commodity markets (Acosta, 2016b; Giraldo, 2018).

A common criticism against neoextractivism is related to the "paradox of plenty" (or "resource curse"), a trendy idea in the 1980s, according to which plentiful natural resources produce economic and political distortions that hamper the development of a country. As Sinnott, Nash and Torre (2010, 42) point out, "mining and farming carried out in enclaves hardly require much institutional development and manage to accommodate well in environments where lack of good governance and weak rule of law prevail." However, for these authors, more than the abundance of resources, it is the "rent-seeking" pattern of accumulation that impedes overcoming the archaic institutional arrangements that legitimize illegal forms of control of resources. In other words, against the geographic and ecological determinism, a more institutional understanding of the factors that lead to the reproduction of these practices is necessary (Acosta, 2016a).

Over the past two decades, these practices have been reinvigorated due to the so-called "China effect." Pressure on natural resources was largely due to growing Chinese demand for cheap raw materials to sustain China's high rates of economic growth (McMichael, 2019). However, Xí Jínpíng cannot take the blame alone. The reactions of other countries to the new global geopolitics also must be considered. In the case of Russia, for example, its development strategy is anchored in oil and gas exports to Europe, products that accounted for 62% of total exports in 2016 (US$176 billion to US$285 billion). Even the United States, whose economy is mainly backed by financial assets, shows a resumption of neoextractivism, given the Trump Government's initiatives to expand fossil fuel production, including coal extraction (Bonanno, 2017).

A controversy in this debate relates to the institutional basis of these practices. Many authors suggest that the neoextractivist model is supported by a developmental state, acting directly on the production sector by means of state bodies and semi-state agencies, but also by capturing the private sector's income from the spoliation of natural resources (Milanez and Santos, 2013). The cases of China and Russia are perhaps the most paradigmatic in this regard. Gudynas (2012) exposes the promotion of this model also in Latin America over the last two decades, when state action in favor of neoextractivism aimed its own legitimation through partial redistribution of the income generated by the spoliation of natural resources. According to the author, this produced a "compensatory State" that simultaneously promoted dynamics of accumulation typical of predatory capitalism and used the returns to maintain social policies of income transfer aimed at reducing poverty.

For Milanez and Santos (2013), this was the path followed by the Brazilian State between 2002 and 2013, when the state action involved three practices. First, a direct action in expanding the capacity of oil and gas extraction through Petrobras investments, which jumped from US$7.4 billion in 2003 to US$45 billion in 2013. Second, the increase in public financing for extractivist companies – illustrated by the raise in the proportion of projects for oil, mining and energy exploitation in the portfolio of BNDES from 54% to 75%. When including the pulp and paper and the food (particularly meat) sectors, this percentage rises to 89% (Torres and Góes, 2013). Third, the relaxation of rules on the use of natural resources and the maintenance of tax exemptions for exporting companies, especially via the Kandir Law (Complementary Law No. 87/1996), which exempts exports of primary and semi-manufactured goods from sales tax.

However, we must be cautious about associating neoextractivism with a developmental state. The strategy of accumulation via commodities export was also very present in the 1990s, at the height of the neoliberal model in Brazil – as illustrated by the approval of Kandir Law in 1996, closely linked to the lobby for privatization of the state-owned mining company Vale do Rio Doce, during Fernando Henrique Cardoso government. The adoption of the neoliberal narrative by Bolsonaro government also complicates the usual reading of neoextractivism as a feature peculiar to Latin American neodevelopmental states. In the Brazilian case, between 2002 and 2016, a combination of liberal and developmental policies was observed (Sallum, Jr. and Goulart, 2017; Niederle and Grisa, 2019). In fact, neoextractivism relates to a neocolonial logic and, in this regard, developmental and liberal strategies do not differ in the most essential aspect, namely the ideology of development that colonialism carries with it. According to Acosta (2016b, 113), these "different ideological stances keep deeming nature as an element to be tamed and commodified."

In any case, it is commonly known that, over the last two decades, the Brazilian State has pursued an economic growth strategy based on increasing exploitation of natural resources and integration into global markets through the export of low technology manufactures (Figure 3.1). The mining sector comprises a prime example of this type of integration to international markets – no longer based on gold exports to Europe as in the sixteenth century, but on the exports of iron ore to China. Between 2003 and 2011, when it reached its peak, metal ores exports jumped from US$3.4 billion to US$44

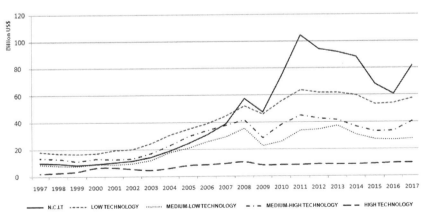

Figure 3.1 Evolution of Brazilian exports by technological intensity (1999–2017).

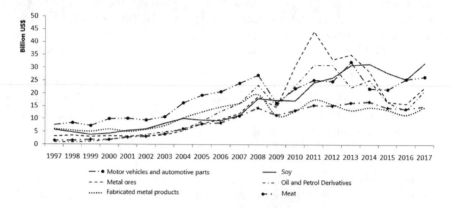

Figure 3.2 Evolution of Brazilian exports (1997–2017), selected products.

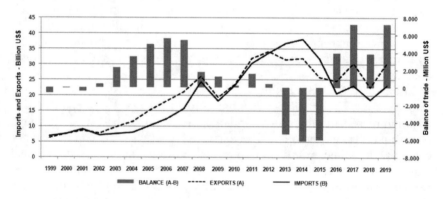

Figure 3.3 Evolution of imports, exports and Brazilian trade balance (1999–2018).

billion. During this period, the product was the major contributor to the Brazilian trade surplus. As of 2013, this position was occupied by the "soy complex" (Figure 3.2).

As of 2011, the value of exports fell for virtually all these sectors, implying a reduction and even a negative balance of trade (Figure 3.3). The crisis of global markets affected all sectors to a greater or lesser extent, tough some endured longer effects – a situation that contributed to the country's institutional destabilization in subsequent years. The mining sector was the most impacted, with exports falling to US$15 billion in 2016 (one-third as compared with 2011). Would this mean a reduction in the rate of exploitation of natural resources? On the contrary. The decreasing value of exports reflected the fall in international commodity prices after the 2008 boom and the partial recovery until 2011. As a result of the fall in prices, and despite a slight reduction in 2012, mineral extraction intensified. Even if under the

Bolsonaro administration this process is increasing at unimaginable rates of spoliation of natural resources, its origins are a bit older and reflect the effects of the international crisis.

The Brazilian State's bet on mining has encouraged several institutional changes in the sector, notably the 2030 National Mining Plan, launched in 2011 by the Ministry of Mines and Energy (MME). This document points out that the 2000s marked a turning point in the mining sector, which became the most dynamic sector in the Brazilian economy, with an average annual growth rate of 10%, mainly due to exports (Brazil, 2011). Aiming at continuing this growth path and at meeting projected growth in both international demand and, to a lesser extent, domestic industry, the plan forecasts that iron and crude steel production, between 2008 and 2030, should increase from 351 Mt to 1,098 Mt, and from 33.7 Mt to 116 Mt, respectively. To this end, in addition to technological improvement and various government incentives (research, financing, tax exemptions), the strategy devises a series of changes in the sector's governance, including the creation of the Mining National Agency (Agência Nacional de Mineração – ANM), enacted in December 2017, and concurrently the revocation of several rules that regulated the sector's activities, on grounds of "creating a favourable environment for attracting investments to the sector and increasing the competitiveness of companies in the mining industry" (Brazil, 2011, 123).

The creation of such "favorable environment" carries a particularly perverse face, namely the relaxation of environmental norms, thus allowing access to preservation areas and, simultaneously, displacing (and killing) original and traditional communities. According to data from the Pastoral Land Commission, a NGO related to the Catholic Church, in south-eastern Pará alone, 80% of the areas surveyed for mining are in lands occupied by settlers, *quilombolas* and indigenous peoples or are areas of environmental preservation (CPT, 2018a). One of the first measures of institutional deregulation was the extinction, in 2017, by decree of President Michel Temer (Decree No. 9142), of the *Reserva Nacional de Cobre e Associados* (RENCA) (the Copper and related ores National Reserve), an area between Pará and Amapá with 46,450 square kilometers (slightly larger than the Netherlands), situated next to Serra dos Carajás, this latter known for housing some of the largest iron ore, gold and manganese deposits in the world (Carneiro, 2013). The decree reviewed the position of the Military Government which, in 1984, established that only the *Companhia de Pesquisa de Recursos Minerais* (CPRM) (Mineral Resources Research Company, a state-owned company accountable to the MME) could conduct geological surveys to assess the occurrence of ores at RENCA. The new law made room for private companies to exploit the area, thus threatening two indigenous reserves, a national park, a national forest reserve, a state forest reserve and four ecological reserves that make up the RENCA area. Although Temer government suspended the decree following public outcry and international repercussions of the case, the sector's strategy to respond to the crisis was clear.

The fall in ore prices was accompanied by intensification of extraction. If, previously, the stimulus to increase exports volume was based on the opportunity posed by high prices, now the motivation has been reversed: a greater volume of products must be exported to obtain the same value as in previous years. This is possible because investments for mineral extraction are relatively low compared to other sectors and, therefore, even with falling prices, the spoliation of natural resources allows for margins to cover capital investments and variable costs (given the low pay of labor). So, to increase and guarantee profit margins in a context of price reductions, there was increased pressure to open new areas for exploitation, entailing intensified degradation of natural resources and more precarious working conditions.

In January 2019, four years after a similar tragedy in the Brazilian city of Mariana, the rupture of the Brumadinho mineral tailings dam in the state of Minas Gerais causing hundreds of deaths, decimating rural communities and devastating rivers and agricultural lands. Since then, it became undeniable that tragedies like those were direct outcomes from the State's permissive attitude regarding the inspection of the sector, especially concerning environmental norms. Nevertheless, rather than tightening inspections, the new Brazilian government became even more conniving at this kind of plundering strategy, which, as we shall see further on, brings together other harmful practices such as deforestation and precarious labor.

Where there's smoke, there's fire

Deforestation is at the origin of Brazil's colonial occupation and has never ceased since. First area occupied by the European immigrants, situated in the coastal zone of the territory, only 12% remains of the original Brazilian Atlantic Forest. In turn, the Cerrado, the "richest savanna in the world" (El País, 2018), has already lost about half of its native cover because of the grain production expansion (Silva, 2013). Nevertheless, over the last decades, any mention of deforestation turns attention fundamentally to the Amazon, whose area has already lost 20% of its forest (Prodes, 2017). In this biome, large-scale deforestation occurs both to feed the logging and mining industries and to introduce livestock and grain crops (Frizo, 2018).

The 2000s showed a gradual reduction in the pace of deforestation, as a result of the control exerted by public agencies and the reaction of international buyers to criticism from environmental and consumer movements (Carneiro, 2013). Among initiatives aimed at reducing deforestation in the Amazon, one of the best known is the "soy moratorium," a joint action of NGOs, notably Greenpeace, and representatives of the major grain companies and of cereals and vegetable oils exporters. Studies suggest that between 2001 and 2006, about 14% of deforested areas were occupied by soybeans, and after the ban, in October 2006, this rate fell to 5.6% (Table 3.1; Kastens et al., 2017). Another example of initiatives like this is the project *Pecuária Verde* (Green Livestock), in which the municipality of Paragominas (Pará) stands

Table 3.1 Municipalities with largest area of deforestation from 2000 to 2018 in the Amazon region

Municipality (State)	Deforested area (km²)			Variation (%)		Deforested area over the total (%)		
	2000	2010	2018	2010/ 2000	2018/ 2010	2000	2010	2018
São Félix do Xingu (PA)	7,037,4	17,004,3	18,733,9	141.6	10.2	8.4	20.2	22.2
Porto Velho (RO)	3,888,3	7,797,0	10,199,6	100.5	30.8	11.2	22.5	29.5
Altamira (PA)	2,058,8	6,726,0	9,162,1	226.7	36.2	1.3	4.2	5.7
Paragominas (PA)	7,212,3	8,605,0	8,791,7	19.3	2.2	37.1	44.2	45.2
Marabá (PA)	5,818,9	8,250,5	8,726,8	41.8	5.8	38.4	54.4	57.6
Novo Repartimento (PA)	3,105,8	7,002,0	8,127,1	125.4	16.1	20.1	45.4	52.7
Juara (MT)	5,520,7	7,813,6	8,053,0	41.5	3.1	24.3	34.4	35.6
Cumaru do Norte (PA)	4,172,5	7,041,7	7,367,8	68.8	4.6	24.3	41.7	43.0
Santana do Araguaia (PA)	4,614,7	7,067,4	7,251,6	53.1	2.6	39.7	60.9	62.4
Novo Progresso (PA)	1,789,8	5,317,9	6,288,8	197.1	18.3	4.7	13.9	16.4

Source: INPE – PRODES (2020).

out as a good example. Third in the ranking of the worst deforesters in the country, with 44% of its total area deforested by 2016, this municipality was the first to leave the "list of Amazon municipalities for priority prevention, monitoring and control of illegal deforestation," known as the "Dirty List of Deforestation." This was a result of several coordinated actions aimed at changing livestock practices to allow for the recomposition of deforested areas. Municipalities figured in the list, which was published in 2008 by the Ministry of the Environment, have restricted their access to public financing, including rural credit for farmers. According to Carneiro and Assis (2015), the case of Paragominas reveals a "partial and conservative experience of ecological modernization" that managed to halt further deforestation by adopting the main legal environmental norms.

The slowdown does not mean that deforestation has ceased to exist. On the contrary, some municipalities continued to rapidly expand this practice. This is the case of the municipality of Apuí (Amazonas), where the total deforested area jumped from 1.7 thousand hectares in 2010 to 2,300 in 2016. The same occurred in Altamira (Pará) – which expanded from 6,700 to 8,500ha– and of Lábrea (Amazonas) – from 3,200 to 4,200ha. These three municipalities remain among the 39 figuring in the most recent list of municipalities for priority deforestation prevention, monitoring and control (Portaria MMA no 361/2017). In addition to these, 21 other municipalities, including

Paragominas, have "deforestation under control and are being monitored" (Portaria MMA no 362/2017), that is, they have been on the "dirty list" and have now moved to this new monitoring condition.

More recently, especially after 2012, deforestation has once again intensified, initially, as a result of the enactment of the new Forest Code (Law no. 12651/2012), which besides relaxing environmental norms, has pardoned infringements previous to June 2008, thus creating an expectation among deforesters that this could happen again in the coming years (Figure 3.4). Following a legal action against this amnesty, on February 28, 2018, the Federal Supreme Court ruled by a 6-to-5 vote that the amnesty of millionaire fines was constitutional. The ten largest deforesters had cleared 98,000 ha and were expected to pay R$166 million in fines. Among the deforesters, 48 farmers also face lawsuits for environmental crimes and ten have been prosecuted for keeping labor analogous to slavery.

After Jair Bolsonaro taking office, in January 2019, the expansion of deforestation has also been legitimized by the president and his cabinet, including the environment minister. Initially, the new government challenged official data concerning this and other environmental issues, such as climate change. Soon the government proceeded with directly disrupting the environmental monitoring and control bodies, such as the National Institute for Space Research (INPE), whose president was fired for defending the veracity of the data produced by the agency. Finally, when international organizations ratified the data, providing irrefutable evidence of the progress of deforestation, the government then accused NGOs of promoting such practices in a kind of international plot to politically destabilize it.

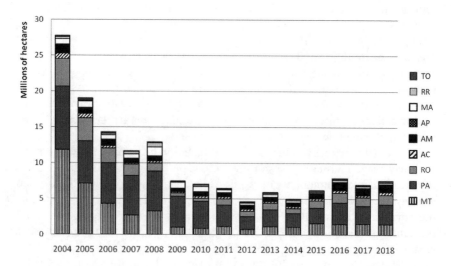

Figure 3.4 New deforested areas by state in the Legal Amazon (2004–2018).

Following the massive fires in the Amazon rainforest in August 2019, the reaction of the international community to the Brazilian government discourse became so strong that it pushed other governments and international companies to break political and trade relations with Brazil. Boycott threats to Brazilian products have worried agribusiness segments that are trying to identify themselves as highly productive and technology-based businesses. A former agriculture minister and owner of Amaggi, the largest trading company with a Brazilian majority stock, Blairo Maggi has been one among many agribusiness representatives who, formerly a supporter of this government, now say that after years striving to create an image of "environmental preservation with production," the new government's speech led the country back to square one in the environmental agenda, thus affecting badly the image of Brazilian agribusiness (Valor Econômico, August 15, 2019). Although such said efforts have always been challenged, since Blairo Maggi himself has already won the Greenpeace "Golden Chainsaw" award, the fact is that now these actors find increasingly difficult to disentangle their image from environmental degradation.

Conflicts over land and territory

The practices discussed so far in this chapter have in common a specific connection to land. As a strategy of accumulation, extractivism is associated with the spoliation of relatively cheap land, what enables earning extraordinary incomes without significant investments in technology and innovation. Data presented by Reydon and Plata (2000) indicate that, in 1997, the price of land in the northern region of Brazil was equivalent to 16% of its average price in the southern states. Since then, on the one hand, this practice has been somewhat limited due to rise in prices driven by both the expansion of the agricultural frontiers and the global land rush (Borras, Jr. et al., 2011; Oliveira, 2016). On the other hand, however, it was fomented by the rise in commodity prices (Chapter 2); the appreciation of land as a financial asset (Chapter 7); and, especially, by access to and control of land through grabbing, an extremely profitable form of primitive accumulation, which is discussed in this section.

Land grabbing can be characterized in many ways. In Brazilian history, one of the best-known forms is called *grilagem* (Motta, 2011). The cases that occurred in the state of Bahia, thoroughly documented by the Association of Lawyers of Rural Workers (AATR, 2017), illustrate the intricate set of institutional arrangements around this practice. As the document points out, *grilagem* is generally carried out by means of forgery of property deeds, for the purpose of faking property rights. Most often, this involves alteration in the original source of the title or in the size of the property. In the first case, land without previous title is registered for the first time. This type of practice was identified in most cases analyzed by AATR, involving judgments in legal actions over inheritance and acquisitive prescription. In the second case, *grilagem* occurs through the "expansion of the original dimensions of the property, without merging with another property into a duly deed of conveyance" (AATR, 2017, 60).

In Brazil, the most widely used institutional mechanisms for expanding the area of a property are the extrajudicial rectification of boundaries (register made by the notary public), the judicial rectification (ordered by a Court following a legal proceeding) and the rough falsification of the property deeds. Although rectification of boundaries is provided for by law, it cannot be used to increase the extent of the property without grounds based on evidence. Nevertheless, as AATR demonstrates, this practice has been employed to illegally advance over public lands or over land occupied by traditional communities. Finally, other documented practices involve the appropriation and register of public lands by individuals; and settlements following discriminative proceedings involving public vacant lands. In this case, the study shows that the state of Bahia, "after confirming the occurrence of land grabbing in the course of the Administrative Discriminative Proceeding, has given up vacant land traditionally occupied by grassland communities in favor of companies that did not comply with legal requirements for land regularization" (AATR, 2017, 61).

The main actors involved in these practices are farmers, agricultural companies, power generation companies and financial market investors, but also real estate registrars, judges, prosecutors, state solicitors and public officials responsible for managing land tenure (AATR, 2017). At the opposite side, people affected by such practices are mainly the indigenous and traditional communities that, even occupying these lands for generations, never had the ownership properly regulated by the state. What is at stake in this conflict is the control of "land," a valuable object for both sides, though with different meanings. While the formers conceive it as a commodity subject to private expropriation, for the second ones, land is a common good that defines a way of life (Wagner, 2004). The implications of this semantic distinction on the same "object" reveal that the agrarian question assumes dimensions that are beyond the dispute for a "factor of production."

This situation is not specific to a single state. The problem reaches the whole country to varying degrees, including (and especially) those lands where the new generation of "modern" Brazilian agribusiness is putting down roots. This is the case of MATOPIBA, a territory under heavy pressure from the expansion of the agricultural frontier supported by the Brazilian State that, in 2015, through Decree No. 8447, created the MATOPIBA Agricultural Development Plan. The Plan covers an area of 73 million hectares in the states of Maranhão, Tocantins, Piauí and Bahia, where numerous traditional communities are being displaced to make way for soy, eucalyptus and livestock. This created such a critical situation that, in 2017, FIAN Brazil (an organization that advocates for the human right to food and nutrition), with the support of the Federal Public Prosecution Service (MPF), organized the "Matopiba International Caravan" for inquiry into land grabbing.

This type of practice is also common in the Amazon, where "vacant" lands amount to 114 million hectares, equivalent to 13.5% of Brazilian lands. The state of Pará stands out in the region, for counting 495 million irregularly registered hectares, an area four times larger than the own area of the state (Treccani, 2017). Also noteworthy is the fact that 25 municipalities within this state have a sum of registered lands that exceeds their own territory. São Félix do Xingu is illustrative in this regard – having twice the territorial area of the state of Rio de Janeiro, it ranked first in the 2016 deforestation list. In June 2006, Pará State Court of Justice issued the Provision No. 013/2006-CJCI, which ordered the halt on rural properties registers. Although provisional, this administrative measure unveiled the extensive character of the land problem in the region. A year later, in 2007, the State Legislative Assembly set up a Parliamentary Commission of Inquiry, which was tasked with overseeing cases related to illegal occupation. In São Félix do Xingu, it was found that irregularly registered area was 2.6 times the total area of the municipality.

In 2009, aiming to mitigate the agrarian chaos created in the Amazon, the now extinct Ministry of Agrarian Development (MDA) launched the *Programa Terra Legal* (Legal Land Programme), which provides for duly register and allocation of land and real estate located in federal public lands. Until 2017, the program served farmers who occupied, since before December 2004, a maximum of 1,500 ha. However, in 2017, the Law no. 13465 promulgated by President Temer – and supplemented in 2018 by Decrees no. 9309, 9310 and 9311 – provided for the regularization of areas of up to 2,500 hectares, occupied since before July 2008, or even after, if the occupancy period of five years or more is proven, by means of "direct, cultivated and peaceful exploitation." According to Gerson Teixeira, former president of the Brazilian Association of Agrarian Reform (ABRA), these institutional arrangements suggest that "the government has set its political purpose by implementing a land policy capable of depleting the stock of public lands by privatizing them not only in the Legal Amazon, but all over Brazil" (Teixeira, 2018, 1).

For Sauer (2018), besides "formalizing a market for public lands by creating and relaxing rules, another purpose is to exempt the State from implementing programmatic rural policies, but especially to remove its capacity to do so" (Sauer, 2018, 3). According to the author, by allowing direct alienation (sale or transference) of public lands without a bidding, the new legal framework certainly makes room for regularization of very recent illegal appropriations, even allowing the purchase of neighboring areas so that to legalize land grabbing, and favoring land concentration. Moreover, by setting the reference values of land far below the market value (less than half) as well as facilitating various forms for payment, the government encourages real estate speculation and illegal occupation of public lands, turning "land grabbing into an even more profitable business" (ibid., 7).

These measures have been challenged not only by social movements and academics, but also by the Federal Prosecution Service, which considers that the new legislation transfers land to individuals "under very advantageous

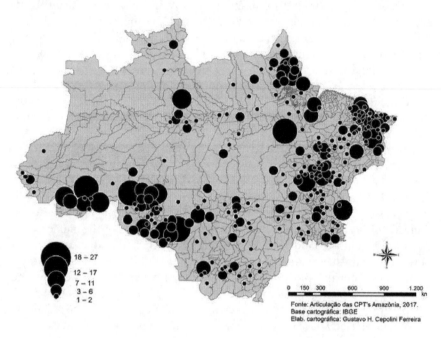

18 – 27
12 – 17
7 – 11
3 – 6
1 – 2

0   150   300   600   900   1.200
                                                 km

Fonte: Articulação das CPT's Amazônia, 2017.
Base cartográfica: IBGE
Elab. cartográfica: Gustavo H. Cepolini Ferreira

Figure 3.5 Conflicts in rural areas in the Amazon region (2000–2017).

economic conditions"; authorizes "the private appropriation of most valuable public assets"; establishes "unjustifiable privileges in favor of land grabbers who, in the past, have illegally appropriated vast tracts of public land"; and that "these land grabs have often involved extensive use of violence, use of slave labor and widespread environmental degradation." Furthermore, "the norm under consideration induces, when it should inhibit, real estate speculation in the Amazon region"; "will lead to the increase of agrarian conflicts (with consequent increase in associated deaths), deforestation (affecting the goals set in the Paris Agreement) and the expansion of situations of total disrespect for the law" (Brazil, Ministério Público Federal, 2017).

Such concerns of the Federal Prosecution Service are justified, since the Amazon concentrated 44% of conflicts over land tenure in Brazil between 2000 and 2015 (Figure 3.5; CPT 2018b). This is even more worrying, insofar as this percentage raised to 50% between 2008 and 2015, and in 2016 alone, 57% of conflicts over land and 54% of the families involved in them were in this region. In Pará – the "land of contract killings"– the signs of violence perpetrated on grounds of dispute over land are historical. The most well-known cases are the slaughter at the Ubá farm in São Geraldo do Araguaia (1985), the massacre at Eldorado do Carajás (1996), the assassinations of Expedito Ribeiro and João Canuto de Oliveira, former presidents of the Rural Workers Union of Rio Maria (1985) and the murder of Sister Dorothy

Stang in Anapu (2005). One of the most recent cases, which took place in May 2017, was the massacre at Pau D'Arco, in the same region where, 20 years before, had been perpetrated the massacre at Eldorado dos Carajás. As is well known, most of these cases are characterized by impunity and slowness in agrarian structuring of the land, which turns the state into complicit in these crimes (Feitosa, 2017).

The perpetuation of land conflicts in rural Brazil is just one – the most devastating – outcome of the collapse of land governance system in the country. According to Reydon et al. (2017), the causes of this situation are historical and diverse: (a) detailed and confusing legislation; (b) lack of a governing body; (c) existence of different registration systems, each with different parameters;[2] (d) excessive concentration of land ownership; (e) incentive to speculation due to price increases that are not accompanied by tax increases (ITR); (f) insecure system of register and lack of integrated control of notaries public information; (g) lack of legal guarantees for most lease and partnership practices, among others. There is hardly any prospect of improvement in this situation, which tends rather to aggravate in view of the "retrogressive stance of the current government, which is handing lots of reserve land over to private individuals and adopting the worst possible measures" (Reydon, 2017, 1).

The irregularity rate of title deeds is alarming – for nearly 20% of Brazilian territory, there are no formal records in any of the official land titling instruments (Sauer and Leite, 2012). Over the past decade, some efforts have attempted to mitigate the effects of this institutional collapse. In addition to the already mentioned *Programa Terra Legal*, also noteworthy is the program for land registration and agrarian regularization implemented in partnership between the federal government and agrarian agencies of state and municipal administrations. These efforts were in line with the approval of the Voluntary Guidelines on Responsible Governance of Tenure of Land, Fisheries and Forests. These guidelines were approved at the 38th Extraordinary Session of the Committee on World Food Security (CFS) in 2012 and have since been the leading international policy on land issues. Besides, it is important to underline that these guidelines were formulated following intense debate among all UN member countries, among which, curiously, Brazil played a prominent role in its negotiation and approval (França, Marques, and Del Grossi, 2016)

However, since the 2016 crisis precipitated by the institutional rupture in the country, the situation has changed rapidly. Instead of responsible governance, the rise of a conservative political coalition has led to an irresponsible attempt to expand land availability for all kinds of usurpation (Niederle et al., 2019). Two examples are particularly relevant in this regard. First, the authorization granted by the already mentioned Law No. 13.465 of 2017, to grant land title to rural settlers as of the tenth year of settlement, a criterion met by 80% of the 1.3 million families settled until 2016. Titling is an old demand of most settlers and, at first glance, is a measure that improves land governance. However, the enactment of this law is, first and foremost, an attempt by the government to increase land availability to the market. Insofar as the sale of lands is conditioned to title deeds, the regulation of these lands makes available to buyers a huge amount of land previously "blocked." In addition, as Sauer and Leite (2017, 32) point out, such measures "also point to exhaustion of the agrarian reform in Brazil, for privileging allocations of public lands that weaken both the creation of settlements projects, and regularization of lands occupied by traditional communities."

The second example refers to changes in the rules regarding demarcation of indigenous and *quilombola* lands. A bill that has been under consideration in the National Congress since 2000 (PEC No. 215/2000) proposes that demarcation should be exclusive attribution of the Congress (removing the decision from the executive power), which would make it hostage to the negotiation of interests in a space where the ruralist legislators – over 200 federal deputies out of the total 513 – is the largest organized group in the House. Adding to this, the Opinion issued by the Office of the Attorney-General (Parecer no. 119/07/2017), which states that an indigenous land can only be recognized and demarcated if it was occupied by its original people in 1988, when the current Federal Constitution was enacted, was a step backwards. Something similar was also defended by the ruralist legislators regarding the recognition of *quilombola* lands. However, in February 2018, the Supreme Court decided in favor of the *quilombolas*. Despite this, since 2019, the federal government took a hostile stance towards indigenous and *quilombola* communities, repeatedly declaring that no new areas will be allocated to them. Thus, if previously the problem resided in the transference of this attribution to a congress controlled by conservative agrarian elites, now the main difficulty lies in that they control this process directly from within the executive power.

Precarious work and contemporary slavery

Among the precarious work practices most discussed currently are the different forms of debt bondage, which combine both the indirect control mechanisms exercised by lenders and the employers' direct control over their employees. In this regard, data published by the International Labour Organization (ILO) based on the National Household Sample Survey (IBGE, 2015), indicate that in Brazil 1.5 million people were prevented from leaving their jobs due to some type of debt with their employers. That is, among the 52 million workers in the private sector or in domestic services, 2.9% were prevented from leaving work due to some kind of financial debt contracted with the employer. Most of these debts are associated with food (948,000 workers), transportation (774,000), working instruments (373,000) and rent (266,000) (ILO, 2017)

These data transcend the universe of workers considered to be under "contemporary slave labor," a condition that, after more than 200 years of the enactment of the law that ended slavery in Brazil, returned to the Brazilian public agenda. In 1995, under pressure from organizations such as the Pastoral Land Commission, and the ILO, the government acknowledged the existence of this violation of human rights and created the Special Itinerant Inspection Group within the Ministry of Labour, responsible for overseeing the properties and releasing enslaved workers. Since then, a series of facts and events has marked the struggle for the institutional recognition of this practice, what entails a dispute over meanings that affects the delimitation of precise criteria to characterize it and, thereafter, to guarantee the supervision and punishment of perpetrators.

The main advances occurred as of 2003, the first year of the Lula Government, when the First National Plan for the Eradication of Slave Labour was approved; the National Commission for the Eradication of Slave Labour (Conatrae) was created, subordinate to the Secretariat of Human Rights of the Presidency of the Republic; the Article 149 of the Penal Code was reformulated, to establish penalties and define what a condition analogous to that of slave is (Law No. 10803); and the "dirty list" of slave labor was established – a public register of employers found guilty of enslaving workers. Two other important institutional advances occurred in 2008, with the creation of the II Plan, and in 2014, following the approval of Constitutional Amendment no. 81, which provides for the expropriation without compensation of rural and urban properties caught in slave labor; these properties, then, should be destined to land reform and housing programs (Repórter Brasil, 2017).

Brazilian Penal Code defines slave labor as the crime that put

> somebody to a condition analogous to that of slave, either by subjecting the person to forced labor or exhausting workday, or by subjecting him/her to degrading working conditions, or by restricting, by any means, the person's locomotion due to debt contracted with his/her employer or agent.
>
> (Law n. 10,903/2003)

Four basic criteria define this type of practice: (a) *forced labor*, when the person is subjected to exploitation and is unable to leave the place because of threat or physical and psychological violence; (b) *exhausting workday*, characterized by excessive workloads that endangers the worker's health integrity; (c) *debt bondage*, which traps the worker in an abusive system of exchanges, in which his/her salary is discounted to pay illegal debts; (d) *degrading conditions*, which define the precariousness of working and living conditions due to poor housing, lack of medical care, ill-treatment or insufficient and inadequate nutrition.

According to data from the Ministry of Labour and Employment, between 1995 and 2016, 52,000 workers found under conditions analogous to slavery were released. Most of them were men, migrants, aged between 18 and 44 years (83%) and had low education (32% was illiterate and 39% reached the fourth grade of elementary school). In recent years, however, the number of rescued workers has been declining. On the one hand, this may be due to an effective reduction of this practice, in view of public repercussion of the issue, which made companies afraid of seeing their brands associated with slave labor. For instance, Carneiro (2013) shows that, during the period of appreciation of pig iron in the international market, steel companies changed their operating patterns, formalizing working relations in the production of coal (raw material in iron processing) and, especially, creating their own sources of coal supply from reforestation. These changes were institutionalized in the "Letter of Commitment to the end of slave labor in charcoal production and to the promotion of decent, formalized and modern labor in the steel production chain." However, the recent crisis in the sector, which has led to the closure of several industrial plants, associated with the institutional changes underway in the country, raises doubts as to the continuity of this process (Carneiro, 2013).

On the other hand, nongovernmental organizations have denounced that such reduction reflects a decrease in inspection operations, due to federal government budget cuts that reduced resources allocated to these actions (Repórter Brasil, 2017). According to data from the Labour Prosecutor's Office, while in 2016 there were 106 control operations carried out and 658 workers were rescued, in 2017 these figures fell to 88 and 341, respectively. Moreover, besides a reduction in the number of auditors, also worrying has been the security conditions for the exercise of their duties. A much publicized event in this regard was the "slaughter at Unaí," occurred in 2004, when three auditors of the Ministry of Labour, who were investigating allegations of slave labor in that region, were killed in an ambush commissioned by a group of farmers and grain dealers, among which was Norberto Mânica, former mayor of Unaí, considered the "King of Beans," and who, despite convicted, remained free by the end of 2018.

A detailed overview of this practice was published in 2009 by the NGO Friends of the Earth. It highlights migrant movements that feeds slave-like labor, and which is carried out by agents who take advantage of social vulnerability of workers in their regions of origin (including violence and insecurity regarding land ownership) to attract them to other regions where they will be subject to all kinds of illegal controls. The largest flows across Brazilian states has been from Maranhão towards Pará, Tocantins to Pará, Maranhão to Tocantins and finally from Paraná, Distrito Federal, Bahia, Alagoas and Maranhão to Mato Grosso (Théry et al., 2009). The main places of recruiting coincide with areas where poverty and killings show high rates, while the release of enslaved workers occurs in areas where, besides these factors, activities such as deforestation, illegal logging and coal and extensive livestock farming predominate.

As Girardi et al. (2014) note, "contemporary slave labor is part of a broader scenario of the Brazilian agrarian question, rooted in the way land and political and economic power have been concentrated." It comes as no surprise, then, that most workers rescued between 1995 and 2016 were employed in activities involving livestock (29%), sugarcane production (24%), coal extraction

(8%) and deforestation (5%). Yet, a "novelty" revealed by recent data is the increase in cases in nonagricultural sectors and in the urban context. In recent years, several reports documented the growth of this phenomenon in cities, revealing its association with the agency of immigrants from other countries, especially Bolivians and Haitians, employed in the construction industry (5% of cases registered by MTE) and clothing (1%).

Although predominant in the most remote rural areas and in traditional agricultural activities, the association between the agrifood sector and contemporary slave labor is wide-ranging. The presence, for example, of meat processors in the "dirty list" evidences that the problem permeates "modern" agribusiness. These cases have been recurrent in the media. In 2012, the Labour Prosecutor's Office (MPT) found 71 irregular Paraguayan immigrants in the Nostra meat processing plant, owned by VL Agro-Industrial Ltda., in the municipality of Cambira, state of Paraná. In 2013, FrigoNorte meat processing plant, installed in Cruzeiro do Sul, Acre, was fined for the practice of slave labor. In 2017, three truck drivers that worked for Minerva Foods reported conditions analogous to slave labor in Várzea Grande, Mato Grosso. The latter case was still under investigation during our research.

In recent years, meat processing plants have become a major focus of attention. The seriousness of allegations of offenses in this sector has been on a level with those found in agricultural activities historically associated with the exploitation of rural workers, such as sugarcane, which is object of important studies (Silva, Bueno, and Melo, 2014). In 2012, the NGO Repórter Brasil investigated the conditions under which employees of the then three largest Brazilian meat processors were subjected: Brasil Foods (BRF), JBS and Marfrig. These three companies are among the top 20 exporting groups in Brazil, the world's largest exporter of beef and poultry. As documented by Repórter Brasil, at the processing plant of BRF in Rio Verde (GO), 90,000 requests for sick leaves were registered between January 2009 and September 2011. "It is as if every 10 months all eight thousand employees of the plant had to be absent for at least one time due to work-related health problems" (Repórter Brasil, 2012).

The prominence acquired by the issue has upset a lot of people, generating reactions and institutional disputes. At the end of 2014, following a claim from the Brazilian Association of Real Estate Developers, the Supreme Federal Court suspended the publication of the national register of employers implicated in this crime (the "dirty list" of slave labor). However, in December 2016, following the publication of a new Interministerial Ordinance (*Portaria Interministerial n. 4, 11/05/2016*), the Labour Court, by means of a preliminary ruling, ordered the publication of the list. The government appealed and obtained from the president of the Superior Labour Court a preliminary injunction suspending its obligation to disclose the list, because of the need to adjust the criteria for inclusion and exclusion of names. Also, in December 2016, the Ministry of Labour and Employment (MTE) created a working group to discuss these criteria. At last, the list, in which employers from the agro-industrial sector prevailed, was made public only thanks to the action of NGOs, which released it in the absence of publication by the MTE.

Another institutional battle involves the very definition of contemporary slave labor. Under pressure from agribusiness lobby, in 2015, the Committee on Agriculture, Livestock, Supply and Rural Development of the Chamber of Deputies issued opinion in favor of the Bill no. 3842/2012, which changes the article that defines slave labor in the Penal Code, by excluding the terms "exhaustive workday" and "degrading working conditions." According to the presented rationale, these terms lack legal support, thus "breaching the established constitutional-penal order." In October 2017, MTE Ordinance 1129 annulled the definition of "degrading condition" as a criterion for defining slave labor. According to a note released by the Ministry, the purpose of the Ordinance is "to improve and confer legal security to Brazilian State's action." Such legal provisions attracted strong opposition from religious organizations, the labor prosecution service, social movements and even ILO. As a result, a few days after its publication, it was suspended by the Supreme Court, which, in a preliminary ruling, considered that it violates constitutional principles. However, the institutional instability caused by several preliminary (reviewable) rulings keeps the issue latent.

Exhaust, drain and destroy

There are different ways to measure the level of depletion of natural resources that are needed to support current consumption patterns. One of the most recurrent in contemporary literature is the so-called "ecological footprint" and, in connection with this concept, the "water footprint." This measure compares products, based on the average volume of freshwater used for their production, including that for the required raw materials. Thus, according to Mekonnen and Hoekstra (2012), while an apple "costs" 125 liters of water, the production of just 1 kg of meat requires 15,400 liters. These data draw attention to the fact that much international trade in commodities is only advantageous insofar as we do not effectively appraise the spoliation of natural resources. In other words, from the monetary point of view, a positive trade balance hides a huge deficit in terms of transfer of natural resources that, if valued, would not justify the export of low value-added products. According to Mekonnen et al. (2015), between 1996 and 2005, five products accounted for three-quarters of all "virtual water" exported by Latin America: soy (36%), coffee (14%), cotton (10%), meat (10%) and sugarcane (8%).

Livestock has been one of the activities most criticized by consumer movements, not only because of the incredible volume of water needed to produce 1 kg of meat, but also for the way it occurs. Yet, to understand the specific relationship between cattle ranching and trade, it is important to note that this sector is formed by different production practices, that is, different livestock models. These models cover, for example, intensive animal farming with use of technology, labor and inputs (industrial order), rational cattle breeding (civic order), farm animal breeding aimed at competitions (aesthetic order) and extensive livestock farming with low technology, low productivity of both labor and capital and practices that deplete natural resources. This latter model is precisely the one that defines the relationship between livestock farming and the commercial order.

The growth of this model of cattle ranching responds to the increase in world consumption of beef. According to data from the US Department of Agriculture (USDA), in 2000, 52.9 million tons of beef were consumed worldwide. In 2017, consumption in absolute values was expected to be record, reaching 59.4 million tons, and representing 7.9 kg per person per year. Currently, the main world consumers are the United States, the European Union, China, Brazil and India. United States alone is responsible for 20% of world demand (11.6 million tons). However, in terms of per capita consumption, the ranking is led by Uruguay, followed by Argentina and Hong Kong, all them with a per capita consumption of beef over 50 kg per inhabitant per year. The United States comes next (36 kg) and Brazil is the fifth (35.8 kg).

China ranks 47th in per capita beef consumption, with an average of 4.07 kg per capita per year. However, the country has shown, between 2000 and 2017, a cumulative rise of 39.3% in per capita consumption, or about 2.0% per year on average. Thus, it becomes obvious why the attention of exporters increasingly turns to the eastern giant (OECD, 2017). USDA (2018) estimates that Chinese beef imports are expected to grow by 73% by 2024, reaching 1.6 million tons. At this rate, it is expected that by 2024 the Chinese will have already surpassed the Americans, taking the world lead in foreign beef purchases. It is this kind of prediction that encourages countries like India and Brazil to expand their herds. Currently, both share the first position among the world's largest exporters of beef and buffalo (22%), being followed by Australia (16%), the United States (13%) and New Zealand (7%). Together these five countries account for almost three-quarters of world exports.

In the early 2000s, increasing pressure from buyers for quality certifications suggested that the more despoiling cattle ranching models would lose ground in international markets to more technology-intensive and sustainable models.[3] New standards were imposed mainly by European and North American buyers, who were forced to respond to criticism from consumer movements. Meanwhile, other buyers have remained much more flexible and compliant with ecologically and socially questionable practices (deforestation, slave labor, animal abuse etc.). This made room for the export of products from this predatory commercial livestock farming model and, albeit it is not possible to quantify the size of this market, its growth can be illustrated by taking as an example the export of live cattle, a product with no value added that is only profitable forbearing low production costs, what in turn entails overexploitation of natural resources.

In 2003, Brazil exported 2,000 live oxen. In 2013, when the country competed with Australia, the world's largest exporter of live cattle (631,000 heads in 2016), these exports reached 688,000. From then on, Brazilian exports fell due to the reduction in demand from Venezuela, until then the main buyer, which started to experience a strong economic crisis. In 2017, 407,000 heads were exported, most of which produced in the state of Pará (about 60%), followed by Rio Grande do Sul and São Paulo. The main buyers were Turkey (55%), Egypt (14%), Lebanon (10%) and Jordan (10%) and sales were intermediated by companies such as Minerva Live Cattle Exports, a subsidiary of Minerva Foods, which in 2016 was already the second largest meat processing company in the country (R$6.3 billion in net sales). Created in 2003 and owned by the Vilela Queiroz family, Minerva Live Cattle Exports has become one of the largest live cattle exporters in the world.

A vivid example of a rent-seeking model of accumulation, the practice developed by this company has been widely criticized by environmental organizations. In 2018, the National Forum for Animal Protection and Defence, which gathers 136 Brazilian NGOs, won a preliminary injunction preventing the departure of a livestock carrier docked in the port of Santos with more than 25,000 heads (exactly! in a single ship!). The cattle had been sold by Minerva to a Turkish company. Due to the allegations, the court requested an expert report from a veterinarian, who identified "abundant evidence of abuse and explicit violation of animal dignity." However, under pressure from the company and worried about the risk posed by this embargo to Brazilian foreign trade, the Minister of Agriculture interfered: "We can guarantee that there is no mistreatment. It is a kind of out-of-control activism" said Blairo Maggi, then minister of agriculture (Folha de São Paulo, April 2, 2018). According to him, "other companies may stop buying from Brazil because of this; it is an intangible commercial loss" (*ibid.*). Finally, the Federal Regional Court accepted the request of the government and authorized the export. It is worth noting that Minerva's transportation of live cattle had already been featured in the press in 2015, when a ship with five thousand oxen sank in Pará and many animals drowned.

The present makes future look like the past

The commercial order is defined by a certain arrangement of practices and institutions whose reinvention has made the future of the agrifood system looks like its past (Figure 3.6). Throughout this chapter, a close connection became crystal-clear linking intensive depletion of mineral resources, Brazilian integration within international commodity markets, deforestation, violence, land grabbing, displacement of traditional communities and the maintenance of precarious forms of labor, including contemporary slavery. As noted by Delgado (2012) in the case of agricultural expansion, there is an intrinsic relationship between the appropriation of land rent (based on different mechanisms of control over the land) and the overexploitation of natural resources and of human work, what is true also regarding mineral

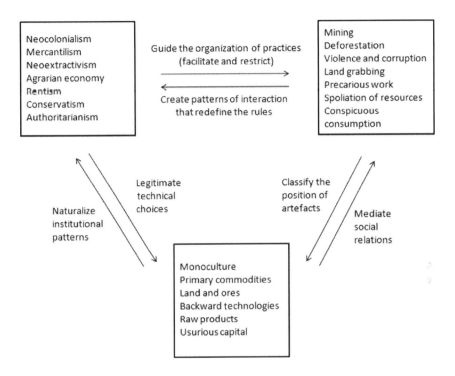

Figure 3.6 Components of the commercial order.

exploitation. This is the classic example of private (economic) returns from collective (social and environmental) costs.

Moreover, we demonstrate that these practices are not only connected with each other, but also with an institutional structure that legitimates them. This structure involves: (i) regulatory frameworks such as laws regarding land tenure registration and criteria for indigenous land demarcation; (ii) public policy instruments such as land regularization programs; (iii) undemocratic values that authorize conservative, authoritarian and violent practices; and (iv) a set of cultural-cognitive conceptions expressed, for example, in the ideas of an "agroexport vocation."

The ubiquity of such practices corroborates the perpetuation of forms of "primitive accumulation" that take place, as Rosa Luxemburg (1988, 86) pointed out, between "capital and noncapitalist forms of production"; "its predominant methods are colonial policy, an international loan system – a policy of spheres of interest – and war. Force, fraud, oppression, looting are openly displayed without any attempt at concealment" (*Ibid.*). The recognition that this kind of accumulation is not just an original and primitive stage of capitalism, nor something external to it, is fundamental to understand how it operates in different social formations. As Perelman (2000) points out, the "new enclosures" of the fields (or, more broadly, of the "territories") constitute a continuous historical process, which, like everything in history, takes on new configurations over time.

This perspective is shared by Harvey (2004), who adopts the concept of "accumulation by dispossession" to demarcate his disagreement with the idea that this process would be only primitive or original. The practices identified by Harvey for defining this logic of "vulture capitalism" are very similar to those presented in this chapter. The differences lie in the financial dynamics. Harvey emphasizes, more than we did in this chapter, the mechanisms of spoliation that are catalyzed by financialization (a practice that is key for his argument is the systemic devaluation of capital whereby capitalists try to circumvent crises of overaccumulation). We agree that the land grabbing practices discussed here are closely linked to the financialization of agriculture. The same is true of contemporary forms of slave labor, given that, for example, the same meat processing plants that employ these practices can be controlled by global investment funds. Slave labor in the farthest municipality of Pará may in some way be connected to a modern agro-industrial processing plant located in São Paulo, which, in turn, reacts to the fluctuations of the Beijing stock exchange.

Such connections, however, can be extended to virtually every sector of the economy, from the US automotive industry that employs Mexican workers, to European electronic circuit board manufacturers in China, or even to Spanish clothing factories using Bolivian workers in São Paulo. This demonstrates, on the one hand, that the logic of accumulation by dispossession is not specific to agriculture and, on the other hand, that, among different varieties of capitalism, it is possible to recognize many "commonalities" (Streeck, 2012). So, if everything is so interconnected, why treat these practices specifically in this chapter? We have already discussed this issue. The choice stems from the need for an analytical model able to reveal the heterogeneity of contemporary (agrarian) capitalism. In the end, of course, we are still talking about capitalism and not about any other kind of sociohistorical formation – although, within it, older practices and institutions are reproduced.

The problem is that a unitary view of this sociohistorical formation tends easily towards sweeping generalizations, what would lead to infer that deforestation, land grabbing or the assassination of the president of rural workers' union are first and foremost caused by the financialization of agriculture, a process far more complex and erratic than generally assumed (cf. Chapter 7). Furthermore, it is worth remembering that our focus is on "practices and their actors." The fact that international banks finance companies that use slave labor only suggests that those actors can move across different social orders, resorting to different practices. The meat processing plant based on slave labor can also be the one that holds cutting-edge informational technology for financial management. Contradictions are so many in such movement of actors across different orders that, for example, the Norwegian government, which in 2017 announced a cut in donations to the Amazon Fund because of increased deforestation, is the majority shareholder of Hydro, a mining company accused by the Public Prosecution Service of contaminating rivers and communities in Barcarena (PA), a municipality located in one of the most polluted regions of the Amazon rainforest. Interestingly, according to information from the Institute of Socioeconomic Studies (INESC), the company has enjoyed tax exemptions in Brazil that amount to R$7 billion.

The contradictions involved in the actors' movement can introduce instability, favor criticism and lead to changes in both institutions and practices. While nobody is astounded by the presence of land grabbers or miners in the commercial order pictured here, chance of reaction is much greater when the Norwegian government is involved in serious environmental disasters or when clothing manufacturers that supply internationally famous brands like Zara are convicted of using slave labor. When this happens, not only do these actors put themselves in disadvantageous political and economic positions, but also the relevant order is put to the test by criticisms. Even so, significant changes in practices will depend on the potential of such criticisms for transformation in view of the window of opportunity opened by the institutional delegitimization of the social order, what will entail political struggles between different actors.

In the situations analyzed here, the main criticisms against the commercial order come from social movements, environmental organizations and religious entities, which denounce the despoilment of nature as typical of this order. On the other hand, agribusiness representatives do everything to ensure the "order of things," preventing a window of opportunity to open for these criticisms. In fact, more recently, it was these actors that seized the opportunity offered by a strengthened conservative political coalition in the country, by proposing institutional changes that reinforce the mercantile-extractive model of appropriation of natural resources, consolidate a path to subordinate integration of the country into international markets, and emphasize the regressive specialization of Brazilian exports. However, among farmers and agro-industrial companies, there are also critics of these practices, just as some governments, social and religious organizations are quite permissive about them.

Notes

1 Marx had already warned of the error of understanding history as subsequent steps:

> The so-called historical presentation of development is founded, as a rule, on the fact that the latest form regards the previous ones as steps leading up to itself, and, since it is only rarely and only under quite specific conditions able to criticize itself – leaving aside, of course, the historical periods which appear to themselves as times of decadence – it always conceives them one-sidedly.
> (Marx, 1973, 106)

2 In the case of the state of Pará, for example, while INCRA's records (2012) accounted for 99,400 properties, with a total area of 33 million ha, data from the

Rural Environmental Registry (CAR, 2017) accounted for 163,500 properties and a total area of 58.2 million hectares. In turn, data from CRI (2017) counted 11,000 properties and 97.1 million hectares (Treccani, 2017).

3 Due to the high costs of confinement, as a result of rising commodity prices, the expansion of these systems has been slower than expected by the sector. In 2017, the National Association of Intensive Livestock Farming (ASSOCON) projected a 25% growth in the number of confined cattle in Brazil. The effective growth, however, was only 5.5%. Strictly speaking, the 5.02 million head confined that year did not even reach the same level of 2015 (5.19 million). Even so, the number is higher than in 2010, when the confined herd was 3.05 million.

References

AATR. 2017. *No rastro da grilagem.* Salvador: AATR.

Acosta, A. 2016a. "Extrativismo e neoextrativismo." In *Descolonizar o imaginário*, edited by G. Dilger, M. Lang and J. Pereira Filho. São Paulo: Rosa Luxemburgo Foundation.

Acosta, A. 2016b. *O bem viver.* São Paulo: Elefante

Boltanski, L. and Chiapello, È. 2005. *The New Spirit of Capitalism.* London: Verso.

Bonanno, A. *The Legitimation Crisis of Neoliberalism.* New York: Palgrave-Macmillan, 2017.

Bonanno, A. and Wolf, S. (eds). 2017. *Resistance to Neoliberal Food Regime.* New York: Routledge.

Borras, Jr., S., Franco, J., Isakson, S., Levidow, L. and Vervest, P. 2016. "The rise of flex crops and commodities: implications for research." *Journal of Peasant Studies*, 43(1): 93–115.

Borras, Jr., S., Hall, R., Scoones, I., White, B. and Wolford, W. 2011. "Towards a better understanding of global land grabbing: an editorial introduction." *Journal of Peasant Studies*, 32(2): 209–16.

Brazil. 2011. *Plano Nacional de Mineração 2030.* Brasília: MME.

Carneiro, M. S. 2013. *Terra, trabalho e poder: conflitos e lutas sociais no Maranhão contemporâneo.* São Paulo: Annablume.

Carneiro, M. S. and Assis, W. S. 2015. "O controle do desmatamento na Amazônia como um processo de modernização ecológica: a experiência do Projeto Município Verde." *Pós-Ciências Sociais*, 12(24): 53–76.

CPT. 2018a. *Atlas de Conflitos na Amazônia.* São Paulo: CPT.

CPT. 2018b. *Conflitos no Campo 2017.* São Paulo: CPT.

Dardot, P. and Laval, C. 2009. *La nouvelle raison du monde: essai sur la société néolibérale.* Paris: La Découverte.

Delgado, G. C. 2012. *Do capital financeiro na agricultura à economia do agronegócio.* Porto Alegre: UFRGS.

El País. 2018. *No Brasil, o tesouro escondido não é uma praia ou uma selva, é uma savana.* Accessed May 22, 2018. www.brasil.elpais.com/brasil/2018/03/21/politica/1521648714_928895.html

Faoro, R. 1989. *Os donos do poder.* Rio de Janeiro: Globo.

Feitosa, T. 2017. *Direito e justiça na Amazônia.* São Paulo: Paco Editorial.

Fragoso, J. L. 1992. *Homens de grossa aventura.* Rio de Janeiro: Civilização Brasileira.

França, C., Marques, V. and Del Grossi, M. 2016. *Superação da Fome e da Pobreza Rural: iniciativas brasileiras. Brasília: FAO.*

Friedmann, H. and McMichael, P. 1989. "Agriculture and the State system: the rise and decline of national agricultures, 1870 to the Present." *Sociologia Ruralis*, 29(2): 93–117.

Frizo, P. 2018. *Os fundamentos institucionais para o gerenciamento dos bens comuns na Amazônia Central*. Master Dissertation. Porto Alegre: UFRGS.

Furtado, C. 1963. *The Economic Growth of Brazil: A Survey from Colonial to Modern Times*. Los Angeles: University of California Press.

Furtado, C. 1974. *O Mito do Desenvolvimento Econômico*. Rio de Janeiro: Paz e Terra.

Furtado, C. 1992. "O subdesenvolvimento revisitado." *Economia e Sociedade*, 1(1): 5–19.

Giraldo, O. 2018 *Ecología política de la agricultura: agroecología y posdesarrollo*. México: Ecosur.

Girardi, E., Mello, N., Hervé, T. and Hato, J. 2014. "Mapeamento do trabalho escravo contemporâneo no Brasil: dinâmicas recentes." *Espaço e Economia*, 2(4).

Gudynas, E. 2012. "Estado compensador y nuevos extractivismos: las ambivalencias del progresismo sudamericano." *Nueva Sociedad*, 237: 128–46.

Guimarães, A. P. 1963. *Quatro séculos de latifúndio*. Rio de Janeiro: Paz e Terra.

Harvey, D. 2004. "The 'new' imperialism: Accumulation by dispossession." *Socialist Register*, 40: 63–87.

Houaiss, A. 1963. Prefácio. In: *Quatro Séculos de Latifúndio*. A. Guimarães. Rio de Janeiro: Paz e Terra.

IBGE. 1924. *Agricultural Census*. Rio de Janeiro: IBGE.

IBGE. 2015. *Pesquisa Nacional por Amostra de Domícilo*. Rio de Janeiro: IBGE.

ILO. 2017. *Estatísticas do trabalho escravo*. Brasília: ILO.

Kastens, J., Brown, J., Coutinho, A., Bishop, C. and Esquerdo, J. 2017. "Soy moratorium impacts on soybean and deforestation dynamics in MatoGrosso, Brazil." *PlosOne*, 12(4): e0176168.

Lang, T. and Heasman, M. 2015. *Food Wars: The Global Battle for Mouths, Minds and Markets*. London: Routledge.

Levitsky, S. and Ziblatt, D. 2018. *How Democracies Die*. Cambridge: Harvard University Press.

Linhares, M. Y. and Silva, F. C. 1979. *História política do abastecimento*. Brasília: Binagri.

Luxemburg, R. 1988. *A acumulação do capital*. São Paulo: Nova Cultural.

Marcondes, R. L. 2012. "O mercado brasileiro do século XIX: uma visão por meio do comércio de cabotagem." *Revista de Economia Política*, 32(1): 142–66.

McMichael, P. 2016. "Commentary: Food regime for thought." *Journal of Peasant Studies*, 43(3): 648–70.

McMichael, P. 2019. "Does China's 'going out' strategy prefigure a new food regime?" *Journal of Peasant Studies*, 1–39.

MDIC. 2018. *Estatísticas do comércio exterior*. Brasília: MDIC.

Mekonnen, M. M. and Hoekstra, A. Y. 2012. "A global assessment of the water footprint of farm animal products." *Ecosystems*, 15(3): 401–15.

Mekonnen, M. M., Pahlow, M., Aldaya, M., Zarate, E. and Hoekstra, A. 2015. "Sustainability, efficiency and equitability of water consumption and pollution in Latin America and the Caribbean." *Sustainability*, 7(2): 2086–112.

Milanez, B. and Santos, R. 2013 "Neodesenvolvimentismo e neoextrativismo: duas faces da mesma moeda?" In *Proceedings of the Annual Meeting of Anppocs*. Caxambu, MG: Anpocs.

Motta, M. 2011. "A grilagem como legado." In *Voluntariado e universo rural*, edited by M. Motta and T. Piñeiro. Rio de Janeiro: Vício de Leitura.

Niederle, P. and Grisa, C. 2019. "From the neoliberal to the developmental state? The ambiguous political paradigm shift in Brazil." In: *State Capitalism Under Neoliberalism: The Case of Agriculture and Food in Brazil*, edited by A. Bonanno and S.Cavalcanti, 43–58. Baltimore: Rowman and Littlefield.

Niederle, P., Grisa, C., Picolotto, E. and Soldera, D. 2019. "Narrative disputes over family-farming public policies in Brazil: conservative attacks and restricted countermovements."*Latin American Research Review*, 54: 707–20.

OECD. 2017. *Meat Consumption*. Accessed December 17, 2017. www.data.oecd.org/agroutput/meat-consumption.htm.

Oliveira, F. 1977. *Questionando a economia brasileira: crítica à razão dualista*. São Paulo: Cebrap.

Oliveira, G. 2016. "Regularização fundiária e a 'corrida mundial por terras' no Brasil." *Campo – Território*, 11(23): 43–75.

Prado, Jr., C. 1979. *Formação do Brasil contemporâneo*. 16th ed. São Paulo: Brasiliense.

Perelman, M. 2000. *The Invention of Capitalism*. Durham: Duke University Press.

Peters, M. 2017. "The end of neoliberal globalisation and the rise of authoritarian populism." *Educational Philosophy and Theory*, 50 4): 323–25.

Prodes. 2017. *Projeto de Monitoramento do Desmatamento na Amazônia Legal por Satélite*. Brasília: INPE.

Repórter Brasil. 2012. *Moendo Gente*. Accessed February 16, 2016. http://moendogente.org.br/#lat=-23.378341326108416&lng=-49.881663489746245&zoom=5>

Repórter Brasil. 2017. *Trabalho escravo contemporâneo*. Accessed February 10, 2018. https://reporterbrasil.org.br/wp-content/uploads/2015/02/folder20anos_versaoWEB.pdf.

Reydon, B. P. 2017. "Especialista alerta para concessões do governo na área fundiária." *Jornal da Unicamp*. June 20.

Reydon, B. P. and Plata, L. (eds). 2000. *Intervenção estatal no mercado de terras, a experiência recente do Brasil*. Brasília: NEAD.

Reydon, B. P. et al. (eds). 2017. *Governança de terras: da teoria à realidade brasileira*. Brasília: FAO.

Sallum, Jr., B. and Goulart, J. 2017. "O Estado brasileiro contemporâneo: liberalização econômica, política e sociedade nos governos FHC e Lula." *Revista de Sociologia Política*, 24 (60): 115–35.

Sauer, S. 2018. *Medida provisória ou de exceção? Decreto regulamentando a grilagem de terras*. Brasília: UnB.

Sauer, S. and Leite, A. Z. 2017. "Medida Provisória 759: Descaminhos da reforma agrária e legalização da grilagem de terras no Brasil." *Retratos de Assentamentos*, 20(1): 14–40.

Sauer, S. and Leite, S. P. 2012. "Expansão agrícola, preços e apropriação de terra por estrangeiros no Brasil." *Revista de Economia e Sociologia Rural*, 50(3): 503–24.

Scoones, I., Edelman, M., Borras, Jr., S., Hall, R., Wolford, W. and White, B. 2018. "Emancipatory rural politics: Confronting authoritarian populism." *Journal of Peasant Studies*, 45(1): 1–20.

Silva, E. B. 2013. *A dinâmica socioespacial e as mudanças na cobertura e uso da terra no bioma cerrado*. PhD Thesis. Goiânia: UFG.

Silva, M. A. M., Bueno, J. D. and Melo, B. M. 2014. "Quando a máquina 'desfila', os corpos silenciam: tecnologia e degradação do trabalho nos canaviais paulistas." *Contemporânea*, 4(1): 85–116.

Sinnott, E., Nash, J. and Torre, A. 2010. *Recursos naturais na América Latina: indo além das altas e baixas*. Rio de Janeiro: Elsevier.

Streeck, W. 2012. "How to study contemporary capitalism?" *European Journal of Sociology*, 53(1): 1–28.

Teixeira, G. 2018. *Nota sobre o Decreto nº 9.309, de 15 de março de 2018*. Brasília: Câmara dos Deputados.

Théry, H., Mello, N., Hato, J. and Girardi, E. 2009. *Atlas do trabalho escravo no Brasil*. São Paulo: Amigos da Terra.

Torres, F. and Góes, F. 2013. "BNDESPar concentra 89% dos investimentos em apenas 5 setores." *Valor Econômico*, March 14.

Treccani, G. 2017. "Políticas de terras na região norte." In *Proceedings of the Jornada de Agricultura Familiar*. Brasília: UnB.

USDA. 2018. *Livestock and Poultry: World Markets and Trade*. Washington: USDA.

Valor Econômico. 2019. *Retórica do governo levará agronegócio à estaca zero, diz Blairo*. Accessed October 9, 2019. https://valor.globo.com/brasil/noticia/2019/08/15/retorica-do-governo-levara-agronegocio-a-estaca-zero-diz-blairo.ghtml.

Wagner, A. 2004. "Terras tradicionalmente ocupadas. Processos de territorialização e movimentos sociais." *Revista Brasileira de Estudos Urbanos e Regionais*, 6(1): 9–32.

4 Crisis and resilience of the domestic order

The practices that constitute the domestic order have long been denied or made invisible in Brazil. It was the large estate and its production aimed at foreign markets that have historically been privileged not only by agricultural policies but also by the social imaginary constructed along the "economic cycles" (sugarcane, cotton, coffee, soy). According to Delgado (2004, 7), this social imaginary deems the subsistence farming "as a kind of counterpoint to modernity, to the modern, dynamic, capitalist sector." Indeed, the main purpose of this sector is not profit, but the production of what "is socially necessary for the physical and social reproduction of the worker and his family" (Garcia, Jr., 1983, 16). Relations with markets are usually restricted to some products that must be traded in order to provide cash, for enabling the purchase of items that are not produced into the farm, but which are necessary for the family's livelihoods, such as salt, tools and clothing (Woortmann and Woortmann, 1997). It does not mean, however, these practices are incompatible with the contemporary capitalist societies.

Caio Prado, Jr., a leading Brazilian economic historian, in his *Formação do Brasil Contemporâneo* (Formation of Contemporary Brazil) (1979 [1942]), dedicated a whole chapter to the analysis of "subsistence farming." In his view, the fundamental economic activities of the country were based on a tripod constituted by large estates, slave labor and monoculture, which underpinned the production of goods for the foreign market. Subsistence farming was only intended for the consumption and maintenance of the colony; it was present in smallholdings or in small-scale exploitation carried out by agricultural workers in the large estates, where food was produced through own/family labor, without either slave or wage labor, using rudimentary technologies, often made by workers themselves. In terms of economic relevance, these activities appear as a second-class category, designed to support and enable the fulfilment of the large cash crops: "They do not have an autonomous life of their own, rather following those to which they are added as a mere accessory" (Prado, Jr., 1979, 124).

From another perspective, the historian Maria Isaura Pereira de Queiroz (2009 [1963]), in her article *Uma categoria rural esquecida* (A forgotten rural category), opposes the idea that the subsistence sector or the actors who practiced it were residual or numerically modest in the rural space. The author draws attention to the existence of a large category of smallholders present in all Brazilian regions, which constitutes the "most important part of the land-bound population in our country" (Queiroz, 2009, 67). They are characterized by a particular way of life, based on sociability within small neighborhood groups. They were disregarded because of both their small surplus production and their distance from towns. Furthermore, they were viewed negatively for their mode of organization, considered as nonproducers and nonconsumers, and therefore excluded from the development processes of modern capitalist society.

Subsistence farming has historically been associated with small farms, which were ignored by statistics not on account of numerical insignificance, but rather for the criteria used for assessing national agricultural production. A problem that persists today, this has been evident since the 1920 Agricultural Census, the first carried out in the country, for which "kitchen gardens, small plots and nurseries belonging to town houses and villas, as well as rural smallholdings, provided that their production is intended for domestic consumption, i.e., has a low value and does not constitute an actual and special business branch" were not considered as rural establishments. Otherwise, in the 1940 Agricultural Census, all agricultural establishments were registered, irrespective of area or value of production. It was possible, then, to observe a 194% growth in the number of establishments in relation to the 1920 data (from 648,153 to 1,904,589), even though the area had increased by only 13% (from 175,104,675 to 197,720,247 ha). While the number of farms over 1,000 ha grew by only 5.7% during that period, those under 100 ha increased by over 250%, confirming that most of them had not been included in the 1920 Census. In addition, based on this new criteria, it was possible to observe that while coffee and sugarcane were present in only 15.8% and 13.3% of the country's rural establishments, respectively, a wide range of domestic farming activities were spread throughout Brazil: poultry (in 80% of the farms), maize (77%), beans (64%), swine (63%), horses (57%), cattle (51%), cassava (45%) and rice (35%) – that is, all these with higher incidence as compared with the commercial products of the large crops.

Queiroz (2009) emphasized the numerical relevance of this subsistence farming in the mid-twentieth century. Opposing Prado, Jr.'s claim that 27.2% of the total Brazilian area consisted of large estates dedicated to monocultures and that the remainder would be "uninhabited," the author demonstrated that the vast majority of the national territory, which was not occupied by large farms, belonged to the subsistence farming regime, that is, plots of independent smallholders, settlers, leaseholders etc. Therefore, drawing on a 1959 study by Jacques Lambert, Queiroz (2009, 61) points out that "Brazil, unlike what is commonly said, is not a country predominantly of monocultures, but rather a country of polycultures; the smallholding's polyculture farming provides food for Brazil's sixty million inhabitants and employs the majority of rural men."

Since the 1960s, this subsistence farming has been faced with the expansion of the industrial order. The introduction of a new set of technical artifacts (oil, pesticides and hybrid varieties) and institutional arrangements (rural credit, banks, cooperatives, rural extension, agricultural research) entailed the growing integration of farmers into markets. In the 1980s, one interpretation of this process characterized the neo-Marxist debate on "commodification of agriculture," which highlighted the effects of this phenomenon on the disintegration of the peasant way of life (Bernstein,1986; Friedman,1978; Goodman and Redcliff,1985). Based on this literature, Abramovay (1998) argued that these trade relations altered peasants' rationality, changing them into producers of exchange values subordinated to the social and economic dynamics of the capitalist mode of production. The most direct effect of this would be the transformation of the practices, artifacts and institutions that guide the organization of farming units and farmers' social life. The commodification of agriculture, as an effect of the penetration of capitalist relations in the countryside, affected the organization of subsistence farming practices by transforming the productive base and building a new organizational logic that prescribes farmers' continuous relationship with markets. In this process, Abramovay noticed the main evidence of the peasant's transformation into a family farmer.

However, subsequent research on the subject showed that there was no complete "subordination to market" or a complete loss of autonomy and individualization (Ploeg, 1990). Farmers have rather developed various strategies for modifying, neutralising, resisting and sometimes even accelerating the results of commodification according to their own social and economic condition. According to Wanderley (2003, 47), "rather than an irreversible and absolute transition from the traditional peasant condition to the 'modern' family farmer, we should consider simultaneously the elements of rupture and continuity between these two social categories." On the one hand, it is important to consider the most significant weight of production for the market, the increasingly widespread use of modern artifacts of production, and the professionalization of the activities. On the other hand, the main line of continuity in this whole process lies in the permanence of family logic as an organizing institution of social practices.

Subsistence farming has changed by combining old and new practices, without completely opposing the changes in the "encompassing society" (Mendras, 1953) and in the economic system to which it is integrated. Traditional peasant knowledge, passed from generation to generation, although being no longer sufficient to guide the practices of a social actor more integrated into markets, remains present and is activated in several situations: the small farmer of the south of the country, who, despite using the technological package, considers the moon phases at the time of sowing; the goat farmer of Brazilian semi-arid, who prefers to sell his animals to the local buyer, even knowing that other traders would pay more for the product; the riverine who monitors the variation in river level, rather taking note of the signs of nature than of the weather forecast daily presented on television; the family that resorts to the community's healer even when they have access to the hospital.

Thus, while, on the one hand, it is undisputed that there has been a growing integration of family farming into markets, on the other, it is also certain that these farmers still mobilize numerous resources outside markets, what reflects room for maneuver and strategies designed to keep a relative autonomy (Ploeg, 2003). Therefore, these farmers' daily practices of resistance and adaptation in the face of the general transformations of capitalist society must be highlighted. They often involve access to artifacts through non-market circuits, making reciprocity one of the key elements in understanding the resilience of a domestic order in the agrifood system (Sabourin, 2011). In addition, this chapter also debate the maintenance of production for the family's own consumption, the improvement of food processing in rural establishments and the social revival of artisanal homemade products as a new market integration strategy.

The reemergence of production for own consumption

As peasantry entered the capitalist markets, production for farmers own consumption began to be interpreted as a remnant of the past, being synonymous with backwardness or with practice averse to modernization. However, several studies have shown that, while often being supplementary in relation to market-oriented farming, agricultural production for own consumption remains a recurring practice that plays several roles in family farming: it keeps food under the control of the family, contributing to food sovereignty and security; diversifies the families' livelihoods; saves resources and improves the use of labor and land; restores the coproduction between society and nature; promotes sociability among family, neighbors and community members; and enhances the social identity of farmers (Carneiro and Maluf, 2003; Grisa and Schneider, 2008; Leite, 2004; Menasche, 2007).

The study by Grisa, Schneider and Conterato (2013) on the characteristics and importance of agricultural production for own consumption in Brazilian farms, based on data from the 2006 Agricultural Census, represented one of the first efforts in the country to measure this practice at the national level. Research findings provided three particularly relevant results. The first one refers to the high incidence of this practice in rural areas – it is found in seven out of ten Brazilian rural establishments. The second finding concerns its monetary importance – it was estimated to sum R$12.7 billion in 2006, which means that, on average, 8% of all agricultural production remains in the farm for consumption by either the family or the production unit. Finally, the third result refers to its dispersion – the practice is widespread from North to South of the country and is present in establishments of all sizes and with different levels of technification and of integration into markets. Accordingly, the authors emphasized that production for own consumption is not foreign to the most modernized, industrialized regions that are integrated into global commodity chains.

Although the practice has greater relevance to food security in rural smallholdings showing higher rates of socioeconomic vulnerability, it also has an important role for families with better economic conditions. Moreover, in some regions of the country, the total value of production for own consumption is higher in better structured family farms. This is explained, in part, by the availability of resources to produce (land, seeds, water etc.), but also by sociocultural factors, such as the eating habits and customs of certain social groups. "This means that production for own consumption is not a hindrance or a traditional trait to be removed from Brazilian agricultural establishments" (Grisa, Schneider and Conterato, 2013, 34). While it guarantee food security for the small and most vulnerable units that could hardly increase their scale, this production represents

> an alternative to obtain healthy and fresh food products harvested from the orchard and the vegetable garden by those farmers who produce for the market but who have not abandoned the self-sufficiency provided by the production for own consumption, which bestows autonomy and identity on them.
>
> (Idem, 34)

The 2017 Agricultural Census included for the first time a question about the main purpose of the establishment's agricultural production: for consumption of the own family of the farmer and their relatives or for commercialization (including exchange or barter). Although no results are available yet about the monetary value of this production, data published so far point to a significant proportion of rural establishments (around 2/5) where production for own consumption is the main purpose (IBGE, 2019). This relevance is also observed in data of the National Household Sample Survey (PNAD). Balsadi and Del Grossi (2016) report a decrease in the Economically Active Population (EAP) employed in agriculture between 2004 and 2014, from 18 million to 14.5 million, which represents a reduction of 20%. "However, the very high growth in the category production for own consumption draws attention, with an increase of almost one million employed persons in the period 2004–2014" (Balsadi and Del Grossi, 2016, 85). This 28.8% increase in the number of people employed in production for own consumption in 2014 mean that this category was established as the main occupation in agriculture, accounting for 30.6% of the total working people.

Among the factors that explain this process, Anjos, Del Grossi and Caldas (2020) and Buainain and Dedecca (2010) highlight the role of public policies to encourage production by family farmers (*Pronaf B*, *Garantia Safra*, *Cisternas*), as well as the income transfer policies (such as *Bolsa Familia* and *Previdência Rural*). Trentin (2015), in turn, emphasizes the contribution of the Brazil Without Misery Plan (*Plano Brasil Sem Miséria*), which stimulated production for own consumption coupled with a set of policies to fight extreme poverty. A similar effect, which we will discuss in the next chapter, is observed in regard to the public food procurement policies, especially the Food Acquisition Programme (*Programa de Aquisição de Alimentos*– PAA) and the National School Feeding Programme (*Programa Nacional de Alimentação Escolar* PNAE), which, while creating a market for family farming by means of public procurement, stimulate the diversification of production in family farms and, indirectly, the household consumption of these foods (Triches, 2010).

In brief, production for own consumption endures as an absolutely current practice in the Brazilian rural areas, one that is constitutive of the *peasant ethos* still present in family farmers (Wanderley, 2003). Although often prejudicially deemed an archaic and backward production practice, limited to the poorest segment of farmers, having low economic relevance and being on the verge of extinction, recent researches suggest the opposite way: high incidence among agricultural establishments, monetary relevance and both geographical and social breadth. Neither the commercial order that prevailed in the early twentieth century nor the consolidation of the postwar industrial order were able to rule out this practice. Considering history, one can imagine that this is also unlikely to happen with the rapid expansion of the financial order.

Small-scale food processing in rural areas

Artisanal small-scale processing of food products has been essential for the socioeconomic reproduction of family farmers. In Brazil, information on this type of activity is available since the 1920 Agricultural Census (IBGE, 1924), which registered more than 150,000 rural establishments carrying out some form of processing of agricultural production, representing 23.8% of total rural establishments in the country. Currently, despite the difficulty of measuring this practice with precision, since informal or clandestine processes lead many farmers to omit it in surveys, 2017 data show that 30.1% of rural establishments processed and/or manufactured some kind of raw material in 2017, with an output that amounted to R$14.8 billion (IBGE, 2019).

Over time, when comparing data from the main products registered in the Censuses from 1975 to 2006, a drop is observed in the number of establishments that processed cassava flour, cheese/curd, sausages, sugarcane treacle, wine and *cachaça*, especially after the 1990s. The same occurred regarding the yield of these products, except for *cachaça* that showed increasing yield over this period of 30 years. This reduction has numerous causes. One of them refers to the 15% drop in the number of agricultural establishments with less than 100 ha between 1985 and 2006, and it is precisely in this stratum that more than 90% of the farms that process food fall (Fernandes Filho and Campos, 2003). Moreover, in a context of reduction in the number of household members, part of the farmers has adopted a logic of productive specialization. Since the 1990s, these small-scale processing initiatives have also been faced with

Table 4.1 Number of agricultural establishments and yield of processed and/or manufactured products according to selected products and years

Products	Number of producer rural establishments				
	1975	*1985*	*1995/1996*	*2006*	*2017*
Cassava flour	495,129	471,243	653,739	264,882	355,207
Cheese and curd	147,670	299,323	358,619	80,825	175,198
Sausages	106,766	304,488	112,813	17,722	44,870
Sugarcane treacle	30,462	95,338	69,412	17,436	20,298
Wine	29,619	46,956	19,906	8,383	8,081
Cachaça	5,273	13,956	21,765	11,124	11,028
Products	Total yield				
	1975	*1985*	*1995/1996*	*2006*	*2017*
Cassava flour	1,811,895	1,648,342	1,478,979	1,332,874	706,752
Cheese and curd	51,737	105,746	202,262	111,463	222,652
Sausages	6,938	14,435	9,477	2,953	7,278
Sugarcane treacle	2,182	20,782	20,682	6,393	9,539
Wine	43,830	42,792	25,363	18,679	24,210
Cachaça	24,410	45,135	106,980	113,208	83,409

Source: Brazilian Agricultural Censuses (various years).

rapid expansion of large agro-industries and supermarkets. Associated with this, one of the most important causes of exclusion was institutional pressure from new food safety standards and regulations. As legislation adapted to the dynamics of large enterprises, household food processing has been pushed underground.

In the last 10 years, however, this downward trend seems to have been reversed. Data from the last Agricultural Census point to an increase in both the number of producers and the quantity produced (Table 4.1). Indeed, despite a widespread image of agricultural specialization, what is seen in many regions is the emergence of a more diverse rural environment, where artisanal food processing is once again gaining ground. This result from several factors, particularly the growing demand for artisanal, homemade, peasant and local foods, which reveals the emergence of a new logic of consumption (Wilkinson, 2008). This process makes room for family farmers to enter markets that value not only their productive practices, but also their identities and values.

The social recognition of both products and family farmers has pushed for this practice to become object of public policies. At the municipal scale, several programs have been created to support family agro-industries, one of the most well-known cases being the Fonte Nova Crissiumal Pact in the north-western region of Rio Grande do Sul (Sausen, Patias and Allebrandt, 2011). At the state level, the pioneer was the Programme for Verticalization of Small-scale Agricultural Processing (PROVE) of the Federal District, which was implemented from 1995 to 1998. Until 2009, taking into account all state programs (DF, MS, RS, SC, PR, RJ, MT and MG) directed to family agro-industries, approximately 4,000 enterprises (90% of them in the southern region of the country) benefited from credit, changes in legislation, training courses or assistance in accessing markets (Wesz, Jr., 2009). At the federal level, the most important program was a specific credit line within PRONAF intended for the implementation, support and strengthening of rural agro-industries (Wesz, Jr., 2017).

Regarding the regulatory framework, some efforts have been made to adapt the standards to the characteristics of small-scale food processing. The creation of food safety unified systems (SUASA), the relaxation of social security tax and the reduction of costs of formalizing artisanal food processing facilities were important steps in this direction. Nevertheless, the prevalence of legislation based on hygienist principles pressures for the standardization of artisanal food, making the products run the risk of changing their nature and losing identity. As a result, most initiatives remain informal. Those few who manage to comply with legislation are generally restricted to operating in local markets within municipal boundaries. If, on the one hand, this encourages direct-to-consumers selling, on the other hand, it limits the formation of wider networks. Market expansion often involves accepting the conditions imposed by intermediaries, which assume the risks of marketing by appropriating a considerable margin of value added that could otherwise be retained by the farmers.

Many studies have confirmed the importance of food processing for rural development, given its relevance for generating jobs in the countryside, enhancing household income, reducing farmers' economic vulnerability and rural exodus, preserving local culture and traditions, strengthening local economies and protecting ecological resources (Maluf, 2001, 2004; Mior, 2005; Pelegrini and Gazolla, 2008; Prezotto, 2002; Waquil et al., 2013; Wesz, Jr., Trentin and Filippi, 2009). One of the main effects of this practice is the internalization of productive resources, through which family farmers build an endogenous base of inputs over which they have control (Niederle and Wesz, Jr., 2009). This is a key element for understanding the relationship between small-scale food processing and what Ploeg (2006) calls the "peasant mode of production" aimed at adding value to farm produce and generating productive employment. According to the author, the "peasant condition reflects the constant and endless struggle of family forms of production for autonomy, which aims to create a self-controlled, integrated and multi-use resource base that makes farmer an actor in rural development" (Ploeg, 2006, 60).

As noted by Waquil et al. (2013), an advantage of the food processing by family farmers is the use of its own raw material. According to data presented by the authors, among family farms, the proportion of own raw material reaches 94.1% of the total in the case of starch or tapioca production, 94.0% in cassava flour; and 89.9% in bread products. In smaller percentages are sausages (78.1%), sweet preserves and jams (77.7%), *rapadura* (sweet made from sugarcane treacle) (75.2%), cheese and curd (67.9%) and maize flour (64, 0%). Among the products selected by the authors, only *cachaça* (the Brazilian national drink) manufactured by family farming uses own raw materials in a lower proportion (43.4%) than that acquired in the markets (56.6%). However, even when raw materials are purchased, this usually occurs in local markets, where trust and reciprocity reduce prices and make payment conditions more flexible.

In short, the expansion of small-scale processing in rural areas has challenged the idea that these practices – often using family farmers' household structures and tools – would be nothing but remnant of an outdated model of development, fated to be (inevitably) overthrown by expansion of large agro-industrial conglomerates integrated into transnational supermarket chains. On the contrary, despite all the economic and institutional constraints on this type of alternative food system (especially legislation inadequacy and lack of structuring public policies), they have expanded, becoming an important strategy for social reproduction of many rural families, for building new market circuits and boosting local economies, while valuing the territories' biodiversity and cultural heritage.

The revival of artisanal foods

As we have shown so far, agricultural production and small-scale processing (both for the market and for own consumption) have been historically deemed as irrelevant. Perceived as remnants of the past, since they do not resort to "modern" artifacts, they have also been recurrently associated with poorer segments of family farming. However, as we also showed, these interpretations have been changing, insofar as we take note of both the recurrence of these practices and their economic, social and cultural relevance. What deserves further examination, however, is the redefinition of these practices as a result of growing consumer demand focused on "exploring the past" (Boltanski and Esquerre, 2017). This section looks into a specific aspect of this dynamic, which is associated with the demand for artisanal food.

The meaning of artisanal evidences a distinctive characteristic that differentiates and individualizes each product. In markets, artisanal foods are presented in opposition to standardized and mass industrial production, since their distinction lies in highlighting product characteristics that could hardly be achieved in large-scale production driven by automatic machines, based on uniform ingredients and rootless recipes. Conversely, the practices that support their meaning often involve production on small scales, with technologies that are not fully automated, the use of local ingredients and the use of traditional recipes. In fact,

> the artisanal way of producing means that the production process implies
> a dimension of art and not merely a technical one. The special touch each

producer gives to his/her product is the distinctiveness and the foundation of the craft, that which makes each product unique.

(Silveira and Heinz, 2005, 2–3)

Champredonde (2016) suggests that the difference between artisanal and industrial production lies mainly in three aspects: the craftsperson's know how; the characteristics or style of the product (singularity); and the social recognition of the producer. In this sense, according to the author, the distribution of knowledge is a distinctive feature of artisanal practices in relation to industrial ones. While in this latter case there is a specialization of knowledge, in the artisanal production the actors involved master a range of knowledge that allows them to participate in all or almost all stages of elaboration. Indeed, this also denotes differences in the way this knowledge is acquired by social actors. Regarding the recognition of the connection between product and producer, the author emphasizes the individualization of this process, which is revealed, for example, in the identification of the product with the artisan's name or surname.

This brings about, still according to the author, a difference between handcrafted products and products typical of a given culture or territory. In the case of typical products there is a strong association with a community or territory. That is, knowledge is distributed in a specific social group that may or may not be concentrated in a territory. Moreover, according to this idea, a typical product may be industrial, although this is not common due to the standardization process. Otherwise, in the case of artisanal products, knowledge may be concentrated in just one person. "The product bears the style that this person imprints upon it and identified with her/him, regardless of its location" (Champredonde, 2016, 44). When both qualities overlap – artisanal and typical – singularities emerge such as the artisanal cheeses from Serra da Canastra or the artisanal wines from Vales da Uva Goethe (see Chapter 6).

Many products carry this "artisanal" attribute. Some of them have long carried such distinction, especially those produced by the family farmers' food processing facilities (cheese, sausages, beverages, sweets etc.), for which the term refers to a quality arising from the production process that results in tastes, distinctive flavors, textures, aromas and appearances (Nichele and Waquil, 2011). Thus, highlighting the artisanal nature of the production process is a way for farmers to highlight their know-how, generally referring to a cultural heritage and local traditions (Cruz and Schneider, 2010). For these farmers,

these are business strategies that translate into attempts to capture a larger share of the value generated in the main food chains, and also entails the revival of artisanal processes, of a "know-how" associated with a historical and cultural heritage.

(Schneider and Ferrari, 2015, 57)

Cheese is one of the products for which the "artisanal" attribute is most recurrent in Brazil (Cruz, 2012). More than 175,000 rural establishments manufacture this type of product in Brazil[1] (IBGE, 2019). The elaboration of artisanal cheese is a historical cultural method of milk conservation, which is rooted in different territories of the country (Menezes, 2011). They are generally produced by family farmers using household artifacts available in their own kitchen, and from fresh milk supplied by their own cows (Cintrão, 2016). As a result, "the techniques and knowledge involved in their production and processing are connected with the family and have been conveyed through generations, being part of the cultural background of their respective territories" (Menezes, Cruz and Menasche, 2010, 1).

Another key distinguishing feature is that farmers do not use pasteurized milk and consequently, unlike industrial cheeses, "artisanal cheeses made from raw milk are living products that have unique textures, flavors and aromas as a result of their intrinsic connections with the different territories, climates, pastures, modes and traditions of craft making in each region" (Slow Food, 2015, 1). According to a survey conducted by the Slow Food movement (2017), there are over 30 different types of traditional cheeses made from raw milk in Brazil. This diversity stems from the place of origin; type of milk; amount of fat, different elaboration procedures; texture; time of maturation; type of finishing; form; size; color; taste; aroma; type of rind etc. Among the best-known are the Canastra, Salitre, Araxá and Serro, from Minas Gerais; Colonial and Serrano from southern Brazil; curd and butter cheeses from the Northeast; and Marajó cheese from Pará.

A problem that directly affects artisanal cheese production in Brazil and elsewhere refers to food hygiene regulation, which is based on the standards of large-scale industrial production. As highlighted by Cruz (2012), due to regulatory inadequacy, many artisanal cheeses continue to be traded informally, risking being seized by inspection agents and causing serious losses to producers. Such situations have been recurrent in the country, albeit little publicized, except when involving greater social conflict or gastronomic celebrities – for example, the seizure of 160 kg of artisan cheeses and sausages at Chef Roberta Sudbrack's booth, during Rock in Rio 2017. As pointed out by Menezes (2011), framing this artisanal activity as illegal means the preponderance of boundaries built by disproportionate or discriminatory norms governing the exercise of artisanal food production.

In Brazil, the state of Minas Gerais pioneered a first regulatory alternative for these products. The State Law 14.185/2002 "is deemed a national milestone, as it is the first one that seeks to legally allow rural properties to make cheeses from unpasteurized milk, by renaming them to 'Queijos Minas Artesanais' (Minas Artisanal Cheeses)" (Cintrão, 2016, 2). Still regarding state legislations, more recently, there have been other similar advances, such as the enactment of the Nivardo Mello law, in July 2017, in Rio Grande do Norte, which regulated artisanal cheeses made from fresh and raw milk according to traditional methods. In early 2018, Law number 4486 was also approved, which regulates the production and sale of artisanal cheeses made from raw milk in the state of Santa Catarina. The problem is that these state legislations are still bound to confusing and inconsistent federal rules, increasing institutional instability and hindering markets expansion.

In 2011, in response to pressures and criticism from social movements, the Ministry of Agriculture, Livestock and Supply (MAPA) issued a normative act (IN 57), whereby artisanal cheeses made from raw milk should be ripened for less than sixty days (period then in force and which dates back to Decree 30691/1952 of Getúlio Vargas government). However, the new standard conditioned this to technical studies to prove that such practice does not compromise the safety of the product. At the same time, it established that this production "is restricted to cheesemaking located in a region of certified or traditionally recognized geographical indication." These standards would prevent this market from operating, mainly because of the impossibility of small-scale artisanal producers to adapt to the new requirements. As a result, a new movement of criticism has started, leading to the need for new mechanisms. In August 2013, MAPA issued the normative act IN 30, repealing the previous one and resolving that "the definition of a new maturation period for artisanal cheeses will follow the evaluation of studies by the state and/or municipal agency of industrial and food hygiene inspection recognized by the Brazilian Inspection System for Animal Products – SISBI/POA" (IN 30/2013, Art.1 §1°). The most recent chapter of this institutional saga was the approval by the National Congress, in the first half of 2018, of the Bill no. 3859, which allows the commercialization of artisanal products of animal origin between the states. The proposal also provides for these products to be identified nationwide with a seal "ARTE" (*Artesanal do Brasil*), which will be awarded by public health agencies in each state.[2]

Other artisanal products face the same kind of problem, although without the same repercussion. This is the case of cachaça, for example, a typical Brazilian distilled spirit manufactured by about 40,000 producers in the country, 98% of which are classified as small and microentrepreneurs, and 85% out of which are estimated to be operating informally. In terms of production volume, 70% of Brazilian cachaça come from the industrial sector – being mostly produced in São Paulo. The rest is artisanal, with the state of Minas Gerais leading the production (Cervieri, Jr. et al., 2014). While the industrial product is controlled by large economic groups, by means of modern distillation columns, usually made of stainless steel – a material that compromises some sensory characteristics of the final product – and sophisticated laboratory techniques, the artisanal cachaça is produced in copper stills – a material that enhances flavors and aromas – and generally by small-scale producers. In addition, in the production of artisanal cachaça, distillation is carried out discontinuously, allowing only the noblest part of the product to be selected, whereas industrial production makes this separation unfeasible, resulting in a final product with lower quality (Verdi, 2006).

Cachaça and cheese are classic examples of the prevalent perception of what would be artisanal foods – those that are associated with rural families that produce them in the farms using artifacts available there, which usually involve a know-how conveyed through generations whose product is an expression of a culturally localized practice. However, there is another dynamic also associated with artisanal food production, which we can find in the processing of beers and baked goods. These "new crafts" are produced mainly in the urban areas, using ingredients not necessarily nearby and modern technological artifacts. Even so, they also retain as their artisanal attributes the use of traditional recipes (although searched on the Internet) and differentiated ingredients (although often imported), small-scale production, and only partially mechanized processes.

The most prominent example here is the production of craft beers, which has drawn the attention of many producers and consumers in Brazil (Gewehr, 2019).[3] The origin of craft brewery in the country dates back to the first decades of the nineteenth century, when microbreweries began to compete with the product imported from England. Located mainly in the south-eastern and southern regions of the country, these microbreweries were actually the homes of immigrants who, after producing for their own consumption, began to trade the surplus in local markets, until production becomes primarily aimed to market. In the late nineteenth century, the development of these ventures was facilitated by increased taxes on British beer imports, so that "foreign beer has practically disappeared, making room for the already emerging large national breweries" (Giorgi, 2015, 102). In fact, in 1888 the two main brewing industries of the country emerged: Antarctica and Brahma. However, with the expansion of the industrial model, beer became a mass standardized product.

According to a survey by MAPA (2019), the number of breweries has seen an almost eightfold increase in the country in the last 10 years, reaching 889 enterprises in 2018, most of them concentrated in the south and southeast of the country. Out of the 5,570 Brazilian municipalities, 479 already have at least one registered brewery. The Brazilian Association of Craft Beer (Abracerva) attributes this growth to the expansion of differentiated beers, especially craft beers. These data are even more relevant considering that the volume of this beverage sold in the country decreased by 7% between 2015 and 2017 (New Trade, 2018). In 2017, the drop in production volume was 0.64%, while the craft beer segment advanced 17.7% (Globo, 2018). As pointed out by one of the leading experts of the new "brewing culture," the American brewer and chief editor of The Oxford Companion to Beer, Garret Oliver, "what we are doing is leading beer back to food condition, so people stop drinking in quantity. Those who drink quality beer will drink less because they are drinking better" (Oliver, 2013, 23).

The revival of Brazilian craft beer is still an incipient process. Abracerva estimates that artisanal production accounts for only 1% of the total volume and about 2.5% of sales revenue in the country (New Trade, 2018). However, it also estimates that this market could triple or even experience a fourfold increase in the next decade. In any case, it is interesting to note how this process has encouraged new practices and engagements, such as Slow Beer, a movement that emphasizes the culture of pleasure in producing and drinking quality beers, thus blending the domestic and aesthetic logic. Tasting beer involves several rituals (circular movement of the glass, inhaling the drink, observing its color, foam and label) that bring the market closer to the world of wine (Giorgi, 2015). Moreover, as important as the expansion of this market is the way the new brewing culture impacts on the production of meanings, contributing to the revival of not only of this product, but of "artisanal" as the quality of distinct foods (Gewehr, 2019).

As in the case of *cachaça*, craft beer does not have a legal framework defining the category criteria and mode of production. The term is usually referred to those beers produced on a small scale by independent producers and under the aegis of a certain tradition that can be understood as the perpetuation of unique product characteristics. Regarding the length of production process, it tends to exceed 20 days, since very particular characteristics of aroma and flavor are sought, while large-scale beer production can be completed within 10 days (Piato and Révillion, 2014). The executive director of Fritz Cervejaria Artesanal, also notes that "craft beer is a concept that implies more malt, higher care and superior quality in relation to commercial beer, and therefore its whole process is differentiated, including finalisation of the product" (Abras, 2012). As we will see in Chapter 6, this logic reveals overlapping areas between the domestic and aesthetic orders.

Another sector that has recently stood out is the artisan bakery and confectionery products, whose visibility seems to be even more recent and less widespread than that of beers. The best known are gourmet bakeries or boutique bakeries that also revealing an aesthetic logic. In the case of these products, handicraft is expressed, for example, in the use of natural yeast, usually without the use of chemical additives, preservatives, colorings and flavorings. This choice also implies adapting the machines and utensils, as the timing and preparation are different. Another feature is the recovery of traditional knowledge and practices, which combine old recipes with a (post)modern aesthetic. Finally, when it comes to the management of signs and meanings, many follow the logic that "product names should convey a familiar and traditional message to customers": "Mother Benta's carrot cake, Granny Anastacia's cheese bread, Aunt Rita's pie, Granny Ana's drumstick" (Montar um Negócio, 2016)

The major challenge for most craft products is the absence (except for cheese and wine) of a legal definition of "artisanal" in Brazil, which paves the way for the appropriation of this distinction by large companies in the sector and, more recently, by agribusiness organizations like the National Confederation of Agriculture and Livestock (CNA) that, once critical of this practice, is now attracted by the expansion of the market. As so far there is nothing legally defining and no institution for controlling whether, for example, the baked goods sold as artisanal do not really use chemical yeast, or if artisanal *cachaça* comes from a traditional alembic, some companies have unscrupulously appropriated this concept. In the cases mentioned here, this situation is more frequent among large brewing industries, which have bet on both the use of special recipes and the acquisition of artisanal microbreweries, which quickly incorporate industrial practices.

This practice is even used (and perhaps mainly) by leading companies in the national beer production ranking such as Ambev, Heineken, Petrópolis Group and Therezópolis. In the case of Ambev, for example, after acquiring craft breweries (such as Colorado in 2015) and launching new labels, the company is now investing in this segment via establishments such as Goose Island Brew House and Wäls. Another investment is a partnership with Yaguara, a cachaça distillery, to ferment the beer with sugarcane and a yeast used in the production of spirits. In turn, Therezópolis bought the microbrewery of Maguje restaurant, located inside Rio de Janeiro Jockey Club. The Petrópolis Group will allocate R$59 million to the construction of a microbrewery in Teresópolis, RJ. Also on the list is Heineken, which aims to strengthen the visibility of its "special" beer brands (Eisenbahn and Baden Baden). Briefly, these examples show how attributes of the Domestic Order are being appropriated by industry and, thus, connected with another arrangement of production practices. If, on the one hand, this results in considerable economic gains for companies, on the other hand, it raises suspicion among consumers about the meaning of artisanal products, what may lead such qualitative concept to lose distinctiveness, thus entailing, sooner or later, decrease in economic gains and the need to create new differentiation strategies.

The diaspora of colonial products

In Brazil, the term *colonial* as an attribute of food is related to the practices and identities of European immigrants and their descendants, especially those of Italian and German origin, who settled in Southern region as of the nineteenth century, establishing the "colonies," where farmers are deemed and recognize themselves as *"colonos."* Thus, instead of referring to the period of Brazilian colonial period under control of the Portuguese crown, in this case, "colonial refers to a certain culture and tradition, associated with the know-how of non-Iberian Europe immigrants, their way of life, their specific forms of land occupation and farming" (Dorigon, 2008, 1). In sum, colonial refers to a link between these farmers' social, historical, cultural, ethnic and regional identity and a production mode based on their knowledge and practices (Menasche, 2015).

This distinction has historically defined the image of a set of products that were generally processed in farms by family farmers, such as salami, cheese, jams and jellies, pasta and biscuits, brown sugar, juices, wine, among others. According to Dorigon and Renk (2011), historically the distance from consumer centers has impelled farmers to produce in the colonies a wide range of both raw and processed foods. The absence of electricity and appliances for the storage and conservation of products led to the use of old conservation practices. Initially, most products were intended for domestic consumption, with a small part being marketed. However, from the 1990s onward, a revival of colonial products has been observed because for consumers these products are considered healthier and more natural. Besides, for many consumers, especially those with rural backgrounds (who have been farmers or are the children and grandchildren of farmers), these products also bear a familiar past. In this case, consumption incorporates an affective dimension, so that the aromas, textures and flavors of colonial products refer to a somewhat idyllic childhood (Dorigon, 2008).

Although the term *colonial* is linked to numerous food products, cheese and wine are among the most recognized ones. In the case of cheese, as we discussed in the previous section, among the variety of Brazilian artisanal cheeses, the colonial cheese is the one that prevails in the south of the country. Therefore, we will briefly refer to colonial wines, whose image is mainly associated with the culture of Italian immigrants, who, to maintain their viticulture tradition, were forced to develop specific styles of growing vineyards so that to adapt to local climate conditions. Regarding the European wine tradition, the main adaptation was the introduction of hybrid grapes (resulting from the cross between European and American varieties of grapes), which are more resistant to pests and diseases. Thus, instead of the renowned Sangiovese, Barbera, Merlot or Cabernet Sauvignon, it was the Isabel, Bordô, Rubi and Niagara varieties that became the expression of an "Italian culture" reinvented by immigrants.

What is the place of colonial wines within the world of wines? In line with the approach of the "worlds of production" by Salais and Storper (1992), Niederle et al. (2016) distinguished four worlds of wine, each with a more or less specific set of logics, actors and artifacts. The classification follows two basic lines (Figure 4.1), which differentiate the mode of production (artisanal × industrial) and the wine category (fine × table). Among "fine wines," that is, those produced from European grapes, the "industrial fine wine" resulted from the entry of the business and cooperative sector in the production and processing of European wine grapes, which led to the creation of a "differentiated commodity" especially aimed at large retailers and nonspecialized consumers. On the other hand, the new world of "artisanal fine wines" emerges from the practices of a new generation of winemakers and oenologists who seek to introduce the product into the specialties circuits, that is, the specialized consumer segments associated with wine and gastronomy (see Chapter 6). In turn, the "industrial table wines" reflect the process of modernization of artisanal production, led by large cooperatives and companies that technified and expanded production scale to reach a commodity that supplies undifferentiated markets and inexpert consumers. Finally, "artisanal table wines" are those usually produced by family farmers, following traditional knowledge and modes of production, deeply rooted in rural territories and generally

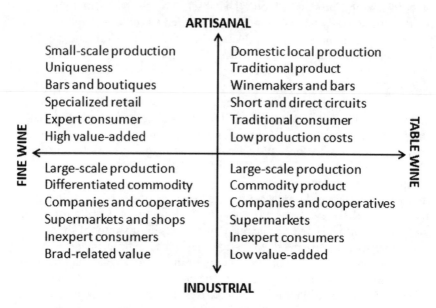

Figure 4.1 Worlds of production in Brazilian viticulture.

aimed at consumers in their own region. This later "world" is the one that houses the so-called "colonial wines"– at least it was until the table wine industry has also appropriated this image.

Despite being the most popular type of wine in the country and that preferred by the farmers themselves, "the term 'colonial' has always carried an ambiguous sense and, despite efforts to assert its association with the values of artisanal production, pejorative connotations persisted" (Wilkinson, Cerdan and Dorigon, 2016). On the one hand, this happens because modernity has created a misrepresented image of rurality and agriculture as an expression of backwardness. In the case of wines, this is not restricted to Brazil, but also happened in renowned producing countries such as France, where, until the nineteenth century, the *"terroir wine,"* now considered synonymous of quality, was deemed a "peasant wine" unfit for the consumption of citizens (city dwellers). In Brazil, the "table wines," among which is the colonial wine, are those that carry this pejorative connotation.

In 2014, Law No. 12959 amended the Wine Law (Law No. 7678/1988 updated by Law No. 10970/2004) to regulate the denomination "colonial wine" or "colonial product," the "wine produced by a family farmer or rural family entrepreneur," which was defined as the drink elaborated according to the cultural, historical and social characteristics of viticulture developed by family farmers. According to the new law, to be entitled to use this designation, the winery shall have a maximum production of 20,000 liters per year, 70% of the grapes used in its production shall be harvested from the producer's own vineyards, and it shall be sold "directly to the final consumer, either in the farm where it was produced, or in an establishment maintained by a farmers' association or cooperative or at family farming fairs." The new regulation, that became known as the Artisanal Wine Law, besides recognizing and legitimizing the activity, also prescribed marketing spaces (Bruch, Vieira and Buainain, 2015). Consequently, the new institutional arrangement tries to restrict the appropriation of the term "colonial" by large agro-industrial companies and cooperatives, a practice that is still recurrent.

Although grounded in local traditions and customs, the production and consumption of colonial products has gone beyond the limits of the European colonization regions of Southern Brazil. Although this is still a modest movement, the diaspora of colonial products reveals a spread to markets much larger than the proximity networks of trust and kinship. From the analysis of the Western region of the state of Santa Catarina, Dorigon (2008) notes that colonial products follow, in geographical terms, two main paths. The first involves the migratory route of the *colonos*. In small quantities, as they are generally informal markets, the products go to Mato Grosso do Sul, Mato Grosso, south-western Bahia and, more recently, to the new agricultural frontiers of Matopiba. The second path is towards the large consumer centers, where they usually supply restaurants and steakhouses whose owners also have cultural links with the region of origin of the products.

The fact that this attribute still refers to a territorialized sociocultural formation allows for its association with both agrifood products and various social practices. An example is the Colonial Product Festival, held annually (25th edition in 2018) in the municipality of São Martinho, Santa Catarina. These festivals always include gastronomy, music, dance and exhibitions. In southern Brazil, there are also numerous "colonial product fairs." Although many of them lack visibility or are not much valued locally, there has been a growing movement of such fairs even in large cities. Thus, once associated with local community festivals, colonial products have now become a new type of enterprise, especially in towns, where many restaurants specialize in serving *café colonial*, a meal that offers a wide variety of products typical of colonial agriculture.

Dorigon (2008) argues that the market of *colonial* products is still in construction and, at the same time, under "risk of losing its character." It is in construction, because it is a dense attribute full of symbols and meanings, by means of which farmers can talk to consumers to promote their practices and ways of life. "Thus, the production of 'trifles,' a typical activity of poor *colonos*, thus associated with a derogatory image, acquires another meaning insofar as consumers perceive their value, associating them with a distinct quality" (Dorigon, 2008, 395). In turn, the loss of its character can occur in two ways. The first is that related to the appropriation of its meaning by agro-industrial companies and cooperatives, leading to the trivialization of the image of these products. The second involves the pressure of food safety legislation, which forces farmers to incorporate industrial practices and artifacts, which alter the characteristics of their products, breaking with traditional know-how.

"New" food qualities

In addition to artisanal and colonial, other meanings also mobilize artifacts and practices that characterize the domestic order. Among the best known are the "homemade" products (*caseiros*), which seek to emphasize their careful elaboration, generally using traditional techniques and kitchen utensils, and which are deemed as being less industrialized, more natural and having more flavor. Because this term highlights the space where certain food is prepared, "homemade" is often attached to various products that are associated with expressions that, in labels and packaging, refer to the home and family, such as "Grandma's homemade cookies." However, what draws attention in this concept is that to some extent, unlike the previous concepts, it has been heavily incorporated by catering establishments. Seeking a differentiation strategy amid standardized diets and tastes, many restaurants began to focus on "home cooking." While often this only involves the denomination (marketing strategy), it is increasingly common to find restaurants that effectively bet on practices and artifacts that fulfil this meaning: "wood-fired pizza," "clay pot *feijoada*," "wood-stove-cooked *comida mineira*" (food typical of Minas Gerais), "iron-pan-cooked *arroz carreteiro*" (beef and rice with vegetables), among many others.

As in previous cases, it took not long until large food companies to appropriate the "homemade" concept. One example that stands out for its explicit contradiction is the advertisement "We are homemade" for Tang, the brand of an artificial powdered soft drink, owned by Kraft Heinz, the world's fifth largest food company. Indeed, in the case of this concept, examples abound. One of the Cargill Group's mayonnaise lines, Lisa, highlights on its label: "Homemade Recipe." Hellmann's, the brand owned by giant Unilever, has a "Homemade Salad Dressing." In the tomato sauces segment, Pomarola, also owned by Cargill, highlights on its label: "Your Homemade Touch"; and Predilecta, which also has its homemade line, announces "special sauces inspired by our grandmas' recipes." And what about Coke's "homemade" orange juice with bits? Finally, there is a whole sector of "homemade" frozen ready meals, which can be served after a few minutes in the microwave oven. This is the case of Ciel Alimentos, whose products such as stroganoff, yakisoba, pancake, stuffed potato and lasagna carry labels that say: "Yummy as homemade." According to the company, "everything, from the ingredients used, purchased from rural producers in the region, to the whole production process, follows strictly the techniques of home preparation taught by Grandma" (Ciel, 2018).

Kanematsu (2017) conducted a relevant study on this subject, comparing the presence of food additives among processed foods with and without reference to the "homemade" concept. She analyzed the labels of all processed foods (5,620) available for sale in a supermarket in Southern Brazil and identified 65 foodstuffs carrying the term "homemade" on the label. Then, other 172 similar foods were selected, which had no reference to that term, to compare the groups. Unsurprising, the results confirmed that, in general, the attribute is merely a marketing strategy for the industry to appropriate the market niche without changing production practices. The study showed that additives were found in

> 81.5% of foodstuffs that used the term homemade, and in 78.5% of those foods that did not use it. Despite the reference to homemade preparation, no significant difference was observed regarding the presence of additives in processed foods with and without reference to homemade.
>
> (Kanematsu, 2017, 7)

A very similar logic is followed by the so-called *comida caipira* (yokel foods), which generally refer to a set of typical dishes: *tutu com torresmo* (cooked and mashed beans with pork rinds), *leitão pururuca* (baked piglet), *cuscuz caipira de legumes* (rustic couscous with vegetables), *pamonha* (sweet corn paste), among many others. Although it has spread throughout the country, the *caipira* identity is strongly associated with the rural culture of the southeastern region of the country. The main reference is the gastronomic tradition of the *caipira* (yokel), as the rural worker was known, which is marked by the assimilation, combination and adaptation of herbs, roots and fruits used by the indigenous people with the grains and vegetables brought by the Portuguese colonizers. In addition, food preparation involves the use of characteristic artifacts such as pestles, bowls, *poiás* (rustic stove) and clay pots (Belluzzo, 2008).

The term *caipira* is also used to identify specific products, among which the most common are the *caipira* chicken and eggs. In this case, due to the confusion caused by a plethora of terms, the Brazilian National Standards Association (ABNT) published, in 2015, a specific regulation regarding the production of "*frango caipira, colonial ou capoeira*" (rustic, colonial poultry). Even so, also in this case, large companies in the sector started to bet on this niche, such as Seara, that pertain to the JBS group, whose packaging of the Nhô Bento chicken breast fillet shows a typical *caipira* pattern and highlights the term *frango caipira*. According to the company, the food is made from poultry raised free and "brings that taste of childhood." By the way, speaking of contradictions, there would probably be no more interesting example than the *caipira* chicken flavor of instant noodles.

Other attributes that refer to the domestic order highlight the production site with terms used in Portuguese (*da roça, do sitio, da fazenda*) to refer the rural origin of the products or who produced it (peasant, family farmer, land reform settler). It is needless to go into the analysis of these denominations, which generally add to the previous ones to compose a set of domestic concepts mobilized by farmers, associations, cooperatives and restaurants for building new markets. Moreover, also in these cases, we note a controversial relationship of the domestic order with other food orders, characterized by both overlapping practices, such as the aestheticization of artisanal products (see Chapter 6), and dynamics that could be best characterized as "invasion," given the way industrial order appropriate terms that, when linked to another set of practices and artifacts, are resignified to the point that, in some cases, there is almost no relation to its original content.

Domestic order: from invisibility to appropriation

In the early twentieth century, the commercial order of large export plantations rendered the domestic order invisible. Then, at the height of the industrial order, it came to be understood as an initial and transitory phase of development, based on archaic institutions and practices, which was doomed to disappear in the course of the agricultural modernization. Nevertheless, the crisis of the industrial model revealed the resilience of domestic forms of food production and consumption. Currently, despite the advance of financialization, domestic forms remain relevant and, in some cases, are revalued either as a strategy for gaining autonomy and providing food security, by means of increased production for own consumption by farmers, or as a new form of integration into new markets. In the latter case, it is noted that consumer demands for artisanal, homemade or traditional products have made room for both farmers to create new strategies for social reproduction, especially by means of food processing, and for new actors to appropriate practices, artifacts and meanings of the domestic order to add value to their own products.

Several continuities are perceived in the conformation of these orders over time, among which the peasant logic of production diversification and the mechanisms of coproduction between society and nature, based on the connections between local knowledge and artisanal objects stand out (Ploeg, 2009). This is noticeable in practices that are organized aiming at ensuring the subsistence of the household, though also envisaging alternatives (Garcia, Jr., 1983), by favoring crops that can be either consumed or traded according to the family needs and market conditions. As to the consumption practices, these are organized around the household, value conviviality and often involve nonmarket exchange systems based on reciprocity (Figure 4.2).

However, as social orders are not fixed institutional configurations, changes may be noticed also in the domestic order. In this chapter, the prime example highlighted was the food processing by family farmers (more specifically by women farmers, as these activities are mostly conduct by them). If this practice was once developed in the home kitchen and was primarily aimed at family consumption, now these products comprise an important source of income and are increasingly fulfilled in specific processing structures. This closer connection with markets implies a rearrangement of practices, not in the sense of losing identity (though this may occur), but of adapting to new

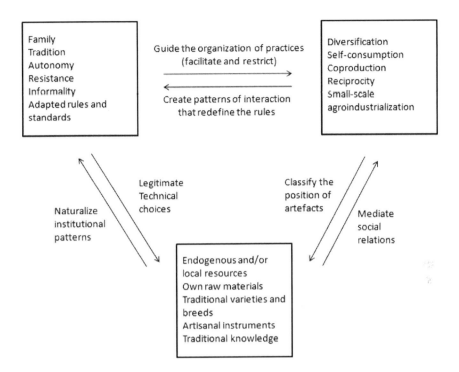

Figure 4.2 Components of the domestic order.

technological and institutional contexts (legislation, consumer preferences, pricing, bargaining with traders etc.).

The transformations of the domestic order were intensified by the growing demand for regional, traditional, artisanal and homemade products. As we will see in the next chapters, this movement has also made room for the emergence of civic and aesthetic orders. In the context of the civic order, the appeal for artisanal, colonial and homemade foods comprises a valuable opportunity to incorporate regional ingredients and flavors, creating alternatives for family farms (Menasche, 2015). Several changes already suggest this in different regions of the country: *manta de cordeiro* (a cut of lamb meat stuffed with seasoned curd or other stuffs), *manteiga de garrafa* (processed butter similar to Indian Ghee) and *queijo coalho* (the north-eastern curd cheese); *açaí*, *guaraná*, Brazilian nuts and cassava flour from the Amazon region; *cuca* (kuchen, a German cake), *queijo serrano* and Goethe wine in the southern region (Wilkinson, Niederle and Mascarenhas, 2016).

Regarding the interfaces with the aestheticization process, the new gastronomic movements are noteworthy. They have driven the emergence of microbreweries, cheese boutiques, bakery boutiques and many other such enterprises (including the spread of food trucks). In this case, the entry of family farming is still marginal, either in the creation of processing facilities capable of serving these new markets, or even in supplying raw materials. This leads many such companies to seek (often import) ingredients in distant markets, what represents a waste of opportunity to develop local innovation capacity based on territorial assets. As a result, the craft beer segment, for example, still lacks a greater Brazilian identity, since even the craft brewing (and its brands) still have strong reference to imported similar products.

Among the challenges for the reproduction of the practices analyzed in this chapter, a critical one involves the readjustment of public policies, mainly in the institutional regulation of production and commercialization, which, often based on standards of the industrial order, hinders the market of artisanal products or steals their identities. Despite new regulations issued in recent years, especially regarding food safety standards, there is still a long way left until the characteristics of each attribute (artisanal, colonial, homemade, rustic) are clearly defined so that this sociocultural legacy from the various forms of peasant occupation of the Brazilian territory can be effectively protected and valued. This regulatory weakness allows large industries to appropriate the image of this legacy to take advantage of the growing demand for these "new" products. As Wilkinson (2002, 9) summarizes, the threats come from both the pressures to adapt this production to hygiene standards and the "competition with the mainstream markets trying to appropriate these niches of traditional products."

This dynamic is even more worrying when these misappropriation practices are recognized, accepted and encouraged by the state. An emblematic case occurred in April 2018, when Law No. 13648 was enacted, which provides for the production of artisanal fruit pulp and juice. The bill (PL 63/2016) proposed to simplify the rural establishment registration procedures and the labelling requirements for the products, allowing the use of the denominations "artisanal," "homemade" and "colonial" in the packaging. However, the original bill also had provisions for ensuring that production, standardization and bottling of fruit pulp or juice would be exclusive of family farmers and their cooperatives and associations (as in the case of the "Colonial Wine Law" of 2014). This bill was approved in the Senate, but President Michel Temer vetoed the exclusive entitlement of family farming, claiming that it would "dismantle the sector and exclude from the market those who use other avenues for the production and marketing of products, such as cooperatives, associations and supermarkets" (Brazil, Senado Federal, 2018). In other words, instead of building a legal framework to protect and value each product without spoiling its identity, the government made room for any interest to appropriate social values historically characteristic of family and peasant agriculture.

Notes

1 For further details on artisanal cheeses, see the doctoral thesis by Fabiana Thomé da Cruz (2012).

2 While legal battles are on the agenda, a parallel path for recognition and institution-alization followed by artisanal cheese producers is the registration of the product as Intangible Cultural Heritage with the Institute of National Historical Heritage (IPHAN). In this regard, see Chapter 6.

3 Our thanks to Bruna Gewehr, whose Masters' dissertation (*Qualidade lupulada: o significado de artesanal na rede cervejeira gaúcha*) contributed to inform our analysis of the craft beer market.

References

Abramovay, R. 1998. *Paradigmas do capitalismo agrário em questão*. 2nd ed. São Paulo: Hucitec.

Abras. 2012. *Cervejaria artesanal avança 84%*, 2012. Accessed February 23, 2016. www.abrasnet.com.br/clipping.php?area=10&clipping=29454.

Anjos, F. S., Del Grossi, M. and Caldas, N. 2020. "La seguridad alimentaria bajo otra mirada: análisis sobre la evolución de la población brasileña ocupada en actividades de autoconsumo." *Investigaciones geográficas*, 73: 103–118.

Balsadi, O. and Del Grossi, M. 2016. "Trabalho e emprego na agricultura brasileira: um olhar para o período 2004–2014." *Revista de Política Agrícola*, 25(4): 82–96.

Belluzzo, R. 2008. *São Paulo: memória e sabor*. São Paulo: Unesp.

Bernstein, H. 1986. "Capitalism and petty commodity production." *Social Analysis*, 20: 11–28.

Boltanski, L., and Esquerre, A. 2017. *Enrichissement: une critique de la marchandise*. Paris: Gallimard.

Brasil. Senado Federal. 2018. *Sancionada com veto lei que regulamenta produção de polpa e suco de frutas*. Accessed May 25, 2018. www12.senado.leg.br/noticias/materias/2018/04/12/sancionada-com-veto-lei-que-regulamenta-producao-de-polpa-e-suco-de-frutas/tablet.

Bruch, K., Vieira, A. and Buainain, A. M. 2015. "Uma análise acerca da construção da lei do vinho artesanal do Brasil." *Revista Brasileira de Direito do Agronegócio*, 8: 39–57.

Buainain, A. M. and Dedecca, C. S. 2010. "Mudanças e reiteração da heterogeneidade do mercado de trabalho agrícola." In: *A agricultura brasileira: desempenho, desafios e perspectivas*, edited by J. Gasques, J. Vieira Filho and Z. Navarro, 123–56. Brasília: IPEA.

Carneiro, M. J. and Maluf, R. 2003. *Para além da produção: multifuncionalidade e agricultura familiar*. Rio de Janeiro: Mauad.

Cervieri Júnior, O., Teixeira Júnior, J., Galinari, R., Rawet, E. and Silveira, C. 2014. "O setor de bebidas no Brasil." BNDES Setorial, 40: 93–130.

Champredonde, M. 2016. "A qualidade vinculada à origem: da imersão à tipicidade territorial." In: *O Sabor da Origem*, edited by J. Wilkinson, P. Niederle and G. Mascarenhas, 21–50. Porto Alegre: Escritos.

Ciel. 2018. *Ciel Alimentos*. Accessed April 15, 2018. www.cielalimentos.ind.br

Cintrão, R. 2016. *Segurança, qualidade e riscos: a regulação sanitária e os processos de (i)legalização dos queijos artesanais de leite cru em Minas Gerais*. PhD Thesis. Rio de Janeiro: UFRRJ.

Cruz, F. T. 2012. *Produtores, consumidores e valorização de produtos tradicionais: um estudo sobre qualidade de alimentos a partir do caso do Queijo Serrano dos Campos de Cima da Serra*. PhD Thesis. Porto Alegre: UFRGS.

Cruz, F. T. and Schneider, S. 2010. "Qualidade dos alimentos, escalas de produção e valorização de produtos tradicionais." *Revista Brasileira de Agroecologia*, 5(2).

Delgado, G. C. 2004. *O setor de subsistência na economia e na sociedade brasileira: gênese histórica, reprodução e configuração contemporânea*. Brasília: IPEA.

Dorigon, C. 2008. *Mercados de produtos coloniais da Região Oeste de Santa Catarina: em construção*. PhD Thesis. Rio de Janeiro: UFRJ.

Dorigon, C. and Renk, A. 2011. "Técnicas e métodos tradicionais de processamento de produtos coloniais: de "miudezas de colonos pobres" aos mercados de qualidade diferenciada." *Revista de Economia Agrícola*, 58(1): 101–113.

Fernandes Filho, J. F. and Campos, F. R. 2003. "A indústria rural no Brasil." *Revista de Economia e Sociologia Rural*, 41(4): 859–880.

Friedman, H. 1978. "World market, state, and family farm: Social bases of household production in the era of wage labor." *Comparative Studies in Society and History*, 20(4): 545–586.

Garcia, Jr., A. R. 1983. *Terra de trabalho: trabalho familiar de pequenos produtores*. Rio de Janeiro: Paz e Terra.

Gazolla, M. and Schneider, S. 2005. "As duas "caras" do PRONAF: produtivismo ou fortalecimento da produção para autoconsumo?" In *Proceedings of the 43 Brazilian Congress of Rural Economy and Sociology*. Brasília: SOBER.

Gewehr, B. 2019. *Qualidade lupulada: o significado de artesanal na rede cervejeira gaúcha*. Master Dissertation. Porto Alegre: UFRGS.

Giorgi, V. 2015. "Cultos em cerveja: discursos sobre a cerveja artesanal no Brasil." *Sociedade e Cultura*, 18(1): 101–11.

Globo. 2018. *Grandes cervejarias apostam em estratégia das artesanais*. Accessed May 22, 2018. www.oglobo.globo.com/economia/negocios/grandes-cervejarias-apostam-em-estrategia-das-artesanais-22543060.

Goodman, D. and Redcliff, M. 1985. "Capitalism, petty commodity production, and the farm enterprise." *Sociologia Ruralis*, 15(3): 231–47.

Grisa, C. and Schneider, S. 2008. "Plantar pro gasto: a importância do autoconsumo entre famílias de agricultores do Rio Grande do Sul." *Revista de Economia e Sociologia Rural*, 46(2): 481–515.

Grisa, C., Schneider, S. and Conterato, M. 2013. *A produção para autoconsumo no Brasil: uma análise a partir do Censo Agropecuário 2006*.Brasília: IPEA.

IBGE. 1924. *Censo Agropecuário*. Rio de Janeiro: IBGE.

IBGE. 2019. *Censo Agropecuário*. Rio de Janeiro: IBGE.

Kanematsu, L. 2017. Comparação entre alimentos industrializados com e sem terminologia de caseiro em relação aos aditivos alimentares. Master Dissertation. Florianópolis: UFSC.

Leite, S. 2004. "Autoconsumo y sustentabilidad en la agricultura familiar: una aproximación a la experiencia brasileña." In: *Políticas de seguridad alimentaria y nutrición en América Latina*, edited by W.Belik,123–81.São Paulo: Hucitec.

Maluf, R. S. 2001. "Políticas agrícolas e de desenvolvimento rural e a segurança alimentar." In: *Políticas Públicas e Agricultura no Brasil*, edited by S. Leite, 145–68. Porto Alegre: UFRGS.

Maluf, R. S. 2004. "Mercados agroalimentares e agricultura familiar no Brasil: agregação de valor, cadeias integradas e circuitos regionais." *Ensaios FEE*, 25(1): 299–322.

Mapa. 2019. *A Cerveja no Brasil*. Brasília: Ministério da Agricultura, Pecuária e Abastecimento.

Menasche, R. 2007. *A agricultura familiar à mesa: saberes e práticas da alimentação no Vale do Taquari*. Porto Alegre: UFRGS.

Menasche, R. (ed.). 2015. *Saberes e Sabores da Colônia: alimentação e cultura como abordagem para o estudo rural*. Porto Alegre: UFRGS.

Mendras, H. 1953.*Études de sociologie rurale*. Paris: Armand Colin.

Menezes, S. 2011. "Queijo artesanal: identidade, prática cultural e estratégia de reprodução social em países da América Latina." *Revista Geográfica de América Central*, 2: 1–16.

Mior, L. C. 2005. *Agricultura familiar, agroindústria e redes no desenvolvimento rural*. Chapecó: Argos.

Montar Um Negócio. 2016. *O lucrativo mundo das padarias artesanais*. Accessed July 17, 2016. www.comomontar.com.br/como-montar/o-lucrativo-mundo-das-padarias-artesanais.

New Trade. 2018. *Número de cervejarias no Brasil quase dobra em 3 anos e setor volta criar empregos*. Accessed January 31, 2018. www.newtrade.com.br/industria/numero-de-cervejarias-no-brasil-quase-dobra-em-3-anos-e-setor-volta-criar-empregos.

Nichele, F. S. and Waquil, P. D. 2011. "Agroindústria familiar rural, qualidade da produção artesanal e o enfoque da teoria das convenções." *Ciência Rural*, 41(12): 2230–35.

Niederle, P. and Wesz, Jr., V. 2009. "A agroindústria familiar na região Missões: construção de autonomia e diversificação dos meios de vida." *Redes*, 14(3): 75–102.

Niederle, P., Bruch, K., Vieira, A. and Schneider, E. 2016. "Vinhos do Brasil: a tipicidade territorial entre tradições e inovações." In: *Sabor da Origem*, edited by J. Wilkinson, P. Niederle and G. Mascarenhas, 161–212. Porto Alegre: Escritos.

Oliver, G. 2013. "Cerveja, gastronomia e criatividade." *Revista da Cerveja*, 4: 23.

Pelegrini, G. and Gazolla, M. 2008. *A agroindústria familiar no Rio Grande do Sul*. Frederico Westphalen, RS: URI.

Piato, M. S. and Révillion, J. 2014. "Restrições ao desenvolvimento das microcervejarias informais no Brasil." *Revista Acta Ambiental Catarinense*, 10(1): 7–18.

Ploeg, J. D. van der. 1990. *Labor, Markets, and Agricultural Production*. Boulder: Westview.

Ploeg, J. D. van der. 2003. *The Virtual Farmer*. Assen: Van Gorcum.

Ploeg, J. D. van der. 2006. "O modo de produção camponês revisitado." In *A diversidade da agricultura familiar*, edited by S. Schneider, 13–54.Porto Alegre: UFRGS.

Ploeg, J. D. van der. 2009. *The New Peasantries: Struggles for Autonomy and Sustainability in an Era of Empire and Globalization*. New York: Routledge.

Prado, Jr., C. 1979. *Formação do Brasil contemporâneo*. 16 ed. São Paulo: Brasiliense.

Prezotto, L. L. 2002. "Uma concepção de agroindústria rural de pequeno porte." *Revista de Ciências Humanas*, 31: 133–154.

Queiroz, M. I. 2009. "Uma categoria rural esquecida." In: *Camponeses brasileiros: leituras e interpretações clássicas*, edited by C. Welch, 57–72. São Paulo: UNESP.

Sabourin, E. 2009. *Camponeses do Brasil: entre a troca mercantil e a reciprocidade*. Rio de Janeiro: Garamond.

Sabourin, E. 2011. *Sociedades e organizações camponesas: uma leitura através da reciprocidade*. Porto Alegre: UFRGS.

Salais, R. and Storper, M. 1992. "The four worlds of contemporary industry". Cambridge *Journal of Economics*, 16: 169–93.

Sausen, J., Patias, I. A. and Allebrandt, S. 2011. "Desenvolvimento local e estratégia de pequenos empreendimentos agroindustriais – a lógica da cooperação e do associativismo: o Pacto Fonte Nova." *Cadernos EBAPE.BR*, 9(3): 868–94.

Schneider, S. and Ferrari, D. L. 2015. "Cadeias curtas, cooperação e produtos de qualidade na agricultura familiar – o processo de relocalização da produção agroalimentar em Santa Catarina." *Organizações Rurais & Agroindustriais*, 17(1): 56–71.

Silveira, R. and Heinz, C. 2005. Controle de qualidade normativo e qualidade ampla: princípios para re-estruturação e qualificação da produção artesanal de alimentos. In *Proceedings of International Congress of Rural Development and Familiar Agro-industry*. São Luiz Gonzaga, RS: UERGS.

SlowFood. 2015. *O que são queijos artesanais.* Accessed June 22, 2016. www.slowfoodbrasil.com/queijos-artesanais

SlowFood. 2017. *Mapas dos queijos artesanais.* Accessed November 22, 2019. www.queijocoalhobrasil.com/wp-content/uploads/2019/06/mapa-dos-queijos-artesanais-do-brasil-junho2019.jpg

Trentin, I. C. L. 2015. *Política pública Brasil Sin Miseria: ¿promoviendo la agroecología y el desarrollo en Rio Grande del Sur?* PhD Thesis. Medellin: Universidad de Antioquia.

Triches, R. 2010. *Reconectando a produção ao consumo: a aquisição de gêneros alimentícios da agricultura familiar para o programa de alimentação escolar.* PhD Thesis. Porto Alegre: UFRGS.

Verdi, A. R. 2006. "Dinâmicas e perspectivas do mercado da cachaça." *Informações Econômicas*, 36(2); 93–98.

Wanderley, M. N. 2003. "Agricultura familiar e campesinato: rupturas e continuidade." *Estudos Sociedade e Agricultura*, 21: 42–61.

Waquil, D. et al. 2013. *O perfil da agroindústria rural no Brasil: uma análise com base nos dados do Censo Agropecuário 2006.* Brasília: IPEA.

Wesz, Jr., V. 2009. *As políticas públicas de agroindustrialização na agricultura familiar – análise e avaliação da experiência brasileira.* Master Dissertation. Rio de Janeiro: UFRRJ.

Wesz, Jr., V. 2017. "A trajetória do Pronaf Agroindústria no Brasil (1998/99–2016/17): um olhar sobre as condições de financiamento e o público beneficiado." In *Questões agrárias, agrícolas e rurais*, edited by G. Flexor and R. Maluf, 112–23. Rio De Janeiro: E-papers.

Wesz, Jr., V., Trentin, I. and Filippi, E. 2009. "Os reflexos das agroindústrias familiares para o desenvolvimento das áreas rurais no Sul do Brasil." *Cuadernos de Desarrollo Rural*, 6(63): 59–85.

Wilkinson, J. 2002. "Sociologia econômica, a teoria das convenções e o funcionamento dos mercados: inputs para analisar os micro e pequenos empreendimentos agroindustriais no Brasil." *Ensaios FEE*, 23(2): 805–24.

Wilkinson, J. 2008. "Global value chains and networks in dialogue with consumption and social movements." *International Journal of Technological Learning, Innovation and Development*, 1: 536–57.

Wilkinson, J., Cerdan, C. and Dorigon, C. 2016. "Indicações geográficas e produtos de origem no Brasil: instituições e redes em ação recíproca." In *Sabor da Origem*, edited by J. Wilkinson, P. Niederle and G. Mascarenhas, 73–105.Porto Alegre: Escritos.

Wilkinson, J., Niederle, P. and Mascarenhas, G. (eds). 2016. *O Sabor da Origem.* Porto Alegre: Escritos.

Woortmann, E. and Woortmann, K. 1997. *O trabalho da terra: a lógica e a simbólica da lavoura camponesa.* Brasília: UnB.

5 Ethical criticism and the construction of a civic order

Obsession with productivity renders the industrial food order unable to recognize forms of production that represents the diverse cultural and eco- logical heritage of Brazilian rural world. The effects of making productivity a value that override any other kind of normative principle are varied. It has contributed, for example, to belittle a broader reflection on the "social function of land," since it privileged only productive aspects over the social and envir- onmental ones, which are also provided for in the Federal Constitution of 1988. Thus, despite its somewhat noble purposes (land reform in "unpro- ductive" areas), the discussion on productivity consolidated a perception of land (and, more broadly, of nature) as a commodity (Polanyi, 1957). This mis- representation is so strong that even some social movements that are critical of agricultural modernization reproduce the discourse of agricultural pro- duction as the only function of land, finding problem simply in its unequal distribution (Delgado, 2017).

The more radical contestation over this process converges to an "ethical criticism" against industrialization of agriculture. Besides questioning the social, environmental and even economic effects of productivity gains of modern agriculture, this criticism turns to the moral values that made this model the only one legitimized by the State and, to some extent, by society. A model that is unable to recognize the contribution of alternative farming systems and of the diverse social groups that inhabit rural areas to building a sustainable development path in which the promotion of sociobiodiversity (as a common good) holds a value as legitimate as that held by productivity in the industrial order.

Over the past two decades, such contestation made room for the emergence of alternative food networks. It can be verified in the proliferation of short circuits, street markets, consumer groups, decentralized associations and cooperatives, experiences of urban agriculture, local consumption and strat- egies of valorization of traditional food, which shape innovative rural devel- opmental trajectories (Gazolla and Schneider, 2017; Goodman, Dupuis and Goodman, 2012). In these new markets, more than differentiated goods, there are values in circulation, which stem from a political construction that brings together a set of social movements that increasingly direct their agendas towards the promotion of new food practices (Niederle, 2014; Picolotto, 2008). These practices emphasize new meanings for food and, more broadly, for the rural, which are associated with societal demands for equity, justice, social participation and sustainability.

The notion of "civic food networks" has been mobilized in the literature to characterize alternative markets that emerge from the engagement of civil society organizations, thus highlighting new conceptions of both food democracy and citizenship (Renting, Schermer and Rossi, 2012; Andre, 2019). According to Cucco and Fonte (2015), these markets "refer to the network of all actors involved in the local food system that, as ecological citizens, partake of the responsibility for the sustainability of the food economy and endorse the value of food as a commons and a right." In this perspective, the definition of a civic order puts collective action – particularly the political construction of markets by social movements and in dialogue with the State – at the forefront in defense of the "common goods" (land, ecological resources, cultural heritage etc.) and of food democracy (especially regarding access to healthy food) as normative pillars.

Building these markets involves both the daily efforts of farmers to create new forms of manage natural resources and the political action of economic social organizations and movements at different territorial scales, from local consumer groups to global networks such as Via Campesina and Slow Food. Although these markets express no more than a component of "alternativeness" in view of the prevalence of industrial and financial orders, they have become a relevant option for many social groups. Indeed, these markets may not be responsible for trade balance records, but, as we will discuss in this chapter, their dynamism seems even more impressive given their potential for turning common goods and productive inclusion of social segments on the fringes of progress into the basis for new models of sustainable development (Blay-Palmer et al., 2019; Marsden, 2016; Hebinck, Ploeg and Schneider, 2014; Lockie and Carpenter, 2010).

We will begin this chapter by discussing the struggle of smallholders for recognition and redistribution, which led to the emergence of the "family farming" category as a subject of rights in the Brazilian countryside. Next, we will analyze the political construction of civic markets by the agroecological social movements and, based on this, we will illustrate with the case of Ecovida Agroecology Network in creating markets and participatory certification processes. This is followed by the debate on the agenda of Food Sovereignty and Security (FSS) as one of the main contemporary expressions of an ethical movement aimed at reconfiguring agrifood systems and, within it, public procurement as an important State-led "redistribution" practice. Finally, we propose a discussion on the construction of new conventions of quality within food markets, emphasizing the notions of "healthy food" and "real food."

The struggle of family farmers for redistribution and recognition

The ethical criticism against the model of capitalist accumulation in agriculture that prevailed in the second half of the twentieth century emphasized the social exclusion. It was not a criticism over the ideology of progress per se, but rather over inequality in access to it. In Brazil, one of the targets of this criticism was the income concentration during the period of the "economic miracle." From 1974 to 1980, Brazil kept an average annual growth rate of about 7%, reaching 14% in 1973 and 10.3% in 1976. However, this growth was not accompanied by rising wages for the working class. On the contrary, to control inflation, the military government kept low wages by means of strong repression. As a result, inflation rate fell from 25.5% a year in 1968 to 15.6% in 1973, though social inequality soared. Whereas in 1960, before the military dictatorship, the Gini Index, used to measure income concentration, was 0.54, in 1977, it had advanced to 0.63 (Soldera, 2017).

This growth regime faced its first setback with the international crisis of 1973. Conflicts between OPEC member countries cut down the oil supply, tripling its price. A new shock in the late 1970s, this time mainly related to the Islamic rebellion in Iran, and the debt crisis in the early 1980s represented the *coup de grâce* for a growth model sustained by widespread availability of cheap credit and oil. Even so, Brazilian military governments, trying to maintain growth and not lose political power, rather than controlling spending, accelerated it, thus escalating the country's debt level. When the military left power in 1984, they left a public debt that represented 54% of GDP, four times greater than that of 1964 (15.7%). Inflation, in turn, reached 223% in 1985 and, despite numerous economic recovery plans of Jose Sarney's government, it continued to worsen, reaching 1,782% in 1989. In short, from a purely economic point of view, debt and inflation comprised the "damn legacies" left by military governments (Schwarcz and Starling, 2015).

The crisis had a strong impact on agricultural modernization policies. Plentiful and highly subsidized credit was gradually reduced throughout the 1980s until reaching, in 1990, a total (US$7.9 billion) lower than that available in 1970 (US$8.2 billion). At its peak, in 1979, it had reached US$34.9 billion. The same occurred to the policy of price guarantee. While, from 1975 to 1979, for example, 61% of cotton production was secured by state loans, in 1990 this percentage fell to 15.9%. Agricultural research and rural extension systems have also been disrupted. Under pressure from the IMF, the government began to implement the neoliberal doctrine of fiscal adjustment, which meant a shrinking of the public structure and the gradual transfer of responsibilities from the state to the private sector. In the case of rural credit, for instance, the funds from the National Treasury, which accounted for 65% of the total credit available in 1985, were replaced by other sources of financing. In 1997, 45% of the funds already came from bank liabilities, while the treasury contributed only 1.5% (Leite, 2001).

The crisis of the compulsory modernization model, however, did not represent the end of inequality. On the contrary: the large commodity producers promptly renegotiated their debts with the state and sought new sources of financing, including private securities traded on stock markets. They also sought support from cooperatives and agricultural companies, which began to offer credit, technical assistance and agricultural inputs. Meanwhile, smallholders began to experience the hardships of a completely absent state and faced with an abrupt process of trade liberalization. This process became a great opportunity for the exporting agro-industrial sectors to leverage their comparative advantages in global commodity chains. However, this has come at the cost of endangering local agrarian systems and small family farmers' production, which has been exposed to competition from more structured foreign producers. Many farmers and cooperatives that in previous decades had survived thanks to domestic market protection were suddenly exposed to adverse economic conditions, being unable to compete with producers that benefited from larger-scale production and lower costs, and that had easy access to modern technologies and to markets.

Although in all Mercosur countries producers felt the effects of trade liberalization, it was initially among small farmers in southern Brazil that the consequences of liberal policies were most evident. At least, this was the region that became the epicenter of several mobilizations claiming specific policies for smallholders and that, over time, gave rise to a new sociopolitical category in the Brazilian countryside: the family farmers (Grisa and Schneider, 2015; Picolotto, 2014). To this end, the traditional movements that struggled for land, established in previous decades, were joined by new union movements, whose demands were mainly focused on differentiated credit lines, agricultural insurance, rural social security, price guarantee, rural extension programs and rural settlements for landless rural workers. Initially episodic, these claims grew into ever larger demonstrations, leading to the 1994 *Grito da Terra Brasil* (Cry of the Land Brasil), led by the National Confederation of Agricultural Workers (CONTAG), and, from that, to the creation of the National Program for Strengthening Family Agriculture – PRONAF, in 1996.

The creation of PRONAF was the beginning of the trajectory of public policies for family farming in Brazil (Table 5.1). The creation of the Ministry of Agrarian Development (MDA), in 1999, affirmed the struggles for family farming's recognition, increasing visibility and legitimacy vis-à-vis the society and the state. As of 2003, the political reconfiguration engendered by the election of President Lula gave a fundamental boost to this trajectory (Grisa and Schneider, 2015; Niederle et al., 2019). In addition to PRONAF and other agrarian and agricultural policies (e.g., Agrarian Reform National Plan – PNRA; National Policy of Technical Assistance and Rural Extension PNATER), a new generation of policies was created focusing issues such as territorial development (Support for Sustainable Development for Rural Territories – PRONAT), agroecology (National Policy

Table 5.1 Main public policies for family farming in Brazil

Public policy	Year	Description	Situation in December 2019
PRONAF – National Program for Strengthening Family Agriculture	1996	The most important in terms of resources allocated, PRONAF is a credit program financing family farming productive modernization with highly subsided interest rates.	After Dilma Roussef's impeachment, PRONAF lost a part of its resources and the interest rates became higher. Yet, this is almost the only program with expressive financial resources. It is still more concentrated in the most capitalized family farmers.
PNRA – Agrarian Reform National Plan	2003	The second national plan for agrarian reform embraced land acquisition programs, support to settlements, and legal regularization of land irregularly occupied by small farmers.	Most part of the resources was applied in the improvement of the previously established rural settlements or in land property rights regularization. Since Jair Bolsonaro came to the presidency, in 2019, however, all actions of agrarian reform have been completely blocked.
PNATER – National Policy of Technical Assistance and Rural Extension	2004	This policy embraces several programs of rural extension focusing different segments of family farming, rural settlers, indigenous and traditional communities	Resources for rural extension have been strongly reduced since 2015. While some programs still support very specific productive activities, technical and social assistance for indigenous and traditional communities were practically abandoned.
PRONAT – Support for sustainable development for rural territories	2003	This program supported the construction of initiatives of territorial development such as collective infrastructures and projects of State in partnership with civil society organizations.	This program was ended after the political rupture that replaced president Dilma Roussef. Since then, all discussions about territorial development were removed from the governmental agenda.
PAA – Food Acquisition Programme	2003	Public procurement initiative that buys food from family farmers to feed people in situation of social vulnerability. It is considered one of the most innovative policies for food security.	Even though it has never been very expressive in terms of resources, this program was strongly criticized by liberal politicians and agribusiness corporations because of the way it legitimated State intervention in food markets. Because of that, it is now almost completely paralyzed.

(*continued*)

Table 5.1 Continued

Public policy	Year	Description	Situation in December 2019
PNAE – National School Feeding Programme	2009	After passing the Law n. 11.947, Brazilian State was obliged to spend at least 30% of the resources of the School Feeding Programme with acquisition of foods from family farmers.	Considering this program has a law as an enforcement institutional mechanism, it is still among those are operating without substantial changes. However, in most part of cases, there is no more the State stimulus to go beyond the 30%. Besides, some actors started to question the exclusivity of family farmers in the program.
PNAPO – National Policy on Agroecology and Organic Production	2012	This policy oriented the National Plan on Agroecology and Organic Production (Planapo), which articulated more than one hundred different actions offered by several government agencies.	Some programs that integrated the Planapo are still operating, but the most part of the actions were interrupted by the government after 2019. While still very present in the discourses of social movements, agroecology is no longer a meaningful reference for the action of the national government.

Source: Elaborated by the authors.

on Agroecology and Organic Production – PNAPO) and food security and nutrition (Food Acquisition Programme – PAA; National School Feeding Programme – PNAE)

Claims for redistribution soon coupled with struggles for recognition which were based, more than on economic inequality, on the perception of disrespect and contempt for the small producers (Fraser and Honneth, 2003). As Picolotto (2014) points out, at that moment, the social movements and trade unions began to lead processes for giving shape to "family farming," which sought to socially legitimize itself as a "subject of rights." In the context of the inflationary crisis and urban-industrial unemployment of the 1990s, the first justification mobilized was the ability of this social segment to produce food and absorb labor. Through this struggle, the old subsistence agriculture was resignified as "the hands that feed the nation" (Picolotto, 2014). As José Graziano da Silva, FAO's president, pointed out during the celebrations of the 2014 International Year of Family Farming, "where family farming was deemed as a problem, it is now seen as part of the solution" (FAO, 2014).

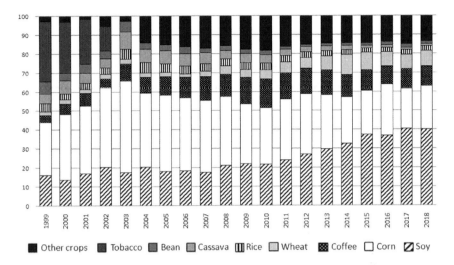

Figure 5.1 Percentage of resources of the PRONAF applied in different cropping systems from 1999 to 2018 in Brazil.

Nevertheless, the prevalence of a modernization logic even within distinct rural development policies has, over time, widened the asymmetries within family farm itself (Aquino and Schneider, 2015). Seeking to demonstrate that "modern family farming" could either replace or complement agribusiness and provide the basis for a new cycle of economic development in rural areas, policies such as the PRONAF favored those family farmers who were already established and integrated into commodity markets, counting on better technological resources (Grisa, Wesz, Jr. and Buchweitz, 2014). That is, these policies contributed to make part of the family farming functional to the industrial and financial orders. This functionality has become the target of criticism over rural development policies from important social movements, especially those related to agroecology and food security. In this regard, PRONAF has been pointed out as a program with this type of negative externality, since it concentrates resources on crops such as maize, soybeans and coffee, encouraging productive specialization (Figure 5.1).

The approach of family farming to the industrial order has been the subject of intense debates, insofar as it endangers the legitimacy of the struggles for redistribution and recognition of this social category. Some researchers, including us, suggest that maintaining this legitimacy requires the ability to meet new civic (and aesthetic) aspirations of contemporary societies. That is, the ability to demonstrate, beyond economic contribution, that family farming is responsible for producing "real food"– and not food alone, but food associated with other cultural expressions, knowledge, values and ways of life. More than a production sector, family farming must legitimize itself as a "way of life" (Wanderley, 2000). This is why some family farming social movements begun to discuss the place of this social segment within food markets: What to produce? How to process? Where to sell the products? For what consumers? While answering these questions, these movements demand public policies that more than enabling the necessary food production and absorbing labor, pay equal attention to social demands for health, sustainability, diversity and equity.

As we will see later in this chapter, these issues underlie the debates on FSS and the creation of public procurement programs. We will also see that strengthening these new demands makes room for different modes of family farming. While the emphasis on the productive capacity of a modernized family farming has deepened social asymmetries, the recognition of a wide range of "traditional communities" catalyzes the emergence of new, more sustainable and inclusive rural development strategies. Central to this process is the gradual and controversial incorporation of the environmental issue into the agenda of family farming social movements (Picolotto and Brandenburg, 2013).

The construction of civic markets by agroecological movements

While criticism from agrarian social movements has privileged the problem of inequality in access to resources (especially to land and credit), that from agroecological movements has always been more radical in questioning the institutional foundations of the industrial order. Over time, the legitimation of this criticism has brought agrarian social movements closer to agroecology. The Landless Movement (MST) adopted it as a guiding principle in 2000. Two years later, the creation of ANA (National Articulation of Agroecology) expanded this convergence to other movements and organizations, such as CONTAG (National Confederation of Agricultural Workers) and FETRAF (National Federation of Family Farm Workers). Therewith, agroecology became one of the main normative bases for the actions of these actors (Lamine, Niederle and Ollivier, 2019; Picolotto and Brandenburg, 2013).

In Brazil, agroecology emerged from a set of practices that, situated on the periphery of agricultural modernization processes – and precisely for this marginal position – have managed to boost innovative forms of production, marketing and consumption. One of the main focuses of these practices is the reconnection between humans and the environment and, concerning the sphere of markets, between producers and consumers. This reconnection is not just spatial (relocation), but also involves the collective appropriation of the values and imaginaries that define agroecological foods. Based on principles of reciprocity, solidarity and communality, these practices demonstrate that economic exchanges can incorporate logics that transcend the utilitarian interest (Sabourin, 2011). One of the spaces where it is most evident is the farmers' markets.

In 2012, a survey conducted by the Brazilian Institute of Consumer Protection (IDEC) identified 140 organic and agroecological farmers' markets in 22 out of the 27 Brazilian state capitals. By November 2019, there were nearly 900 such initiatives spread across the country (IDEC, 2018). For agroecological organizations, these markets are a kind of hub for a wider range of new markets. It is often from these that farmers begin to build mechanisms for direct selling to consumers through the delivery of food baskets, as well as to establish contact with shops and restaurants that become regular buyers. Moreover, besides exchange of products, these farmers' markets are also a place where information and knowledge are exchanged and where agroecological movements develop their political connections. They serve as a means to convey values and principles to visitors, playing a crucial role in promoting agroecology in the public arena (Niederle and Radomsky, 2017; Lamine, 2020).

Another circuit based on similar principles and that is also expanding is one structured around consumer groups. Spread across the world taking different organizational formats, these groups share the goal of securing income for farmers in exchange for regular food supplies. In general, their actions include "politicized" or "reflexive" consumption practices (Michelletti, 2003).[1] However, compared to other countries such as France, Japan, the United States and Canada, the practice of collective purchasing is still incipient in Brazil. In 2014, Preiss (2017) identified 46 such initiatives in 33 Brazilian cities. However, as the author points out in her thesis on the various formats of collective purchasing practices, there are no consistent surveys on these practices, and they can probably be much more relevant than we guess.

According to Preiss (2017), among the common characteristics of consumer groups, the following stand out: the priority given to family farmers as suppliers; the preference for locally produced and agroecological foods; the use of online tools to place orders; and the possibility of a closer relationship between consumers and producers as their key motivation. In addition, "consumer engagement is justified on the grounds of health concerns and of desire to contribute to a different food system" (Preiss, 2017, 51). To this end, besides food supply these groups organize spaces for integration between participants (shared meals, visits to farmers and celebration of special occasions) and for sharing knowledge about food and cooking practices (cooking workshops, lectures and debates on consumption and production). "Most of these experiences were also integrated into networks and partnerships with a variety of institutions, such as schools, universities, research institutes, churches, non-governmental organizations, social movements and foundations" (ibid., 51).

The organization of more democratic food supply systems is also a feature of the Peasant Programme proposed by the Small Farmers Movement (MPA), which is a member of the Via Campesina. This program not only points to agricultural strategies for production of healthy food and for quality of life in the countryside, but also to the need to promote new consumption circuits. One of its central proposals concerns the structuring of small food supply units that gathers the food and redistribute it to families, soup kitchens, small grocery shops and government acquisition programs. The Plan also proposes a direct sale circuit of food baskets that, on the one hand, promotes the production of land reform settlements and, on the other hand, facilitates the purchase of food by consumers organized around urban union movements. The main novelty of the Plan is the attempt to connect rural and urban movements, aiming to make food a means of mediation between the countryside and the city, peasants and workers.

Building these markets requires considerable social engineering. To overcome the scarcity of transport and storage infrastructures that affects most farmers and associations, agroecological movements had to innovate in distribution practices. By actively involving farmers and consumers in this process, they created circuits that ultimately proved to be more efficient than the centralized distribution systems that prevail in Brazil, not only because they reduce operating costs, but also for enabling lower levels of food loss and waste (Belik and Cunha, 2015). An example in this regard is that of the Ecovida Agroecology Network. Established in 1998, through an articulation between various ecological farming organizations in southern Brazil, whose trajectories date back to the protests over the Green Revolution of the 1970s and 1980s, this network focuses on the promotion of agroecological transition based on participatory processes (Brandenburg, 2008). To this end, groups and hubs are articulated according to territorial proximity, usually encompassing a community within the same municipality, although not limited to the strict official boundaries. The connection between the groups also involves a coordinating entity – cooperative, association or NGO – responsible for the interaction between farmers, technicians and consumers. The network is currently comprised of 30 regional nucleus covering 300 farmer groups in about 170 municipalities, 130 small-scale food processing facilities, 35 NGOs and 8 consumer cooperatives (Lamine, 2020; Ploeg, Jingzhong and Schneider, 2012; Radomsky, Niederle and Schneider, 2014).

Network organization and territorial embeddedness allow Ecovida to maintain a dynamics of information and knowledge exchange that is fundamental for the agroecological transition and for the interaction *within* and *between* markets. In 2019, Ecovida held more than 250 farmers' markets, distributed in about 70 municipalities. In addition, Ecovida's farmers also use various other circuits, including more conventional ones such as large supermarket chains (Figure 5.1). The choice of one circuit over another depends on several factors such as preestablished contractual obligations, price variation and quantity demanded. In the case of proximity markets and short circuits, their development often depends on the ability to integrate two or more circuits, what allows for reducing logistics costs. Thus, for example, deliveries to restaurants are made on the same day of the farmers' market, to avoid the need to travel twice to the city, which would also mean losing time of farming.

In fact, Ecovida does not produce or sell any product. Farmers, associations and cooperatives have their own marketing structures that assume three main

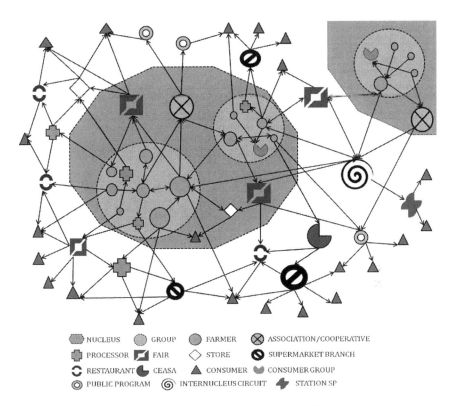

Figure 5.2 Marketing circuits of the Ecovida Agroecology Network.

organizational forms (Figure 5.2). In the first and most frequent case, each farmer distributes his/her own products individually (including exchanges with other farmers) and Ecovida only facilitates the connection between sellers and buyers. In the second form, a "group" of farmers organizes the distribution so that one farmer transports the products of the whole group. In the case of farmers' markets, for example, one or two farmers may be chosen by the group to undertake marketing activities. Finally, associations and cooperatives can manage small storage and distribution facilities. In this case, the most important circuits are public acquisition programs, which are usually accessed by means of a collective organization. These different modes of operation are often combined.

One of the most important innovations of Ecovida is an internucleus circuit for food distribution and marketing. The Southern Circuit (*Circuito Sul*) consists of eight distribution routes through which food is exchanged between groups and nucleuses (Figure 5.3). The main objective is to provide greater diversity of products for farmers and associations to supply different markets. Basic operation involves farmers' participation in the collection and delivery

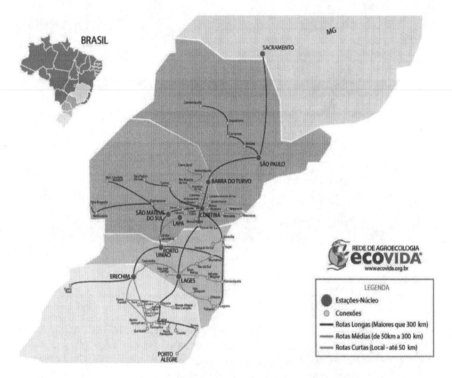

Figure 5.3 Ecovida network circuit for food distribution and marketing.

of products *from* and *to* different groups and nucleus. Thus, the same truck (owned by a farmer) that takes the bananas from Cooperafloresta (Paraná) to the farmers of Ecocitrus (Rio Grande do Sul) who will sell the product at the Porto Alegre farmers' market returns with the oranges of the latter, which will be delivered by Cooperafloresta to school meals in Curitiba. Exchanges take place in some association or cooperative, directly at the farmers' homes, or even at the roadside.

A set of rules and principles organize the distribution practices of the Ecovida Network: (a) the circuit has neither infrastructure nor legal personality; (b) priority is given to intranetwork circulation aiming at increasing food security (quantity, quality and diversity) for Ecovida members; (c) priority (but not exclusivity) is given to Ecovida certified products (see below); (d) those who sell must also buy (it is not possible for a group or nucleus just to offer products); (e) by adopting a fair trade logic, prices do not necessarily follow market volatility, which implies that a farmer may exit the circuit if he/she opportunistically decides to sell his/her products to the occasionally more lucrative market. Given these rules and principles, one can imagine that economic gain would be a secondary objective for farmers. However, the issue is far more complex. While the example of Ecovida suggests the embeddedness of economic action in a complex web of social relations, we are still talking about economic action, in which actors weigh utilitarian values as profit, and other social values like participation in a community.

One of the great challenges of Ecovida and other similar experiences of political market-building is to operate a continuous mediation between the civic principles of the social movement and the self-interest, calculability and instrumentality that are also present (though not exclusively) in economic action of individuals and organizations (Caliskan and Callon, 2009). One example in this regard is the almost continuous and unsolvable debate over price formation. While some actors argue that Ecovida should have a stronger regulatory role, setting a similar price for the same product in all regions, the currently prevailing view favors a more flexible coordination. In general, all price negotiations are made directly between farmers and consumers. Whereas this enhances the possibility for individualist logics, it is argued that it is impossible to disregard the different relations between supply and demand in each region. According to that perspective, it would be unrealistic to expect a farmer in the metropolitan region of Florianópolis, close to consumers with higher purchasing power, to apply the same price that most farmers use in small towns. In other words, the "fair price" would necessarily be distinct from one social context to another.

In fact, farmers, as individual actors, and Ecovida, as a collective social actor, move between different orders and deal with different principles. Even practices may lie in a zone where distinct social orders overlap. The practice of pricing a product is one of the most debated in contemporary economic sociology. Beckert (2011), Boltanski and Thévenot (1991) and Beckert and Aspers (2011) are among those who argue for the existence of different value regimes, each supported by distinct conceptions of justice. Based on this understanding, it can be said that, in the civic order, the attribution of price to a product involves an idea of justice that requires to consider the social conditions of the actors involved in a transaction (sometimes even individually), rather than ensuring the highest possible profit. Evidently, not all farmers of the Ecovida Network act accordingly and, strictly speaking, the same farmer takes on very different conceptions of justice when negotiating prices with an old customer of the local market or a supermarket manager.

Marketing at a local market also cannot be understood per se as a guarantee of civic values. Such markets are frequently appropriated by intermediaries not related to collective movements or committed to common goods. In this case, local markets serve as channels very similar to conventional markets. Various authors draw attention to this misconception of confusing locality with justice and democracy (Hinrichs, 2000). According to Goodman, Dupuis and Goodman (2012, 16), "we have to move away from the idea that food systems become just simply by virtue of making them local and toward a conversation about the work needed to make them more just." Local markets can hold profoundly unfair and conservative practices that accentuate social inequality. Therefore, what situates practices in a civic order is not the place where they develop, but the principles that guide them and, pragmatically, the effects they produce in terms of social and environmental justice. In this sense, some long-distance markets structured around the notion of fair trade may be as much or even more relevant than local markets as spaces that promote these practices and principles.

Participatory certification as a civic practice

In 2009, the informal organization established by the Ecovida Agroecology Network was formalized as the Ecovida Participatory Certification Association, which started to directly operate assessing the conformity of products to organic quality standard. As a result, Ecovida is now also the leading body for participatory assessment of organic production in Brazil, and one of the most recognized worldwide. By November 2019, 4,300 farmers were eligible to use its seal, what represents 63% of the 6,800 Brazilian farmers using this certification (and 21% of the 20,390 who followed some type of control for organic products in the same year). Just by way of comparison to show the expansion of Ecovida, two years earlier, in 2017, there were 2,500 farmers out of a total of 15,000 that held some type of control, or about 15%.

The creation of this mechanism stemmed from the institutionalization of the organic market in Brazil. One of the initial milestones of this process was the attempt by the Brazilian government, as of the 1990s, to establish a set of norms and standards to meet the requirements of the European market while keeping in line with the normative framework defined by World Trade Organization. To this end, in 1995, the Ministry of Agriculture created the CNPO (National Committee of Organic Products). Formed mainly by government officials and technical experts, this committee produced a first normative framework, published in 1998 (Ordinance No. 505/1998) and then submitted to public deliberation. The discussion of this milestone resulted in the Normative Act 07/1999, which defined organic production. However, as it did not define certification mechanisms, its capacity for market coordination was limited.

Most social organizations involved with agroecology opposed both the institutionalization and the certification of organic food. According to them, as agroecology comprises a complex process of transition towards more sustainable food systems, it is impossible to synthesize its various aspects into a seal. In other words, certification of organic products would not only be unable to recognize the different levels of agroecological transition (from the simple replacement of synthetic chemical inputs with organic ones to the complete restructuring of the entire territory) but also would not be able to encompass the nonproductive dimensions of this process, that is, the ethical, social and cultural elements that define the agroecological movement. These criticisms were at the heart of the debates that opposed supporters of agroecology and those of organic production (Petersen, Mussoi and Dal Soglio, 2013).

As institutionalization proved an inescapable avenue, agroecological organizations sought to create alternatives to reduce the risk of small family farmers being excluded from the new rising market (Lamine, Niederle and Ollivier, 2019). The repertoire of actions of the agroecological movement moved from social criticism to the production of institutional novelties, including participatory certification schemes. Another effort in this direction involved a symbolic dimension. Even though the technomercantile logic of organic agriculture has ultimately prevailed in legislation, becoming the only designation officially recognized, the social movements managed to guarantee the possibility of using associated terms, such as ecological, biodynamic, natural, regenerative, biological and agroecological (provided that the rules for organic production are met). A very common practice today, these alternative designations allow farmers to handle different meanings so that to ascribe distinctive values to their products.

Building participatory certification was a highly contentious process. Acceptance of a guarantee system other than the conventional external audit was surrounded by disagreement. Many technical experts and companies accused social movements of promoting a supposedly weak system of control that would discredit Brazilian organic production in international markets. Considering the lobbying power of these actors over MAPA, the alternative mechanisms were admitted just because, at that time, agroecological movements were not only important actors in this social field, but also, since 2003, they enjoyed greater support from state actors, especially from the MDA (Ministry of Agrarian Development). These movements took advantage of the window of opportunity opened by Lula's election in 2002, which allowed them to strengthen their discourses and positions in public spaces and, thereby, to influence the construction of the institutional arrangement (Schmitt et al., 2017).

Although the Law of Organic Products (Law No. 10831/2003) was enacted in the first year of the Lula Government – carrying parameters quite similar to those of the Normative Act 07/1999 – it was only in 2007 that Decree No. 6323 regulated its implementation, establishing more precise norms for production and marketing, especially regarding the creation of the Brazilian Organic Conformity Assessment System (SISOrg). It means that between the law and the decree, it took four years of intense negotiation to reach a normative framework able to serve the interests of different actors (Niederle and Almeida, 2013). To this end, the Decree made adjustments that relaxed the previous rule. For example: while the Normative Act 07/1999 established fixed periods for "conversion" of the farms to organic production systems (12 and 18 months for annual and perennial crops, respectively), Art. 6 of the Decree stipulated that "the conversion period will vary according to the type of exploration and the previous use of the land, considering the current social and environmental situation" and that "the activities to be developed during the conversion period should be established in the organic system plan of the production unit." This wording was reached after a long debate that reflected conceptual and political differences about the processes of agroecological "conversion" (which suggests a rupture) and "transition" (gradual adaptation).

Nonetheless, the main merit of Decree No. 6323 was the regulation of the three currently accepted organic conformity assessment mechanisms. First, the one used worldwide, which is based on external auditing and transfers control to a public or private third-party body. Second, the Participatory Guarantee Systems (PGS), in which the control is exercised by a legal entity that resorts to the direct participation of farmers and, less often, consumers, in the monitoring and evaluation processes. This is the case of Ecovida. Finally, the decree also provided for the existence of Social Monitoring Organizations, which can attest the organic quality of products from family farming, which are intended exclusively for direct sale to consumers. Like participatory certification, this has become an important civic mechanism. By November 2019, 4,736 family farmers were eligible to use it in Brazil.

In the case of Ecovida, the participatory certification process operates according to three levels of control. The first level occurs in the own family production unit. The second involves the community responsibility, so that the whole group can lose the right to certification if any irregularity is verified in a single farm and not reported to the Network coordination structures. Finally, the third level consists of the "external observation," that is, the inspection of production units by farmers from other groups (usually from the same nucleus), who are responsible for analyzing not only the compliance with the official standards for organic production but also the conformity of the practices with the principles of the Ecovida Network. This is one of the reasons why community (group) and territorial (nucleus) scales are so important to Ecovida.

Participatory certification comprises a civic practice in at least two senses. First, because it was built as an alternative for the inclusion of family farmers into the organic food market, since they otherwise would be unable to afford the audited certification. It should be noted that, in the case of Ecovida, the cost incurred by farmers with certification basically refers to travel and food expenses of farmers responsible for the "external observation." Second, because the very operation of participatory certification presupposes collective engagement in the process, including breaking with the asymmetry between the expert knowledge of the appraiser and the farmers' knowledge, which characterizes the third-part auditory. In participatory certification, everyone is coresponsible for the process.

Each certification system has a relatively specific logic, which is expressed by the different rules, practices, actors and artifacts. This entails a differentiation regarding both the trajectory of certified products and the values that they carry along their social trajectories. Generally, products certified by external audit are demanded by supermarkets and processing companies, which are primarily interested in meeting the technical standards required by legislation. Otherwise, foods that undergo participatory certification are more recurrent in alternative networks that operate as more direct inter-mediaries between producers and consumers. However, due to the increased demand for organic products, these logics have often overlapped. Actors and artifacts have increasingly crossed borders, creating contradictory dynamics and making room for social criticism. A prime example is the gradual entry of products carrying participatory certification into the shelves of the lar-gest transnational retail conglomerates (Niederle and Marques, 2016). While some actors argue that this practice further legitimates participatory certifi-cation, proving that it is as safe as third-part auditory, others see in it a new expression of "conventionalization." According to this argument, besides the appropriation of the ethical values of the agroecological movement by supermarkets, these latter continue to require standards of scale and quality that force farmers to productive specialization (cf. Chapter 2). In the same vein, the association of the agroecological product with artifacts character-istic of the industrial order, such as plastic packaging, is noteworthy.

Right to food, food security and public procurement

One of the most striking criticisms over the industrial food order is that, des-pite promoting the growth of world agricultural production, it was unable to overcome the problem of hunger. Not even the continued incorporation of thousands of hectares into the new agricultural frontiers suggests that the problem will come to be solved. On the contrary, with the advance of the financial order, this problem will probably be aggravated. One cause, as we will see in Chapter 7, is the increasing volatility of food prices in global markets (Belik and Correa, 2013; Speranza and Kato, 2017). According to FAO data, between 2010 and 2011, one of the moments when this phenomenon was most evident, 70 million people crossed the poverty line towards absolute misery worldwide (Maluf, 2017). Coupled with this, there is also an expansion of food waste, as a result of the supply model built under the auspices of the industrial and financial orders. In another report, FAO (2015) estimated that 1.3 billion tons of food is wasted each year worldwide, which corresponds to one-third of all that is produced, and which could feed 2 billion people (i.e., more than enough to end hunger on the planet).

The issue of food waste has been gaining traction in the agenda of different governments, companies, social movements and NGOs. In several countries, it is already possible to identify practices aimed at reducing this problem. In France, the Intermarché supermarket chain has launched a marketing strategy focused on "ugly fruits and vegetables." The intention is to stimulate the consumption of foods that do not have the aesthetic standard established by the industrial order, but which, even so, have no less nutritional value or cause any health problems. The same practice was adopted by the Canadian company Loblaw, whose brand is called "Naturally Imperfect." Portugal also has experiences focused on the revaluation of this type of "imperfect" product. In Brazil, similar initiatives that could be related to the Ugly Produce

Movement are found, for example, in the strategy used by the online store *Fruta Imperfeita*, a website that receives orders and delivers baskets of fruits and vegetables in the city of São Paulo. The baskets are assembled with aesthetically imperfect products, purchased directly from farmers and delivered to consumers at home. Another initiative is the Food Banks created by non-profit organizations, based on voluntary work, to receive food donations, recover surpluses, assess quality and redistribute the food to charities that attend socially vulnerable people (Belik, Cunha and Costa, 2012).

However, despite the relevance of these actions, one of the main limits to the development of such practices in Brazil is the rules that, based on an industrial safety concern, inhibit food donation. While countries such as France and Italy are advancing legislation that prohibits food waste, forcing large retail establishments to sign contracts with charities for donation of leftovers, in Brazil there are few supermarkets or restaurants that risk donating food, for they fear being fined. In fact, Brazil has been walking the wrong way regarding this concern with food waste. A prime example is the proliferation of all-you-can-eat buffets. If per kilo restaurants were once a fantastic innovation to massify food consumption away from home, now the chance of paying a lump sum and eat as much as you want (or can) has become the individual happiness of many and the collective torment of a few concerned with the effects of this practice in terms of public health and sustainable development. Besides generating a huge food waste, it encourages excessive consumption of processed, hypercaloric and nutritionally "empty" foods.

On the grounds of fighting hunger and food shortages, the industrial order encouraged a consumption model that has sparked a public health crisis, given the alarming indicators of obesity, diabetes, hypertension and a wide range of associated diseases. In 2016, one-fifth of the world's population was considered obese. In Brazil, in the last 10 years, obesity has increased by 60%. Diabetes, in turn, has quadrupled in the last three decades worldwide, from 108 million people in 1980 to 422 million in 2014. Currently, more than 16 million adult Brazilians suffer from the disease. Along the same line is the association between the rising of cancer cases and the use of pesticides in food (Abrasco, 2015). Over the last decade, Brazil has not only become the world's largest consumer of pesticides, but also the eighth largest world market for medicines (while in 2011, the sector's turnover in Brazil was R$38 billion, in 2016 it reached R$64 billion and, in 2017, projections pointed to R$85 billion) (Anvisa, 2017).

The point of convergence of various movements criticizing the industrial order is the recognition of the Human Right to Adequate Food (HRAF) and, based on that, the principles of Food Sovereignty and Security (FSS). Article 25 of the Universal Declaration of Human Rights adopted by the United Nations in 1948 provides for the HRAF. Nevertheless, in Brazil, only in 2010 a broad process of social mobilization succeeded in accomplishing Constitutional Amendment No. 64 that includes in Article 6 of the Federal Constitution the right to food. As food becomes a right, the state must guarantee access to it by means of public policies. Actions and policies aimed at Food and Nutrition Security, thus, consist in fulfilling this right. According to Law No. 11.346/2006, which created the National Food and Nutrition Security System (SISAN), food and nutrition security is the fulfilment of the right of all to regular and permanent access to sufficient quality food, based on health-promoting dietary practices that consider cultural diversity and are environmentally, culturally, economically and socially sustainable.

Additionally or alternatively to the concept of food security, various social movements and organizations, most of them members of the Brazilian Forum on Food and Nutrition Sovereignty and Security (FBSSAN) created in 1998, have incorporated the notion of food sovereignty, which emphasizes the right of countries and territories to autonomously define their own policies and strategies to ensure food for their populations, considering the cultural specificities of each social group. After a broad debate in civil society, mainly led by Via Campesina, this definition was ratified by the 2001 World Forum on Food Sovereignty held in Havana. The Forum has defined food sovereignty as

> the peoples' right to define their own policies and strategies for the sustainable production, distribution and consumption of food that guarantee the right to food for the entire population, on the basis of small and medium-sized production, respecting their own cultures and the diversity of peasant, fishing and indigenous forms of agricultural production, marketing and management of rural areas, in which women play a fundamental role ... Food sovereignty is the means to eradicate hunger and malnutrition and to guarantee lasting and sustainable food security for all of the peoples.
>
> (World Forum on Food Sovereignty, 2001)

The civic principles that underpin the right to adequate food guided the formulation of public policies by the National Council for Food and Nutrition Security (CONSEA). Created in 1993, during the government of Itamar Franco, CONSEA was extinguished by Fernando Henrique Cardoso administration, recreated in 2003 in the first year of the Lula government and again extinguished in 2019, by President Jair Bolsonaro. Among other incumbencies, the Council was responsible for setting the guidelines of the National Food and Nutrition Security Policy and Plan, based on the deliberations of the National Food and Nutrition Security Conferences. It was within this public forum, composed of state and civil society actors, that some of the most innovative practices in terms of promoting food democracy were produced. Among them are the public food procurement privileging family farming, especially the Food Acquisition Program (PAA), created in 2003, and the National School Feeding Program (PNAE), reformulated in 2009. Both exemplify the importance of "redistribution" as a principle of social integration.

At different times in history, the Brazilian state has acted towards redistribution by means of food purchasing policies (Menezes, Porto and Grisa, 2015).
The innovation pioneered by PAA and PNAE lies in the way these purchases
involve civil society participation and are guided by the right to food and
the civic principles underlying policies for food and nutrition sovereignty and
security (Niederle and Grisa, 2013). Our interest, here, resides precisely in this
relationship between the instruments of public action and the institutional
arrangements that support them. In this sense, a first aspect to highlight is the
priority ascribed by these programs to food purchase from family farmers,
including in this category land reform settlers, *quilombolas*, artisanal fishers
and all other groups included in Law 11326/2006. So, this is about a policy
of democratizing access to public resources that were once almost exclusively
granted to large producers, cooperatives and agro-industrial companies.

In 2012, when it reached the maximum amount (R$886 million) of annual
resources invested since its creation, in 2003, the PAA encompassed 186,000
family farmers, which, in that year, supplied 529,000 tons of food to 24,000
social organizations. It is true that, considering the country's 4.3 million family
farms, this number is relatively modest. However, despite its small scale, the
program drew attention for its institutional innovation, which represented,
for the social movements of family farming, the gateway to a new generation
of rural development public policies focused on the political construction
of food markets with great potential for social inclusion. This explains why
PAA has become the target of strong criticism from agribusiness corporations
(Triches and Grisa, 2015). These actors endeavored to demonstrate that the
new distribution models in which the state, in partnership with civil society
organizations, mediates relations between producers and consumers would
be economically inefficient and subject to fraud. As a result, not only the
program was questioned – hence, being virtually extinguished due to a significant reduction in budget allocation – but also the very logic of economic
mechanisms based on redistribution and the centrality of the state in this
process were challenged. In other words, for these actors, more dangerous
than losing a few million reais to family farmers was the fact that the PAA
legitimized state action in the markets (Niederle et al., 2019).

Because of its institutional logic, the situation of the National School
Feeding Programme (PNAE) is slightly different, though it also confirms the
importance of coordination between state and social organizations in the con-
struction of food markets (Belik and Chain, 2009). Created in 1954, as School
Lunch Program, as of 2009, through the enactment of Law No. 11947/2009,
PNAE establishes that at least 30% of the funds transferred by the National
Fund for Development of Education (FNDE) to states and municipalities
must be used to purchase food from family farmers and their associations.
In 2015, the program reached about 40 million public school students, with a
budget of R$3.8 billion allocated to purchases from family farming (22.8% of
the total budget for school meals). However, since then, it has not been able to
expand participation of family farming. By 2016, 15% of the municipalities

still did not make this type of purchase and only 43.5% were able to meet the prescribed minimum. As a result, also in the case of PNAE, agribusiness representatives are pressuring Congress to remove from the legislation the obligation to purchase from family farms, thus creating one of the main confrontations with the movements for food security that, until now, have managed to block the proposals presented to the legislative.

The way PAA and PNAE were structured implied the reorganization of a broad set of social practices. Firstly, the guarantee of selling and of a minimum price encouraged farmers to expand the cultivation of staple foods, and also the revaluation of traditional products that were once only destined for own consumption or not even used (Triches, 2010). Second, insofar as farmers and their associations and cooperatives dealt themselves with food distribution, new marketing practices have been created, as the case of Ecovida Network illustrates. Furthermore, significant changes took place in food preparation within the benefited entities. Instead of precooked industrialized foods and instant refreshments, the inclusion of fresh produce from family farms required new preparation practices, creating new interfaces between technical knowledge of nutritionists and the cooks' knowledge. From this meeting, demands emerged for farmers to process some products, which encouraged the creation of small-scale processing facilities.

Both programs favored regional food purchases and, as a result, were able to recognize alternative farming practices and include farmers who find it difficult (or refuse) to adopt conventional farming systems. In this sense, although the acquisition of organic foods, for which both programs guarantee a 30% premium price, represents a small proportion of the allocated resources,[2] it means a fundamental contribution to the promotion of agroecology, which, as we emphasized earlier, is not reduced to the logic of certification (Perez-Cassarino et al., 2016; Schmitt and Grisa, 2013). An example is the enhancement of product from Brazilian sociobiodiversity, which is evident not only in procurement (*redistribution*) but also in contests organized by the FNDE to reward the best school meal recipes (*recognition*). The inclusion of these products has an important effect of reconnecting farmers and consumers with local food crops, which in turn impacts on the dynamics of mutual recognition among actors. By introducing typical regional foods into the school diet (tapioca and cassava flour in the Northeast, artisanal cake and crackers in the South), these programs break with the sense of disrespect and contempt perceived by many farmers, especially those who are stigmatized for adopting alternative farming systems such as the indigenous and traditional communities.

As Triches (2010) suggests, the geographical and cultural rapprochement between producers and consumers reveals relationships based on an ethics that transcends economic gain: while farmers are concerned with producing healthy food for students, who may be their own children, these latter recognize and value the food of farmers who, in small municipalities, are their parents, relatives or neighbors. Another aspect highlighted by the author is how changes in eating habits of students foster a demand for healthy food that spreads to other spaces of food consumption, including the household. According to the author, this is due to changes in tastes and palate of students, which leads to greater acceptability of this type of product at home. In turn, this process encourages parents to look for fresh and healthy products, which implies a virtuous relationship between public procurement and the promotion of direct markets such as farmers' markets. In this sense, another indirect effect is the pressure that the purchase of fresh and healthy food by public schools exerts on the quality of food in private schools, which also began to adjust their menus to meet demands that often came from the students' parents and the school community.

From healthy food to "real food"

In the 2000s, a new quality convention came to light in the speeches of actors engaged in forums for discussion about food sovereignty and security, which builds on the notion of "healthy food." Its origin is related to at least two types of criticism. On the one hand, the idea that, to be healthy, it is not enough for food to be produced by family farmers, considering that public policies aimed at this category led part of these farmers to incorporate practices characteristic of the industrial order, such as cultivation of transgenic crops and use of all sort of chemicals. On the other hand, as a criticism over the conventionalization process impelled by the industry that filled supermarket shelves with organic junk food.

This new convention began to guide the practices of various social movements. The Small Farmers Movement (MPA), for example, incorporated it into the Peasant Plan. In 2013, AS-PTA, a nonprofit association that works towards rural sustainable development, coordinated an urban and periburban agriculture project in the metropolitan region of Rio de Janeiro called "Healthy Foods from Local Markets." A year earlier, the National Articulation of Agroecology (ANA) and the Ecovida Agroecological Network organized a seminar on "building local markets and democratizing access to healthy food." That same year, the manifesto approved at the National Seminar of Social Organizations of the Countryside, which brought together in Brasilia the main rural social movements and unions, defined the production and access to healthy food as one of the four pillars of the struggle for "sustainable development focused on food and territorial sovereignty."

The notion of healthy food was also incorporated by CONSEA, especially during the organization of the Third National Conference on Food and Nutrition Security, held in 2007. According to the document issue from this conference, this convention "must meet the principles of variety, quality, balance, moderation and pleasure (taste), the dimensions of gender, race and ethnicity, and the environmentally sustainable forms of production, free from physical, chemical and biological contaminants and from genetically modified organisms" (CONSEA (2007, 31). In that moment, the discourse originated from the farmers' movements converged with that of the organizations representing nutrition and public health interests, such as the Federal Council of Nutritionists (CFN), which even launched a campaign whose motto was "adequate and healthy food: less waste, more food!." This convergence led to the consolidation of the notion of "adequate and healthy food" as the main pillar of the Fourth Conference, held in 2011.

However, at that moment, there were already several signs of a process of endogenization and appropriation of this convention by the industrial order, what generated a new dispute of meanings, similar to that occurred with organic products and that is in progress now with artisanal products (see Chapter 4). This dispute is expressed in the new practices of production, marketing and certification of (supposedly) healthy foods. A main evidence of this is the widespread news about the growth of the healthy food market, including not only organic products, but also the whole generation of gluten free, lactose free and sugar free foods; nutrient-added and biofortified foods; besides the so-called "natural foods."

Two types of practices characterize the process of appropriation by the food industry of the notion healthy. The first is related to changes in production processes of certain products in response to pressures from consumption practices and/or regulatory requirements. An example was the closure in 2017 of Fonte Ijuí, a company located in northwestern Rio Grande do Sul. Purchased by The Coca-Cola Company in 2012, Fonte Ijuí processed the mineral water that was distributed in southern Brazil under the brand name Crystal. Criticized by consumers and experts for its high sodium content (103.6 mg/L), the product found it difficult to face competitors. Thus, for the southern market, the brand started to sell water bottled at the spring Fonte José Gregório (Bauru-SP), which has 80% less sodium (17.7 mg/L). Another measure adopted by the company, and widely publicized as a practice of "environmental responsibility," was the launch of the Ecoflex packaging, which uses 20% less plastic than the previous one. Both practices used by Coca-Cola could be considered opportunistic strategies, given that they were adopted not because of the company's ethical values, but rather for consumer pressures and, above all, for the impact this was having on sales. Even so, their positive effect on public health and the environment is undeniable.

Otherwise, the situation is completely different when we consider the second type of appropriation of "healthy," which is expressed in discourses that have no effective correspondence with production practices. This is noticeable, for example, in the advertising of certain brands of vegetable oils that declare the absence of cholesterol, that is, a feature common to any product of this type. Moreover, the absence of a single component is not a sufficient criterion of healthiness, an argument that can be illustrated by the very vegetable oil. Recent studies suggest that, although not containing cholesterol, oils derived from some types of seeds may increase too much the presence of other components (omega 6 and transfat) that are potentially carcinogenic and cause heart diseases. Indeed, contrary to decades of scientific discourse on the benefits of these products, some studies have suggested the consumption of animal fat (butter and lard) as a substitute for certain oils and margarines (Erasmus, 1996; Fallon and Enig, 2000). Interestingly, the replacement of butter by margarine was one of the prime examples mobilized by Goodman, Sorj, and Wilkinson (1987) to explain the process of "substitutionism" set in motion by the industrialization of agriculture (cf. Chapter 2).

Among the food markets where the discourse of healthiness is most evident is that of the so-called "heart-healthy products." The best-known example in Brazil is the margarine Becel, a brand controlled by Unilever. In addition to the direct advertising to consumers about the supposed health benefits of this product, what is more interesting is that this practice was based on the legitimacy of the "seal of approval" granted by the Brazilian Society of Cardiology (SBC). The political and scientific controversies about this certification instrument were analyzed by David (2016), whose doctoral thesis reveals the game of economic interests behind this process: as companies increased sales, SBC made about R$600,000 per year with the granting of the seal. For being highly contested and misleading, this practice was banned by the Federal Council of Medicine in 2011.

This kind of distortion of the notion of "healthy" has led organizations such as FBSSAN and CONSEA itself to sharpen criticism against appropriation processes of this convention by the food industry. An example in this regard involves the so-called biofortified products (FBSSAN, 2016), which are being considered by the food industry as the new extraordinary solution for hunger and malnutrition. Biofortification corresponds to genetic modification of seeds to produce foods with higher content of some specific micronutrient. In Brazil, the main experience in this direction is the BioFORT Project, coordinated by Embrapa, which aims to "reduce malnutrition and ensure greater food security by increasing iron, zinc and vitamin A levels in the diet of the poorest population" (Embrapa, 2015). However, according to Consea (2015, 106), "there is no guarantee that a highest concentration of a specific nutrient will be beneficial and safe for health. Furthermore, high consumption of a micronutrient can undermine health."

In 2015, during the Fifth National Conference on Food and Nutrition Security, concerns over the misuse of the discourse of healthy food led CONSEA to propose a new convention: "real food" (*comida de verdade*). It does not break with the idea of healthy food but strengthens other dimensions such as the respect for regional food cultures and identities, the protection of sociobiodiversity and even the recognition of the sacred dimension of food. In addition, this convention also contributes to counteract the paranoia or social neurosis involving healthy eating, a phenomenon that has already gained a term: orthorexia. First described by physician Steven Bratman, in 1997, this eating disorder that has no official diagnosis characterizes the compulsive obsession with eating healthy foods. Unlike anorexia and bulimia, in this case, the consumer avoids anything deemed unhealthy and therefore dangerous to the body. The problem arises because self-imposed dietary restrictions often result in more or less severe malnutrition.

New food policies

The configuration of a civic order in the agrifood system can be interpreted as one of the most important expressions of political construction of markets. State actors also play a relevant role in structuring this food order. However, unlike the classic model of a centralized state, acting upon well-defined and delimited sectors, here we note the design of new formats of public action, which highlight the interactions between the various actors who participate in the construction and implementation of civic redistribution mechanisms. "This notion does not reduce the role of the state but defines it in its increasingly evident interface with other institutional frameworks" (Niederle and Grisa, 2013, 98). Indeed, the new generation of food sovereignty and security policies demonstrates that the boundary between state, market and civil society is becoming increasingly blurred.

This new policy format leans on public spaces and social participation processes. To exemplify this, in this chapter we highlighted the relevance of CONSEA, a public arena that became one of the most plural and diverse forums among those aimed at recommending public policies.[3] The influence of CONSEA on the design of public procurement programs is exemplary of how the interaction between state actors and social organizations is essential to produce innovation in public action. Among all the policies formulated in Brazil in the last two decades for supporting family farming, the food sovereignty and security policies are those that attracted the most attention from governments and multilateral organizations around the world, even boosting the transference of ideas and policy instruments to other countries and continents (FAO, 2014; Grisa and Niederle, 2019).[4]

Figure 5.4 summarizes the main components of the civic order discussed in this chapter. In addition to those already noted in the preceding paragraphs, it is important to emphasize principles such as the right to food and the protection of the common goods as two institutional foundations of food sovereignty and security policies and, more broadly, of civic markets. These principles are also equally significant for agroecological movements, justifying participatory certification practices and the efforts for reconnection between producers and consumers by means of direct marketing circuits. Moreover, they organize and give coherence to the discourse of these movements, allowing them to distinguish themselves from the technomercantile perspective of organic agriculture.

As in the other chapters, here we presented a partial view of the architecture of a civic order. Among the gaps that remain to be filled are, for example, solidarity economy practices: associativism, self-management, microfinance, social currencies etc. While some of these artifacts and practices were mentioned in discussions about local marketing experiences such as farmers' markets and consumer groups, we were unable to deepen, for example, the discussion on the organization of global fair-trade networks. According to the literature on the subject, the practices that develop in these networks are illustrative of a civic order, but also reveal the underlying tensions, given the

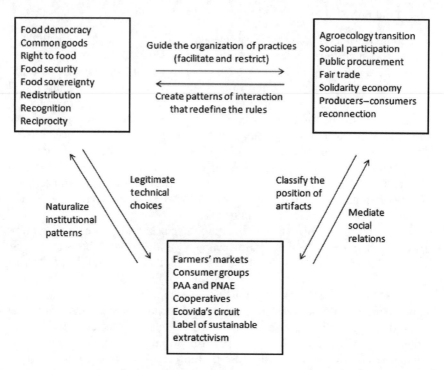

Figure 5.4 Components of the civic order.

conflicts that, in Brazil, mark the relations between local movements of solidarity economy and the international fair trade certification organizations (Wilkinson; Mascarenhas, 2007).

Another issue that deserves greater attention is the ethical criticism from the various animal rights movements, which has increasingly significant impacts on food consumption. A survey conducted by the Datafolha Institute in 2017 found that 63% of Brazilians want to reduce meat consumption. Part of this reduction is associated with the impact of the discourse of these movements. Coupled with it are the practices of vegetarianism and veganism, which, in addition to individual health concerns, are also associated with civic rules and principles. In 2018, a survey revealed that in Brazil, 14% of the population declares themselves vegetarian, which would represent 22 million people (in 2012, they were 8%, or 15.2 million people). In another survey of vegan restaurants in Porto Alegre, Niederle and Schubert (2020) identified strong interfaces between veganism and sustainable food practices, such as preference for organic food, direct purchase from family farmers, adoption of practices for the reduction of food waste and the connection of food with its various sociocultural dimensions.

Despite these gaps, the analyzes presented in this chapter seem sufficient to argue that there is a specific space in the agrifood system, where production and consumption practices follow a logic that is distinct from those defined by any other mode of social ordering analyzed in this book. The strong association of these practices with what some authors call "food democracy" (Hassanein, 2003; Lang and Heasman, 2015), and which involves the construction of collective action mechanisms in defense of the common goods – be they the natural resources of the agroforestry systems, the cultural heritage of native peoples or even human health as a collective responsibility – is the main reason, following a grammar very similar to that proposed by the worlds of Boltanski and Thévenot (1991), to group these practices into a civic order.

Notes

1 Instead of "politicized consumer," we prefer the notion of "politicized consumer practices," so that to avoid ascribing an excessively rigid substance to social actors (consumers) who are guided by different principles in different contexts (sometimes buying organic at an open market, sometimes transgenic snacks at Wal-Mart). We also avoid "an elitist understanding of reflexivity" (Guthman, 2002, 299), according to which popular taste would be predetermined and unconscious, whereas only green food consumers would be reflexive. This understanding clearly overlooks the distributive differences regarding access to food (Goodmann, 2017).

2 Considering PNAE, the purchase of these products in 2016 was of R$97.5 million, representing only 2.63% of the total program budget (R$3.8 billion). In the case of PAA, between 2009 and 2015, the annual amount spent on organic foods ranged from R$5 to R$10 million, i.e., less than 2% of the total.

3 Other spaces worth highlighting here are the Sustainable Rural Development Councils and their different levels (municipal, state and federal), the National Council of Traditional Peoples and Communities (CNPCT), the Municipal School Feeding Councils and the Territorial Committees, all equally extinguished by the Bolsonaro government in 2019.

4 An example is the Purchase from Africans for Africa (PAA), an initiative of the Brazilian government in partnership with the World Food Program (WFP), the United Nations Food and Agriculture Organization (FAO) and the Department for International Development (DFID) of the United Kingdom.

References

Abrasco. 2015. *Dossiê Abrasco: um alerta sobre os impactos dos agrotóxicos na saúde.* São Paulo: Expressão Popular.

Andre, P., Clark, J., Levkoe, C. and Lowitt, K. (eds). 2019. *Civil Society and Social Movements in Food System Governance.* New York: Routledge.

Anvisa. 2017. *Anuário Estatístico do Mercado Farmacêutico 2016.* Brasília: Agência Nacional de Vigilância Sanitária.

Aquino, J. R. and Schneider, S. 2015. "O Pronaf e o desenvolvimento rural brasileiro: avanços, contradições e desafios para o futuro." In: *Políticas Públicas de Desenvolvimento Rural,* edited by C. Grisa and S. Schneider, 53–81. Porto Alegre: UFRGS.

Beckert, J. 2011. "The transcending power of goods: imaginative value in the economy." In: *The Worth of Goods,* edited by J. Beckert and P. Aspers, 106–28. Oxford: Oxford University Press.

Beckert, J. and Aspers, P. (eds) 2011. *The Worth of Goods*. Oxford: Oxford University Press.

Belik, W. and Chaim, N. A. 2009. "O programa nacional de alimentação escolar e a gestão municipal: eficiência administrativa, controle social e desenvolvimento local." *Revista de Nutrição*, 22: 595–607.

Belik, W. and Correa, V. C. 2013. "A crise dos alimentos e os agravantes para a fome mundial." *Mundo Agrário*, 14(27): 1–28.

Belik, W. and Cunha, A. 2015. "Abastecimento no Brasil: o desafio de alimentar as cidadese promover o Desenvolvimento Rural." In: *Políticas públicas de desenvolvimento rural no Brasil*, edited by C. Grisa and S. Schneider, 217–38. Porto Alegre: UFRGS.

Belik, W., Cunha, A. and Costa, L. A. 2012. "Crise dos alimentos e estratégias para a redução do desperdício no contexto alimentar e nutricional do Brasil." *Planejamento e Políticas Publicas*, 38: 107–132.

Blay-Palmer, A., Conaré, D., Meter, K., Di Battista, A. and Johnston, C. (eds). 2019. *Sustainable Food System Assessment*. New York: Routledge.

Boltanski, L. and Thevenot, L. 1991. *De la Justification*. Paris: Gallimard.

Brandenburg, A. 2008. "Mouvement agroécologique au Brésil: trajectoire, contradictions et perspectives." *Natures Sciences Sociétés*, 16: 142–147.

Caliskan, K. and Callon, M. 2009. "Economization Part 1: Shifting attention from the economy towards processes of economization." *Economy and Society*, 38(3): 369–98.

Consea. 2007. *III Conferência Nacional de Segurança Alimentar e Nutricional*. Relatório Final. Brasília: Consea.

Consea. 2015. *V Conferência Nacional de Segurança Alimentar e Nutricional*. Relatório Final. Brasília: Consea.

Cucco, I. and Fonte, M. 2015. "Local food and civic food networks as a real utopias project." *Socio.Hu*, 3: 22–36.

David, M. 2016. *Certificação de alimentos e práticas científicas: o caso da Sociedade Brasileira de Cardiologia*. PhD Thesis. Florianópolis: UFSC.

Delgado, G. C. 2017. "Questão agrária hoje". In: *Agricultura familiar brasileira*: desafios e perspectivas de futuro, edited by G .Delgado and S. Bergamasco, 12–21. Brasília: NEAD.

Embrapa. 2015. *Alimentos biofortificados buscam reduzir a desnutrição da população*. Accessed May 24, 2016. www.embrapa.br/busca-de-noticias/-/noticia/3254365/alimentos-biofortificados-buscam-reduzir-a-desnutricao-da-populacao.

Erasmus, U. 1996. *From Seed to Oil: Fats That Heal, Fats That Kill*. Burnaby, BC: Alive.

Fallon, S. and Enig, M. 2000. *Why Butter is Better*. The Weston A. Price Foundation.

FAO. 2014. *Scaling Up the Brazilian School Feeding Model*. Rome: FAO.

FAO. 2015. *The State of Food and Agriculture*. Rome: FAO.

FBSSAN. 2016. *Biofortificação: as controvérsias e as ameaças à soberania e segurança alimentar e nutricional*. Brasília: Fórum Brasileiro de Soberania e Segurança Alimentar e Nutricional.

Fraser, N. and Honneth, A. 2003. *Redistribution or Recognition? A Political-Philosophical Exchange*. London: Verso.

Gazolla, M. and Schneider, S. (eds). 2017. *Cadeias curtas e redes agroalimentares alternativas*. Porto Alegre: UFRGS.

Goodman, D., Dupuis, E. M. and Goodman, M. 2012. Alternative Food Networks: *Knowledge, Practice and Politics*. London: Routledge.

Goodman, D., Sorj, B. and Wilkinson, J. 1987. *From Farming to Biotechnology*. London: Basil Blackwell.

Grisa, C. and Niederle, P. 2019. "Transferência, Convergência e Tradução de Políticas Públicas: A Experiência da Reunião Especializada sobre Agricultura Familiar do Mercosul."*Dados*,62(2), e20160099.

Grisa, C., Schmitt, C., Mattei, L., Maluf, R. and Leite, S. 2011. "Contribuições do Programa de Aquisição de Alimentos à segurança alimentar e nutricional e a criação de mercados para a agricultura familiar." *Revista Agriculturas*, 8: 34–41.

Grisa, C. and Schneider. S. (eds). 2015. *Políticas de Desenvolvimento Rural no Brasil*. Porto Alegre, UFRGS.

Grisa, C., Wesz, Jr., V. J. and Buchweitz, V. 2014. "Revisitando o Pronaf: velhos questionamentos, novas interpretações." *Revista de Economia e Sociologia Rural*, 52(2): 323–346.

Hassanein, N. 2003. "Practicing food democracy: A pragmatic politics of transformation."*Journal of Rural Studies*, 19(1): 77–86.

Hebinck, P., Ploeg, J. D. van der and Schneider, S. (eds). 2014. *Rural Development and The Construction of New Markets*. London: Routledge.

Hinrichs, C. 2000. "Embeddedness and local food systems: Notes on two types of direct agricultural market." *Journal of Rural Studies*, 16: 295–303.

IDEC. 2018. *Mapa das Feiras Orgânicas*. Rio de Janeiro: IDEC.

Lamine, C. 2020. *Sustainable Agri-Food Systems: Case Studies in Transitions Towards Sustainability from France and Brazil*. New York: Bloomsbury Publishing.

Lamine, C., Niederle, P. and Ollivier, G. 2019. "Alliances et controverses dans la mise en politique de l'agroécologie au Brésil et en France." *Natures Sciences Sociétés*, 27(1): 6–19.

Lang, T. and Heasman, M. 2015. *Foodwars: The Global Battle for Mouths, Minds and Markets*. London: Routledge.

Leite, S. 2001. "Padrão de financiamento, setor público e agricultura no Brasil." In *Políticas Públicas e Agricultura no Brasil*, edited by S. Leite, 53–94. Porto Alegre: UFRGS.

Lockie, S. and Carpenter, D. (eds). 2010. *Agriculture, Biodiversity and Markets*. London: Earthscan.

Maluf, R. S. 2017. "Abastecimento alimentar, inflação de alimentos e o contexto urbano no Brasil." In *Questões agrárias, agrícolas e rurais,*, edited by G. Flexor and R. Maluf, 177–91. Rio de Janeiro: E-papers.

Marsden, T. 2016. "Exploring the rural eco-economy: Beyond neoliberalism." *Sociologia Ruralis*, 56(4): 597–615.

Menezes, F., Porto, S. and Grisa, C. 2015. *Abastecimento alimentar e compras públicas no Brasil: um resgate histórico*. Brasília: Centro de Excelência Contra a Fome.

Micheletti, M. 2003. *Political Virtue and Shopping: Individuals, Consumerism and Collective Action*. Basingstoke: Palgrave Macmillan.

Niederle, P. A. 2014. "Os agricultores ecologistas nos mercados para alimentos orgânicos: contramovimentose novos circuitos de comércio." *Sustentabilidade em Debate*, 5: 79–96.

Niederle, P. A. and Almeida, L. 2013. "A nova arquitetura dos mercados para produtos orgânicos: o debate da convencionalização." In: *Agroecologia*: práticas, mercados e políticas para uma nova agricultura, edited by P. Niederle, L. Almeida and F. Vezzani, 23–67. Curitiba: Kayrós.

Niederle, P. A. and Grisa, C. 2013. "Ideias e valores: a análise da ação pública a partir das interfaces entre a abordagem cognitiva e a economia das convenções." *Política & Sociedade*, 12: 97–136.

Niederle, P. A. and Marques, F. C. 2016. "Produção ecológica de alimentos e mudanças institucionais: implicações para a construção de novos mercados." In *Construção de mercados e agricultura familiar*, edited by F. Marques, M. Conterato and S. Schneider, 275–310. Porto Alegre: UFRGS.

Niederle, P. A. and Radomsky, G. F. 2017. "Quem governa por dispositivos? A produção das normas e padrões para os alimentos orgânicos no Brasil." *Tomo*, 30: 227–265.

Niederle, P. A. and Schubert, M. 2020. "How does veganism contribute to shape sustainable food systems? Practices, meanings and identities of vegan restaurants in Porto Alegre, Brazil." *Journal of Rural Studies*, 78: 304–313.

Niederle, P. A., Grisa, C., Picolotto, E. and Soldera, D. 2019. "Narrative disputes over family-farming public policies in Brazil: conservative attacks and restricted countermovements." *Latin American Research Review*, 54: 707–720.

Perez-Cassarino, J. et al. 2016. "Promoção da Soberania e Segurança Alimentar e Nutricional (SSAN) por meio do mercado institucional: a experiência brasileira." In: *Soberania Alimentar (SOBAL) e Segurança Alimentar Nutricional (SAN) na América Latina e Caribe*, edited by I. Bezerra and J. Perez-Cassarino, 223–246. Curitiba: UFPR.

Petersen, P., Mussoi, E. and Dal Soglio, F. 2013. "Institutionalization of the agroecological approach in Brazil: advances and challenges." *Agroecology and Sustainable Food Systems*, 37(1): 103–114.

Picolotto, E. L. 2008. "Novos movimentos sociais econômicos: economia solidária e comércio justo." *Outra Economía*, 2: 74–92.

Picolotto, E. L. 2014. "Os atores da construção da categoria agricultura familiar no Brasil." *Revista de Economia e Sociologia Rural*, 52: 63–84.

Picolotto, E. L. and Brandenburg, A. 2013. "Sindicalismo da agricultura familiar, modelos de desenvolvimento e o tema ambiental." In *Agroecologia: práticas, mercados e políticas para uma nova agricultura*, edited by P. Niederle, L. Almeida and F. Vezzani, 105–36. Curitiba: Kayrós.

Ploeg, J. D. van der., Jingzhong, Y. and Schneider, S. 2012. "Rural development through the construction of new, nested, markets: Comparative perspectives from China, Brazil and the European Union." *Journal of Peasant Studies*, 39(1): 133–173.

Polanyi, K. 1957. *The Great Transformation: The Political and Economic Origins of Our Time*. Boston: Beacon Press.

Preiss, P. V. 2017. *As alianças alimentares colaborativas em uma perspectiva internacional: afetos, conhecimento incorporado e ativismo político*. PhD Thesis. Porto Alegre: UFRGS.

Radomsky, G. F., Niederle, P. A. and Schneider, S. 2014. "Participatory systems of certification and alternative marketing networks: The case of Ecovida Agroecology Network in South Brazil." In *Rural Development and the Construction of New Markets*, edited by P. Hebinck, J. D. Ploeg and S. Schneider, 79–98. The Hague: Routledge.

Renting, H., Schermer, M. and Rossi, A. 2012. "Building food democracy: exploring civic food networks and newly emerging forms of food citizenship." *International Journal of Sociology of Agriculture and Food*, 19(3): 289–307.

Sabourin, E. 2011. *Sociedades e organizações camponesas: uma leitura através da reciprocidade*. Porto Alegre: UFRGS.

Schmitt, C. and Grisa, C. 2013. "Agroecologia, mercados e políticas públicas: uma análise a partir dos instrumentos de ação governamental." In *Agroecologia: práticas, mercados e políticas para uma nova agricultura*, edited by P. Niederle, L. Almeida and F. Vezzani, 215–65. Curitiba: Kairós.

Schmitt, C., Niederle, P., Avila, M., Sabourin, E., Petersen, P., Silveira, L., Assis, W., Palm, J. and Fernandes, G. 2017. "La experiencia brasileña de construcción de políticas públicas en favor de la Agroecología." In *Políticas públicas a favor de la agroecología en América Latina y El Caribe*, edited by E. Sabourin et al., 73–122. Porto Alegre: FAO.

Schubert, M. 2017. Comer fora de casa, as práticas e as rotinas do comer nos contextos da modernidade: uma leitura comparada entre Brasil, Reino Unido e Espanha. PhD Thesis. Porto Alegre: UFRGS.

Schwarcz, L. M. and Starling, H. M. 2015. *Brasil: uma biografia*. São Paulo: Cia das Letras.

Soldera, D. 2017. *A instabilidade do referencial de políticas públicas para a agricultura familiar no Brasil: uma análise das narrativas dualistas*. Master Dissertation. Porto Alegre: UFRGS.

Speranza, J. and Kato, K. 2017. Tendências atuais dos preços dos alimentos e repercussões sobre a segurança alimentar no Brasil. In: Questões *A*grárias, *A*grícolas e *R*urais: conjunturas e políticas públicas, edited by R. Maluf and G. Flexor, 192–211. Rio de Janeiro: E-papers.

Triches, R. 2010. Reconectando a produção ao consumo: a aquisição de gêneros alimentícios da agricultura familiar para o programa de alimentação escolar. PhD Thesis. Porto Alegre: UFRGS.

Triches, R. and Grisa, C. 2015. "Entre mudanças e conservadorismos: uma análise dos Programas de Aquisição de Alimentos (PAA e PNAE) a partir da retórica de intransigência." *Revista NERA*, 26: 10–27.

Wanderley, M. N. B. 2000. "A valorização da agricultura familiar e a reivindicação da ruralidade no Brasil." *Desenvolvimento e Meio Ambiente*, 2: 29–37.

Wilkinson, J. and Mascarenhas, G. 2007. "The making of the fair-trade movement in the South: the Brazilian case." In *Fair Trade: The Challenges of Transforming Globalization*, edited by L. Raynolds, D. Murray and J. Wilkinson, 157–79. London: Routledge.

6   Aesthetic order
Immaterializing of food

Besides the ethical criticism, mainly voiced by the agrarian social movements and, more recently, the agroecological movements, there is another kind of dynamic in the food markets that reflects what Boltanski and Chiapello (2007) call the "aesthetic critique" of capitalism. Promoted by new social movements, but also by a more dispersed multitude of relatively dispersed individuals, sometimes only virtually interconnected, such criticism is also directed to the industrial food order, but not so much for the socioeconomic inequity it produces. The central issue here is its inability to respond to the new lifestyles that emerged with the advent of postmodernism, the cultural face of late modernity.

According to Jameson (1996), the emergence of this dynamic is related to both the commodification of culture and the culturalization of the economy. The incorporation of culture by the market makes aesthetic a key element of contemporary capitalism, moving it from the periphery to the center of the production and consumption system. Lash and Urry (1994) take a similar stance by claiming that postmodernism emerges as the new cultural pattern of the economic, social and political relations of "disorganized capitalism"– a new multinational, informational and consumerist phase of capitalist society. From this perspective, the current period of the capitalist economy is both post-Fordist, since it succeeds the era of mass production and consumption, and postmodern, considering that production and consumption are increasingly affected by the postmodernist aesthetics. This historical condition makes culture a vehicle for profound transformations in the relations of production, since economic goods reveal themselves essentially as cultural signs. These authors also suggest a process of commodification of culture and emphasize how cultural and aesthetic patterns colonize the economy, revealing the success of postmodernism in enhancing the aesthetic dimensions of modernity.[1]

From a more contemporary perspective, some of these processes could be interpreted following the logic of "enrichment" analyzed by Boltanski and Esquerre (2017). This is the term these authors employ to understand the emergence of a new economy, which rests less on the production of new things than on the enrichment of things that were already available – and which often date back to a rather distant past – by means of new narratives, language games and symbolic reconstructions. As the authors observe,

> cultural enrichment always presupposes the use of a narrative device in order to select, in the multiplicity of phenomena, certain differences presented by a certain thing, differences considered as particularly pertinent and which must therefore be privileged and focused in the discourses that accompany the circulation.
>
> (Boltanski and Esquerre, 2017, 72)

In this economy, time counts in favor of product enrichment, so that past acts as a major semantic device for value creation.

The aesthetic criticism of modernity praises the different, exotic, asymmetrical and singular. It calls for new (more individualized) modes of consumption, promoting convenience, indulgence, personalization and customization. In the case of food consumption, it prompts foodie and gourmet movements. Enjoying different cuisine became as expressive countercultural phenomenon as was the use of illicit drugs among hippies in the 1960s. Food raves are equally marked by frenzies and exaggerations. Food and drink festivals that attract foodies from everywhere have replaced rock festivals or coupled with them. Chefs replaced rock idols on the covers of magazines and even some rockers became chefs and food critics. As highlighted in an extensive article on the subject by Steven Poole in *The Guardian*, in September 2012,

> Food replaces drugs in the gently ageing food-fancier's pantheon of pleasure, and brings along with it traces of the old pharmaceutical vocabulary. You hear talk of taking a "hit" of a dish or its sauce, as though from a spliff or bong; and a food-obsessive in hunter-gatherer mode is thrilled to "score" a few chanterelle mushrooms, as though he has had to buy them from a dodgy-looking gent on a murky Camden street corner. Food is valued for its psychotropic "rush"; Nigella Lawson refers to salted caramel as "this Class A foodstuff". Yes, food is the new drugs for former Britpoppers and the Ecstasy generation, a safer and more respectable hedonic tool, the key to a comfortingly domesticated high. Western industrial civilisation is eating itself stupid. We are living in the Age of Food. Cookery programmes bloat the television schedules, cookbooks strain the bookshop tables, celebrity chefs hawk their own brands of weird mince pies (Heston Blumenthal) or bronze-moulded pasta (Jamie Oliver) in the supermarkets, and cooks in super-expensive restaurants from Chicago to Copenhagen are the subject of hagiographic profiles in serious magazines and newspapers. Food festivals (or, if you will, "Feastivals") are the new rock festivals, featuring thrilling live stage performances of, er, cooking.
>
> (*The Guardian*, 2012)

In Brazil, the sociology of consumption has unveiled this new dynamic of the food markets. In this perspective, Barbosa (2009) draws attention to two fundamental aspects. The first concerns the substantial changes both in the discourses about food – so much has never been said and written about it – and in the practice of eating. While aesthetic criticism helps to delegitimize the rushed and mechanical behavior that characterizes industrial society (the argument of reflexivity), the formation of an aesthetic order involves the legitimation of a set of practices that praise commensality as a form of socialization, leisure, distinction and learning. Eating becomes a cultural investment that requires time, knowledge and money: gathering friends, researching restaurants, tasting new flavors, enjoying different culinary traditions, challenging the stomach and brain to experience new sensations and emotions.

From a habitual and futile activity that hardly deserved the attention of sociologists (Poulain, 2013), eating has become so complicated that requires asking for help. New actors, objects and artifacts come into play. The aesthetic order reserves a prominent place for guides and manuals, newspaper and magazine, gastronomy blogs, television programs, specialized YouTube channels, and, more recently, smartphone applications. Consumers are surrounded by artifacts that daily influence their food choices. We are not talking about manipulation of individuals, who would be driven by new propaganda strategies of food empires (what would lead us to the old Frankfurtian thesis of the cultural industry). Nor are we saying that this does not exist. Right now, we are just drawing attention to sociotechnical devices that are shaping new eating practices.

Added to this are the new indices, rankings, ratings and certifications. Quality assessment mechanisms that prevail in the Industrial Order (HACCP, ISO, GMP, Codex Alimentarius), which privilege the so-called "objective" characteristics of products, now coexist with subjective, uncertain and controversial appraisals of perception. Such appraisals make room for new "experts" like Robert Parker and his famous wine rating, but also for the opinion of "ordinary people," who give four stars for a good restaurant or hundreds of "likes" for a culinary blog. If, until recently, these ratings were just fun, today they are amongst the main concerns for the commercial strategies of companies (in some cases, even more than be quoted in the Michelin Guide). Global exposure on the Internet can be either the salvation or the nightmare of producers, industries, supermarkets and restaurants.

While in the industrial order people trust the instruments produced by modern science, and in the ethical order they place their hopes in the Habermasian public sphere, here "trust" is transferred to a new, more fluid and dynamic type of space, which mixes the public and the private. This space connects completely anonymous individuals with new celebrities. In Brazil, chefs such as Alex Atala, Bela Gil, Rita Lobo and Henrique Fogaça are followed by consumer groups, foster social movements, create trends and define the public agenda (Gueneau et al., 2017; Zaneti and Balestro, 2015). Internationally, the most well-known expression may be the global star Jamie

Oliver and his (failed?) food revolution. The fame of these actors is such that artists now want to be cooks. The kitchen has become the new setting for the actors. Cooking has definitely become an art and, like on stage, aesthetics plays a central role in contemporary cooking. After all, food becomes a mixture of spices and meanings, ingredients and images, served in plates and portraits.

This dynamic is not exclusive to the virtual world, which, here, is no longer distinguished from the "real" one. These changes involve people's daily lives. The lifeworld (*lebenswelt*) is filled with aesthetics everywhere. As Miele and Murdoch (2002, 312) note, "there seems little doubt that modern societies are now strongly configured by the application of an aesthetic sensibility to a whole variety of economic and social activities." According to the authors, one of the most evident faces of phenomena is its ability to sell even nontradable things. In Brazil, for example, this was seen when the sacred art of Ouro Preto became home decoration. In turn, those things that were already marketed have gained new shapes, components, packaging, as well as prices two or three times higher. The *beiju* found in farmers' markets of Olinda, of Tupi-Guarani indigenous origin, becomes the gourmet *tapioca*, stuffed with salmon tartar and guacamole, by the hands of a chef in São Paulo.

If, in this food order, more than in any other, the revolution begins in the kitchen, at some point it reaches the countryside. Increasingly, instead of the old aristocratic emphasis on overly ornate dishes, the *nouvelle cuisine* is approaching farmers and rural territories (Zaneti, 2017). The demand for fresh and seasonal produce brought with it a rhetoric of *terroir* and typicality, as well as the valuation (and appropriation) of local knowledge, craft skills, traditional heritage and social identities. This created "an aesthetic of 'connectedness' or 'embeddedness' in which the food is seen as a reflection of surrounding socio-economic and ecological relationships" (Miele and Murdoch, 2002, 325). Globally, the main expression of this is Slow Food, an international movement with over 100,000 members in 150 countries, whose basic principle is "the right to enjoy food, using special quality handcrafted products that are produced in a way that respects both the environment and the people responsible for production, the producers."

This approach to the rural territories reveals a growing overlap between the aesthetic and civic orders. The gourmet movement fostered by chefs, at first, embraced a concern about a sustainability and locality, which led to the appreciation of fresh produce, biodiversity and organics. Afterwards came the search for products from family farming and traditional communities (Zaneti, 2017). The new frontier lies in the way of access to these products: shopping at farmers' markets, for example, is modern again. Just as eating out became a complex practice for being associated with many others whose meaning goes far beyond eating (Schubert, 2017), going to farmers' markets turned into a total aesthetic fact, especially as the consumer finds there an environment of leisure, entertainment and sociability. People don't go to this kind of marketplace just for the food, not even for its price. Some go to the there and don't even buy food. What matters is the whole experience provided by these environments (what is also true of a shopping center).

When this kind of practice also combines the intent of being a political act – in the sense of supporting a certain type of farmer or production system, as in agroecological farmers' markets – an approximation is noted between aesthetic criticism and its ethical analogous. Levi-Strauss was right: food is good for thinking; but also to communicate and to protest. This leads us to the second fundamental aspect analyzed by Barbosa (2016, 2), namely, the "ethicization of the aesthetics" concurrently with an "aestheticization of ethics." As Barbosa (2009, 55) suggests, "the gastronomisation of eating, which so far we depicted as focused on pleasure, sensoriality and sociability, has also changed in conjunction with other trends. It became green and politicised and it is difficult to tell apart these influences." As we will see later, the incorporation of the socioenvironmental agenda by supporters of the sustainable gastronomy is a major expression of this new synthesis (Dias, 2016).

In this chapter, after discussing the importance of instruments for qualification and valuation of goods, we analyze the aestheticization of the rural world, demonstrating how gastronomy has been associated with the rhetoric of *terroir*. Using the example of Geographical Indications of origin, we analyze how aesthetic criticism can be mobilized from an eminently reformist perspective, which is prone to be appropriated by the industrial order. In a way, this is why we keep civic and aesthetic orders apart: the fact that, despite comprising processes that are increasingly connected, the aesthetic turn of food markets does not necessarily encompass a civic component. Precisely because of this, several authors consider the aesthetic movement as an expression of new strategies of the food industry to maintain its profit margins. That is, it would appear as a simulacrum of the "true" social relations of production. In this case, the Marxist debate on the fetishization reemerges. Against this argument, and coming back to Boltanski and Esquerre's logic of enrichment, at the end of this chapter, we argue for a distinct reading of valuative struggles in food markets.

Intermediaries and judgment artifacts

Like the world of art, there are food markets whose operation can hardly be explained by the mainstream economic science. These are markets where the balance between supply and demand is far from being a sufficient parameter to guide the action of producers and consumers. What makes them so different is that the qualities of the goods that circulate within them do not reveal an objective "basket of attributes"– as Lancaster (1966) believed – from which individuals could choose in line with exogenous and previously formed preferences. Instead, in these markets, the goods are first and foremost immaterial and symbolic constructions. They are "singularities" (Karpic, 2007).

Among the best-known food products, wine is an emblematic example of singularity. After all, how to distinguish a good wine? What kind of quality attribute has the best wines in the world? What makes a bottle of Romanée-Conti be sold for US$10,000 at a London restaurant, while the same amount of a Brazilian table wine is sold for less than a dollar for Japanese buyers. Certainly, there are differences in the organoleptic quality of the product, as well as in the conditions of production and processing. Quality is also a material attribute. Even so, in this type of market, it is impossible to explain price formation – much less consumer choice, which is not based solely on this criterion – without understanding the role of numerous intermediaries and judgment artifacts that act in the social construction of the value (Aspers and Beckert, 2011; Beckert, 2011).

The role of these intermediaries and artifacts is not to present products as they are, but as they are being interpreted by certain social actors (Callon, Meadel and Rabeharisoa, 2012). They alter the functioning of markets, influencing values, beliefs and social representations. Its importance is even greater when consumers are unable to choose based on comparison between products. They choose, instead, by comparing brands, certificates, seals, indexes, guides or rankings. More than the product, what is at stake is its reputation. The image becomes more real than the product itself. Therefore, the naturalized conception of quality that prevails in the traditional economy is overcome, and, by highlighting the cognitive, valuative and emotive dimensions of action, productive strategies are rather focused on manipulation of cultural meanings than on changes in production systems (Lash and Urry, 1994).

As Allaire (2004) noted, the recognition of this immaterial configuration shows that some foods only acquire qualities through the mobilization of mental images provided by the social networks in which they circulate. This reading resembles the cultural approach proposed by Appadurai (1998), an anthropologist dedicated to analyzing the "social life of things." For this author, "we must follow things in themselves, for their meanings are inscribed in their forms, their uses, their trajectories. Only by analysing these trajectories can we interpret the human transactions and calculations that give life to things" (Appadurai, 1998, 17). Thus, the quality associated with the origin of a food is not reduced to its physical characteristics that stem from the peculiar edaphoclimatic conditions under which it was produced. This comprises natural, social, cultural and economic attributes of the territory, which operate through socially constructed images that make the product identity recognizable. Aesthetics becomes fundamental in this process of "food immaterialization" (Harvey, McMeekin and Ward, 2004).

Issued from the discussions of the Convention Theory, the "economics of singularities" model became known worldwide. More recently, the model has even been extrapolated to the idea of a *societé singulariste* (Martuccelli, 2010). However, while meeting new interlocutors in various areas of knowledge and countries, Karpic was criticized by his French counterparts. The problem, according to them, lies in the very notion of singularity. For Karpic (2007, 166), singularities "are structured, uncertain and incommensurable goods and services ... which cannot be confused with the 'determined' goods of the perfect competition model." For his critics, the truth is that no good can be understood through the neoclassical model (Beckert, 2011; Eymard-Duvernay, 2009). The way it is enunciated, therefore, the definition creates an unsustainable asymmetry between the singularities and commodities markets: these latter perfect, the former impure.

Over the past two decades, economic sociology and anthropology have attempted to break this dualism (Aspers and Beckert, 2011). If fine wines, specialty coffees, craft beers, medicinal herbs, chocolates and olive oils are much more than just "exchange value," the same can be said for commodities that, by definition, would be undifferentiated goods (Allaire, 2013). This is noticeable when we follow, for example, the social trajectory of soybeans, which Menasche (2005) called the "grain of discord": the "green gold" of modern farming undergoes a series of both physical and symbolic movements until turning into tofu – the "healthy soy curd"– on the plate of a vegan restaurant, the. The same is true of corn: the image of the gourmet tortilla bears no resemblance to the grain concealed in almost all processed food products.

For Eymard-Duvernay (2009, 154), "uniqueness is not a substantial feature of the good, but rather of the way of judging it." Therefore, although the term may have been the most widely captured aspect of Karpic's theory, in our view, more relevant is the singular way the author and, more broadly, economic sociology incorporate the role of social intermediaries and judgment devices (Aspers and Beckert, 2011; Callon, Meadel and Rabeharisoa, 2012). So, what is unique about these markets is not the fact that they work differently than the neoclassical model suggests (which, strictly speaking, does not adequately explain any market), but rather the importance of a myriad of humans and artifacts in the process of social construction of quality. In this sense, what changes is the intensity of this process. If these humans and artifacts are key to organizing trade circuits for wines and coffees, the same is true of commodity markets (Busch, 2011).

Earlier here, we highlighted the role of chefs in this process, but there are other human intermediaries. In the wine world, for example, winemakers and sommeliers have established themselves as important mediators, given consumers' inability to value this "credence good" whose qualities they cannot measure even after buying and tasting it. Other segments such as coffees, chocolates, olive oils and beers also have already such market professionals (Cochoy and Dubuisson-Quellier, 2000). The expansion of gastronomic literature and the popularization of contests, rankings and labels have given these actors a position as true spokespersons who speak on behalf of the product, what enhances their ability to influence both consumer habits and producers' strategies (Ali, Lecocq and Visser, 2010). As in the fashion universe, one of the most recent phenomena in this regard is the influence of youtubers of gastronomy, some of whom, without any specialized training in the field, have their recipe tips, dishes, combinations and ingredients followed by millions of people.

Considerable criticism has already been centered on the way a select group of professionals decisively interferes "desingularizing" food, since its indices and classifications create homogeneous global standards. In the wine market, the emblematic case is that of Michel Rolland, consultant to a hundred wineries, including Miolo Wine Group, the largest wine conglomerate in Brazil. This French oenologist became particularly famous for being one of the main contributors to the spread of technological processes that enable producers to quickly obtain characteristics of a wine that, otherwise, would only be achieved after a long and costly period of aging. Furthermore, these processes enable wines from different *terroirs* to bear relatively similar characteristics, thus creating a standardized flavor. Through these techniques, the diversity between wine regions is no longer important. What prevail are the innovations in winemaking methods, making room for the so-called "technological wines" (Niederle, 2011).

However, the presence of this kind of actor and artifact creates disorder and instability within the aesthetic order. Whereas in the industrial order its presence is quite legitimate and, more than that, necessary, here it is subject to criticism and opposition. This allows to infer that it is not the presence of the chef or the oenologist (actor), the seal or certificate (artifact), the norm or standard (institution) that characterize a particular process (aestheticization) resulting in the formation of an order (aesthetics). The question is how these factors connect to the arrangement of entities that shape the social practices. It is these practices that produce meaning, define the image of a food and ascribe value to it. The same actor or artifact may compose different practices, which become the expression of different modes of ordering (and qualification). This may, for example, cause some discomfort to fans of new celebrities of the gastronomic world, when faced with the fact that practices (including discourses) can be contradictory, sometimes expressing an ethical–aesthetical criticism, other times approaching the industrial–financial logics. Rather than defining rationalities, identities and qualities as innate substances that individuals and objects carry with them everywhere, it is preferable to consider the context in which practices develop, and then relationally interpret what are the rationalities, identities and qualities that are being mobilized in that particular context.

Feeding the body and the market

The main driver of the aesthetic order in the food system has been the social obsession with the body. Roughly speaking, while the civic order rests on *'consommateurs solidaires,'* concerned with the common good, in this case we are faced with *'consommateurs solitaires,'* worried about their health and image – often more about their image than the health. Guivant's (2003) study on consumers of organic products is exemplary. The author demonstrates how the expansion of this market is associated with the growth of an "egotrip lifestyle" that encompasses consumption practices that do not respond primarily to environmental concerns – the feature of green consumers – but rather to the hedonic ethics of body worship.

It is not only, and not mainly, the markets for organic products that the fitness generation has been driving in Brazil. Data from the Brazilian Franchising Association point to over 6,000 franchises related to "healthy life," such as gyms, restaurants, clothing and footwear. While in 2013 the sector represented 3% of the total franchises in the country, in 2016 it already reached 8% (Exame, 2016). With 35,000 gyms in 2018, Brazil is the second largest world market in this sector, second only to the United States. But what is most striking is the growing consumption of protein, energy, diet and light, zero gluten, enriched, fortified and functional foods. There are several examples: whey proteins, cereal bars, protein shakes, fortified flours and countless energy drinks. One of the newest markets is the so-called "superfoods," a controversial attribute associated with the use of products for regulating organic processes. Celebrities in this market include traditional seeds like quinoa and chia. In Brazil, açaí also gained this status.

Aestheticization has made room for a variety of staple foods. Low-carb diets have encouraged the replacement of simple carbohydrates like white rice, pasta and bread with protein sources like meat and eggs, as well as cholesterol by "good fats" present in foods like avocado, nuts, olive oil and tuna. Rising prices for products such as avocados, nuts and cereal bars illustrate the increased demand. Added to this is the demand for foods that supposedly have some functionality for metabolism: flaxseed, almonds, blueberries, broccoli, litchi, pitaia … even soy or, more specifically, soy isoflavone. This latter is sold as a rather miraculous product, able to fight osteoporosis, strengthen the immune system, prevent cancer, reduce cholesterol, among many other miraculous possibilities.

The expansion of these markets reveals that the very concept of health has changed. It is no longer understood as the absence of disease or infirmity, but as a task, a set of practices and behaviors to feel good, light, lively and happy. That is, it is no longer necessarily about preventing or treating illness, but about an effort – rather painful and obsessive – to access new sensations, new ways of experiencing the body. "Such perspectives are in line with the youth-health-beauty trilogy in which health discourses, aesthetic discourses as well as hedonistic discourses are fully convergent" (Santos, 2008, 28). Along with the satisfaction of duty fulfilled there is the anxiety, anguish and suffering to keep fit, be it hypertrophied muscles or anorexic thinness.

If, as suggests Fischler's "incorporation principle" (1990, 66), "we become what we eat," we also eat what we want to become. And what we want to become depends on a collective social construction. Santos (2008) noted that, currently, the belly has become the epicenter of our concerns. To cope with this fear, the consumption of all that can increase the "paunch" is reduced, and at the same time, everything that contributes to its reduction and "better functioning" is consumed. In turn, the media explores its image: the abdomen dominates the covers of health magazines; functional products display it on packaging; on the internet countless websites give food tips and exercises to "lose belly fat" or to achieve a "negative belly." To this end, there is even a kind of "aestheticization of hunger," insofar as society values those who are strong to "starve," even having the possibility of eating everything they want.

These new forms of disciplinary regime over the body, which Foucault (2008) would probably include in "biopolitics," are produced by means of intricate games of knowledge and power, in which

> the new forms of control are not exerted against human nature – that is, it is not about disciplining rebellious or indifferent bodies – but with it, in its favor, since the values of pleasure, self-care and healthy body are part of the range of people's desires.
>
> (Niederle and Radomsky, 2017, 255)

Indeed, the new forms of domination also intensify individualism, while turning it into a praise to freedom. Based on a discourse of guarantee of individuals' freedom, the body becomes the focus of the new techniques of power and pleasure.

Among the many devices that contribute to this discipline of the body and that, therefrom, impact on eating habits, one of the main novelties are the mHealth applications. These digital artifacts offer new ways to monitor, measure and represent human body through detailed biometric data from each person. They are based on a voluntary strategy of individuals to self-track their daily spending (exercise) and food intake practices (Lupton, 2013). Popular apps include MyFitness Pal, My Diet Coach, Diet and Health, Technutri and Diet and Weight Loss. According to Barbosa, Roesler and Cazella (2016), the main features of these devices involve: calculators for body mass index, percentage of fat and weight; reminders for water consumption, mealtimes, registration of meals and physical activity; performance charts and tracking of results; "healthy" recipes and tables showing nutrient availability in food; motivational tips and food education programs, possibility of interaction with other users on social networks; and, more recently, "gamification," that is, the ability to enter games, seeking better rankings among users community or performance awards.

The main interest of the social sciences regarding these devices is associated with the emergence of new processes of biopolitical control. In this sense, Lupton (2013) highlights how the "healthist" discourse incorporated by applications supports forms of liberal governmentality that transfer to the individual the responsibility for taking care of his/her own health. According to the author, "this discourse tends to gloss over the social and economic determinants of health states for a focus on 'empowerment' and 'taking charge' of one's own health" (Lupton, 2013, 397). Therefore, this type os discourse "value those who take such responsibility and represent them as ideal citizens, while people who are viewed as lacking self-responsibility or who are ill are positioned as inferior and morally deficient" (idem, 397).

The impacts of this aesthetic phenomenon on the organization of food systems are diverse. On the one hand, although adherents of the diet of sweet potatoes, eggs and chicken are not primarily interested in supporting small farmers, indirectly, the aestheticization process creates alternatives of income for this social group, as well as for the traditional communities that live, for example, from the extraction of açaí or Brazil nuts. At the same time, and especially in the case of extractivism, they create new challenges in managing common resources. The risk of overexploitation due to increased demand is very present in the markets of guarana, Brazil nut, acai and palmetto.

The appropriation by food corporations of these natural resources and, more broadly, of the image of healthiness that they carry, is another challenge to aesthetization, being target of ethical criticism. The main example discussed in the literature in this regard is the "conventionalization of organic agriculture" (Buck, Getz and Guthman, 1997). This process is based on increasing specialization, growing production scales and replacement of synthetic inputs with organic inputs without, however, including more complex levels of agroecological transition. It is not restricted to production since it also involves the growing participation of large processing and distribution networks in the organic food market.

In the United States, data presented by Howard (2016) reveal a rapid concentration of the organic food industry – the presence of corporations such as Coca-Cola, Nestlé, Pepsi, Cargil and ConAgra is noteworthy. The newest entrant in this market is Amazon. In 2017, this e-commerce giant announced the purchase of Whole Foods, one of the nation's largest "healthy" food chains, for US$13.7 billion. In Brazil, one of the most recent examples was the purchase, also in 2017, of Mãe Terra, a company of natural and organic products based in São Paulo, by Unilever. The acquisition is linked to the strategy of the Anglo-Dutch multinational in Brazil, which has become the largest market for healthy foods and drinks in the world, where 79% of consumers consider health and nutrition their food priorities (Estadão, 2017).

The new aesthetics of the rural world

Although led by consumers, aesthetic criticism has reached the farmers. Among these, the first that began to change their practices to meet the new demands were those most directly connected with the urban space. Our research on the organic food market suggests three distinct groups: (1) farmers who have contractual links with businesses, supermarkets and restaurants; (2) farmers who sell directly to consumers; (3) neorurals who ingressed into food production after some kind of urban experience. Three different logics of appropriation of aesthetic discourse characterize these groups. In the first case, this is basically due to the imposition of formal rules and standards by buyers, usually retail chains. In the second case, it occurs in a much more negotiated and tacit way, through interaction and proximity between producers and consumers. Finally, in the third case, we note the initiative of new farmers to identify, and even anticipate urban consumption trends by virtue of their own experience. Whatever the particular logic of this process, these actors began to develop new social practices, aiming at responding to the process of aestheticization not only of food, but also of the rural world itself.

A new arrangement of artifacts and meanings is created in response to this process. *Caipira* food is resignified and enriched along with crock pots, wood stove, wooden spoons, antique knives and enamelware (Boltanski and Esquerre, 2017). By means of various semantic and symbolic movements, these tokens of the past and rural life become the nostalgic expression of an "ancient time" when the food was authentic, smelled and tasted "for real." "Objects evoke fantasies based on symbolic associations with desired events, people, places, or values" (Beckert, 2011). In a way, the rural is no longer a space, but a time and a quality; that precedes the arrival of the industry, canned food, pressure cooker, stainless steel and microwave oven. It becomes synonymous with nostalgia, tradition, diversity, craftsmanship and locality. And it enters the urban environment, which is provided not only with food, but also with countless elements of rurality. In the cities, restaurants incorporate rustic artifacts that support this rural aesthetics.

The aestheticized rural is not the same as that of the industrial order (modern, technological, efficient), nor even that of the domestic order (traditional, old). This process of resignification becomes a means for farmers and their communities to fight the feelings of disrespect and contempt embedded in the image of an uncivilized rural cultivated by urban citizens. As the rural becomes a space for consumption, the rural practices, identities and landscapes are reconstructed. More than a place where the artisanal cheeses and beers are once again produced, the rural becomes the space of new identities, aspirations and life projects. It is no surprise that many young people who return to the countryside do so for glimpsing the opportunities offered by gastronomy and tourism. Although it still involves investments in agricultural production, these are aimed at new food products.

The link between tourism and gastronomy is essential to understand how these practices are structured. In the *Serras Verdes* (Green Mountains) of southern Minas Gerais or in the *Caminhos dos Engenhos* (Mills Trails) in the wetlands of Paraiba, the aestheticization process is directly related to the expansion of rural tourism and rural space. The importance of this practice in the formation of food memories is already widely demonstrated (Souza, 2017) – needless to deepen this argument here. However, it is worth noting an increasingly important change: if, previously, history and landscape were the main attractions in many regions, and gastronomy benefited from externality gains, now food has gained a place at the desk of travel agencies. There are circuits specifically focused on eating experiences. Consumers want to taste the place, the ecological and sociocultural environment that produces the food.

Several contradictions mark this process. Generally, the first question that emerges in this discussion is the relation between aesthetics and elitism. After all, who can afford it? Sociology has already dealt with this link between consumer practices and the phenomenon of social distinction (Bourdieu, 1979; Veblen, 1957). Among other things, it has shown that where, what, and with whom to eat are social markers used to manage identities, resources and powers (Warde, 2015). Nevertheless, the emergence of an aesthetic order in food markets has impacts on different social strata – it should not be confused with production and consumption of *foie gras* by a wealthy elite. The matter is not the product itself, but the practices and representations it engenders. Obviously, some products are more prone to aestheticization and others resist it, but insofar as even popcorn has entered the gourmet universe, one can understand the plasticity of the phenomenon.

The criticism of elitism stems from the limited effect of social inclusion of this process, either regarding the universe of consumers who can afford these foods, or in relation to the type of farmer who can produce it. The term "niche" is recurrently used to characterize the circuits for these products, as if this tricky concept could grasp the complexity of the phenomenon. Based on the analysis of the link between gastronomy and family farming, Zaneti (2017) suggests the existence of at least two distinct dynamics. The first one refers to a mediation of the relationship between consumers and farmers by a third actor who appropriates most of the added value. In this case, farmers are paid little, consumers pay a lot, and the difference between these pays for the chef's expertise and/or the restaurant's created atmosphere (the cultural tokens). The second dynamics involves more symmetrical connections generally found in proximity markets: farmers get more, consumers pay less and remuneration acknowledges the specialized knowledge of chefs, but also the traditional know-how of farmers; the investments made by the restaurant to create a friendly environment, but also the community's collective efforts to conserve the rural landscape. In this case, the ethicization of aesthetics is a more evident ingredient.

Another contradiction is analyzed by Miele and Murdoch (2002), based on the differentiation between "entertainment aesthetics" and "gastronomic food esthetics." The first notion underlines the processes of aesthetic reconstruction in which the focus is not on food but on the environment where practices develop. It shows that new eating experiences can be created without changing a single ingredient or product. The attention is primarily on the reconstruction of the eating environment to create new entertainment experiences. Differently, the second type of food aesthetics favors the quality of food. Here, the narrative is associated with the flavor, freshness and typicality of the ingredients, which are connected with the characteristics of the place where they were produced and their social trajectories. Although the authors focus their analyses on this second type of experiment, there is often a hybridization between these logics.

Finally, there is the issue of imbrication of sectoral and territorial dynamics. As we discussed above, the aesthetic components that differentiate a food often refer to attributes of the rural space and, more broadly, of the whole territory. These attributes encompass the landscape and the knowledge collectively produced and shared across generations. However, to what extent does food aesthetics recognize (and remunerate) the commons? The situations are diverse. Bowen and Zapatta's (2009) analysis of tequila and mezcal production in Mexico draws attention to the risks of private appropriation of the commons. In this case, large companies have benefited from a process that focuses on the product itself, while territories serve as the physical and cultural basis for their economic strategies. On the other hand, the studies by Pecqueur (2001) and Delfosse (2007), in France, reveal situations in which the attributes of territories are placed in the foreground to produce strategies for the qualification and valorization of a wide "basket of goods."

Regarding the Brazilian context, this discussion had already caught our attention when we analyzed the effects of territorial overflow caused by the expansion of viticulture and wine tourism in the Vale dos Vinhedos (Niederle et al., 2016). Over the past two decades, this small territory embedded in the heart of the Serra Gaucha (Rio Grande do Sul) has become the most renowned wine producer in Brazil. This was undoubtedly due to investments made by wineries to improve product quality. Likewise, it is recognized that landscapes, traditions and all other commons of the territory were essential to leverage this process, especially through wine tourism. However, while data on the economic gains of wineries, as well as of the hotel and food industry are beyond reproach, numerous controversies surround the discussion about the impacts on farmers. For example, some local actors see land price appreciation as an indicator of the success of this trajectory; while others point to this as one of the main risks to their sustainability, as it increases too much the opportunity costs of agriculture and attracts real estate investments that, according to them, mischaracterizing not only the landscape but also the historical sociocultural conformation.

Nevertheless, this is not the only type of dynamics encompassed by the new aesthetics of the rural. The experience of rural tourism that began about a decade ago in Santa Rosa de Lima, a municipality in the South of Santa Catarina, has a stronger territorial logic. Led by family farmers themselves, with the support of various social organizations, the *Acolhida na Colônia* embraces a wide range of products and services, aiming to provide tourists a unique experience of rural life. Currently disseminated across several other municipalities, the initiative undertakes practices and meanings that go far beyond the commodification of culture. Homemade recipes highlight domestic practices, while the focus on agroecological production and ecotourism could also be associated with the civic order. Still, under the influence of gastronomic tourism, many of these practices also carry aesthetic components, which are expressed in culinary specialties, local crafts and the environment created to accommodate tourists, that is, the farmers' own house.

The taste of origin

According to Wilkinson, Niederle and Mascarenhas (2016, 11), "a new dynamics has been drawing attention in several food markets: the growing

Figure 6.1 Examples of Brazilian Geographical Indications labels.

appreciation of attributes related to the origin of products." Among devices that institutionalize this bond, the best-known is the Geographical Indication (GI), a sign of intellectual property that distinguishes the territorial origin of a product or service (Figure 6.1). The first Brazilian GI was recognized in 2002 (Vale dos Vinhedos for wines in Rio Grande do Sul). Since then, encouraged by the results of this experience, and by the incentive of different public and private actors, the demands for recognition have expanded and diversified across other territories and products. By December 2019, there were already 65 geographical names registered in the National Institute of Industrial Property (INPI) as Indications of Provenance (54) or Designations of Origin (11). In addition to wines, the list of recognized agrifood products includes cheeses, coffees, cotton, rice, propolis, shrimp, honey, fruits, *cachaça*, sweets, saffron, yerba mate, cassava flour, guarana, among others.

GIs are hybrid and contradictory devices. On the one hand, they emphasize the sociocultural embeddedness of the product in its territory and, by valuing intangible assets that are difficult to transpose to other territories, are even defined as tools of territorial development (Cerdan 2009; Pecqueur, 2001). On the other hand, they are adjusted to act as catalysts for technical innovations that lead to standardization and often endanger the products' link with the *terroir* (Niederle and Vitrolles, 2010). The specific way in which a GI is linked to the dynamics of the territory depends on the format that this device takes after a lengthy negotiation about its institutional and sociotechnical configuration. This process is carried out by different actors whose distinct interests must be mediated to produce a compromise, which defines the institutional basis for stabilizing a system of common rules and standards. The focus of the controversies is the Code of Practices (*Cahiers des Charges*), a document approved by the producers themselves that specifies production, processing, marketing, monitoring and control practices.

Despite the high institutional plasticity of this device, in this section, we are specifically interested in the way GIs connect to the conformation of an aesthetic order. This does not mean that they are specific to this form of ordering. On the contrary, previous studies have already demonstrated GIs close connection with the domestic order, given its potential for valuing a range of traditional practices; their rapid appropriation by the industrial order, which implies the redesign to meet modernization and standardization strategies; as well as the controversial relationship their establishes with the civic order, because of the contradictory effects of appreciation of the territory and the product, on the one hand, and the risk of overexploitation caused by the expansion of demand, on the other (Niederle, 2011). However, compared to other devices mentioned in the previous chapters, GIs are those that most clearly incorporate a gastronomic food aesthetic (Miele and Murdoch, 2002).

First, the link between this device and the formation of an aesthetic order stems from the fact that the formal registration of a GI demands the renown of the geographical name. In Brazil, in the case of an Indication of Provenance, the only legal requirement for registration is the recognition of the geographical name that identifies the territory as a producing center of a given good, regardless of the intrinsic characteristics of this latter. Even if coffee or cheese with similar physicochemical characteristics is produced in another territory – what would make it impossible to distinguish the origin of the product by these criteria – the prevailing factor of differentiation in an Indication of Provenance is the image of the territory, which will always be a sociocultural and identitary construction, even if it is based on both physical factors such as climate and landscape, and human factors such as customs and traditions.

An important aspect of the interaction between GIs and aesthetics is the way that movements for revaluation of origin foster certain practices that go beyond the production. This is the case, for example, of festivals, fairs, contests and religious celebrations that, whether to mark the event of extra virgin olive oil extraction at the Mantiqueira Mountains or the beginning of the grapes harvest in Farroupilha, help to incorporate symbolic elements into the territory and product images. These practices play an important role in "anchoring" (Warde, 2015) other food practices, for consolidating their value bases (knowledge, traditions, customs). Therefore, they are key to building collective identity and demarcating the uniqueness of products, thus creating a stronger bond between these and their territories.

Investments in the valuation of the origin of foods have expanded the possibilities of meeting a new demand from the gastronomic movements, namely, to add "brasility" to a universe historically dominated by practices that privilege knowledge, ingredients and artifacts from other countries and cultures. From baru ice cream to yerba mate beer, Brazilian cuisine reinvents itself, and in doing so creates alternatives for family farmers and traditional communities. Often considered unviable by rural economists because of low agricultural productivity, these farmers are heirs to resources of biodiversity, knowledge and traditional production methods (Gueneau et al., 2017). Examples abound: guarana of Maués; clay pots of Goiabeiras; the golden grass of Jalapão; the red propolis of Alagoas, the artisanal cheeses of Minas Gerais, the acai of Baixo-Tocantins.

However, there are also plenty examples of appropriation of knowledge and other material and immaterial resources by other actors. Besides valuing the territories, GIs can be redefined to serve many other purposes, including the imposition of strict industrial quality standards, which leads to the exclusion of less competitive producers, as occurred in the case of Pampa Gaúcho meat. It was indeed for the malleability of this device that it became the object of attention of commodity producers. For them, GI comprises a market repositioning strategy to move from the price competition, which is increasingly linked to the possibility of reducing production costs, towards a post-Fordist competition regime, in which the watchwords are segmentation and differentiation. This is what rice farmers did in the North Coast of Rio Grande do Sul, when they set up the project for the first Brazilian Denomination of Origin, registered in 2010. The same can be said for coffee GIs, which reveal the efforts of Brazilian producers to create new market circuits, so that to meet the growing demand for specialty coffees (Wilkinson, Niederle and Mascarenhas, 2016).

Would it be appropriate to consider the use of GIs in these segments as a process of "misappropriation" simply because they are linked to commodities? Or, otherwise, should we recognize that this phenomenon challenges the very frontier between commodity and singularity? GI experiences in Brazil seem to be evidence that the differentiation between these markets does not lie in the type of product but in the process of singularization. Besides, it is not only the boundary between commodity and singularities that GIs call into question, but also the one between markets. In various territories, GIs were built with a view to enhancing the access of large producers to export markets, suggesting that strategies of valorization of origin do not emerge in opposition to globalization processes. But there is nothing a priori to make GI a specific mechanism for this type of circuit, since some results have even been ineffective (Niederle and Silva, 2017). On the other hand, when a GI is more strongly linked to a territorial development strategy, its potential to boost proximity circuits is revealed. Despite the particularities of each case, this is noticeable both in Goiabeiras, in Espírito Santo – where a small association of artisans from the outskirts of the capital, Vitória, started to be visited daily by tourists in search of clay pots – and in the Vale of Uva Goethe, in Santa Catarina – whose traditional table wine supplies the growing local wine tourism.

Aesthetics and cultural heritage: interfaces and conflicts

There are other devices for recognition and protection of territorialized goods besides Geographical Indications. This is the case, for example, with the catalog of cultural heritage, a public instrument aimed at safeguarding traditional knowledge and practices. This device that cross the boundaries between domestic (traditions) and civic (commons) orders is managed by the National Institute of National Historical and Artistic Heritage (IPHAN), which is responsible for assessing the factors that justify the inclusion of a particular practice as an "immaterial good." It does not focus on the product, but on the immaterial components of the social practices through which they are produced. That is why registration is not granted to cheese or acarajé, but to the "craft of making artisanal *minas* cheese" or the "craft of the *baianas de acarajé*," that is, to the knowledge associated with the practices managed by social actors.

For having a logic that does not primarily concern the protection of property and the commercial valuation of the product, heritage making holds a controversial relationship with both the qualification devices that arise from the industrial order, and with those associated with the aesthetic order. This relationship was analyzed by Belas (2015), whose research shows how the action of designers produced substantial changes in the traditional handcraft of the golden grass of Jalapão, which is also object of recognition via GI. According to the author, the growing demand for this good has increased the "risk of reification and homogenization of traditional crafts as a reflection of an eminently market perspective, which prioritizes products over producers and their production contexts" (Belas, 2015). It does not mean that traditions should be "protected from the market." However, in this case, innovation is only acceptable when the product continues to "make sense" to its producers (Bérard and Marchenay, 2007). That is, when the community continues to recognize in it the knowledge and practices socially shared over time (Champredonde, 2016).

Among all food products suitable as an example of this type of dynamics, the case of artisanal cheeses was the one that has drawn most attention of the academic and political fields in Brazil. Discussions involving norms of production led to the formation of a network movement for valorization of artisanal cheeses (see Chapter 4). Dialogue between producers, researchers, nongovernmental organizations, public managers, chefs and consumers has enhanced this movement's ability to publicize and legitimize its criticism, forcing changes in institutional arrangements (Cruz, 2012). In fact, despite pressures from major agro-industries against the production of artisanal cheeses, the circulation of these products grew and reached new circuits. This process resulted from the way heritage-making discourse was incorporated by gastronomic movements, gaining more space in newspapers, blogs and magazines. As a result, if, on the one hand, there is still substantial resistance to the recognition of this type of product, on the other hand, there has never been such a significant movement in its defense as a Brazilian cultural heritage (Cruz and Menasche, 2014).

One of the most obvious contradictions in this discussion concerns the fact that, while Brazilian law sets various obstacles to the manufacture and marketing of artisanal cheeses, it has long allowed the importation of similar products from other countries, especially France and Italy. In these countries, artisanal cheeses are part of the national identity and are expressions of a secular culture. Furthermore, they constitute a consumer good quite representative in terms of trading, either due to domestic market demand, or to its participation in exports. In fact, in order to promote and protect this heritage, until March 2017, France and Italy have already registered, respectively, 54 and 51 GIs of cheeses in the European Union – almost half of the 232 European GIs. Many of these registers concern raw milk products: Roquefort, Camembert de Normandie, Mâconnais, Pelardon, Asiago, Pecorino, Grana Padano, Parmigiano Reggiano, among others.

In Brazil, if until recently these names were found almost exclusively in small specialty stores, they have now entered large retail chains interested in their significant price differentials. In addition, there is an image appropriation carried out by most of the large dairy industries, which sell *"tipo"* (similar to) roquefort, camembert, parmesan, provolone cheeses. Unlike wines, which have additional protection, approved by the World Trade Organization at the Marrakesh Ministerial Meeting in 1994, in the case of cheese and other foodstuffs, the use of translated names and accompanied by expressions such as class, type, style and imitation is still authorized. The matter has been the subject of recurring conflicts in multilateral negotiations involving industrial property and is now one of the main obstacles to the signing of the Mercosur-European Union agreement.

Criticism over this situation only gained ground in the public debate when the first projects for cheese GI began to be discussed. The recognition of Serro and Canastra GIs in 2011 and 2012, respectively, made the institutional arrangement unsustainable. For the INPI, responsible for the registration of GIs, the existence in these territories of traditional products, whose first historical records date back to the eighteenth century and which are widely recognized by producers and consumers, was unquestionable. This view was corroborated by the registration already granted by IPHAN, in 2008, to the Artisanal Way of Making Cheese in Minas Gerais, in the regions of Serro, Serra da Canastra and Serra do Salitre, as a cultural heritage. Nevertheless, it is precisely these traditional methods and processes that have been criticized by large dairy companies and agroindustrial cooperatives that, generally, seek legitimation in values of the industrial order. Like several other artisanal Brazilian cheeses, Serro and Canastra cheeses are made from unpasteurized milk, use natural rennet yeast extracted from the milk itself and are matured on wooden benches. All these characteristics pose obstacles to their recognition and marketing due to safety food legislation which, besides restricting these practices, established maturation periods incompatible with the production methods, the characteristics of the product and the ways of selling it. In sum, both the GI recognized by the INPI and the IPHAN heritage registration focused on a product that, according to the norms that was then in force, was prevented from being produced and traded.

The debates raised by this type of controversy broadened when other territories began to discuss their strategies of recognition and differentiation. Influenced by the experiences of Serro and Canastra, other Brazilian regions also began to discuss singularization devices for their artisanal cheeses: Araxá, Serrano, Salitre, Catauá. The movement also sparked discussions about types of artisanal cheeses that spread across various territories: *colonial*, *coalho*, *manteiga*, *cabacinha* and several others. In view of the institutional obstacles that have arisen to the valorization of these cheeses, several actors assumed a critical stance regarding not only health standards (spurring the aforementioned normative changes), but also the GIs themselves. According to them, in various situations, the Code of Practices incorporated parameters of the food safety, what allowed the formalization of agro-industries, but at the cost of excluding smallholders and endangering traditional practices and knowledge.

The fact that no other GI registration has been granted in Brazil for artisanal cheeses in recent years results in part, from the understanding that this device can mischaracterize, desingularize and standardize the product (Cintrão, 2016). As Cruz and Menasche (2014) note, more than the organoleptic attributes of artisanal cheese (e.g., the elimination of certain beneficial bacteria due to pasteurization), the modes of production, knowledge, the images and social representations associated with them are also at stake. Nevertheless, even if this understanding converges with the criticism against the legislation in force, it still holds significant divergences when it comes to the strategies of valorization and commercialization of artisanal cheeses. In some contexts, the constructed narrative suggests that the "market logic" (*sic*) present in GIs would be corrupting the culture, promoting a process of "disenchantment," turning artisanal cheeses into mere "commodities." In other situations, however, the construction of (new) markets is presented as the most feasible alternative for preserving and, what is more, strengthening the artisanal cheese culture. One of the main dilemmas of the actors involved in this debate has been to reconcile the aesthetic, ethical and domestic values that underlie these different positions.

In the case of France, some research holds that granting economic value to a traditional cheese was an effective means of protecting it (Delfosse, 2007). From this perspective, if the product obtains a differential value in the market, it can reproduce itself, so that the know-how to produce it is preserved. It means that, if consumers value products deeply rooted in local cultures, the possibilities of reproducing the knowledge and customs that differentiate this product would be greater (Brunori, 2006). Otherwise, the product runs a serious risk of giving way to industrial imitations. Accordingly, European policies for recognition of traditional products focused on the reformulation of production norms and standards, so that to build a kind of valuative compromise – always subject to criticism and contestation – between the aesthetic and ethical principles that are at stake in these markets.

In Brazil, there is still a long way to go in this direction. Firstly, this would entail reconsidering the very conception of "market" that prevails in social theory, as well as in the imaginary of producers, public officials and social movements. Thereon, it may be possible to connect GIs with the policy of safeguarding immaterial heritage. Since registering a product as a cultural heritage does not protect it against use and copying, anyone can take advantage of its reputation for commercial purposes. GIs constitute a possibility of partial protection of this heritage, at least as regards the exclusivity of the geographical name by the local community. Although a GI does not forbid anyone from producing artisanal *minas* cheese, it can restrict the use of the Serro and Canastra names to those producers who conform to the Code of Practices. What is protected is not the product per se, but the reputation, the renown, the "image" of the territory.

New bottles for old wines?

In the late 2000s, the fast food chain McDonalds launched a quality differentiation strategy focused on incorporating typical regional and national products into its hamburgers. In Italy, McParmeggiano-Reggiano was produced with one of the most reputed cheeses in the world, originated from provinces of Emilia-Romagna and Lombardy, and McItaly, made entirely from products with Geographical Indication (Italian meat, lettuce, artichoke cream and Asiago cheese). This strategy has become the subject of numerous public controversies (Niederle and Cruz, 2010). Luca Zaia, then Italian Minister of Agriculture, defended the initiative, arguing that it "promotes the taste of Italy" among younger consumers. Moreover, according to him, the strategy would require thousands of tons of Italian agricultural products per month, favoring the farmers. Carlo Petrini, founder of the Slow Food Movement, on the other hand, countered: "This has nothing to do with supporting Italian farmers and products, this is about making money by working with a multinational that actively seizes power from local producers" (*The Telegraph*, 2010).

McDonald's strategy could be interpreted as the creation of a "gourmet capitalism" that makes it more palatable, as occurs with its "greening" when it comes to appropriating the sustainability discourse. Therefore, according to Petrini, the strategy of the company implies appropriation, desingularization and standardization of the Italian gastronomic heritage. McDonald's action would simply be transforming food heritage into a commodity, resulting in a degradation of the values and cultural representations carried by the products. The "fetishization" of these commodities would reveal the mechanisms by which the food industry manipulates signs and meanings, tastes and desires. Advertising leads consumers, trapped in an illusion, to believe to be eating something unique, while in fact they help to consolidate the same pattern of social relations of production and labor that is hidden behind the commodity.

This is not exclusive to fast food. To some extent, it is a more general trend of the agrifood system. When it comes to food, writes Poulain (2013, 38), the fetishization movement would tend "towards the standardisation of a limited number of dishes." Thus, behind its apparent diversity, "the great contemporary cuisine, even when revisiting some classic dishes, would be characterized by a relative reduction in the foods options." In this sense, another case with international repercussions was the frozen food scandal that shook the reputation of French cuisine. Considering that it is the only country in the world whose gastronomy is considered as world heritage by UNESCO, the information that, in 2013, 31% of the restaurants were using ready-made dishes, turned the stomach of many consumers, including those in the French parliament, where a group of 40 deputies filed bills for regulation of the sector (Fernandes, 2013).

One noticeable aspect in the French debate was the way it pervaded the relationship between diversity and gastronomy. According to media reports published at the time, the phenomenon of frozen food was directly associated with the diversification of the offer and the entry of sophisticated dishes in the menus. Small restaurants have offered a wide range of dishes at very low prices, including French classics such as duck with orange and *boeuf bourguignon* (beef cooked with burgundy red wine). Everything was produced outside the restaurant by major industries that specialized in offering the same variety to dozens of restaurants. As a result, restaurant critics began to point out to tourists, the main targets of these restaurants, establishments with limited menus with few starters, and only three or four main dishes. That is, in a somewhat paradoxical way, "a menu with very few dishes is interpreted by experts as a sign of quality, which indicates a higher probability of using fresh ingredients, bought daily" (BBC, 2013).

In Brazil, the use of premade food by restaurants still deserves a thorough study. This type of practice is known to exist, but there are no data to assess its relevance, perhaps because the issue has not yet attracted public attention. What has already entered the agenda, however, is the current gourmet offensive by large agro-industrial conglomerates. Recent examples are the strategies of two giants of the Brazilian and global agrifood sector. In 2016, BRF Foods, owner of the Sadia and Perdigão brands, launched a partnership with the British chef Jamie Oliver to promote "healthy and gourmet" products: basically, the same type of frozen chicken in different recipes. Hitherto applauded for his "food revolution," the chef suddenly became *persona non grata* to the militants of the movements for good, clean and fair food. In the same year, JBS Foods hired *haute cuisine* fan Robert de Niro to promote the "Seara Gourmet" product line.

The importance acquired by the theme in Brazilian society is revealed, for example, in the numerous television programs aimed at gastronomy. Zaneti (2017) points to about 160 television programs in Brazil about food and eating. It was mainly through these means that the theme spread, although the new media also play a significant role. As highlighted in a report in Caderno Paladar (Estadão, 2014), the "gourmet shock" that went viral in social networks makes a hypothetical traditional *pamonha* become "organic green corn dough, agglutinated with coconut milk and sugar." The price grows as much as the name, from R$2.00 to R$15.00. Would this be the proof that everything is a matter of making money, business as usual? The food-truck revolution would also be nothing but a new way for capitalism to reinvent the hot dog cart and widen its profit margins, though now through the entrepreneurial initiative of some hipster who, as the American journalist Christian Lorentzen would say, "fetishises the authenticity"? (TimeOut, 2007).

If everything is nothing but old wine in new bottles, it is up to social movements to fight for the decommodification of these foods that would be, taking Polanyi's (1957) terms, just "fictitious commodities." And that exactly is what many have done. Slow Food is the main expression of this countermovement on a global scale. According to its supporters, it is not just about defending good food and gastronomic pleasure, but also about protecting traditional foods and ingredients, conserving production and processing methods and defending biodiversity. Resingularization (or reenchantment), therefore, does not involve the type of food, but rather the arrangement of entities and practices that define its image. From this perspective, it is impossible to say that we are talking about the same Asiago cheese when it is found in a mayonnaise-filled hamburger served on the fast food chain, or in a traditional *panini* from a small Venetian restaurant.

A new generation of social research has focused on the ability of new consumer movements to recontextualize foods, giving them meanings that are distinct from those they carried "originally" (Stolle, Hooghe and Micheletti, 2005). This is accompanied by an important discussion about the consumer–citizen and the forms of "politicized consumption," which are expressed, for example, in boycott and buycott practices (Portilho and Micheletti, 2018). Among the reference authors in this discussion, Miller (2007) analyzes the political dimension of these processes, suggesting that understanding the trajectories of the goods allows to defetishize them, since the human relationships that underpin their socially constructed images are unveiled. In turn, Campbell (2005) builds a notion of "craft consumer" to analyze how consumers, in the act of consuming, transform standardized goods into personalized objects.

Research has shown that these processes are far more intricate and less noticeable than is evident in the extreme case of fast food and slow food. What to say about the strategies of valorization of artisanal cheeses and the uses of GIs in Brazil? Our research on the subject brought us closer to somewhat different approaches, closer to the new economic socioanthropology (Niederle, 2014). From this perspective, Zelizer (1994) has attempted to overcome the opposition between these "hostile worlds." Bringing moral values that are strange to capitalism back to the center of explanations about the functioning of modern markets, she suggests that it is necessary to understand the symbolic plasticity of these commodities and the consequences of route deviations caused by certain circuits in which impersonal social relations predominate (Zelizer, 1994).

Zelizer's multimarket model suggests that the two worlds should not be diametrically opposed, as if Parmeggian-Reggian cheese had intrinsic qualities that prevented it from entering the commodity universe, whereas every hamburger produced by a fast food restaurant was the *ex-machina* expression of the pure commodity, free from any kind of symbolic representation. If, on the one hand, life itself is the object of commodification (life insurance, health insurance), on the other, not even money escapes the moral values that define its form and use. In the same vein, Allaire (2013, 76) suggests that, while it is true that the monetary assessment of Champagne's intangible quality does not violate its magic bubbles, which are still impregnated with cultural beliefs and representations, "the same is also true of the simple chips a child is eating at a fast food restaurant that provokes his/her imagination."

Such plasticity does not mean extreme relativization. Here the typically Polanyian political program returns to debate with Zelizer's model. Recognizing that an industrial frozen lasagna served by a Roman restaurant still carries meanings that go far beyond its exchange value does not contradict the political struggles that emerge from the value crisis arisen when the consumer feels "deluded." To a large extent, this depends on the ability of the new social movements to denounce, and thereupon on public regulation initiatives. What is certain is that the relationship between ethics and aesthetics remains a dilemma for movements that criticize the industrial food order. Deeper changes in food markets seem to increasingly depend on the ability of these movements to produce compromises between the values emanating from these two worlds (Boltanski and Thévenot, 1991), what also implies the development of new practices, technical artifacts and institutional arrangements.

Beyond fetishism

The main components of the aesthetic order can be summarized as follows: practices such as gastronomization, immaterializing of food and various forms of immaterial work supported by artifacts such as certification

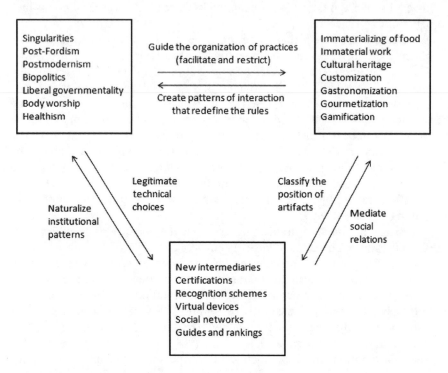

Figure 6.2 Components of the aesthetic order.

and recognition instruments, virtual devices that support the discourse of healthism, as well as a paraphernalia of guides, indexes, rankings and social networks (Figure 6.2). In addition, all of these artifacts, as well as new market professionals (youtubers, chefs, winemakers etc.), are legitimized by institutional standards that have been consolidated with the advent of post-Fordism, postmodernity and biopolitics.

If the emergence of this mode of ordering was rooted on the aesthetic critique of the standardization and homogenization of production and consumption promoted by the industrial capitalism, its consolidation is largely due to the way capitalism was able to internalize such criticism (Boltanski and Chiapello, 2007). This appropriation, however, produces new movements of contestation. One of these reactions highlights the aesthetic of simplicity, for which less is more. Rather than brands, stamps, rankings, likes, it is the food that appears in the foreground, and without much refinement. Still, like minimalism in art and design, this is an aesthetic criticism that suggests changes within the order without contesting its institutional foundations. It is a reformist criticism.

Another kind of criticism, a more radical one, questions the authenticity of the whole aesthetic phenomenon. While the distinction between a mass product and a differentiated product is relatively easy, the same is not true when it comes to goods that are marketed as images. How to know whether a product is effectively natural? What business strategies hide behind the advertising of healthy products? Is it sound to believe that a chocolate covered cereal bar can be healthy? As Boltanski and Chiapello (2007, 449) point out,

> the tension between the truth of the original and the artificiality of what has been "fabricated" in its image inflects what it means to characterize something as authentic in a direction that makes reference not so much to the object itself, as to the intentions of those it is procured from. Now what is authentic is that which has been made without a secondary strategic intention.

As the growing interest of industries in the markets of singularities becomes more evident, there is an increasing skepticism toward the spectacle and the simulacrum created by the aesthetic phenomenon. The fear that everything may be fake heightens the tensions between the image of individual freedom held by the aesthetic critique and the mechanisms of domination and control of feelings and bodies created by this same order.

The most prevalent understanding of the aesthetic phenomenon, which is heir to Frankfurtian sociology, is one that accentuates the way capitalist industry, pursuing profits, uses media, marketing and now big data to manipulate tastes and desires of consumers. "It's label, stupid!," wrote a political columnist for a Brazilian leftist magazine (Vieira, 2014). Synthesized in the idea of "fetishization," this understanding has already been opposed by authors such as Fischler (1990) and Poulain (2013), for whom food modernity is, above all, the result of processes of blend and hybridism, in which homogenization and commoditization coexist with increasing food variety, and the strategies of industries are fed back by the emergence of new practices and motivations that do not depend entirely and sometimes not even mainly on their interests. Hence, it is not just "label," but the recognition of the symbolic dimensions of food (Barbosa, 2009).

An example is the growth of meals had in the workplace. This phenomenon, directly associated with changes in the world of work, including the growing female presence, is inducing new production and distribution practices, such as the return of lunchboxes, now increasingly diverse and gourmetized. Besides being an alternative for those who can't afford to eat at a restaurant, the lunchbox has become the option of those who don't want to eat at a restaurant, either because they do not have enough time, or because they prefer to adjust their eating times (even breaking the Brazilian pattern of three meals a day), or because they prefer to produce their own food by selecting foods suitable to their current diet. The dissemination of this type of practice has even led famous restaurants and chefs such as Alex Atala, who runs the Mercadinho Dalva and Dito, in São Paulo, to sell a gourmet lunchbox. Although some insist that it contains merely rice, beans, eggs and collard greens in a common aluminum box, the fact is that there is a symbolic dimension that distinguishes it from other dishes with the same ingredients (and, of course, it is used as a marketing strategy to make money).

Even though carrying your lunchbox to work has become modern and cool, there are those who prefer to resort to food delivery systems, both at work and at home. In fact, the growth and diversification of specialized food delivery applications (Just-Eat, iFood, PedidosJá, Uber Eats, among others) is astonishing. The largest company in this field is currently Just-Eat. Founded in 2001, it already operates in 15 countries, including Brazil, where it established a joint venture with iFood, created in 2011, which already counts over 5,000 restaurants registered across the country (Schubert, 2017). If, on the one hand, these new artifacts affect the behavior of consumers, who are "enticed" by advertisements and conditioned by the algorithms that organize their buying options, on the other hand, these allow them to access a variety of food they would probably not find if they had to look for a restaurant near their workplaces or homes. In addition, the artifacts themselves are modified over time to adapt to emerging consumer demands.

These last two examples, among many others that we will not be able to examine in this chapter, reveal that the aesthetic phenomenon is more widespread and complex than we generally consider. As we noted earlier, the emergence of an aesthetic order in the agrifood system, beyond the exquisite dishes of a Michelin Guide three-stars restaurant – which has also been strongly contested in the gastronomic world for its supposed surrender to economic interests – is seen also in the domestic universe, where, for example, it promotes the gourmet balcony integrated to the kitchen; reshapes the countryside and the gastronomy of the farm to attract tourists; and even introduces gourmet food for dogs and cats. The development of this phenomenon obviously favors social groups with greater purchasing power and promotes social distinction and differentiation. However, besides being not limited to these groups, what is more evident is that these examples can no longer be treated as small and insignificant "niche."

Note

1　Lash and Urry's perception differs from that of Jameson regarding the consequences of commodification not only of culture but also of consumption as a cultural practice. While the latter ascribes greater analytical relevance to the strength of appropriation of culture and consumption by corporations and the media, as if every act of consumption in late capitalism was controlled by the irresistible force of the market, the former see a more significant space for countering this process, what would be related to the greater reflexivity of the late modern societies.

References

Ali, H. H., Lecocq, S. and Visser, M. 2010. "The impact of gurus: Parker grades and en primeur wine prices." *Journal of Wine Economics*, 5(1): 22–39.

Allaire, G. 2004. "Quality in economics: a cognitive perspective." In *Qualities of Food*, edited by M. Harvey, A. Mcmeekin and A. Ward, 66–92. Manchester: Manchester University Press.

Allaire, G. 2013. "A contribuição da sociologia econômica para compreender o significado da qualidade nos mercados alimentares." In *Indicações geográficas: qualidade e origem nos mercados alimentares*, edited by P. Niederle, 55–80. Porto Alegre: UFRGS.

Appadurai, A. (ed.). 1988. *The Social Life of Things: Commodities in Cultural Perspective*. Cambridge: Cambridge University Press.

Aspers, P. and Beckert, J. 2011. Value in markets. In *The Worth of Goods: Valuation and Pricing in the Economy*, edited by J. Beckert and P. Aspers,3–38. Oxford: Oxford University Press.

Barbosa, L. 2009. "Tendências da alimentação contemporânea." In *Juventude, Consumo & Educação*, edited by M. Pinto and J. Pacheco, 15–64. Porto Alegre: ESPM.

Barbosa, L. 2016. "A ética e a estética na alimentação contemporânea." In *Produção, consumo e abastecimento de alimentos*, edited by F. Cruz, A. Matte and S. Schneider. Porto Alegre: UFRGS.

Barbosa, M., Roesler, V. and Cazella, S. 2016. "Aplicativos móveis para controle da obesidade e modelagem do emagreça@saudável." *Novas Tecnologias da Educação*, 14(1).

BBC. 2013. *Escândalo' da comida congelada ameaça reputação de restaurantes franceses*. Accessed May 21, 2017. www.bbc.com/portuguese/noticias/2013/05/130531_restaurates_franca_df#:~:text=Um%20card%C3%A1pio%20com%20pouqu%C3%ADssimos%20pratos,de%20ingredientes%20frescos%2C%20comprados%20diariamente.

Beckert, J. 2011. "The transcending power of goods: imaginative value in the economy." In The *Worth of Goods: Valuation and Pricing in the Economy*, edited by J. Beckert and P. Aspers, 106–28. Oxford: Oxford University Press.

Belas, C. 2015. "Entre a salvaguarda e o mercado: estratégias para a valorização comercial do artesanato de povos e comunidades tradicionais." In *Proceedings of the VII Jornada Internacional de Políticas Públicas*. São Luís: UFMA.

Bérard, L. and Marchenay, P. 2007. "Localized products in France: definition, protection and value-adding." *Anthropology of Food*, s2.

Boltanski, L. and Chiapello, È. 2007. *The New Spirit of Capitalism*. London: Verso.

Boltanski, L. and Esquerre, A. 2017. *Enrichissement: une critique de la marchandise*. Paris: Gallimard.

Boltanski, L. and Thevenot, L. 1991. *De la Justification*. Paris: Gallimard.

Bourdieu, P. 1979. *La distinction*. Paris: Les Éditions de Minuit.

Bowen, S. and Zapata, A. 2009. "Geographical indications, terroir, and socioeconomic and ecological sustainability: The case of tequila." *Journal of Rural Studies*, 25(1): 108–19.

Brunori, G. 2006. "Post-rural processes in wealthy rural areas: Hybrid networks and symbolic capital." In *Between the Local and the Global*, edited by T. Marsdenand J. Murdoch, 121–45. London: Emerald.

Buck, D., Getz, C. and Guthman, J. 1997. "From farm to table: the organic vegetable commodity chain of northern California."*Sociologia Ruralis*, 37(1): 3–20.

Busch, L. 2011. *Standards: Recipes for Reality*. Cambridge: MIT Press.

Callon, M., Meadel, C. and Rabeharisoa, V. 2012. "The economy of qualities". *Economy and Society*, 31(2): 194–217.

Campbell, C. 2005. "The craft consumer: Culture, craft and consumption in a post-modern society." *Journal of Consumer Culture*, 5(1): 23–42.

Cerdan, C. 2009. "Valorização dos produtos de origem e do patrimônio dos territórios rurais no sul do Brasil: contribuição para o desenvolvimento territorial sustentável." *Política & Sociedade*, 8(14): 277–99.

Champredonde, M. 2016. "A qualidade vinculada à origem: da imersão à tipicidadeterritorial. In *O Sabor da Origem*, edited by J. Wilkinson, P. Niederle and G. Mascarenhas, 21–50. Porto Alegre: Escritos.

Cintrão, R. 2016. *Segurança, qualidade e riscos: a regulação sanitária e os processos de (i)legalização dos queijos artesanais de leite cru em Minas Gerais*. PhD Thesis. Rio de Janeiro: UFRRJ.

Cochoy, F. and Dubuisson-Quellier, S. 2000. "Introduction: Les professionnels du marché: vers une sociologie du travail marchand." *Sociologie du Travail*, 42(3): 359–68.

Cruz, F. T. 2012. *Produtores, consumidores e valorização de produtos tradicionais: um estudo sobre qualidade de alimentos a partir do caso do Queijo Serrano dos Campos de Cima da Serra*. PhD Thesis. Porto Alegre: UFRGS.

Cruz, F. T. and Menasche, R. 2014. "O debate em torno de queijos feitos de leite cru: entre aspectos normativos e a valorização da produção tradicional." *Vigilância Sanitária em Debate*, 2(2): 34–42.

Delfosse, C. 2007. *La France fromagère*. Paris: La Boutique de l'Histoire.

Dias, S. 2016. *Do campo à mesa: limites e possibilidades de uma gastronomia sustentável*. PhD Thesis. Piracicaba: USP.

Estadão. 2014. *Raio gourmetizador vira piada nas redes sociais*. Accessed December 12, 2017. www.paladar.estadao.com.br/noticias/comida,raio-gourmetizador-vira-piada-nas-redes-sociais,10000008206.

Exame. 2016. *Brasil jáé um dos maiores mercados "fitness" do mundo*. Accessed February 24, 2017. www.exame.abril.com.br/revista-exame/brasil-ja-e-um-dos-maiores-mercados-fitness-do-mundo.

Estadão. 2017. *Controlada pelo 3G, dona do Burger King compra rival por US$ 1,64 bi*. Accessed December 22, 2017. www.economia.estadao.com.br/noticias/negocios,controlada-pelo-3g-dona-do-burger-king-compra-rival-por-us-1-64-bi,70001673919.

Eymard-Duvernay, F. 2009. "L'économie des conventions entre économie et sociologie." In *Traité de sociologie économique*, edited by P. Steiner and F. Vatin, 131–64. Paris: Quadrige-PUF.

Fernandes, D. 2013. *'Escândalo' da comida congelada ameaça reputação de restaurantes franceses*. Accessed February 23, 2016. www.bbc.com/portuguese/noticias/2013/05/130531_restaurates_franca_df

Fischler, C. 1990. *L'Homnivore*. Paris: O. Javob.

Foucault, M. 2008. *O nascimento da biopolítica*. São Paulo: Martins Fontes.

Gueneau, S., Diniz, J., Mendonça, S. and Garcia, J. 2017. "Construção social dos mercados de frutos do Cerrado: entre sociobiodiversidade e alta gastronomia." *Século XXI – Revista de Ciências Sociais*, 7(1): 130–56.

Guivant, J. 2003. "Os supermercados na oferta de alimentos orgânicos: apelando ao estilo de vida ego-trip.' *Ambiente & Sociedade*, 6(2): 64–81.

Harvey, M., McMeekin, A. and Ward, A. (eds). 2004. *Qualities of Food*. Manchester: Manchester University Press.

Howard, P. 2016. *Concentration and Power in the Food System: Who Controls What We Eat?* New York: Bloomsbury Academic.

Jameson, F. 1996. *Pós-modernismo: a lógica cultural do capitalismo tardio.* São Paulo: Ática.

Karpic, L. 2007. *L'économie dês singularités.* Paris: Gallimard.

Lancaster, K. 1966. "A new approach to consumer theory." *Journal of Political Economy,* 74(2): 132–57.

Lash, S. and Urry, J. 1994. *"Economies of Signs and Space."* London: Sage.

Lupton, D. 2013. "Quantifying the body: monitoring and measuring health in the age of mHealth technologies." *Critical Public Health,* 23(4): 393–403.

Martuccelli, D. 2010. *La Société Singulariste.* Paris: Armand Colin.

Menasche, R. 2005. "Os grãos da discórdia e o trabalho da mídia." *Opinião Pública,* 11(1): 169–91.

Miele, M. and Murdoch, J. 2002. "The practical aesthetics of traditional cuisines: slow food in Tuscany." *Sociologia Ruralis,* 42(2): 312–28.

Miller, D. 2007. "Consumo como cultura material." *Horizontes Antropológicos,* 13(28): 33–63.

Niederle, P. 2011. *Compromissos para a qualidade: projetos de indicações geográficas para vinhos no Brasil e na França.* PhD Thesis. Rio de Janeiro: UFRRJ.

Niederle, P. 2014. "Os agricultores ecologistas nos mercados para alimentos edânicos: contramovimentos e novos circuitos de comércio." *Sustentabilidade em Debate,* 5(1): 79–96.

Niederle, P. and Cruz, F. T. 2010. "O que muda quando a tradição se torna fast food? As reações dos consumidores italianos e franceses aos hamburgers McParmegiano-Reggiano e Quick Hallal." In *Proceedings of the V Encontro Nacional da Anppas.* Florianópolis: ANPPAS.

Niederle, P. and Radomsky, G. F. 2017. "Quem governa por dispositivos? A produção das normas e padrões para os alimentos orgânicos no Brasil." *Tomo,* 30(1): 227–65.

Niederle, P. and Silva, F. 2017. "As Indicações Geográficas e os novos mercados para os vinhos brasileiros." In *Cadeias curtas e redes agroalimentares alternativas,* edited by M. Gazolla and S. Schneider, 219–40. Porto Alegre: UFRGS.

Niederle, P. and Vitrolles, D. 2010. "Geographical indications and qualification in the Brazilian wine production." *Estudos Sociedade e Agricultura,* 5(se).

Niederle, P., Bruch, K., Vieira, A. and Schneider, E. 2016. "Vinhos do Brasil: a tipicidade territorial entre tradições e inovações." In: *Sabor da Origem,* edited by J. Wilkinson, P. Niederle and G. Mascarenhas, 161–212. Porto Alegre: Escritos.

Pecqueur, B. 2001. "Qualité et développement territorial: l'hypothèse du panier de biens et de services territorialisés." *Économie Rurale,* 261(1): 37–49.

Polanyi, K. 1957. *The Great Transformation: The Political and Economic Origins of Our Time.* Boston: Beacon Press.

Portilho, F. and Micheletti, M. 2018. "Politicizing consumption in Latin America. In *The Oxford Handbook of Political Consumerism,* edited by M. Boström, M. Micheletti, and P. Oosterveer, 539–57. Oxford: Oxford University Press.

Santos, L. 2008. *O corpo, o comer e a comida: um estudo sobre as práticas corporais e alimentares no mundo contemporâneo.* Salvador: EDUFBA.

Schubert, M. 2017. *Comer fora de casa, as práticas e as rotinas do comer nos contextos da modernidade: uma leitura comparada entre Brasil, Reino Unido e Espanha.* PhD Thesis. Porto Alegre: UFRGS.

Souza, J. C. 2017. "Turismo Rural e Comunitário como vetores para o fortalecimento de cadeias agroalimentares familiares e agroecológicas." *Revista Cenário*, 4(7): 112–27.

Stolle, D., Hooghe, M. and Micheletti, M. 2005. "Politics in the supermarket: Political consumerism as a form of political participation." *International Political Science Review*, 26(3): 245–269.

The Guardian. 2012. *Let's start the foodie backlash*. Accessed June 2, 2016. www.theguardiacom/books/2012/sep/28/lets-start-foodie-backlash

The Telegraph. 2010. *McDonalds' McItaly burger fails to impress Italian critics*. Accessed February 22, 2016. www.telegraph.co.uk/news/worldnews/europe/italy/7168066/McDonalds-McItaly-burger-fails-to-impress-Italian-critics.html

Timeout. 2007. *Why the hipster must die*. Accessed August 22, 2018. www.timeout.com/newyork/things-to-do/why-the-hipster-must-die

Veblen, T. 1957. *The Theory of the Leisure Class*. New York: Mentor Book.

Vieira, W. 2014. "É o rótulo, estúpido! Do brigadeiro gourmet ao cinema vip, a banalização da 'exclusividade'." *Carta Capital*. Accessed August 4, 2017. www.cartacapital.com.br/revista/809/e-o-rotulo-estupido-5851.html.

Warde, A. 2015. *The Practice of Eating*. Cambridge: Polity.

Wilkinson, J., Niederle, P. and Mascarenhas, G. C. (eds). 2016. *O Sabor da Origem*. Porto Alegre: Escritos.

Zaneti, T. B. 2017. *Cozinha de raiz: as relações entre chefs, produtores e consumidores a partir do uso de produtos agroalimentares singulares na gastronomia contemporânea*. PhD Thesis. Porto Alegre: UFRGS.

Zaneti, T. B. and Balestro, M. 2015. "Valoração de produtos tradicionais no circuito gastronômico: lições do Cerrado." *Sustentabilidade em Debate*, 6(1): 22–36.

Zelizer, V. 1994. *The Social Meaning of Money*. New York: Basic Books.

7　From the agribusiness economy to the new financial order

The presence of financial capital is not new to the agricultural sector. As we saw in Chapter 2, the process of agricultural modernization and the formation of the industrial order after World War II were anchored in a set of financial instruments whose large amounts directly benefited farmers, processers and distributors (Delgado, 1985). In recent years, however, there have been qualitative changes in financial practices associated with certain dynamics of the agrifood system, revealing a deeper process of "financialization," which is, in turn, associated with important institutional transformations of capitalism (Streeck, 2013; Sassen, 2016).

Financialization was made possible by the emergence of neoliberalism, the new political ideology that gained ground in the 1970s with the decline of welfare state in Western Europe, the end of the New Deal legacy in the United States and the crisis of the developmental state in the Global South (Bonanno and Wolf, 2017; Brenner, 2003). This process surpasses the borders of nations; makes use of but does not respect national governments; and acts, as Hardt and Negri (2001) define, by the hands of the new "empires," that is, through mechanisms of decentralization and deterritorialization of capital. Along with this, not only new productive practices were established, but also new forms of domination at a global scale, whereby money acts as the ether that dissolves the democratic institutions and governance mechanisms characteristic of twentieth-century industrial societies.[1]

In the economic sphere, the advancement of the financial system gained momentum when Bretton Woods agreements were unilaterally abandoned by the United States. This was followed by a new monetary system, which was marked by floating exchange rate and the end of US dollar's gold convertibility standard (Harvey, 2005). A simultaneous and interrelated movement was the liberalization of capital, marked by the increase in foreign direct investments (FDI) inflows (Freitas and Prates, 1998). The progressive withdrawal of nation states from the control over the international financial system constituted a key institutional change towards integration of markets on a global scale (Gomes, 2017). For Chesnais (2005, 47), three processes were constitutive of this dynamic: the "monetary and financial deregulation or liberalization, the decompartmentalization of the national financial markets, and the disintermediation, that is, the opening of lending operations, previously reserved for banks, to all types of institutional investors."

These three processes were crucial for the emergence of both new financial practices (securitization, derivatives) and actors (insurance companies and pension funds, mutual funds, hedge funds, sovereign wealth funds) (Belluzzo, 1995; Carvalho et al., 2007). New artifacts were created, so that governments, companies and investors (individual and collective) could obtain rapid and substantial capital gains. Moreover, these artifacts allowed to detach involved parties (debtor and creditor) from each other and to transfer transaction risks to third parties. Indeed, either a building, a product or a debt, all can be bought and sold countless times without the agents involved having any knowledge of the other parties (Sassen, 2016). They often do not even know what type of operation their resources are being invested in, as it seems to have been the case, reported by The New York Times (2015), of North-American professors, whose pension fund (TIAA – Teachers Insurance and Annuity Association) was investing in grabbed lands in Brazil.

As to investors, banks are no longer the only intermediaries between financial capital seeking investment and entrepreneurs looking for credit for their businesses. A relatively heterogeneous set of private initiatives as investment funds became pools of resources for financial investment (Carvalho et al., 2007). As Frederico and Gras (2017, 20) note, this interest-bearing capital "is characterized by a myriad of capitalists that have distinct goals and strategies, as well as different, often obscure, forms of interconnection." Though, these investors are often looking for high short-term returns and, therefore, prone to greater risks, what makes the financial system more unstable (Paula, Santos and Pereira, 2015).

Financialization is characterized essentially by the fact that financial gain is detached from the production of goods and services. It was Adam Smith who first proposed this debate, distinguishing real wealth from fictitious wealth. Marx deepened it proposing the concept of "fictitious capital," which despite having nominal monetary value and existing as paper, has no ballast in terms of actual productive activity or physical assets. With financialization, fictitious capital appreciates relatively independently of the productive assets, thus profoundly changing the dynamics of the capitalist system. As Bresser-Pereira (2010, 57) shows, "between 1980 and 2007 financial assets grew about four times more than real wealth, the GDP." This demonstrates that financialization is the process, legitimized by neoliberalism, whereby the financial system, which is not only capitalist but also liberal, creates artificial financial wealth.

Financial capital seeks more profitability without leaving the financial realm, resorting to different means, such as corporate capital (when a firm goes public and sells its products on the stock exchange), state debt (when banks sell debt-based securities), workers' wages (when part of the earnings goes directly to a social security fund), among other possibilities. This ability of the financial system to generate revenue without producing anything at all has intensified speculative practices, leading to the formation of financial bubbles, such as the one that characterized the subprime crisis in the United States in 2007 – a result of the big bet that consisted of granting high risk mortgage loans to American consumers. These complex speculative practices are mediated by different technological and institutional artifacts, which guarantee the speed of financial transactions and complicated risk calculations, and which enable more scope, and strategies for mobility and appreciation of fictitious capital (Sassen, 2016).

Bresser-Pereira (2010, 56) argues that the 2007–2008 global crisis was a reflection of the rise in credit in the form of bonds, resulting in an artificial expansion of the "financial wealth or fictitious capital, which has expanded at a much higher rate than that of production, or real wealth." For the author, the crisis was caused by the deregulation of financial markets and the wild speculation allowed by such deregulation. One of several consequences of this crisis, which directly affected the agrifood system, was the migration of large investors from the real estate and credit markets to commodity futures markets, and the purchase and lease of large areas of land, thus intensifying the transformation of land and food in financial assets freely traded as fictitious capital (Goldfarb, 2014; Gomes 2017; Martin and Clapp, 2015).

Financialization of the agrifood system

There is a longstanding connection between the agricultural and the financial sectors, which takes various forms: agricultural production loans, price support, agricultural insurance, mortgage, contract farming, among others. The technical and institutional devices, however, as well as the way and intensity of the practices that connect these sectors have changed dramatically in recent decades. If, in the past, as noted by Martin and Clapp (2015), governments set up institutions to financially support farmers and established regulations to curb excessive speculation and to limit speculators' action in agricultural commodity markets, now they dismantle public financial support agencies and remove protection mechanisms for farmers while easing the rules to facilitate operations by private financial agents.

In such a context of financial deregulation and liberalization, several actors – banks, brokerage and securitization companies, investment funds and corporations from other sectors of the economy – which so far had not been interested in agrifood, started to invest heavily in this sector, many of them in association with national agricultural companies and large-scale farmers. As Frederico and Gras (2017, 12) point out, "in most cases, their strategies couple earning profits from grain crops, agrofuels and planted forests, and capturing land income through real estate speculation." Encouraged by the boom in commodity and land prices in the 2000s, these actors saw an opportunity to diversify their investments, reduce their risks (as other markets were more volatile) and increase their returns. In fact, the convergence of multiple crises – financial, energy, environmental and food – sparked the interest of financial agents in agricultural commodities, land acquisition and appropriation of natural resources (Borras, Jr. and Franco, 2010; Borras, Jr. et al., 2011).

The financial crisis led the so-called "traditional markets" (stocks, bonds, cash and cash equivalents) to lose value and become highly unstable, thus leading investors to seek safer and more profitable businesses, diversifying their investment portfolios to better manage risks (Sauer and Borras, Jr., 2016). The energy crisis deepened due to the dramatic increase in oil price (the price per barrel jumped from US$39 to US$133 between December 2004 and July 2008), as a result, among other things, of political instability in the main producing countries (Pereira, 2017). These factors led to the search for alternative energy sources, such as corn, sugarcane, soybean, palm and canola, what pushed the prices of these crops up and stirred up the search for new agricultural areas (Oliveira, 2011; Sauer and Leite, 2012). The environmental crisis, in turn, gained publicity in the context of global warming and climate change, leading to growing interest in markets that meet the environmental agenda, especially investments in the purchase of carbon credits and the production of "clean energy," as well as in the agreements to reduce emissions from deforestation and forest degradation (Sauer and Borras, Jr., 2016).

The food crisis was mainly associated with the global rise in food prices (Borras, Jr. and Franco, 2010), whose index doubled between 2006 and 2008. Maluf and Speranza (2014) note that the wide fluctuation in food commodity prices is explained not only by circumstantial factors, such as short-term imbalances between supply and demand, but, above all, by systemic factors as: continued rising in demand for food in large emerging countries, including grains for animal feed in view of increased consumption of protein foods due to greater incomes; allocation of increasing amount of grains such as corn and soybeans, as well as other foodstuffs, to the production of agrofuels; rising oil prices that affected prices generally and, particularly, the costs of agricultural production and transportation; effects of global climate, especially extreme events such as prolonged droughts and floods; decreasing growth rates of cereal harvests coupled with low levels of stocks as a result of about 30 years of underinvestment in agriculture.

The confluence of rising global food demand, declining stocks, lack of regulatory instruments and lower risk in commodity and land markets has provided excellent prospects of speculative gain for finance capital. In the aftermath of losses resulting from the subprime mortgage crisis, the fall in Wall Street stock values and the sharp devaluation of US dollar (Herreros, Barros and Bentes, 2010), global financial market investments underwent a major change, with a significant and constant growth of funds allocated to the global agrifood sector (Frederico and Gras, 2017; Spadotto, 2017). According to information provided by the consulting firm Valoral Advisors (2019), which specializes in agricultural and food investments worldwide, there were 534 funds earmarked for investments in the agrifood sector by 2018, which means an impressive growth compared to the 38 identified in 2005 (Figure 7.1). In

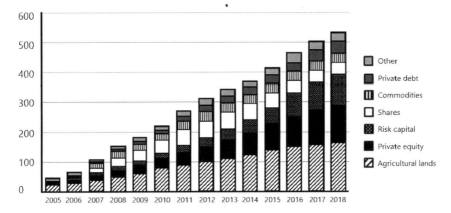

Figure 7.1 Number of food and agriculture investment funds by asset class (2005–2018).

this regard, it is worth noting, besides insurance companies, pension funds, mutual, hedge and sovereign wealth funds, also large agribusiness companies has created their own funds, such as the soy processing giants: ADM, Bunge, Cargill and Dreyfus (Goldfarb, 2014; Murphy, Burch and Clapp, 2012).

Valoral Advisors (2018) also inform that Latin America, and especially Brazil, offer a "fertile soil" for these investments, whose total value in the region exceeds US$70 billion. Regarding the areas of operation of these funds, the acquisition of farm land stands out, showing a growth of 587% between 2005 and 2018, and comprising the most important segment, focus of one-third of the funds. The second and third most relevant areas are private equity and venture capital funds, which accounted for 25% and 20% of investments in 2018, respectively. Both are segments aimed at total or partial acquisition of privately held companies. Such investments seek to increase the market value of these companies, so that to obtain substantial returns by later selling them. The funds that account for 6% or 8% of the total, are those focused on shares of stock of publicly traded companies (listed equities), which in recent years have tended to fall; commodities, essentially futures market, with a more stable trend; and private debt, especially agricultural financing, whose value has increased over the analyzed period. Other funds (representing 6% of the total in 2018) focus mainly on land or water recovery or conservation.

A relevant question raised by Murphy, Burch and Clapp (2012) refers to the role these new investors play in agricultural production, food processing and distribution – a role quite different from the traditional operation of the banking sector. Previously, banks offered products and services to farmers, especially credit, but had no interest in appropriating the business or managing a firm in this segment or interfering with business decisions. Conversely, financial institutions now have partial or total control of companies in the sector or even hold large farming areas. Therefore, actors hitherto unrelated to the agrifood sector, now, besides offering financial resources, also participate in – and, depending on the degree of control, define – strategic decisions of firms. As a result, land, natural resources, agricultural commodities and food become financial assets highly valued and less risky as compared with other markets and products, which has enabled the rapid and intense process of financialization of the agrifood system (Gomes, 2017).

The financialization of agrifood companies

Amid the intensification of financialization processes, agrifood companies became a focus of the investments (Anseeuw et al., 2017). If, on the one hand, there are investors interested in putting their money in these companies (institutional, individual and corporate investors), on the other, the companies face the need for increasing capitalization. Among the possibilities is a restructuring that allow the entry of external resources, which has been done either through initial public offering (IPO) (by issuing shares to trade on the stock exchange) or via participation of investors in the company's capital stock (becoming shareholders).

In Brazil, many companies have decided to go public as an alternative to bank financing, since this enables access to both Brazilian and foreign potential investors (Cavalcanti and Misumi, 2001). Besides raising capital, another reason to do so is to enhance strategic flexibility, to increase prestige through greater market visibility, to implement corporate restructuring and improve management (Souza, 2003; Bomfim, Santos and Pimenta, Jr., 2007). Concerning the different economic sectors, Balestro and Lourenço (2014) noted that agribusiness is the one that holds the largest number of participating firms (21.2%) in the São Paulo Stock Exchange – BM&F Bovespa, followed by information technology services (19.2%), construction (13.5%), machinery and equipment (9.6%), tourism, hospitality and leisure (5.8%), telecommunications (5.8%), among others. In addition, the authors observed an increase in participation of foreign capital in the Brazilian stock exchange, from 24.1% in 2003 to 42.1% in 2013.

Going public for companies directly linked to agriculture is not a recent practice. Some transnational firms (such as ADM, Dow, Unilever, John Deere) started this strategy in the 1970s, while others (AGCO, Mosaic, Nestle, Danone, Bayer, Basf, Heineken) joined them in the following decades. Today, companies such as CNH, Monsanto, Yara, Bunge, Dreyfus, Cofco, Kraft Heinz, among others also have shares traded on stock exchanges worldwide. Data presented by Clapp (2017) show that large multinational conglomerates in the seeds and pesticides sector also have significant part of their shares controlled by investment funds: 33% of DuPont shares (before its merger with Dow, in 2015) and nearly 25% of Monsanto's shares (before being bought by Bayer, in 2016) were controlled by the top six funds operating in this sector: BlackRock, Capital Group, Fidelity, The Vanguard Group Inc.,

State Street Global Advisors and Norges Bank Investment Management (Ipes-Food, 2017).

In Brazil, BM&F Bovespa has listed agrifood companies from various segments: agricultural machinery and equipment (Caterpillar, Metisa and Stara), fertilizers and pesticides (Heringer, Mosaic, Nutriplant), meat (BRF, JBS, Marfrig, Minerva), paper and pulp (Suzano, Fibria, Klabin, Celulose Irani, Santher), sugar and alcohol (Raizen, Biosev, São Martinho), beverages (Ambev, Coca Cola, PepsiCo), miscellaneous foods (Camil, Hershey, J. Macedo, Kraft Heinz, M. Dias Branco, Mondelez and Oderich) and retail (Pão de Açúcar, Carrefour and Walmart). As to agricultural production, although going public was not frequent among companies, it has changed quickly. At the beginning of 2018, five companies of the "agriculture" segment – Aliperti, BrasilAgro, CTC – Centro de Tecnologia Canavieira, Pomifrutas, SLC Agrícola and Terra Santa Agro – were listed on BM&F Bovespa. Among these, SLC Agrícola stands out for its corporate structure.

SLC Agrícola is a company focused on the production of commodities, mainly cotton, soybean and maize, but also wheat, maize seed and sugarcane. The company controls 14 production units in 6 Brazilian states, which amounted to 403,000 ha cultivated in 2017. The SLC Group (owned by Schneider Logemann family) holds the majority control of SLC Agrícola (51.03% of total shares), while mutual funds control 14.5% of the shares and the remainder is traded directly on the stock exchange. The architecture of SLC Agrícola also comprises two joint ventures: with Dois Vales Group, owned by Soares Penido Obras, Construções e Investimentos, a conglomerate that participates in different consortiums of highway, airport, train and bus concessions; and with Mitsui & Co, one of Japan's leading industrial and financial conglomerates. Furthermore, the company has also a "real estate branch," the subsidiary SLC Land Co, focused on acquisition of raw land, opening and clearance of the area, soil correction, construction of infrastructure and sale of the land (SLC Agrícola, 2018).

In addition to going public, another common practice of large companies for raising capital is the search for investors willing to acquire control of part of the company shares. In this regard, a significant growth in the participation of various (pension, social security, mutual, hedge, sovereign) funds is observed. The most emblematic case concerns 3G Capital investment fund. Formed in 2004 by Jorge Paulo Lemann, Marcel Herrmann Telles and Carlos Alberto Sicupira,[2] this fund controls large companies in the agrifood sector, such as AB InBev (the world's largest brewery), Kraft Heinz (resulting from the merger of Kraft Foods and H. J. Heinz, is the fifth largest food and beverage company in the world) and Brands International (third largest fast food operator worldwide, resulting from the merger of Burger King and Tim Hortons coffee shop). In 2017, this fund spearheaded an offer of US$143 for the acquisition of Unilever, which declined the offer.[3]

Sovereign wealth funds, created by some States to use part of their international reserves, also have investments in the agrifood sector. One example is the Singapore Government Investment Corporation, which holds a 5% stake in Bunge and BRF, as well as approximately 3% of Glencore, which operates in ore, agricultural products and energy.[4] This participation of state-controlled sovereign wealth funds is a relevant aspect of financialization. It is not only private capital that makes use of this type of practice – some governments also find mechanisms for accumulation in these investments. The case of Singapore is particularly interesting in this regard, for revealing the logic of different varieties of capitalism. The country was considered by *The Wall Street Journal* and *The Economist* as a successful example of contemporary "capitalism" for its openness to private investment. Nevertheless, 90% of its lands and 85% of all residence buildings are government-owned. In addition, 22% of GDP is produced by public companies. As the economist Ha-Joon Chang recently pointed out, "They have a pragmatic model of economics that mixes elements of free-market capitalism and socialism. They are neither capitalists nor socialists. They are pragmatists" (Oliveira, 2018).

Three companies in the agricultural industry that are listed on BM&F Bovespa (SLC Agrícola, Terra Santa Agro and Brasil Agro) combine publicly traded stocks with the capital raising from varied funds. SLC Agrícola has the participation of investment funds of Odey Asset Management and of Kopernik Global Investors, which hold, respectively, 9.3% and 5.2% of the company's shares. Terra Santa Agro also has among its shareholders different financial institutions (Laplace Investimentos, Gávea Investimentos, EWZ Invest LLC and Sul América Investimentos). The same is true of Brasil Agro (Cape Town LLC, Autonomy Capital and Elie Horn). In addition to these cases, there are several other examples, such as the Argentinian companies El Tejar, Los Grobos, Cresud and Adecoagro, which operate in Brazil and other Southern Cone countries, and which, over the years, have raised capital from various funds for both land purchase and agricultural production (Bernardes et al., 2017; Sosa, 2017).

The choice of these companies of raising capital via IPO and investors mobilization carry a great instability, because those who buy shares or holdings of a firm want to make big (speculative) gains in the short-term, what makes the system very unstable, subject to frequent and abrupt fluctuations in asset prices. Furthermore, there are the inherent risks of farming activity, which can have a direct impact on the company's performance. The volatility of this market, indeed, allows for both formidable profits and extraordinary losses. Two particularly interesting cases in Brazil are those of JBS and BRF. Propelled by huge public loans (see Chapter 2), these companies used the State to become major players in the food markets. Even so, at some point, going public became a requirement to leverage business growth. Now, both companies have fallen prey to their own ambitions. Involved in one of the largest corruption scandals in the country, JBS has seen its market value drop by R$7.5 billion in a single day. On May 22, 2017, JBS shares fell 31.3%. The company shares closed the day at R$5.98, one of the lowest prices in its history, even below, in nominal terms, the value registered at the time of its IPO,

10 years ago (R$6.29). In the case of BRF, the destabilizing factor was the arrest of executives of the company under the Federal Police *Operação Carne Fraca* (Weak Flesh Operation)[5], which found frauds committed by its meat processing plants to evade health control processes. On March 5, 2018, the company's stock plummeted by 20%, leading to a loss of nearly R$5 billion in market value in a single day.

There are other ways for raising capital besides going public and mobilizing investors. Considering the case of farmers, particularly, there are more traditional forms, such as public rural credit (via the National System of Rural Credit) and loans from traders, agribusiness or input retailers. In the face of a sharp reduction in the volume of public resources, another instrument available, and which is strongly integrated into the financial dynamics, refers to agribusiness financial securities, such as the Rural Product Security (CPR), instituted in 1994, and the new securities created in 2004: Agribusiness Credit Rights Certificate (CDCA), Agricultural Deposit Certificate/Agricultural Warrant (CDA/WA), Agribusiness Receivables Certificate (CRA) and Agribusiness Letter of Credit (LCA). According to Oliveira (2010), these agriculture financing alternatives are based on the issuance of bonds, with the participation of banks, insurance companies and commodity exchanges, what helps reduce and diversify the risk. With such bonds representing agricultural produce, it became possible to coordinate the operations carried out in the physical and future markets, attracting investors from other sectors that have resources available.

According to data available in the 2012/2013 Agricultural and Livestock Plan (Brazil, 2012), the volume of agribusiness securities – LCA, CRA and CDCA – in stock was close to R$15 billion at the beginning of 2010, and in 2012 this value doubled. In January 2018, these securities reached a total R$95.5 billion, suggesting a continued expansion in recent years (Cetip, 2018). Considering the whole of Brazilian farmers, the number of those directly involved with financial capital is still small, though it has been growing in some sectors and regions, as shown by data on sources of financing for soy production in Mato Grosso between 2008/2009 and 2018/2019 (Figure 7.2). In the last harvest, financial capital accounted for 18% of the total resources spent on soy production in that state. According to Imea (2017, 1), the increase in this participation "was mainly driven by the increase in the supply of credit with interest rates freely agreed between financial institution and borrower, through Agribusiness Letters of Credit (LCA), among other sources."

The financial logic, indirectly, also infiltrates the capital raising strategies of privately held companies. Cargill, the world's largest privately held company, has been providing different financial services since the 1990s. In addition to operating in the futures market for agricultural commodities (see next section), it has several subsidiaries, such as Cargill Risk Management, Cargill Trade & Structured Finance, CarVal Investors, Black River Asset Management, Cargill Energy and Risk Management Solutions, besides Cargill Bank. In addition to being fundamental to the company's own risk management and

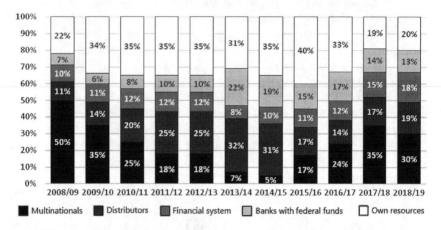

Figure 7.2 Funding for soybean production in Mato Grosso.

capital raising, these subsidiaries offer financial products and services to third parties and manage large investment funds. That is, unlike most companies, which make use of these funds, Cargill also operates as a financial agent, assuming the role of investor. As Goldfarb (2014, 99) notes, the company "acts as a speculator within the sector in which it operates."

Companies such as ADM, Bunge and Dreyfus also have financial services divisions. The ABCD Group is "to some extent, taking advantage of these opportunities with its investment funds, established for internal purposes and for external clients" (Murphy, Burch and Clapp, 2012, 26). Consequently, it has become "very difficult to determine to what extent the traders' good performance is primarily based on their financial activities or on their traditional physical trade. In fact, it is a combination of both" (ibid., 26). In other words, these companies have ceased to compete exclusively within physical markets, increasingly encompassing capital market expectations, what opens new opportunities for raising capital through operating in both the productive/ commercial sphere, which for over a century has been part of their scope, and the financial intermediation for internal purposes and for external clients.

In short, changes in the financial sphere had profound impacts on the corporate strategy of companies. As a result, although not always visible or widely known, there is a group of actors "behind the companies" (institutional, private and state investors), financing their activities, establishing partnerships and controlling them either directly or indirectly (Frederico and Gras, 2017). The growing absorption by firms of the logic of capital markets has encouraged investors to seek immediate results, which often undermine long-term competitive strategies. As pointed out by Balestro and Lourenço (2014, 249), "financialization would be the hegemony of rentiers over entrepreneurs."

The financialization of agricultural commodities

While world production of maize for the 2015/2016 crop totaled 1 billion tons, 345 million out of which in the United States alone, the amount traded on the Chicago stock exchange reached 10.5 billion tons (Heinrich-Böll Foundation, 2017). The financialization of agricultural commodities is directly linked to the fictional expectations surrounding futures market, a type of transaction that is established between two parties, where there is a future obligation to buy or sell a certain amount of a commodity at a previously agreed price. According to Paula, Santos and Pereira (2015), the main function of this practice was initially to protect producers and traders from price fluctuations, ensuring a preestablished return. In this sense, these comprised operations against unforeseen fluctuations, which estimated the future price in view of expectations of changes in supply, demand and stock levels over time. Today, it is much more a speculation practice, in which price volatility is important to accelerate return on investment.

In addition to advances in technological and institutional artifacts that have facilitated and broadened this type of practice, a major innovation emerged when financial agents "came into play" selling to investors derivatives based on agricultural and food commodities (Murphy, Burch and Clapp, 2012). In this case, instead of a direct relationship between actors that pertain to the sector (rural producers interested in selling production and agro-industrial export companies concerned with the acquisition of goods), the transactions are controlled by actors that, until then, were not part of these markets and whose interests are other than stabilizing the supply and demand of raw materials and food. On the contrary, they are even interested in making profits from the forecast of a global food shortage and food insecurity crisis. According to Balestro and Lourenço (2014), many institutional investors saw agricultural production as an opportunity to diversify their investments (in addition to stocks and bonds, they included commodities in their portfolios) and to reduce risks. This became even clearer after the confluence of different crises in 2007–2008 and the persistence of food prices above historical averages in subsequent years.

In Brazil, the futures market started operating at the end of 1977 on the São Paulo Commodity Exchange (BMSP). Initially, coffee and soybean contracts were negotiated (1978) and, over the years, soybean oil and meal, cotton, maize, cattle, sugar, alcohol and ethanol were included (Corrêa and Raíces, 2017). This market "jumped in July 1985, with the creation of the Mercantile and Futures Exchange, BM&F, which would later be called the Commodity and Futures Exchange (BM&F)" (Goldfarb, 2014, 101).[6] In turn, in the 1990s, especially after monetary stabilization, trade liberalization, and the reduction of the interventionist role of the State in providing credit and managing risk, future contracts for agricultural products began to multiply. Another important driver of this market was, then, the launch of the financial settlement modality (without the need to deliver physical goods) valid for fat

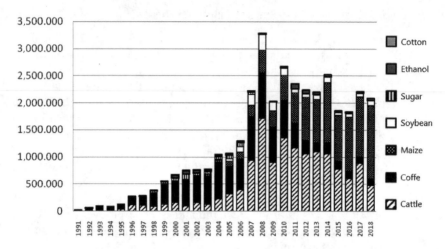

Figure 7.3 Forward and option contracts for agricultural commodities traded on BM&F and BM&F Bovespa (1991–2018).

cattle, in 1994, for soy and sugar, in 1995, and for maize and cotton, in 1996. This possibility substantially increased liquidity and attracted speculators who started to quickly buy and sell these contracts (Amado, 2003).

Figure 7.3 shows the number of forward and option contracts for agricultural commodities traded initially on the BM&F and later on the BM&F Bovespa. An impressive growth is observed, especially between 1991 and 2008, from 15,300 to 3.3 million contracts, representing a jump of 212 times in less than 20 years. Despite being a practically uninterrupted increase over the considered period, 2008 stands out, when there was a great leap in relation to the trend that had prevailed in previous years – between 2006 and 2008 the variation was over 150%. This peak was precisely a result of the greater instability caused by the 2008 financial crisis. Even though this number of contracts, exceeding 3 million a year, was not sustained in the following years, the practice persisted, and the number has never returned to precrisis levels.

Until 2006, coffee was the agricultural commodity with the largest number of contracts traded on the BM&F Bovespa, accounting for more than two-thirds of the total. After that year, fat cattle took the lead (2007–2013) with over 1 million annual contracts. In the most recent period, however, maize has predominated with a growing movement, jumping from 9% to 65% of total contracts, between 2007 and 2018. In the last 10 years, these three products have absorbed over 90% of the total. Soybean peaked between 2006 and 2009 (with 9% of contracts) and after that it has accounted for less than 5% of the total. Sugarcane derivatives (sugar and alcohol/ethanol) were also relevant in the transition from the 1990s to the 2000s, absorbing more than 10%, but currently have a lower presence. Cotton had a modest share until 2007 and then stopped trading on the BM&F Bovespa.

The logic behind this market is based on abstract bases, without product backing. Financialization leads to an autonomous circuit of financial accumulation, which is no longer subject to the limitations of the real economy. This can be seen in the relationship between the traded volume of contracts and other agribusiness financial assets and the actual agricultural production. Paula, Santos and Pereira (2015) point out that, globally, the investments in stocks transformed into derivatives, under the lead of financial investors, accounted for over 20 times the value of transactions with physical stocks. The same dynamics was also observed in the coffee futures market, in which transactions corresponded, on average, to 2.1 national crops – especially 2007, when the volume traded was equivalent to 3.2 crops (Silveira, Maciel and Ballini, 2014).

This abstraction of physical output from agricultural commodity derivatives is based on the possibility that different investors (banks, funds, insurers etc.) add these products to their financial portfolios, since there is no need for physical purchase, what matters is to allow liquidity (Clapp, 2014). This, of course, attracted speculators who, thereafter, have directly influenced the formation of future prices of agricultural commodities. The research presented by Herreros, Barros and Bentes (2010) shows that the behavior of international cotton, sugar, coffee and soybean prices at the Chicago and New York stock exchange, in the period from 2006 to 2009, was significantly related to speculative practices: "for cotton, the speculation level reached, on February 24, 2009, 64.56%; for coffee, on July 17, 2008, 60.60%; for soybeans, on July 3, 2008, 54.87%; and, in the case of sugar, reached 53.72% on July 29, 2008." This means that, despite being a modern trading tool that allows farmers and agrifood companies to mitigate the risks that arise from price fluctuations of some agricultural products, in the contemporary context this markets became increasingly dangerous. It serves the interests of a number of speculators who have no connection with the agricultural sector and who are not interested in price stability or supply security. A similar logic guides the financialization of land and nature, as we will see further on.

Land and nature as financial assets

In the contemporary societies, "land, in its broad sense, has become one of the greatest needs of advanced capitalism — for food and industrial crops, groundwater, traditional and new forms of mining" (Sassen, 2013, 27). The economic pressure on land and, more broadly, on natural resources has reflected in various ways on the configuration of the globally discussed land grabbing phenomenon, that is, the process of acquisition (purchase, lease, concession, supply contract), on a large scale, of land and other associated resources in another country. This process usually involves land that is being used for production or that is potentially arable, where corporate investors aim to grow food or nonfood crops to increase supply in domestic or global markets or achieve a favorable return on investment (Holmes, 2014).

Until the early 2000s, international groups focused their investments primarily on raw material processing activities, rarely seeking control over rural properties (Wilkinson, Reydon and Di Sabbato, 2012). Nevertheless, land acquisition by foreigners is not new. For example, land purchases by Brazilians in Paraguay (Zaar, 2001; Souchaud, 2007; Galeano, 2012) and Bolivia (Urioste, 2011) throughout the second half of the twentieth century is well-known. Another known fact is the acquisition of land by foreigners in Brazil, as for example the sale "to foreign individuals and legal entities in the second half of the 1960s, when more than 28 million hectares were transacted, in most cases, unlawfully" (Oliveira, 2010, 3). Not to mention the concessions and expropriations during the colonial period (Gomes, 2017; Wilkinson, 2018).

Nowadays, however, this phenomenon carries some novelties worth highlighting. The main ones are the rapid growth in transaction volume, geographic expansion and investor diversity (Sassen, 2016). As Sauer (2010) observes, there is a "world's race" for land, accelerated after the 2008 crises. This race is linked to different factors, such as the need for: food production to supply the growing demand motivated by the increase in prices and change in the diet of populous countries like China and India; biofuel production in response to the substantial increase in oil prices; preservation of natural resources, enabling the provision of environmental services (formation of a kind of "environmental market"); construction of extensive infrastructure corridors and Special Economic Zones; investment appreciation and speculative gains (White et al., 2012; Wilkinson, 2018).

It is precisely this last element that we will further explore here, since it represents a specific type of practice characteristic of the institutional dynamics of the financial order. It is based on the growing interest in land control by financial speculators (banking institutions, but especially nonbank ones such as institutional investors and wealthy individuals). This is an important, if not unexpected, shift in the focus of the investments of these actors, from trading in securities (equities, bonds) to fixed capital investment in physical assets – especially because these are "investments made by the financial sector, which has been historically opposed to investments in fixed assets, especially to land purchases, a market characterized by low liquidity" (Flexor and Leite, 2018, 21).

As Harvey (2013) explains, from the investors' perspective, what is transacted is not "land" but the right to the rent of land. This is why land "is a productive asset that moonlights as a financial asset" (Fairbairn, 2014, 779). Therefore, this growing attraction of financial investors to land acquisition, on a global scale, is a novelty that substantially distinguishes these processes from previous ones – that is, from the way land grabbing is structured within the institutional logics of other social orders: either as a mechanism of dispossession of natural resources in the commercial order; or as a control of "factors of production" in the industrial order. In the contemporary context, we can say that

we have witnessed an unprecedented integration between finance capital and land ownership, at least regarding scale – for the global scope
and quantity of land involved – and the guiding logic, with the transformation of land in an asset included in the institutional investment
portfolio.

(Bernardes et al., 2017, 7)

Although we are talking about a phenomenon that is on the agenda for
researchers, governments and multilateral organizations, the available data
are inaccurate and contradictory.[7] A source commonly used for research on
the topic is the Land Matrix portal, created in 2008, as an independent initiative for monitoring large-scale land transactions. At the end of 2019, this
base registered 1,700 transactions on a global scale, covering approximately
50 million hectares, indicating an average of almost 30,000 ha per acquisition. As to the concluded agricultural negotiations, it is observed that the
movement of acquisitions was modest until 2006, rapidly increasing since
then. As of 2014, however, there is greater stability. Regarding land use, 79%
of the contracts and 57% of the area were focused on agricultural purposes
(agrofuels, food crops, livestock and nonfood agricultural products), followed
by forestry (10% and 28%, respectively). The list included areas for tourism,
industry, conservation and renewable energy.

Regarding the type of investors, a great diversity is observed: private companies (which absorb 41% of all land), companies listed on stock exchange
(30%), investment funds (9%), state entities (6%) and individual entrepreneurs
(3%), though there is a significant percentage for which information is not
available (16%). Nevertheless, many situations are difficult or even impossible
to interpret, what leads to underestimation of the actions of these institutional investors. Moreover, with regard to companies, the report even points
to the involvement of ADM, Cargill and Dreyfus in land purchase in Latin
America: ADM acquired a small amount of land in Brazil for palm oil production, in 2012; Cargill, through local subsidiaries, made acquisitions in
Colombia (about 140,000 ha, in 2010 and 2012); Dreyfus, via its subsidiaries
Calyx Agro and Louis Dreyfus Company, acquired land in Argentina, Brazil,
Paraguay and Uruguay (approximately 70,000 ha under 12 agreements signed
between 2005 and 2009) (Land Matrix, 2016).

In turn, concerning the origin of investments, among the first 20 coun-
tries are, from traditional economic powers (United States, United Kingdom,
France, Canada, China) and emerging economies (India, South Africa,
Argentina and Brazil), also tax havens (British Virgin Islands, Jersey,
Luxembourg) and major oil producers (Saudi Arabia, Kazakhstan) (Land
Matrix, 2016). However, as Gomes (2017) points out, these data always refer
to the host country of the company that signed the contract. The problem is
that many of these firms operate as international investment platforms. As
exemplified by Nakatani et al. (2014, 64), "the Portugal-based Quifel Group
acquired one hundred and twenty-six thousand hectares in Sierra Leone,

whose purchase was made in the UK, as well as the Al-Falah Group from Bangladesh, acquired 30,000 hectares in Tanzania, also negotiating from the United Kingdom." In addition, as Bernardes et al. (2017) highlight, investments in land are not restricted to usual North–South movements, as cross-investments between peripheral countries, as in the South American case, become increasingly common.

Brazil assumes a "double personality" in land grabbing dynamics. On the one hand, Brazilian investors acquire land in other countries. In this case, the country ranks 20th on the list, with 17 contracts concluded, covering 360,000 ha, most of which are located in Latin America (Paraguay, Uruguay, Peru, Colombia and Nicaragua) and Africa (Angola, Zambia, Mozambique, Sudan and Ghana). On the other hand, it is the fifth country in extension of area bought by foreign investors (behind Indonesia, Ukraine, Russia and Papua New Guinea), exceeding 3 million hectares[8] in 68 completed acquisitions. The new agriculture frontier of Matopiba has been the main focus of these investments. Based on a detailed search of different data sources, Gomes (2017) mapped land acquisitions in this region since 2000, finding 2.5 million hectares under the control of foreign investors. As to the countries of origin of the investments, the main are the United States, Argentina, Canada, Japan, the Netherlands and the United Kingdom

The increased interest in land acquisition, in a context of commodity appreciation and expansion of the agricultural frontier, impacted directly on prices increase. As Flexor and Leite (2018) illustrate, average land prices in Brazil were R\$4,756/ha in 2010 and reached R\$10,083/ha in 2015. That is, in five years, the average land price raised by 112%. This represents a much higher increase than variations in the Consumer Price Index (IPCA = +48.9%) or in the General Market Price Index (IGPM = +52.55%). The Brasil Agro fund reports (2018), prepared for accountability for attracting new investors, indicate an impressive appreciation of land in the regions where it operates. Between 2006 and 2015, considering grain production areas, prices increased 480% in Mineiros (Goiás), 330% in Ronda Velha (Bahia) and 280% in Sorriso (Mato Grosso).

A central issue regarding land grabbing concerns the role of the state. Since 1960, the Brazilian State has been gradually losing effective control over land acquisition (Castro and Sauer, 2018). In 2010, the LA01 opinion by the Office of the Attorney General (AGU) reinstated rules and limited land grabbing by foreigners, by establishing the "return of quantitative limits, restricting the purchase of land by foreigners to 5,000 hectares and to 25% of the total area of the municipality" (Flexor and Leite, 2018, 46). In the case of areas larger than 5,000 hectares, the purchase is only allowed to companies that have more than 50% of its capital stock composed of Brazilians. However, in face of this new regulation, foreign groups went public, becoming minorities, precisely to evade regulation and continue to buy large areas. Presently, the National Congress is analysing, as a matter of urgency, a bill (No. 4059/ 2012) that, if approved, will mean greater deregulation and liberalization of land purchases (Castro and Sauer, 2018). The speeches and justifications in favor of its approval include arguments on the "need to attract new investment during an economic crisis" (Flexor and Leite, 2018, 29).

Although we have focused on land appropriation especially in areas suitable or with potential for agricultural production, it is important to note that there are other related practices often cited in debates on green grabbing. This discussion fits into the economic context we have already described, and adds to the issues of climate change, natural resources contamination and global agreements focused on ecological agendas (Fairhead, Leach and Scoones, 2012). Sauer and Borras, Jr. (2016) discuss the issue of commodification and appropriation of nature, revealing a wide range of actors involved, as well as a variety of uses – current, future and speculative – in the name of "sustainability," "conservation" or of "green values." For these authors, such practices are directly associated with problems involving the creation of mechanisms said to be more environmentally sustainable, including the creation of forest reserves, through the purchase of carbon credits, agreements for reduction of emissions from deforestation (REDD+), investments in clean energy, ecotourism, among other mechanisms proposed by the environmental agendas.

Related to this is also the practice of water grabbing. Water has become a financial asset for many actors, who envision future gains from a potential global water crisis that could undermine both agricultural production and human consumption (Franco, Mehta and Veldwisch, 2013). Regarding human consumption, data from the International Bottled Water Association indicate that, in 2016, Brazil ranked fourth among world producers. The average annual growth in bottled water consumption in the country was about 10%, exceeding the world average (8.5%), though much lower than that observed in the largest world market, China. With its demand growing 17% per year, the Asian country nearly doubled consumption between 2009 and 2014, when it reached 33 billion liters. As a result, China surpassed the United States, becoming the world's largest bottled water market. This is one of the reasons why major investors in the sector have been pressuring the Brazilian government to discuss the relaxation of national legislation regarding the exploitation and privatization of this resource, as illustrated, for example, by the meetings that President Temer had with the CEOs of these companies during the World Economic Forum in January 2018. The issue was also a focus of concern at the VIII World Water Forum, an event held in Brasilia, in March 2018.

Although the discussion on commodification is quite advanced, a newer and even more far-reaching movement – in terms of the intensity of capitalist relations – refers to "financialization of nature" (Misoczky and Böhm, 2012) or "financialization of the environment" (Salviatti, 2017). This practice is identified by Smith (2007, 24) as the new frontier for expanding financial capital through new markets of green commodities and environmental derivatives. Perhaps the prime example is the carbon credit market, which relies on certificates issued by a person or company that has reduced its greenhouse gas emissions, which can be purchased by countries or industries that fail to meet their goals of carbon emission reductions. In Brazil, the purchase and sale of credit is made through auctions promoted by BM&F Bovespa, in which there are now propositions for the creation of new technical and institutional artifacts such as biodiversity derivatives, modified derivative contracts to sell investors the risk of species extinction (Misoczky and Böhm, 2012).

Flex crops

Another phenomenon that stands out in the contemporary agrifood system refers to flex crops. These are crops that have multiple uses (food, feed, fuel, fiber, industrial input) and that can be easily interchanged, considering the varied relationships between crops, components and uses. Borras, Jr. et al. (2016) bring an important and innovative contribution on this issue, pointing out two distinct and intertwined dimensions of this concept. The first refers to the multiple uses of products for different purposes, such as soybeans, which can be used both in animal feed production and in human food directly, or even as biodiesel raw material. The second concerns flexibility in substitutions, based on interchange of products and components, so that supply gaps can be filled by other flexible crops, such as the replacement of sugar refined from sugarcane with corn syrup in bakery. Therefore, flexible crops are those that can have multiple uses, which means that the product does not have a fixed and exclusive destination, what gives great flexibility to its final use.

Flexible crops play a dual role as they act to reduce uncertainty as well as to stabilize or increase the profitability of sellers and buyers. For being a raw material for a more diversified product portfolio, they allow investors to anticipate and more readily react to price fluctuations (Borras, Jr. et al., 2016). However, this flexibility requires a complex set of technological artifacts that allowed companies to make rapid and inexpensive changes in production processes to use the same raw material for different purposes (use of enzymes, conversion of plants to biorefineries etc.) (Borras, Jr. et al., 2016; McKay et al., 2016). A remarkable aspect is that these technoscientific advances were applied not only to the main products (such as ethanol and sugar in the case of sugarcane), but also to those products that were, until then, deemed as waste (such as sugarcane bagasse, which can now be transformed into bioelectricity, and cane-vinasse, which is already used in the production of biogas and fertilizers). These technological artifacts have become important for companies and their investors, either by reducing production costs or by "greening" their practices, as that generally reduce the negative impact on natural resources.

Flexible crops generally refer to what the literature calls 4F Crops: food, fiber, fuel and forest (Sauer, 2016). One of the most prominent examples is soybeans, whose multiple destinations cover human food, animal feed, biodiesel and industrial use. In terms of human nutrition, the best-known products derive from oil extracted from the grain, such as cooking oil itself, salad dressing, margarine, vegetable shortening and mayonnaise. There is also refined soybean oil, from which lecithin is obtained, a product widely used to produce sausages, mayonnaise, ice cream, cereal bars and frozen foods. In addition, soy is used to produce chocolate, seasonings, pastas, as well as beverage mixes (such as soymilk and fruit juices), baby food and many diet foods. In terms of animal feed, 80% of the feed produced in Brazil comes from soybean meal and maize. As an industrial input, soy is used in products from various segments: cosmetics, pharmaceutical, veterinary, plastics and varnish and paint industries. Soy is also the basis of biodiesel production in Brazil, accounting for about 80% of production (Abiove, 2018).

Sugarcane is another product that fits the logic of flexible crops. In Brazil, its historically known by-product is sugar, which was one of the pillars of the economy in the colonial period and remains an economically important product. According to Brazilian Sugarcane Industry Association (UNICA), the 2016/2017 harvest produced 38.7 million tons of sugar in the country. The other main by-product is ethanol, with a production of 27.3 billion liters, of which 15.7 billion become hydrous ethanol (which is sold at gas stations) and 11.6 billion is anhydrous ethanol (which is blended with gasoline, as Brazil has used a 27% blend since 2015). The percentage destined either to sugar or to ethanol production varies mainly according to the price of the final product. Furthermore, some mills are using vinasse, bagasse and straw in the production of biogas, second-generation ethanol and electricity, and have made investments in the dissemination of bioplastic ("green plastic") obtained from sugarcane (UNICA, 2018). Finally, there is a part of sugarcane production that turns into cachaça.

Considering the higher efficiency of sugarcane, in Brazil maize is still mainly used for animal feed – the basis for poultry, pork, fish and cattle feed – and human – consumed directly or as a component in the manufacture of candies, cookies, breads, chocolates, jellies, ice cream, mayonnaise, beer etc. However, in 2017, Brazil's first maize ethanol plant was inaugurated in Lucas do Rio Verde, Mato Grosso. Designed to produce 240 million liters of ethanol a year, the initiative has the financial and administrative participation of the Summit Agricultural Group, an agricultural investments company based in Iowa, United States.

Planted forests also fit flexible cultivation. According to data from the Brazilian Tree Industry (IBA, 2017), Brazil has 7.8 million hectares of reforestation, an area mainly occupied by eucalyptus and pine (94% of the total). In 2016, 18.8 million tons of pulp were produced, the main destination of planted forests production, which is used for processing various chemicals, such as plastics, varnishes, artificial silk, as well as processed foods such as hamburgers, grated cheese and juices, besides being a source of fibers for whole products. The sector's production included 10.3 million tons of paper, 7.3 million m^3 of timber, 11.8 million m^3 of laminate flooring and 4.5 million tons of charcoal. In addition, planted forests are taking a relevant role in climate change discussions due to their potential carbon absorption capacity.

Besides the dissemination of new technological artifacts that created previously unimaginable practices, thus increasing the possibilities of use and the flexibility of crops (Borras, Jr. et al., 2016), another novelty of this market is the growing interest of financial capital. The variety of destinations and uses and the advantages of risk mitigation and maximization of returns have attracted banks and investment funds to these crops. In addition to the futures market and the participation of financial institutions in the corporate structure of companies involved in flexible crops, the financialization of these crops can also be seen in direct investments in the sector. The most visible example lies in the planted forests market in Brazil. It is currently estimated that 10% of planted forests total area is controlled by financial investors. "Attracted by the great forest potential of the country, these investors started their operations here, over ten years ago, investing in funds specialized in forest assets" (IBA, 2017, 33).

The fact that a single crop can justify multiple uses is also deemed as a reason for taking hold of land, suggesting a synergy between flexible crops and land grabbing, besides financialization proper, since an important part of the resources that drive both practices are, directly or indirectly, linked to financial capital. Therefore, the expansion of flexible crops directly affects global demand for land and natural resources, encouraging the expansion of agricultural frontiers and attracting investors, especially foreign ones, to different countries in Latin America, Africa and Asia (Sauer, 2016). Considering data presented by Land Matrix (2016), for example, the main products grown in lands appropriated by foreign investors worldwide are precisely palm, jatropha, sugarcane, maize, soybean and rubber tree.

The fox guarding the chicken coop

The financialization of the agrifood system has direct consequences for food supply and consumption. One of the most direct effects refers to food prices, as growth in financial investments has not only put pressure on food inflation, but also made price behavior much more volatile. As Flexor and Leite (2018, 25) summarize, this increase "does not result just from increased demand in a context of limited supply. The rising prices also reflect the behaviour of financial markets and the increasing inclusion of agricultural commodities into the logic that guides these markets." If food price volatility directly affects farmers – especially family farmers who do not access the futures market, finding themselves helpless when the selling price of their produce suddenly drops – it is also highly harmful to consumers, as it may quickly reduce their purchasing power, what becomes even more worrying in a context of rising world hunger.

The problem is that the interest of the small number of financial investors lies in both price increases and market volatility, while for the majority of the world's population unregulated financialization has led to severe food security and sovereignty crises. The problem starts at the source, lies in financial capital investments in land assets, which "threatens food security and sovereignty, as they further concentrate agricultural production in few commodities, favoring monopolies in food and agro-energy production" (Sauer and Leite, 2012, 522). Moreover, with the facilities to transform food into fuel and/or industrial input, these risks are increased. The problem also extends to investments on agricultural commodity derivatives. Attracted by speculative gains, these investments directly influence price formation. As Paula, Santos and Pereira (2015, 310) illustrate, "financialization of agricultural trade can provide a nefarious combination between an increase in the malnourished population and expectations of increased returns in the financial sphere."

Rising land prices, driven by land grabbing and commodity valuation, are another outcome that deserves attention, since they pressure, either voluntarily or involuntarily, family farmers to sell or lease their lands. In this case, there is an interference on the production, distribution and consumption of food, due to the role that these actors play in local and regional supply, besides the direct impact on food for own consumption, as these practices remain present and relevant in the contemporary context (see Chapter 4). Moreover, when the land is acquired by a foreign investor, in some cases production is destined to meet food demand in the country of origin (Borras, Jr. and Franco, 2010). This is clear in the case of sovereign wealth fund investments, such as the Saudi Arabian Sovereign Wealth Fund, which has made several land acquisitions in other countries with a view to ensure Saudi Arabia's food security (Gomes, 2017). Chinese investments in land purchases in Africa also reproduces the same logic.

Regarding food consumption practices, the financial order takes a configuration distinct from other orders, since the characteristics of products, food preparation and places of consumption are not decisive elements. What is really determining is the return on investments. This is why institutional investors are focusing on products and companies that have very different (and sometimes opposite) characteristics and proposals. On the one hand, they are acquiring companies that produce standardized and massified products (typical of the industrial order). The example discussed above is that of 3G Capital, the fund that runs Kraft Foods, Heinz, InBev and Burger King. On the other hand, there are investments in "healthy and sustainable" products (characteristic of the civic order). This is the case of the French investment fund Moringa, which in 2017 invested US$5 million in the company Floresta Viva, which grows palm trees based on principles that mix agroecology and agroforestry. Another example is investments in *haute cuisine* (constitutive of the aesthetic order). In 2012, the English fund Aureos Latin American invested US$32 million in the purchase of Astrid y Gastón, a restaurant that was once considered the best in Latin America (Exame, 2014). In the same vein, the Fogo de Chão barbecue chain was acquired in early 2018 by the US investment firm Rhône Capital, in a deal valued at US$560 million (about R$1.8 billion) (Valor Econômico, 2018).

Supply and consumption dynamics have also been changed as the relations between financial capital and the retail sector become closer. As Saltorato and Donadone (2012, 2) point out, the national retail sector is experiencing a

> movement that involves, on the one hand, closer relations with financial institutions and, on the other, an intense process of concentration, entry of foreign capital, initial public offering, internationalization of business, professionalization of management, all of which boost financialization of Brazilian retail.

The dissemination of the financial logic in retail operations in Brazil can be observed in the partnerships between large conglomerates and financial institutions, in the IPO of retail companies and in the equity participation of national and international investment funds in retailers' capital stock (Saltorato et al., 2016).

This is a worrying situation, since supermarkets now concentrate most of the food distribution in Brazil and in the world. Data presented by Reardon and Berdegué (2002), on what the authors call the "supermarketization" process, suggest that in Brazil – a country that has been in the "first wave" of worldwide supermarket expansion in the late 1980s and early 1990s – about three-quarters of food retail sales are concentrated in supermarkets. In addition, while in the 1990s this process was spearheaded by national retail chains, currently the four major groups, Casino, Carrefour, Walmart and Cencosud/ Gbarbosa, which control 60% of the Brazilian market, are transnational and have their shares traded on stock exchanges worldwide.

An example typical of the trajectory of Brazilian retail transformations driven by financialization is that of CBD (Companhia Brasileira de Distribuição), also known as Grupo Pão de Açúcar (GPA). This group, owned by the Brazilian businessman Abilio Diniz, went public in 1995 and, two years later, its shares were traded on the New York Stock Exchange. It became, then, the first company wholly controlled by Brazilian capital to make a global issue of shares. In 1999, the French conglomerate Casino bought 24% of GPA's capital for US$854 million. Following a reengineering process that led the group to lead the ranking of the largest retail chains in the country, Casino decided to expand its stake, investing R$2 billion and, in June 2012, took full control of GPA. Today, this group is the largest distribution and retail network in Brazil, controlling brands such as Extra, Pão de Açúcar, Casas Bahia, Ponto Frio, among others. Casino, in turn, is controlled by Rallye, a holding company that holds 49.4% of the group's capital and 61.2% of the votes on the board.

The interest of financial capital in the retail sector reflects the significant capital gains it has provided for shareholders. Here, the prime example is that of Walmart. With a revenue of US$485 billion in 2017, the group leads – with a significant margin of difference to the second place (the Chinese electric power company, State Grid, US$315 billion) – the Fortune's list of the top

500 companies in the world, considering all sectors. That is, it is easy to understand the advance of financial capital over a sector that, since some years now, is led by a conglomerate that, in terms of annual income, surpasses the automakers and even the giants of the energy and oil sectors.

However, there is at least one more reason for association between capitals. Besides investors being integrated into the corporate structure of retail chains, retailers have established themselves as providers of financial services such as credit cards, insurance, transfer and payment services. In Brazil, due to the high interest rates applied by these players, in some cases these services provide profits even higher than the sales of products. As an analyst at Standard & Poor's rating agency pointed out, while, in the beginning, "banks went into stores primarily to finance the acquisition of goods, they now want virtually to set in-store agency. Retailers already offer more services to customers and earn part of the financial gains" (Folha de São Paulo, 2005). One of the consequences of this new type of relationship is that by linking food purchases to credit provision, consumers have both their financial security and their food security dependent on the same company, what reduces their autonomy to choose and decide (Clapp and Isakson, 2018).

The financial order and its repercussions for the agrifood system

In this chapter, we demonstrated an expansion and intensification of the participation of financial capital in the agrifood system, which spans different areas, actors and regions. Financial order is anchored in important institutional arrangements such as market liberalization, corporate governance and the prevalence of fictitious capital. These new institutional arrangements, backed by an indispensable set of artifacts – notably the widespread use of information technology and the dissemination of financial securities – were instrumental in shaping a new universe of practices such as speculation; formation of investment funds; initial public offering by companies; grabbing of land, natural resources and water; productive flexibility; corporate management etc. While not all of these practices are completely new, they have been strongly catalyzed by the financial capital (Figure 7.4).

An important feature of the financial order refers to its instability (which can be seen in stock value, commodity price, shift in investors' focus etc.), as this order often attracts actors whose practices are focused on rapid and high returns to their capital and who, therefore, take greater risks – what Clapp and Isakson (2018) call "risky returns." In addition, such a "hurry" of interest-bearing capital means that the timing of financial investors is not always at the same pace as the companies' real base (productive/commercial sphere). This has encouraged some executives to seek short-term results to meet investors demand, even though this may compromise the company's long-term competitiveness. According to Balestro and Lourenço (2014), this incentive strategy based on the ideology of maximizing shareholder value generates instability in the markets.

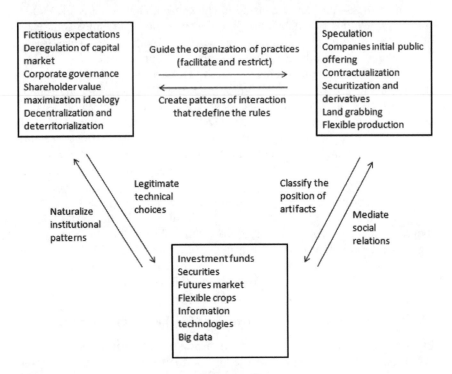

Figure 7.4 Components of the financial order.

The fact is that these investors are usually interested in buying and selling (stocks, commodities, land etc.), according to the prospects of fast and high returns. In this sense, a speculative practice prevails, which is highly detrimental to different actors of the agrifood markets. Furthermore, there is a complex institutional arrangement that allows financial gain to be detached from the production of goods and services (fictitious capital), so that securities or stocks, for example, may appreciate relatively regardless of productive assets, serving the interests and expectations of a number of speculative agents who have no direct link with the sector.

Another key institutional element to the financial order concerns the impact that expectations (as a cognitive device) have on actors' practices. The "fictional expectations" that Beckert (2017) calls "imagined futures" can be perceived in different situations and moments. The prospects of the volume of maize that shall be harvested in the United States impacts its future price, which is set at present; and, even if afterwards the expectation does not materialize, it has already changed its price. Another recurring case concerns the behavior of a company's stocks as a result of speculation. The supposed proposal of ADM to merge with Bunge (it is worth recalling that none of these firms confirmed this information) increased ADM's shares from US$69.6 to

US$82.1 between January 18 and January 22, 2018 – an 18% growth in 5 days. There is also the situation of flexible crops, which is explained, for example, in the oscillations of this market, when companies start investing in biodiesel industries based on the prospects that a new processing technology will be launched or that the country will raise the percentage of the mandatory bio-fuel blend (which is not just a passive expectation but also involves political pressure on the government). In this case, for being a multidestination crop, the advantage is that, while the expectation is not fulfilled, it remains being used as raw material in the more traditional destinations.

The arrangement of practices, artifacts and institutional devices produced configurations that are very specific to this order, especially in what we call the financialization of agrifood companies, of agricultural commodities and of land/nature. Although we have split our analysis into these three major elements, it is worth mentioning that other dimensions could have been incorporated. Moreover, it should be noted that situations that combine these three fronts are not uncommon. An example is Brasil Agro, a publicly traded firm that has 40% of its assets controlled by the Argentinian company Cresud, which is in turn backed by investment funds. This company operates in the purchase, appreciation and sale of land, and is also engaged in agricultural production (soybean, maize, sugarcane and livestock) in its own and in leased lands. Crops are traded in the futures market, and in the last agricultural year 87.4% of its soybean production was traded previously to harvest (BrasilAgro, 2018).

From an analytical standpoint, it is clear that, beyond the perspectives that focus primarily on agro-industries or supermarkets as leading agents in the agrifood sector (Reardon, 2015), it is also necessary to include financial investors, even though their action may be much more difficult to map. As Clapp (2014) argues, the distance between financial investors and their impacts on the food system tends to veil the role played by these actors in the food system, as well as their impacts. In addition,

> these effects are felt unevenly. While big agribusiness firms and financial investors largely benefit from the transformations as their power and wealth increase, the majority of farmers and consumers, as well as the planet, have borne the bulk of the costs associated with the changes.
>
> (Clapp and Isakson, 2018, 2)

These new financial practices in the agrifood system have intensified the process of concentration in different sectors and, associated with this, there has been an increase in inequality. As a result, according to Balestro and Lourenço (2014, 262), "the unregulated action of nonbank financial investments may produce a greater asymmetry in the distribution of resources within the agribusiness value chain in favor of financial market actors [to the detriment of productive capital]." According to the authors, financial agents have appropriated a larger surplus of the value generated within the supply chain, which has clear consequences for key issues such as quality (tends to be lower due to pressures for cost reduction), sustainability (greater pressure on resources contrary to environmental parameters) and working conditions (with an emphasis on low wages to keep production costs low).

(Idem, 255)

From this same perspective, Clapp and Isakson (2018) systematize the effects of the complex interaction between financialization and the agrifood sector on the social and ecological sustainability of food and agricultural supply. Considering the long-term impacts, the authors point out three important consequences of the expansion of these financial practices: it emphasizes the inequality of power and wealth among the actors involved; it increases economic (due to its instability) and ecological (because of overexploitation of natural resources) vulnerability in agrifood systems; and it impedes and minimizes the collective demands for change and resistance. Thus, "taken together, these wider implications of financialization in the agrifood sector present a direct challenge to the ability of food systems to provide livelihoods and food security over the long term" (Clapp and Isakson, 2018, 1).

Notes

1 Among the most effective control mechanisms is the reproduction of "public debt". As Streeck (2013) demonstrates, maintaining the "debt state" is one of the most effective and widespread control means found by the financial capital to define a new kind of "capitalist democracy."

2 A report on the state of inequality released by Oxfam (2017) featured, among the richest people in Brazil, Jorge Paulo Lemann, in the first position (a fortune of R$93.3 billion), Marcel Telles ranking third (R$47.3 billion) and Carlos Sicupira ranking fourth (R$39.9 billion). According to the organization, their fortunes are equivalent to the wealth of one-third of the Brazilian population.

3 The 3G Capital fund also operates outside the agrifood sector, controlling Lojas Americanas, the Brazilian fourth largest retailer, besides owning B2W, the country's largest e-commerce conglomerate (americas.com, shoptime and submarine).

4 In 2016, 49% of Glencore's agricultural operations were bought by two Canadian pension funds, the Canada Pension Plan Investment Board and the British Columbia Investment Management Corp.

5 A Federal Police-led operation named with a pun that takes the word "carne," which translates as both meat and flesh, to play with the expression "The spirit is willing but the flesh is weak" that has its origin in the bible.

6 BM&F Bovespa emerged, in 2008, from the merger of the São Paulo Stock Exchange (Bovespa) and BM&F. In 2017, it merges with the Custodian Bank (Central de Custódia e de Liquidação Financeira de Títulos – Cetip), forming B3, the fifth largest stock exchange in the world.

7 White et al. (2012) argue that, despite some differences in definition and timeframe, estimates of the total area sold, leased or licensed by international investors globally by 2012 amounted to 43 million hectares, according to the World Bank

data, to 80 million, according to The International Land Coalition (ILC), and to 227 million according to a survey by Oxfam International. Despite the huge discrepancy, all these are awesome values.

8 Although previously mentioned, it is important to recall that this data is underestimated. In May 2010, there were already 4,349,074 ha registered with INCRA under foreign ownership, as shown by Sauer and Leite (2012).

References

Abiove. 2018. *Estatística*, 2018. Accessed May 18, 2018. www.abiove.org.br/site/index. php?page=estatistica&area=NC0yLTE=>.

Amado, C. 2003. *Uma análise da eficiência dos mercados futuros agrícolas brasileiros.* Master Dissertation. Recife: UFPE.

Anseeuw, W., Roda, J.-M., Ducastel, A. and Kamaruddin, N. 2017. "Global strategies of firms and the financialization of agriculture." In *Sustainable Development and Tropical Agri-Chains*, edited by E. Biénabe, A. Rival and D. Loeillet, 321–37. Dordrecht: Springer.

Balestro, M. and Lourenço, L. 2014. "Notas para uma análise de financeirização do agronegócio além da volatilidade dos preços das commodities." In *O mundo rural no Brasil do século* 21, edited by A. M. Buainain et al., 241–66. Brasília: Embrapa.

Beckert, J. 2017. *Imagined Futures: Fictional Expectations and Capitalist Dynamics.* Cambridge: Harvard University.

Belluzzo, L. G. 1995. "O declínio de Bretton Woods e a emergência dos mercados globalizados." *Economia e Sociedade*, 4(1): 11–20.

Bernardes, J. A. (ed.). 2017. *Globalização do agronegócio e landgrabbing: a atuação das megaempresas argentinas no Brasil.* Rio de Janeiro: Lamparina.

Bomfim, L. P., Santos, C. M. and Pimenta, Jr., T. 2007. "Processos de abertura de capital de empresas *brasileiras* em 2004 e 2005: razões e percepções." *Revista de Administração*, 42(2): 524–34.

Bonanno, A. and Wolf, S. (eds). 2017. *Resistance to Neoliberal Food Regime: A Critical Analysis* . New York: Routledge.

Borras, Jr., S. and Franco, J. 2010. "La política del acaparamiento mundial de tierras: replanteando las cuestiones de tierras, redefiniendo la resistencia." *ICAS Working Paper Series*, 1.

Borras, Jr., S., Franco, J., Isackson, R., Levidow, L. and Vervest, P. 2016. "The rise of flex crops and commodities: Implications for research." *Journal of Peasant Studies*, 43(1): 93–115.

Borras, Jr., S., Hall, R., Scoones, I, White, B. and Wolford, W. 2011. "Towards a better understanding of global land grabbing: An editorial introduction." *Journal of Peasant Studies*, 32(2): 209–16.

Brasilagro. 2018. *Institutional website.* Accessed January 22, 2018. www.brasil-agro. com.

Brenner, R. 2003. *O boom e a bolha: os Estados Unidos na economia mundial.* Rio de Janeiro: Record.

Bresser-Pereira, L. C. 2010. "A crise financeira global e depois. Um novo capitalismo?" *Novos Estudos CEBRAP*, 86: 51–72.

Carvalho, F. J. C. et al. 2007. *Economia monetária e financeira: teoria e política.* Rio de Janeiro: Elsevier.

Castro, L. F. P. and Sauer, S. 2018. "Marcos legais e a liberação para investimento estrangeiro em terras no Brasil." In *Questões agrárias, agrícolas e rurais: conjunturas e políticas públicas*, edited by R. Maluf and G. Flexor, 39–51. Rio de Janeiro: E-papers.

Cavalcanti, F. S. and Misumi, J. Y. 2001. *Mercado de capitais*. Rio de Janeiro: Campus.

Cetip. 2018. *Estatísticas*. Accessed March 21, 2018. www.cetip.com.br/Estatisticas.

Chesnais, F. 2005. *A finança mundializada*. São Paulo: Boitempo.

Clapp, J. 2014. "Financialization, distance and global food politics." *Journal of Peasant Studies*, 41(5): 797–814.

Clapp, J. 2017. *Bigger Is Not Always Better: The Drivers and Implications of the Recent Agribusiness Megamergers*. Waterloo, ON: University of Waterloo.

Clapp, J. and Isakson, S. R. 2018. "Risky returns: The implications of financialization in the food system." *Development and Change*, 49(2): 437–60.

Corrêa, A. L. and Raíces, C. 2017. *Derivados agrícolas*. Santos: Comunnicar.

Delgado, G. C. 1985. *Capital financeiro e agricultura no Brasil: 1965–1985*. São Paulo: Ícone.

Delgado, G. C. 2012. *Do capital financeiro na agricultura à economia do agronegócio – mudanças cíclicas em meio século*. Porto Alegre: UFRGS.

Exame. 2014. *Dá para ganhar dinheiro com alta gastronomia no Brasil?* Accessed February 16, 2016. www.exame.abril.com.br/revista-exame/ganhar-dinheiro-esta-na-receita.

Fairbairn, M. 2014. "Like gold with yield: Evolving intersections between farmland and finance." *Journal of Peasant Studies*, 41(5): 777–95.

Fairhead, J., Leach, M. and Scoones, I. 2012. "Green grabbing: A new appropriation of nature?" *Journal of Peasant Studies*, 39(2): 237–61.

Flexor, G. and Leite, S. P. 2018. "Mercado de terra, commodities boom e land grabbing no Brasil." In *Questões agrárias, agrícolas e rurais: conjunturas e políticas públicas*, edited by R. Maluf and G. Flexor, 20–38. Rio de Janeiro: E-papers.

Folha de São Paulo. 2005. *Lojas "viram" banco e aumentam os lucros*. Accessed September 22, 2015. www1.folha.uol.com.br/fsp/dinheiro/fi1010200502.htm.

Franco, J., Mehta, L. and Veldwisch, G. J. 2013. "The global politics of water grabbing." *Third World Quarterly*, 34(9): 1651–75.

Frederico, S. and Gras, C. 2017. "Globalização financeira e landgrabbing: constituição e translatinização das megaempresas argentinas." In *Globalização do agronegócio e land grabbing: a atuação das megaempresas argentinas no* Brasil, edited by J. A. Bernardes, 12–31. Rio de Janeiro: Lamparina.

Freitas, M. C. and Prates, D. M. 1998. "Abertura financeira na América Latina: as experiências da Argentina, Brasil e México." *Economia e Sociedade*, 7(2): 173–98.

Galeano, L. A. 2012. El caso del Paraguay. In *Dinámicas del mercado de la tierra en América Latina y el Caribe*, edited by FAO, 407–34. Rome: FAO.

Goldfarb, Y. 2014. *Financeirização, poder corporativo e expansão da soja no estabelecimento do regime alimentar corporativo no Brasil e na Argentina: o caso da Cargill*. PhD Thesis. São Paulo: USP.

Gomes, C. M. 2017. *A financeirização e internacionalização das terras na "última fronteira agrícola"– MATOPIBA: o land grabbing e dinâmicas de expansão do agronegócio*. Rio de Janeiro: UFRRJ.

Hardt, M. and Negri, A. 2001. *Império*. Rio de Janeiro: Record.

Harvey, D. 2005. *O Neoliberalismo: história e implicações*. São Paulo: Loyola.

Harvey, D. 2013. *Os limites do capital*. São Paulo: Boitempo Editorial.

Heinrich-Böll Foundation. 2017. *Agrifood Atlas: Facts and Figures About the Corporations that Control What We Eat*. Berlin: Heinrich Böll Foundation.

Herreros, M. M., Barros, F. G. and Bentes, E. S. 2010. "Atividade especulativa dos fundos de investimento no mercado futuro de commodities agrícolas, 2006–2009." *Revista de Política Agrícola*, 19(1): 24–39.

Holmes, G. 2014. "What is a land grab? Exploring green grabs, conservation, and private protected areas in southern Chile." *Journal of Peasant Studies*, 41(4): 547–67.

IBA. 2017. *Relatório 2017*. Brasilia: IBA.

Imea. 2017. *Composição do funding do custeio da soja para safra 2017/18 em Mato Grosso*. Accessed November 22, 2017. www.imea.com.br/imea-site/relatorios-mercado.

Ipes-Food. 2017. *Too big to feed: exploring the impacts of mega-mergers, consolidation, concentration of power in agri-food sector*. Accessed January 18, 2018. www.ipes-food.org.

Land Matrix. 2016. *International land deals for agriculture: analytical report II*. Accessed May 23, 2018. www.landmatrix.org.

Maluf, R. S. and Speranza, J. S. 2014. *Preços dos alimentos, modelos de agricultura e abastecimento alimentar no Brasil: os casos da soja e do feijão*. Rio De Janeiro: ActionAid.

Martin, S. J. and Clapp, J. 2015. "Finance for agriculture or agriculture for finance?" *Journal of Agrarian Change*, 15(4): 549–59.

Mckay, B., Sauer, S., Richardson, B. and Herre, R. 2016. "The political economy of sugarcane flexing: Initial insights from Brazil, Southern Africa and Cambodia." *Journal of Peasant Studies*, 43(1): 195–223.

Misoczky, M. C. and Böhm, S. 2012. "Do desenvolvimento sustentável à economia verde: a constante e acelerada investida do capital sobre a natureza." *Cadernos EBAPE.BR*, 10(3): 546–68.

Murphy, S., Burch, D. and Clapp, J. 2012. *Cereal Secrets: The World's Largest Grain Traders and Global Agriculture*. London: Oxfam.

Nakatani, P. et al. 2014. "Expansão Internacional da China Através da Compra de Terras no Brasil e no Mundo." *Textos & Contextos*, 13(1): 58–73.

Oliveira, A. U. 2011. "Os agrocombustíveis e a produção de alimentos." In *A (in)sustentabilidade do desenvolvimento*, edited by M. Simonetti, 159–80. São Paulo: Cultura Acadêmica.

Oliveira, C. 2010. "Os títulos do agronegócio brasileiro: uma análise comparativa entre a percepção existente no seu lançamento e a situação atual." In *Proceedings of the Brazilian Congress of Rural Economy and Sociology*. Campo Grande: Sober.

Oliveira, R. 2018. "*O Brasil está experimentando uma das maiores desindustrializações da história da economia*. Entrevista com Ha Joon Chang." Accessed January 5, 2018. www.brasil.elpais.com/brasil/2018/01/05/economia/1515177346_780498

Oxfam. 2017. *A distância que nos une*. Rio de Janeiro: Oxfam.

Paula, M., Santos, F. and Pereira, W. 2015. "A financeirização das commodities agrícolas e o sistema agroalimentar." *Estudos Sociedade e Agricultura*, 23(2): 294–314.

Pereira, L. 2017. "Liberação na aquisição de imóveis rurais por estrangeiros no Brasil e o controle de terras." *Boletim Dataluta*, 112: 1–20.

Reardon, T. 2015. "The hidden middle: the quiet revolution in the midstream of agrifood value chains in developing countries." *Oxford Review of Economic Policy*, 31(1): 45–63.

Reardon, T. and Berdegué, J. 2002. "The rapid rise of supermarkets in Latin America: Challenges and opportunities for development." *Development Policy Review*, 20(4): 317–34.

Saltorato, P. and Donadone, J. C. 2012. "Banqueiros e bancários na construção do varejo financeiro nacional." In *Proceedings of the Annual Meeting of ANPOCS*, Caxambu: ANPOCS.

Saltorato, P., Domingues, L., Donadone, J., Sanches, E. and Sola, F. 2016. "Fusões, aquisições e difusão da lógica financeira sobre as operações de varejo brasileiro." *Gestão & Produção*, 23(1): 84–103.

Salviatti, A. 2017. "Financeirização do Meio Ambiente." *Historia Ambiental Latinoamericana y Caribeña*, 6(2): 311–21.

Sassen, S. 2013. "Landgrabs today: Feeding the disassembling of national territory." *Globalizations*, 10(1): 25–46.

Sassen, S. 2016. *Expulsões: brutalidade e complexidade na economia global*. Rio de Janeiro: Paz e Terra.

Sauer, S. 2010. Demanda Mundial por terras: "landgrabbing" ou oportunidade de negócios no Brasil. *Revista de Estudos e Pesquisas sobre as Américas*, 4(1): 72–88.

Sauer, S. 2016. "Terra no século XXI: Desafios e perspectivas da questão agrária." *Retratos de Assentamentos*, 19(2): 69–97.

Sauer, S. and Borras, Jr., S. 2016. "Land grabbing e Green grabbing: uma leitura da 'corrida na produção acadêmica' sobre a apropriação global de terras." *Campo-Território*, 11(23): 6–42.

Sauer, S. and Leite, S. P. 2012. "Expansão agrícola, preços e apropriação de terra por estrangeiros no Brasil." *Revista de Economia e Sociologia Rural*, 50(3): 503–24.

Silveira, R., Maciel, L. and Ballini, R. 2014."Derivativos sobre commodities influenciam a volatilidade dos preços à vista? Uma análise nos mercados de boi gordo e café arábica no Brasil." *Revista de Economia e Sociologia Rural*, 52(3): 417–36.

SLC Agrícola. 2018. *A empresa*. Accessed February 22, 2018. www.slcagricola.com.br.

Smith, N. 2007. "Nature as accumulation strategy." *Socialist Register*, 43: 16–36.

Sosa, A. P. 2017. *El papel de las megaempresas agropecuarias en la financiarización del régimen alimentario global: los casos del Grupo Los Grobo y El Tejar en Argentina y en Brasil (1996–2015)*. PhD Thesis. Buenos Aires: UBA.

Souchaud, S. 2007. *Geografía de la migración brasileña en Paraguay*. Asunción: UNFPA.

Souza, A. T. 2003. "Bolsa de valores como fonte de financiamento." *FAE Business*, 6: 20–24.

Spadotto, B. R. 2017. "Land grabbing e uso do território: capital financeiro e apropriação de terras no sul do Maranhão e Piauí (MATOPIBA)." In *Proceedings of the Latin American Meeting of Geographers*. La Paz: EGAL.

Streeck, W. 2013. *Tempo Comprado: a crise adiada do capitalismo democrático*. Coimbra: Actual.

Unica. 2018. *Nova linha de plástico verde da Braskem amplia mercado de bioplásticos no país*. Accessed September 29, 2018. www.unica.com.br.

Urioste, M. 2011. *Concentración y extranjerización de la tierra en Bolivia*. La Paz: Fundación Tierra.

Valor Econômico. 2017. *Fertiláqua quer dobrar vendas até 2018*. Accessed August 14, 2018. www.valor.com.br/agro/5055724/fertilaqua-quer-dobrar-vendas-ate-2018.

Valoral Advisors. 2018. *Databases*. Accessed December 12, 2018. www.valoral.com.

White, B., Borras, Jr., S., Hall, R., Scoones, I. and Wolford, W. 2012. "The new enclosures: critical perspectives on corporate land deals." *Journal of Peasant Studies*, 39(3–4): 619–47.

Wilkinson, J. 2018. "Land grabbing e estrangeirização de terras no Brasil." In *Questões agrárias, agrícolas e rurais*, edited by R. Maluf and G. Flexor, 12–29. Rio de Janeiro: E-papers.

Wilkinson, J., Reydon, B. and Di Sabbato, A. 2012. "Concentration and foreign ownership of land in Brazil in the context of global land grabbing." *Canadian Journal of Development Studies*, 33(4): 417–38.

Zaar, M. H. 2001. "A migração rural no Oeste paranaense/Brasil: a trajetória dos 'brasiguaios'." *Scripta Nova*, 94(88).

8 Conclusions

When we began to discuss the project that led to this book, we had two object-ives in mind. The first was to question a homogenizing view of the Brazilian agriculture. It was not long before we realized that this could not be restricted to agricultural production. We should go beyond and reach the practices of consumption, moving through all the links and circuits through which food and raw materials circulate, encompassing what we usually call "the market." The second objective was to build an approach that would allow us to carry out this project. The available models of market analysis were, for various reasons, inadequate. We would not achieve our objectives based on concepts such as supply chain or value chain. Initially, we found in the sociology of agriculture and food some approaches closer to what we needed, especially in the concepts of food regimes and farming styles. However, as discussions progressed, these approaches have also revealed their limits.

The discussions over the two years taken to write this book led us to meet the New Economic Sociology, the Neoinstitutional School and the Practice Theory. The idea of market as a social construction was, then, already fully incorporated into our research. We had also used the grammar of "worlds of justification" from the French Convention Theory. To a large extent, it was from the pragmatist assumptions embraced by this theory that we knitted some of the denser precepts that comprise the argument of this book. Besides, the dialogue between economic sociology and convention theory was already widely known in food studies. The main innovation we introduced into this dialogue lies, on the one hand, in broadening the model to contributions from other institutional approaches, what enabled a more refined view of social institutions, and, on the other hand, in incorporating the practice theory.

Instead of actors and structures, *practices* and *institutions* became the two main entities of a middle-range theory that overcomes the misconceptions of individualism and holism. By integrating these concepts, and associating them with a notion of artifacts, which seeks to capture the materiality of the world, the concept of *social order* was developed. In a way, the orders are similar to the "worlds of justification" occupied by the practices. *Food orders* are arrangements of rules, habits, values, identities, meanings and artifacts associated with particular ways of producing, distributing, selling, buying, preparing and eating. Indeed, based on this concept this book proposes an analytical alternative to the dualist narratives that still prevail in the sociology of agriculture and food, and which are expressed in the oppositions between local and global, sector and territory, family farming and agribusiness food regimes and farming styles.

Rather than starting from the social actors and their interests, or from the way individuals, groups or classes shape practices and institutions according to these interests, our analysis starts from the practices and their actors. Indeed, social orders are not primarily delimited by the presence of one social actor or another. Orders are arrangements of social practices intrinsically associated with institutional mechanisms and material artifacts. Thus, any attempt to understand (or criticize) the configuration of a particular order implies looking at the connections between these three components of our ontology: the doings and sayings that shape practices; the normative (values), regulatory (rules) and cognitive (ideas) institutions; and the materiality of the world (artifacts).

Clearly, once a food order has been delimited, it is important to situate the multiple actors that circulate within it and, more or less skillfully, cross its boundary toward other food orders. As Beckert's analysis (2009, 6) of what he calls "social order of markets" highlights, "the task of market sociology is to study both: the emergence and shaping of the social macrostructures relevant in the market context as well as the structuring of market action – and the distribution of exchange opportunities – by these macrostructures." Although the idea of macrostructure seems inappropriate to our definition of social order, it can be said that it was from this same perspective that we included the power struggles, the conflicts and the material and symbolic resources employed by the actors to attain a dominant position within the social orders, that is, in the markets.

Moreover, our starting point does not begin with individuals, groups or classes predisposed to conflict. Conflict is one of the ever-present options for social action, as are cooperation and compromise. The starting point is the recognition that the same players competing in a particular market – in setting a certification standard or in creating a technology, for instance – may have synergistic and collaborative behaviors in another market, or in the same market at some other time. As North, Wallis and Weingast (2009, 2) note, "because social orders engender different patterns of behaviour, individuals in different social orders form different beliefs," rationalities and identities. Considering that actors move around different orders, if we want to understand their practices, we must escape the hypostasized representations of their identities, in order to consider how these are shaped during the action. Instead of actors, it is the practices that take on specific meanings ("politicized consumption"), though, of course, once actors recurrently reproduce this practice, they will incorporate the associated identity ("politicized consumer"), albeit transitorily.

Actors are not entities functional to practices, which would be defined by some kind of generalizing institutional superstructure – the actors recursively produce the practices and institutions. Nor are they in the social game simply to accept the rules and forms of distribution of resources and identities, which would make them a kind of institutional puppet. Social actors introduce new technologies, create new rules, develop new practices and change their ideas, representations and values. The development of information technologies, for example, affected the configuration of all food orders. The emergence of sustainability as a social value was instrumental to boosting the civic order, but it also affected the financial order, which, by integrating this value with new information technologies, created a global carbon credit market. In turn, the inflow of pension funds as relevant actors in land grabbing processes exemplifies not only the emergence of a new form of integration between financial and commercial orders, but also the ability of certain actors to carry resources and technical devices from one order (financial) to another (commercial).

Thus, it is important to consider issues such as stability and institutional change. As we have repeatedly pointed out throughout the book, the idea of "order" refers to the creation of stability and reduction of uncertainties for actors to carry on their social exchanges. This notion is very close to the most widespread understanding within the institutional debate (Mahoney and Rueschemeyer, 2003; March and Olsen, 2006). In this literature, stability is usually the result of institutional and technological path dependence, which implies that actors offer some level of resistance to change certain rules or introduce new technologies, not only for the additional costs that it may entail, but because of uncertainties about its benefits. However, what is observed in the food markets is increasingly faster institutional, technological and ecological changes. Stability comprises a more transitory and contingent situation than it is commonly deemed. This explains why contemporary expressions of the food orders are not exactly the same as before. Domestic and commercial orders, for example, cannot be imagined in the same terms as they existed a century ago. The family farming small-scale food processing incorporated new productive and commercial practices. It is no longer necessarily restricted to the domestic environment (the kitchen), nor to a surplus economy. Nevertheless, it bears a resemblance to the traditional domestic rural manufacturing, what is expressed in foods that rely on social practices and values that have long characterized peasant communities.

In turn, the contemporary commercial order reinvented slave labor. Although this practice is not carried out in the same way as it did in the nineteenth century, it nevertheless bears the same perverse institutional logic that, yesterday and today, accepts the inhuman exploitation of workers in agricultural and industrial production, not to mention the service sector – either large supermarkets or telemarketing companies, to name only two sectors that concentrate new forms of servitude whose analysis falls beyond the scope of this book. It could be argued that, unlike the nineteenth century, contemporary forms of slavery are not restricted to black people, though this is only partially true. Such practices, in general, do not only hold the same names, but also similar addresses and social groups as those of the past. It is still basically the black populations living in the peripheries (rural and urban) who are victims of racism incorporated as one of the institutional patterns of the commercial order.

Then, what happens when institutional and technological disruptions take place? Beyond these incremental changes, do not orders evolve because of radical changes? Or does this kind of change not exist? Of course, it does. The literature on food regimes has precisely the virtue of highlighting the role of ruptures instead of incremental changes. However, following other strands of institutional analysis (Thelen, 2004) and sociology of techniques (Geels, 2002), our approach has privileged more gradual forms of transition, for three reasons. First, because they are more recurrent. Secondly, because, generally, the effects of this kind of change are largely ignored by the social sciences, which privilege critical moments as markers of new "ages," even if these latter are often very similar to previous ones. Finally, and most significantly, because radical changes lead to the end of an order and/or to the emergence of new orders. This is due to the degree of disruption that a truly radical change entails to the institutional and technical structure of an order, which would not be able to endure it without disintegrating.

It is in this sense that, where adherents of the narrative of food regimes envision the transition from a colonial-mercantile regime toward an industrial-Fordist regime in the 1930s, we observe the emergence of an industrial order that comes to compete with (and prevail over) the commercial order. Although this represented a more or less radical rupture with what existed, the commercial and domestic orders nonetheless did not cease to exist or were fully incorporated into the industrial order. Similarly, when those authors found a new rupture, as of the 1980s, which led to the crisis of the Fordist food regime and its replacement by a new financial-neoliberal regime, we identified the emergence of new food orders: the financial one, which becomes hegemonic, but also the aesthetic and civic orders (Figure 8.1).

We have not identified the complete disappearance of any order. This result differs from that previously presented in Niederle (2018). The criticisms of the idea that practices and institutions of the commercial order had been incorporated by the industrial order led us to a new understanding. Despite the fact that some practices typical of the commercial order have been seriously challenged over the last decades, the recent rise of authoritarian governments and movements has even led to a revival of this order. In the Brazilian context, this is expressed, for example, in the expansion of (un)productive sectors that rely on the spoliation of natural resources, on slave labor and on the institutional legitimacy of illegal and violent forms of land appropriation (Niederle et al., 2019).

Another issue that arises here refers to the way changes are produced. There is a relative consensus around idea that, due to the malleability of institutions, the so-called incremental changes are produced within orders. Therefore, such

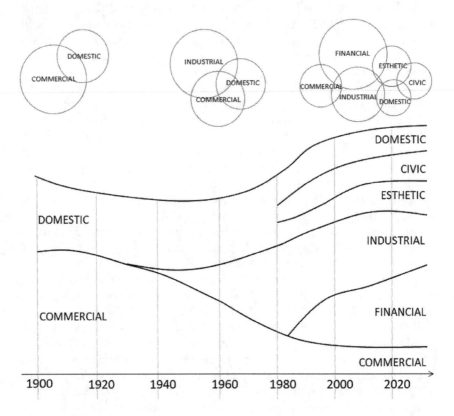

Figure 8.1 Food orders development and diversification in Brazil.

adjustments stem from the reinterpretation of norms by the social actors; the introduction of new norms, standards or artifacts, which alter the arrangement of practices; or the entry of new social actors in the market. The problem lies in understanding the origin of the radical changes. For the approaches based on the concept of food regimes, disruptions are systemic, that is, they are consequences of crises of the very capitalist accumulation-regulation regime (Boyer, 2003). The deeper the crisis, the greater the need for a rupture, not exactly for capitalism to disappear (Marx's terminal crisis) but for the regime to reinvent itself (Schumpeter's creative destruction). The MLP of analysis of sociotechnical transitions, in turn, favors the idea that disruptions in regimes derive from external shocks, usually originating from the upper level of the sociotechnical and institutional landscape (Geels, 2002).

Otherwise, the model of social orders does not work with a hierarchy that places certain institutions at higher levels. In our view, there is no reason to establish, prior to the research, that a new norm on industrial property negotiated at the World Trade Organization will cause changes in farmers' practices deeper than those brought about by the amendment of an informal convention on shared land use. In the first case, we are obviously dealing with a norm that will spread to the 200 member states of this organization, whereas in the second case it is a local convention. It is also plausible to imagine that, throughout the research, strong effects of the global norm on local farming styles will be perceived. Even so, we do not start from a prior conception of these effects. First, because, however global the norms and technologies are, they will be differently tested, interpreted and adapted by local actors. Second, because, in certain contexts, they may turn out to be completely innocuous. In short, it is the social contexts that define the relevance of each institution in shaping practices. Perhaps there is no better example in this regard than the production of artisanal raw milk cheese. If it depended on national food safety regulations, this product would have disappeared from the Brazilian countryside. In fact, in many regions this has happened and continues to occur. In others, however, this practice has expanded and gained space.

If there is no prior hierarchy, and all institutions are potentially important, how can we identify those that most strongly affect the structuring of practices? Somewhat paradoxically, an answer to this question can be found in the work of Ostrom (2007), who coined the concept of "nested institutions" precisely to highlight the existence of multiple "institutional levels" that operate in interrelated ways. However, she also proposed the much less-known and used concept of rules-in-use (or working rules). This draws attention to the need to identify *in loco* what are the rules that effectively guide the actors in the organization of their practices, whether the management of the commons, the choice of a seed or even the purchase of certain food in a supermarket. According to the author, "once we understand the working rules, then, we attempt to understand where those rules come from" (Ostrom, 2007, 36).

Although not following Ostrom's rational view on how actors choose the institutions they would need to solve certain "operational problems"– what seems to us an exaggerated instrumentalism typical of much of the new institutional economy – the notion of "rules-in-use" is close to the pragmatist perspective we employ in our analysis. This perspective brings to the fore the need to understand the way actors consciously or unconsciously mobilize different rules, standards, conventions, understandings, beliefs and values in order to organize their doings (planting, selling, eating etc.) and sayings (discourses and narratives). That is, the action of these institutional elements is object of interpretation in the scope of social interaction.

Rather than taking them as substantial properties derived from vague macrostructures (the "landscape"), these elements should be deemed as relational properties, since it is in interactions that they acquire meaning (Eymard-Duvernay et al., 2005). As no norm is transparent in itself, it can only be understood while in operation (Schatzki, 2002). Moreover, the way social actors understand it does not respond to a rational calculation that leads these actors to opt for the best solution to a given problem, but rather stem from a complex interpretative process in which strategic decisions incorporate, on the one hand, criteria of efficiency other than those specifically "economic," and, on the other hand, the said "habitual" and "nonreflective" behavior may also be a key mechanism of institutional "choice."

This perspective proposes an alternative for the dilemma of social actor's nature: hyperreflexive in some theories, semi-automaton in others. The social actor is neither rational, strategic and calculating, nor an incoherent fool – and, at the same time, is all that (Callon, 1998). What changes is the social context. A pension fund manager that operates in the financial market may be unable to manage a solidarity economy cooperative. At the very least, this implies recognizing that we are faced with "situated rationalities" (Thévenot, 1989), so that an assessment of an actor's behavior must pay attention to the relationships he establishes with his immediate context, be it global or local. Ultimately, each social order has its own parameters for defining what it means to act rationally. The strategy of pursuing the highest profit in the shortest time may be the standard for the financial order, but it is not quite rational to survive in civic markets.

One of the problems of sociological analysis of institutions is the over-emphasis on nonreflective reproduction of behaviors, given, for example, the thesis of "institutional isomorphism" (DiMaggio and Powel, 2005). On the other hand, Boltanski (2009) proposes a different understanding for the supposed trade-off between habitual action and reflective action. This understanding involves the recognition that reflective action is instigated by situations of crisis. Social actors do not spend all the time calculating the best way to produce, buy or talk. Such role is attributed to institutions as references or action guides that organize the most common behaviors. However, in crisis contexts, actors are driven to reflect on their practices. This idea brings up a topic for discussion, which is directly associated with the reconfiguration of social orders: the role of criticism as a trigger of crises. No economic crisis will indeed be a crisis until it is interpreted as such by the social actors. As the recent Brazilian context has made very clear, there are discursive disputes for the production and denial of the crisis. Obviously, it will be far more difficult to produce a crisis if the discourse is not based on the reality of things, that is, on rising unemployment, expanding inflation, food shortages and so on.

Throughout the chapters, we sought to highlight the most relevant criticisms that actors mobilize in order to destabilize a particular food order, either to promote minor adjustments so that to make the rules more appropriate to their interests and values (reformist criticism) or with a view to destroying that mode of social ordering (radical criticism). We also highlighted the discursive game of justifications for either criticizing or reaffirming a particular prac-tice or institution, showing that teams and players are not always the same in such game. Even if they come into play with relatively defined positions and identities, in the course of the game there may be substitutions. There is even the possibility of some players switching sides, though this rarely happens in the same game. Most commonly this occurs from game to game. While some economists see this behavior as a moral hazard that must be controlled by institutions, we deem to be more interesting to recognize that this is a practice relevant to institutional change.

Understanding institutional changes also implies going beyond interactions and overlaps between different food orders to encompass their nexus with other social orders. In their analysis of markets as social fields, Fligstein and McAdam (2012) highlight a recurring tendency of many researches to a "fieldcentric bias," that is, an inclination to study the dynamics of a social field as independent of what occurs in other fields. To avoid this problem, we must associate the internal transformations of the food orders with the dynamics, changes, crises and disturbances that occur in other social orders. Thus, the chapters sought to underline how some factors, such as changes in public policy resulting from change of political party in power; the abrupt devaluation of a currency in the face of international crisis; or the reduction of certain resources, such as oil, due to political and economic conflicts, affect the conformation of food orders, opening and closing windows of opportunity for critical movements and for changes in production and consumption practices.

While the issue of institutions seems well-settled, it is still necessary to look more carefully into the issue of social practices. As we saw above, identifying the institutions that guide the configuration of practices is not a simple task. To this end, many scholars devise complicated models of classification that, however complex they may be, never account for the entire reality. The same is true for social practices. After all, almost anything can be presented as a social practice: eat, pray and love; occupy, resist and produce. Therefore, to try to delimit the place of practices in social orders, three questions need to be answered: How to identify a practice? How to associate it with a certain social order? And, once this has been done, how to measure its relevance?

To answer the first question, it is necessary, first, to delimit the social phenomenon under analysis. In this book, we did not distinguish social orders and food orders, because we dealt with food production and consumption. This choice considerably reduced the universe of practices to be investigated. For the purposes of this book, eating and producing become practices more relevant than others. The second step, as Warde (2015) and Schubert (2017) suggest, is to understand whether eating practices are interconnected in a codependent way, when the performance of one directly affects the other (food preparation and consumption), or are coexistent practices, sharing a same context without affecting substantially one another. This level of association varies from one context to another. In the civic order, for example, eating and producing may be codependent practices of occupying and resisting, but are coexisting practices regarding practices of praying and loving (except, perhaps, for those who define agroecology as a philosophy of life).

The fact that a practice fits into one or another social order is primarily due to the way in which an arrangement of interdependent practices is configured. In this case, the question that needs to be asked is: what practices shape a kind of highly cohesive, codependent central hub of a wider web of social practices? That is, we are faced with a perspective that focuses on the relationship not properly between actors, but between their practices (Shove, Pantzar and Watson, 2012). Based on this, one should argue about the meanings and identities carried by these practices (Schatzki, 2002). As these are also relational properties, they are connected to other meanings and identities that will be either centrally or peripherally positioned, sometimes at the borders where two or more orders overlap. This is the case, for example, with the meaning of "healthy" food, which on the one hand is strongly associated with civic order attributes such as food security and real food, and, on the other hand, maintains a certain level of interconnection with typical semantic constructions of the aesthetic order, such as the standards of body beauty.

The shaping of practice arrangements also stems from how the use of material artifacts to perform a practice can affect the configuration of other practices, reinforcing the level of dependency between them. The seal that supports participatory organic certification, for example, is a central artifact for creating civic markets for agroecological products. The high yield hybrid seeds, which condition the way of planting, demand the use of certain inputs (fertilizers, agrochemicals) that, in turn, condition the cultivation practices. The creation of a new biodiesel processing method can encourage the cultivation of a new raw material, which will require the reorganization of agricultural work practices. In sum, artifacts strengthen the forms of association between certain practices, even creating innovation trajectories that affect the universe of future choices of social actors.

Understanding why certain practices form a coherent arrangement to shape an order also entails recognizing the values that define them as socially legitimate practices. Like institutions, practices are also subject to interpretation and social legitimacy. Mutually coherent practices that define a specific type of ordering, more than sharing artifacts that operate coordinately (hybrid seeds and fertilizers) are consistent with the values that legitimize them before a particular social group. It is in this sense that we can understand the close link between the forms of spoliation of natural resources and contemporary slave labor, not only because one practice is directly connected to the other (the use of workers in degrading mining conditions), but also because they respond to a set of evaluative principles that are consistent with each other, and which even led to the creation of the concept of "environmental racism" (Acselrad, 2002).

Finally, the question remains of the relevance of social practices for shaping modes of ordering. Are all practices equally important for structuring the dynamics of a market? Clearly not. Why, then, when characterizing the civic order, for example, did we privilege an analysis of participatory certification and were silent about the use of social currencies? The identification of the practices most relevant to the analysis – those that, for using Warde's (2015) terms, have greater capacity for "anchoring" other practices for the construction of an orderly arrangement – demands a considerable qualitative research effort. Since there is no ready recipe in qualitative research, it is a matter of sociological practice, that is, of improving the eminently human mechanisms of observation and understanding of social phenomena. Besides, in our case, we were obliged to focus on the examples we had already some research about.

The reader will hardly escape the temptation to ask about the possibility of quantitatively measuring a practice and, more broadly, a social order. However, the kind of metric we are used to in market research makes us quite reticent about this idea. On the one hand, there are no data to allow this type of measurement at more aggregated spatial scales, such as country-level. In localized case studies, it would be possible to quantify, for example, the number of farmers using social currencies and participatory certifications. Indeed, whenever possible, we sought to present data on practices (number of farmers with participatory certification, area of commodities production, number of geographical indications registered, number of workers in slave-like labor conditions etc.). Even so, there are no statistical data available to measure the set of practices that make up an order, what makes it unfeasible to compare the extent of each order.

It is not difficult to anticipate that, among the questions that will concern some critics of this book, one regards to the number of food orders: are these six the only existing in Brazil? We have already answered this question. The delimitation of orders is influenced by the interests of the researcher, without any false pretense of scientific neutrality. As much as orders express arrangements of practices, institutions and artifacts, it is inevitable that the identification of links between these entities will contain a good deal of choice and arbitrariness. Indeed, as in the case of the *cités* or worlds of the convention theory, it would not be unusual if any Latourian wanted to propose an ecological order (Latour, 1995). Moreover, not only the number but also the configuration of the food orders can vary from one social context to another. The practices, institutions, artifacts and meanings of a domestic order in France are not necessarily the same as those found in Brazil. The interpretation by social actors of what is, for example, the conventionalization of agroecology is different from one context to another. That is, unlike the model of worlds of justification, the orders do not have the same "universalist" claim. The orders that we defined to understand the Brazilian reality may not be relevant to analyze the food markets in Russia or China. In addition, they may also be inadequate to describe the specific dynamics of certain Brazilian regions. In this case, how to think of comparative research? First and foremost, comparison starts from the very identification of what are the relevant social orders in each context.

The concept of food orders is a heuristic construct that helps to examine the heterogeneous configuration of the forms of food production and consumption. It allowed us to identify social dynamics that cannot be adequately analyzed by resorting to generalist explanations that attempt to bring together in one definition – such as industrialization and financialization – all the dynamics that characterize agriculture and, more broadly, food markets. Adherents of these explanations will surely reply that there is an overstatement here. After all, they are not meant to explain all processes, but only the most relevant ones, those that "really" define the course of capitalism. In this case, our criticism is not directed to the idea that postwar transformations led to the hegemony of the industrial order, which is consistent with the idea of "industrialization of agriculture." We also agree that, especially since the 1990s, it was the financial order that took the leading role, reflecting the process of "financialization." We just do not agree to reduce the dynamics of capitalism to a single grammar. That is, although it is not difficult to adhere to Fraser's (2017, 68) idea that the "dominant sector in contemporary capitalism is the financial," we remain closer to the proposition of Boltanski and Esquerre's (2017) about the coexistence and aggregation of different economies, each with more or less specific practices, rules, standards, artifacts, values and qualities. The financial order is one of those economies. This understanding goes hand in hand with the neoinstitutional debate about varieties of capitalism (Hall and Thelen, 2009; Thelen, 2004).

What is the contribution of the food orders approach to understanding the reality of Brazilian agriculture? How could one deny the advancement of the financialization and market concentration processes? We do not deem it credible or necessary to deny these processes. The question that needs to be answered involves another level. Can we understand the reality of the forms of food production and consumption in Brazil by looking only at these processes, characteristic of a neoliberal financial regime? The endeavors of McMichael (2016) and other authors to characterize the hegemonic world food regime is fundamental, insofar as it allows to explain essential and broadly general phenomena. However, there is a tendency to consider them in an excessively unitary way. In our view, even what the regimes narrative defines as financialization is a more heterogeneous process. We do not deem appropriate to equate the role of US universities' pension funds in the land grabbing process and the acquisition of Kraft Heinz by the 3G Capital fund. Both practices are, however, associated with processes of financialization of the food markets.

To some extent, the central object of this discord is ontological. Where some authors envision a world moving toward homogenization and standardization, others see chaos, the explosion of differences, fragmentation. The same thing is observed, but two different realities are seen. Our reality is more heterogeneous than the one that sees only one ubiquitous global food regime. However, it is also less fragmented than the interpretative kaleidoscope of farming styles. In a sense, the concept of social order helps "place order" in the fragmented reality of localized styles. Even so, it shares with this concept and with its proponents the concern to draw attention to the diversity of food systems. This diversity, however, is not only expressed in production practices, but also in the consumer universe and in all processing, distribution and marketing practices.

As regards to consumption, Poulain (2013, 27) presents two statements that, at first glance, are diametrically opposed. First, he states that "never in history has an eater had access to such food diversity as now in the West." However, shortly thereafter, he argues that since the "globalization and industrialization of the food sphere, the products have standardized, homogenized." How can diversity and homogenization coexist in the same food system? The answer is relatively simple, though not widely accepted, namely: we do not live in the "same food system." We move around different food orders. This is what explains the apparent "food cacophony" that Poulain describes as the multiplication of contradictory discourses.

A similar explanation allows us to overcome the apparent paradox between the growing concentration in the food markets, increasingly controlled by a small number of companies and the diversification of production and consumption practices. Recurrently, the relevant literature presents hasty conclusions on how oligopolization has generated greater standardization. We are not saying that this phenomenon does not exist. The transnationalization of many food retailer conglomerates, for example, has imposed similar rules and quality standards on farmers and processors in various parts of the world, leading to the conformation of similar practices. However, this phenomenon coexists with the need for these same conglomerates to adopt a more heterogeneous portfolio of practices and rules. The largest agro-industrial conglomerates have also incorporated specific divisions to develop food innovations that respond to new consumer demands.

The existence of dominant trajectories of institutional and technological change is undoubted. These trajectories make certain social practices to spread rapidly while others are unauthorized. However, the evolution of institutions and practices does not have a single linear route (Veblen, 1957). The expansion of authoritarian and violent practices of land appropriation is an example that the evolution does not follow successive stages of modernization as Walt Rostow and all theorists of modernization who followed him imagined. Otherwise, in this case it would be more appropriate to think of circular dynamics, which "make the future look like the past." The increasing consumer demand for butter – and more recently for swine fat – as margarine substitutes is another example. It finds no explanation either in modernization theory or in the narrative of food regimes. Or rather, in both it is thrown to the level of the niches, a kind of purgatory of all practices that do not conform to the dominant trajectories.

The development of different trajectories, which can be interpreted through the evolution and differentiation of food orders, is a result of the agency capacity of social actors (farmers, consumers, agricultural technicians, researchers, retailers, policymakers etc.) to react to institutional and technological pressures, as well as to produce institutions and artifacts that enable them to conform to new social practices and orders. This is a conclusion that had already been highlighted by the actor-oriented perspective, which grounds the farming style studies. As Long and Ploeg (1994) point out, even under strong institutional constraints from both the state and the market, farmers are able to develop farming styles that diverge from the prevailing sociotechnical standards. However, there is a second reason for heterogeneity, which is less considered by these authors: the fact that it also stems from the disjunctions between different practices and institutions. In other words, the state and the market are not uniform macrostructures that impose a single institutional standard, which farmers accept or confront. They are arenas of action governed by contradictory practices and institutions. This was illustrated in this book by the formal recognition by INPI of the geographical indications for artisanal raw milk cheeses, which, according to MAPA food safety standards, could not even exist, much less be marketed. Social actors skillfully leverage and manage these institutional incongruities to create differentiated practices. That is, because of their very nature, these institutions not only constrain, but also create opportunities for deviant actions.

The driver of changes remains being the social struggles around critique and contestation of the institutional patterns that underpin social practices (Boltanski, 2009). These struggles can be diffused and individualized, as is the case with the everyday resistance practices of family farmers, which create productive innovations that allow them to dispense with technological artifacts controlled by the input and processing industries (Ploeg, 2009). On a recurring basis, however, these struggles also engage social organizations and movements, which focus not only on criticizing certain orders, so that to destabilize them, but also on sustaining new social orders based, for example, on civic practices and values. Examples of this type of collective action have drawn attention to the political construction of markets, one of the most innovative and thought-provoking themes in the current research agenda of the economic sociology (Fligstein and McAdam, 2019).

In the Brazilian case, given the deeply critical moment that the country has been experiencing since at least 2013, the sharpening of institutional changes is visible. Currently, the country is perhaps one of the best research laboratories in the world to think about the value of theories on stability and institutional change. The problem is that, for this very reason, this book was written on quicksand. By the time it reaches readers, a more or less significant number of institutional changes will have caused some kind of reconfiguration in the social practices and orders that we analyzed. Therefore, this is an unfinished work, which had to be completed, because no one can predict when and under what conditions a new period of stability will be produced.

References

Acselrad, H. 2002. "Justiça ambiental e construção social do risco." *Desenvolvimento e Meio Ambiente*, 5(1): 49–60.
Beckert, J. 2009. "The social order of markets." *Theory and Society*, 38(3): 245–69.
Boltanski, L. 2009. *De la critique*. Paris: Gallimard.
Boltanski, L. and Esquerre, A. 2017. *Enrichissement: une critique de la marchandise*. Paris: Gallimard.

Boyer, R. 2003. "Les institutions dans la théorie de la régulation." *Cahiers d'Économie Politique*, 44(1): 79–101.

Callon, M. 1998. "An essay on framing and overflowing: Economic externalities revisited by sociology." In *The Laws of the Markets*, edited by M. Callon, 244–69.Oxford: Blackwell.

DiMaggio, P. and Powel, W. 2005. "The iron cage revisited: Institutional isomorphism and collective rationality in organizational fields." *American Sociological Review*, 48(2): 147–60.

Eymard-Duvernay, F., Favereau, O., Salais, R. and Thévenot, L. 2005. "Pluralist integration in the economic and social sciences: The economy of conventions." *Heterodox Economics from the Post-Autistic Economics Review*, n. 34.

Fligstein, N. and McAdam, D. 2012. *A Theory of Fields*. New York: Oxford.

Fligstein, N. and McAdam, D. 2019. "States, social movements and markets." *Socio-Economic Review*, 17(1): 1–6

Fraser, N. 2017. "Una nueva forma de capitalismo? Respuesta a Boltanski y Esquerre." *New Left Review*, 106: 61–70.

Geels, F. 2002. "Technological transitions as evolutionary reconfiguration processes: A multi-level perspective and a case study." *Research Policy*, 31: 1257–74.

Hall, P. and Thelen, K. 2009. "Institutional change in varieties of capitalism." *Socio-economic Review*, 7(1): 7–34.

Latour, B. 1995. "Moderniser ou écologiser? À la recherché de la 'sepième' cité." *Ecologie Politique*, 13: 5–27.

Long, N. and Ploeg, J. D. van der. 1994. "Heterogeneity, actor and structure: Towards a reconstitution of the concept of structure." In *Rethinking Social Development: Theory, Research and Practice*, edited by D. Booth, 62–90. London: Longman.

Mahoney, J. and Rueschemeyer, D. (eds). 2003. *Comparative Historical Analysis in The Social Sciences*. Cambridge: Cambridge University Press.

March, J. and Olsen, J. 2006. "Elaborating the 'new institutionalism'." In *Oxford Handbooks of Political Institutions*, edited by R. Rhodes, S. Binder and B. Rockman, 3–21.Oxford: Oxford University.

McMichael, P. 2016. "Commentary: Food regime for thought." *Journal of Peasant Studies*, 43(3): 648–670.

Niederle, P. 2018. "A pluralist and pragmatist critique of food regime's genealogy: Varieties of social orders in Brazilian agriculture." *Journal of Peasant* Studies, 45(7): 1460–83.

Niederle, P., Grisa, C., Picolotto, E. and Soldera, D. 2019. "Narrative disputes over family-farming public policies in Brazil: Conservative attacks and restricted countermovements."*Latin American Research Review*, 54: 707–20.

North, D., Wallis, J. and Weingast, B. 2009. *Violence and Social Orders*. Cambridge: Cambridge University Press.

Ostrom, E. 2007. "Institutional rational choice: An assessment of the institutional analysis and development framework." In *Theories of the Policy Process*, edited by P. Sabatier, 21–64. Cambridge: Westview Press.

Ploeg, J. D. van der. 2009. *The New Peasantries: Struggles for Autonomy and Sustainability in an Era of Empire and Globalization*. New York: Routledge.

Poulain, J.-P. 2013. *Sociologias da alimentação: os comedores e o espaço social alimentar*. 2nd ed. Florianópolis: UFSC.

Schatzki, T. 2002. *The Site of the Social*. University Park: Pennsylvania State University.

Schubert, M. 2017. *Comer fora de casa, as práticas e as rotinas do comer nos contextos da modernidade: uma leitura comparada entre Brasil, Reino Unido e Espanha*. PhD Thesis. Porto Alegre: UFRGS.

Shove, E., Pantzar, M. and Watson, M. 2012. *The Dynamics of Social Practice: Everyday Life and How It Changes*. London: Sage.

Thelen, K. 2004. *How Institutions Evolve*. Cambridge: Cambridge University Press.

Thévenot, L. 1989. "Equilibre et rationalité dans un univers complexe." *Revue Économique*, 2: 147–97.

Veblen, T. 1957. *The Theory of the Leisure Class*. New York: Mentor Book.

Warde, A. 2015. *The Practice of Eating*. Cambridge: Polity.

Index

Printed in the United States
By Bookmasters